READING LOLITA IN TEHRAN

Reading Lolita in Tehran

A MEMOIR IN BOOKS

Azar Nafisi

RANDOM HOUSE / NEW YORK

Grateful acknowledgment is made to the following for permission to reprint previously published material:

Estate of Vladimir Nabokov: Extracts from the correspondence of Véra Nabokov. All rights reserved. Reprinted by arrangement with the Estate of Vladimir Nabokov.

Faber and Faber, Ltd: From FOUR QUARTETS, part of COLLECTED POEMS, 1909–1962, by T. S. Eliot, reprinted by permission of Faber and Faber, Ltd.

Harcourt, Inc.: Excerpt from "Burnt Norton" in FOUR QUARTETS by T. S. Eliot, copyright © 1936 by Harcourt, Inc., and renewed 1964 by T. S. Eliot. Reprinted by permission of the publisher.

Liveright Publishing Corporation: "somewhere I have never travelled,gladly beyond," from COMPLETE POEMS: 1904–1962 by E. E. Cummings, edited by George J. Firmage, copyright © 1931, 1959, 1991 by the Trustees for the E. E. Cummings Trust, copyright © 1979 by George James Firmage. Reprinted by permission of Liveright Publishing Corporation.

Random House, Inc.: Seven lines from "Letter to Lord Byron" from W. H. AUDEN: THE COLLECTED POEMS by W. H. Auden, copyright © 1937 by W. H. Auden. Reprinted by permission of Random House, Inc.

Vintage Books, a division of Random House, Inc.: Excerpts from LOLITA, by Vladimir Nabokov, copyright © 1955 by Vladimir Nabokov. Reprinted by permission of Vintage Books, a division of Random House, Inc.

Library of Congress Cataloging-in-Publication Data
Nafisi, Azar.
Reading Lolita in Tehran : a memoir in books / Azar Nafisi
p. cm.
ISBN 0-375-50490-7 (acid-free paper)
1. Nafisi, Azar. 2. English teachers—Iran—Biography. 3. English literature—Study and teaching—Iran. 4. American literature—Study and teaching—Iran.
5. Women—Books and reading—Iran. 6. Books and reading—Iran.
7. Group reading—Iran. I. Title.
PE64.N34 A3 2003   820.9—dc21   [B]   2002036724

Printed in the United States of America on acid-free paper
Random House website address: www.atrandom.com
8 9 7

Book design by J. K. Lambert

IN MEMORY OF MY MOTHER, NEZHAT NAFISI

FOR MY FATHER, AHMAD NAFISI,

AND MY FAMILY: BIJAN, NEGAR AND DARA NADERI

To whom do we tell what happened on the
Earth, for whom do we place everywhere huge
Mirrors in the hope that they will be filled up
And will stay so?

Czeslaw Milosz, "Annalena"

AUTHOR'S NOTE

Aspects of characters and events in this story have been changed mainly to protect individuals, not just from the eye of the censor but also from those who read such narratives to discover who's who and who did what to whom, thriving on and filling their own emptiness through others' secrets. The facts in this story are true insofar as any memory is ever truthful, but I have made every effort to protect friends and students, baptizing them with new names and disguising them perhaps even from themselves, changing and interchanging facets of their lives so that their secrets are safe.

CONTENTS

PART I

Lolita

I

In the fall of 1995, after resigning from my last academic post, I decided to indulge myself and fulfill a dream. I chose seven of my best and most committed students and invited them to come to my home every Thursday morning to discuss literature. They were all women—to teach a mixed class in the privacy of my home was too risky, even if we were discussing harmless works of fiction. One persistent male student, although barred from our class, insisted on his rights. So he, Nima, read the assigned material, and on special days he would come to my house to talk about the books we were reading.

I often teasingly reminded my students of Muriel Spark's *The Prime of Miss Jean Brodie* and asked, Which one of you will finally betray me? For I am a pessimist by nature and I was sure at least one would turn against me. Nassrin once responded mischievously, You yourself told us that in the final analysis we are our own betrayers, playing Judas to our own Christ. Manna pointed out that I was no Miss Brodie, and they, well, they were what they were. She reminded me of a warning I was fond of repeating: *do not,* under *any* circumstances, belittle a work of fiction by trying to turn it into a carbon copy of real life; what we search for in fiction is not so much reality but the epiphany of truth. Yet I suppose that if I were to go against my own recommendation and choose a work of fiction that would most resonate with our lives in the Islamic Republic of Iran, it would not be *The Prime of Miss Jean Brodie* or even *1984* but perhaps Nabokov's *Invitation to a Beheading* or better yet, *Lolita*.

A couple of years after we had begun our Thursday-morning seminars, on the last night I was in Tehran, a few friends and students came to say good-bye and to help me pack. When we had deprived the house of all its items, when the objects had vanished and the colors had faded into eight gray suitcases, like errant genies evaporating into their bottles, my students and I stood against the bare white wall of the dining room and took two photographs.

I have the two photographs in front of me now. In the first there are seven women, standing against a white wall. They are, according to the law of the land, dressed in black robes and head scarves, covered except for the oval of their faces and their hands. In the second photograph the same group, in the same position, stands against the same wall. Only they have taken off their coverings. Splashes of color separate one from the next. Each has become distinct through the color and style of her clothes, the color and the length of her hair; not even the two who are still wearing their head scarves look the same.

The one to the far right in the second photograph is our poet, Manna, in a white T-shirt and jeans. She made poetry out of things most people cast aside. The photograph does not reflect the peculiar opacity of Manna's dark eyes, a testament to her withdrawn and private nature.

Next to Manna is Mahshid, whose long black scarf clashes with her delicate features and retreating smile. Mahshid was good at many things, but she had a certain daintiness about her and we took to calling her "my lady." Nassrin used to say that more than defining Mahshid, we had managed to add another dimension to the word *lady*. Mahshid is very sensitive. She's like porcelain, Yassi once told me, easy to crack. That's why she appears fragile to those who don't know her too well; but woe to whoever offends her. As for me, Yassi continued good-naturedly, I'm like good old plastic; I won't crack no matter what you do with me.

Yassi was the youngest in our group. She is the one in yellow, bending forward and bursting with laughter. We used to teasingly call her our comedian. Yassi was shy by nature, but certain things excited her and made her lose her inhibitions. She had a tone of voice that gently mocked and questioned not just others but herself as well.

I am the one in brown, standing next to Yassi, with one arm around her shoulders. Directly behind me stands Azin, my tallest student, with her long blond hair and a pink T-shirt. She is laughing like the rest of us. Azin's smiles never looked like smiles; they appeared more like preludes to an irrepressible and nervous hilarity. She beamed in that peculiar fashion even when she was describing her latest trouble with her husband. Always outrageous and outspoken, Azin relished the shock value of her actions and comments, and often clashed with Mahshid and Manna. We nicknamed her the wild one.

On my other side is Mitra, who was perhaps the calmest among us. Like the pastel colors of her paintings, she seemed to recede and fade into a paler register. Her beauty was saved from predictability by a pair of miraculous dimples, which she could and did use to manipulate many an unsuspecting victim into bending to her will.

Sanaz, who, pressured by family and society, vacillated between her desire for independence and her need for approval, is holding on to Mitra's arm. We are all laughing. And Nima, Manna's husband and my one true literary critic—if only he had had the perseverance to finish the brilliant essays he started to write—is our invisible partner, the photographer.

There was one more: Nassrin. She is not in the photographs—she didn't make it to the end. Yet my tale would be incomplete without those who could not or did not remain with us. Their absences persist, like an acute pain that seems to have no physical source. This is Tehran for me: its absences were more real than its presences.

When I see Nassrin in my mind's eye, she's slightly out of focus, blurred, somehow distant. I've combed through the photographs my students took with me over the years and Nassrin is in many of them, but always hidden behind something—a person, a tree. In one, I am standing with eight of my students in the small garden facing our faculty building, the scene of so many farewell photographs over the years. In the background stands a sheltering willow tree. We are laughing, and in one corner, from behind the tallest student, Nassrin peers out, like an imp intruding roguishly on a scene it was not invited to. In another I can barely make out her face in the small V space behind two other girls' shoulders. In this one she looks absentminded; she is frowning, as if unaware that she is being photographed.

How can I describe Nassrin? I once called her the Cheshire cat, appearing and disappearing at unexpected turns in my academic life. The truth is I can't describe her: she was her own definition. One can only say that Nassrin was Nassrin.

For nearly two years, almost every Thursday morning, rain or shine, they came to my house, and almost every time, I could not get over the shock of seeing them shed their mandatory veils and robes and burst into color. When my students came into that room, they took off more than their scarves and robes. Gradually, each one gained an outline and a shape, becoming her own inimitable self. Our world in that living room with its window framing my beloved Elburz Mountains became our sanctuary, our self-contained universe, mocking the reality of black-scarved, timid faces in the city that sprawled below.

The theme of the class was the relation between fiction and reality. We read Persian classical literature, such as the tales of our own lady of fiction, Scheherazade, from *A Thousand and One Nights,* along with Western classics—*Pride and Prejudice, Madame Bovary, Daisy Miller, The Dean's December* and, yes, *Lolita.* As I write the title of each book, memories whirl in with the wind to disturb the quiet of this fall day in another room in another country.

Here and now in that other world that cropped up so many times in our discussions, I sit and reimagine myself and my students, my girls as I came to call them, reading *Lolita* in a deceptively sunny room in Tehran. But to steal the words from Humbert, the poet/criminal of *Lolita,* I need you, the reader, to imagine us, for we won't really exist if you don't. Against the tyranny of time and politics, imagine us the way we sometimes didn't dare to imagine ourselves: in our most private and secret moments, in the most extraordinarily ordinary instances of life, listening to music, falling in love, walking down the shady streets or reading *Lolita* in Tehran. And then imagine us again with all this confiscated, driven underground, taken away from us.

If I write about Nabokov today, it is to celebrate our reading of Nabokov in Tehran, against all odds. Of all his novels I choose the one I taught last, and the one that is connected to so many memories. It is of *Lolita* that I want to write, but right now there is no way I can write about that novel without also writing about Tehran. This, then, is the story of *Lolita* in Tehran, how *Lolita* gave a different color to Tehran and how Tehran helped redefine Nabokov's novel, turning it into this *Lolita,* our *Lolita.*

2

And so it happened that one Thursday in early September we gathered in my living room for our first meeting. Here they come, one more time. First I hear the bell, a pause, and the closing of the street door. Then I hear footsteps coming up the winding staircase and past my mother's apartment. As I move towards the front door, I register a piece of sky through the side window. Each girl, as soon as she reaches the door, takes off her robe and scarf, sometimes shaking her head from side to side. She pauses before entering the room. Only there is no room, just the teasing void of memory.

More than any other place in our home, the living room was symbolic of my nomadic and borrowed life. Vagrant pieces of furniture from different times and places were thrown together, partly out of financial necessity, and partly because of my eclectic taste. Oddly, these incongruous ingredients created a symmetry that the other, more deliberately furnished rooms in the apartment lacked.

My mother would go crazy each time she saw the paintings leaning against the wall and the vases of flowers on the floor and the curtainless windows, which I refused to dress until I was finally reminded that this was an Islamic country and windows needed to be dressed. I don't know if you really belong to me, she would lament. Didn't I raise you to be orderly and organized? Her tone was serious, but she had repeated the same complaint for so many years that by now it was an almost tender ritual. Azi—that was my nickname—Azi, she would say, you are a grown-up lady now; act like one. Yet there was something in her tone that kept me young and fragile and obstinate, and still, when in memory I hear her voice, I know I never lived up to her expectations. I never did become the lady she tried to will me into being.

That room, which I never paid much attention to at that time, has gained a different status in my mind's eye now that it has become the precious object of memory. It was a spacious room, sparsely furnished and decorated. At one corner was the fireplace, a fanciful creation of my husband, Bijan. There was a love seat against one wall, over which I had thrown a lace cover, my mother's gift from long ago. A pale peach couch faced the window, accompanied by two matching chairs and a big square glass-topped iron table.

My place was always in the chair with its back to the window, which opened onto a wide cul-de-sac called Azar. Opposite the window was the former American Hospital, once small and exclusive, now a noisy, overcrowded medical facility for wounded and disabled veterans of the war. On "weekends"—Thursdays and Fridays in Iran— the small street was crowded with hospital visitors who came as if for a picnic, with sandwiches and children. The neighbor's front yard, his pride and joy, was the main victim of their assaults, especially in summer, when they helped themselves to his beloved roses. We could hear the sound of children shouting, crying and laughing, and, mingled in, their mothers' voices, also shouting, calling out their children's names and threatening them with punishments. Sometimes a child or two would ring our doorbell and run away, repeating their perilous exercise at intervals.

From our second-story apartment—my mother occupied the first floor, and my brother's apartment, on the third floor, was often empty, since he had left for England—we could see the upper branches of a generous tree and, in the distance, over the buildings, the Elburz Mountains. The street, the hospital and its visitors were censored out of sight. We felt their presence only through the disembodied noises emanating from below.

I could not see my favorite mountains from where I sat, but opposite my chair, on the far wall of the dining room, was an antique oval mirror, a gift from my father, and in its reflection, I could see the mountains capped with snow, even in summer, and watch the trees change color. That censored view intensified my impression that the noise came not from the street below but from some far-off place, a place whose persistent hum was our only link to the world we refused, for those few hours, to acknowledge.

That room, for all of us, became a place of transgression. What a wonderland it was! Sitting around the large coffee table covered with bouquets of flowers, we moved in and out of the novels we read. Looking back, I am amazed at how much we learned without even noticing it. We were, to borrow from Nabokov, to experience how the ordinary pebble of ordinary life could be transformed into a jewel through the magic eye of fiction.

3

Six A.M.: the first day of class. I was already up. Too excited to eat breakfast, I put the coffee on and then took a long, leisurely shower. The water caressed my neck, my back, my legs, and I stood there both rooted and light. For the first time in many years, I felt a sense of anticipation that was not marred by tension: I would not need to go through the torturous rituals that had marked my days when I taught at the university—rituals governing what I was forced to wear, how I was expected to act, the gestures I had to remember to control. For this class, I would prepare differently.

Life in the Islamic Republic was as capricious as the month of April, when short periods of sunshine would suddenly give way to showers and storms. It was unpredictable: the regime would go through cycles of some tolerance, followed by a crackdown. Now, after a period of relative calm and so-called liberalization, we had again entered a time of hardships. Universities had once more become the targets of attack by the cultural purists who were busy imposing stricter sets of laws, going so far as to segregate men and women in classes and punishing disobedient professors.

The University of Allameh Tabatabai, where I had been teaching since 1987, had been singled out as the most liberal university in Iran. It was rumored that someone in the Ministry of Higher Education had asked, rhetorically, if the faculty at Allameh thought they lived in Switzerland. *Switzerland* had somehow become a byword for Western laxity: any program or action that was deemed un-Islamic was reproached with a mocking reminder that Iran was by no means Switzerland.

The pressure was hardest on the students. I felt helpless as I listened to their endless tales of woe. Female students were being penalized for running up the stairs when they were late for classes, for laughing in the hallways, for talking to members of the opposite sex. One day Sanaz had barged into class near the end of the session, crying. In between bursts of tears, she explained that she was late because the female guards at the door, finding a blush in her bag, had tried to send her home with a reprimand.

Why did I stop teaching so suddenly? I had asked myself this question many times. Was it the declining quality of the university? The ever-increasing indifference among the remaining faculty and students? The daily struggle against arbitrary rules and restrictions?

I smiled as I rubbed the coarse loofah over my skin, remembering the reaction of the university officials to my letter of resignation. They had harassed and limited me in all manner of ways, monitoring my visitors, controlling my actions, refusing a long-overdue tenure; and when I resigned, they infuriated me by suddenly commiserating and by refusing to accept my resignation. The students had threatened to boycott classes, and it was of some satisfaction to me to find out later that despite threats of reprisals, they in fact did boycott my replacement. Everyone thought I would break down and eventually return.

It took two more years before they finally accepted my resignation. I remember a friend told me, You don't understand their mentality. They won't accept your resignation because they don't think you have the right to quit. *They* are the ones who decide how long you should stay and when you should be dispensed with. More than anything else, it was this arbitrariness that had become unbearable.

What will you do? my friends had asked. Will you just stay home now? Well, I could write another book, I would tell them. But in truth I had no definite plans. I was still dealing with the aftershocks of a book on Nabokov I had just published, and only vague ideas, like vapors, formed when I turned to consider the shape of my next book. I could, for a while at least, continue the pleasant task of studying Persian classics, but one particular project, a notion I had been nurturing for years, was uppermost in my mind. For a long time I had dreamt of creating a special class, one that would give me the freedoms denied me in the classes I taught in the Islamic Republic. I wanted to teach a handful of selected students wholly committed to the study of literature, students who were not handpicked by the government, who had not chosen English literature simply because they had not been accepted in other fields or because they thought an English degree would be a good career move.

Teaching in the Islamic Republic, like any other vocation, was subservient to politics and subject to arbitrary rules. Always, the joy of teaching was marred by diversions and considerations forced on us by the regime—how well could one teach when the main concern of university officials was not the quality of one's work but the color of one's lips, the subversive potential of a single strand of hair? Could one really concentrate on one's job when what preoccupied the faculty was how to excise the word *wine* from a Hemingway story, when they decided not to teach Brontë because she appeared to condone adultery?

I was reminded of a painter friend who had started her career by depicting scenes from life, mainly deserted rooms, abandoned houses and discarded photographs of women. Gradually, her work became more abstract, and in her last exhibition, her paintings were splashes of rebellious color, like the two in my living room, dark patches with little droplets of blue. I asked about her progress from modern realism to abstraction. Reality has become so intolerable, she said, so bleak, that all I can paint now are the colors of my dreams.

The colors of my dreams, I repeated to myself, stepping out of the shower and onto the cool tiles. I liked that. How many people get a chance to paint the colors of their dreams? I put on my oversize bathrobe—it felt good to move from the security of the embracing water to the protective cover of a bathrobe wrapped around my body. I walked barefoot into the kitchen, poured some coffee into my favorite mug, the one with red strawberries, and sat down forgetfully on the divan in the hall.

This class was the color of my dreams. It entailed an active withdrawal from a reality that had turned hostile. I wanted very badly to hold on to my rare mood of jubilance and optimism. For in the back of my mind, I didn't know what awaited me at the end of this project. You are aware, a friend had said, that you are more and more withdrawing into yourself, and now that you have cut your relations with the university, your whole contact with the outside world will be mainly restricted to one room. Where will you go from here? he had asked. Withdrawal into one's dreams could be dangerous, I reflected, padding into the bedroom to change; this I had learned from Nabokov's crazy dreamers, like Kinbote and Humbert.

In selecting my students, I did not take into consideration their ideological or religious backgrounds. Later, I would count it as the class's great achievement that such a mixed group, with different and at times conflicting backgrounds, personal as well as religious and social, remained so loyal to its goals and ideals.

One reason for my choice of these particular girls was the peculiar mixture of fragility and courage I sensed in them. They were what you would call loners, who did not belong to any particular group or sect. I admired their ability to survive not despite but in some ways because of their solitary lives. We can call the class "a space of our own," Manna had suggested, a sort of communal version of Virginia Woolf's room of her own.

I spent longer than usual choosing my clothes that first morning, trying on different outfits, until I finally settled on a red-striped shirt and black corduroy jeans. I applied my makeup with care and put on bright red lipstick. As I fastened my small gold earrings, I suddenly panicked. What if it doesn't work? What if they won't come?

Don't, don't do that! Suspend all fears for the next five or six hours at least. Please, please, I pleaded with myself, putting on my shoes and going into the kitchen.

4

I was making tea when the doorbell rang. I was so preoccupied with my thoughts that I didn't hear it the first time. I opened the door to Mahshid. I thought you weren't home, she said, handing me a bouquet of white and yellow daffodils. As she was taking off her black robe, I told her, There are no men in the house—you can take that off, too. She hesitated before uncoiling her long black scarf. Mahshid and Yassi both observed the veil, but Yassi of late had become more relaxed in the way she wore her scarf. She tied it with a loose knot under her throat, her dark brown hair, untidily parted in the middle, peeping out from underneath. Mahshid's hair, however, was meticulously styled and curled under. Her short bangs gave her a strangely old-fashioned look that struck me as more European than Iranian. She wore a deep blue jacket over her white shirt, with a huge yellow butterfly embroidered on its right side. I pointed to the butterfly: did you wear this in honor of Nabokov?

I no longer remember when Mahshid first began to take my classes at the university. Somehow, it seems as if she had always been there. Her father, a devout Muslim, had been an ardent supporter of the revolution. She wore the scarf even before the revolution, and in her class diary, she wrote about the lonely mornings when she went to a fashionable girls' college, where she felt neglected and ignored—ironically, because of her then-conspicuous attire. After the revolution, she was jailed for five years because of her affiliation with a dissident religious organization and banned from continuing her education for two years after she was out of jail.

I imagine her in those pre-revolutionary days, walking along the uphill street leading to the college on countless sunny mornings. I see her walking alone, her head to the ground. Then, as now, she did not enjoy the day's brilliance. I say "then, as now" because the revolution that imposed the scarf on others did not relieve Mahshid of her loneliness. Before the revolution, she could in a sense take pride in her isolation. At that time, she had worn the scarf as a testament to her faith. Her decision was a voluntary act. When the revolution forced the scarf on others, her action became meaningless.

Mahshid is proper in the true sense of the word: she has grace and a certain dignity. Her skin is the color of moonlight, and she has almond-shaped eyes and jet-black hair. She wears pastel colors and is soft-spoken. Her pious background should have shielded her, but it didn't. I cannot imagine her in jail.

Over the many years I have known Mahshid, she has rarely alluded to her jail experiences, which left her with a permanently impaired kidney. One day in class, as we were talking about our daily terrors and nightmares, she mentioned that her jail memories visited her from time to time and that she had still not found a way to articulate them. But, she added, everyday life does not have fewer horrors than prison.

I asked Mahshid if she wanted some tea. Always considerate, she said she'd rather wait for the others and apologized for being a little early. Can I help? she asked. There's really nothing to help with. Make yourself at home, I told her as I stepped into the kitchen with the flowers and searched for a vase. The bell rang again. I'll get it, Mahshid cried out from the living room. I heard laughter; Manna and Yassi had arrived.

Manna came into the kitchen holding a small bouquet of roses. It's from Nima, she said. He wants to make you feel bad about excluding him from the class. He says he'll carry a bouquet of roses and march in front of your house during class hours, in protest. She was beaming; a few brief sparkles flashed in her eyes and died down again.

Putting the pastries onto a large tray, I asked Manna if she envisioned the words to her poems in colors. Nabokov writes in his autobiography that he and his mother saw the letters of the alphabet in color, I explained. He says of himself that he is a painterly writer.

The Islamic Republic coarsened my taste in colors, Manna said, fingering the discarded leaves of her roses. I want to wear outrageous colors, like shocking pink or tomato red. I feel too greedy for colors to see them in carefully chosen words of poetry. Manna was one of those people who would experience ecstasy but not happiness. Come here, I want to show you something, I said, leading her into our bedroom. When I was very young, I was obsessed with the colors of places and things my father told me about in his nightly stories. I wanted to know the color of Scheherazade's dress, her bedcover, the color of the genie and the magic lamp, and once I asked him about the color of paradise. He said it could be any color I wanted it to be. That was not enough. Then one day when we had guests and I was eating my soup in the dining room, my eyes fell on a painting I had seen on the wall ever since I could remember, and I instantly knew the color of my paradise. And here it is, I said, proudly pointing to a small oil painting in an old wooden frame: a green landscape of lush, leathery leaves with two birds, two deep red apples, a golden pear and a touch of blue.

My paradise is swimming-pool blue! Manna shot in, her eyes still glued to the painting. We lived in a large garden that belonged to my grandparents, she said, turning to me. You know the old Persian gardens, with their fruit trees, peaches, apples, cherries, persimmons and a willow or two. My best memories are of swimming in our huge irregularly shaped swimming pool. I was a swimming champion at our school, a fact my dad was very proud of. About a year after the revolution, my father died of a heart attack, and then the government confiscated our house and our garden and we moved into an apartment. I never swam again. My dream is at the bottom of that pool. I have a recurring dream of diving in to retrieve something of my father's memory and my childhood, she said as we walked to the living room, for the doorbell had rung again.

Azin and Mitra had arrived together. Azin was taking off her black kimonolike robe—Japanese-style robes were all the rage at the time—

revealing a white peasant blouse that made no pretense of covering her shoulders, big golden earrings and pink lipstick. She had a branch of small yellow orchids—from Mitra and myself, she said in that special tone of hers that I can only describe as a flirtatious pout.

Nassrin came in next. She had brought two boxes of nougats: presents from Isfahan, she declared. She was dressed in her usual uniform—navy robe, navy scarf and black heelless shoes. When I had last seen her in class, she was wearing a huge black chador, revealing only the oval of her face and two restless hands, which, when she was not writing or doodling, were constantly in motion, as if trying to escape the confines of the thick black cloth. More recently, she had exchanged the chador for long, shapeless robes in navy, black or dark brown, with thick matching scarves that hid her hair and framed her face. She had a small, pale face, skin so transparent you could count the veins, full eyebrows, long lashes, lively eyes (brown), a small straight nose and an angry mouth: an unfinished miniature by some master who had suddenly been called away from his job and left the meticulously drawn face imprisoned in a careless splash of dark color.

We heard the sound of screeching tires and sudden brakes. I looked out the window: a small old Renault, cream-colored, had pulled up on the curb. Behind the wheel, a young man with fashionable sunglasses and a defiant profile rested his black-sleeved arm on the curve of the open window and gave the impression that he was driving a Porsche. He was staring straight in front of him as he talked to the woman beside him. Only once did he turn his head to his right, with what I could guess was a cross expression, and that was when the woman got out of the car and he angrily slammed the door behind her. As she walked to our front door, he threw his head out and shouted a few words, but she did not turn back to answer. The old Renault was Sanaz's; she had bought it with money saved from her job.

I turned towards the room, blushing for Sanaz. That must be the obnoxious brother, I thought. Seconds later the doorbell rang and I heard Sanaz's hurried steps and opened the door to her. She looked harassed, as if she had been running from a stalker or a thief. As soon as she saw me, she adjusted her face into a smile and said breathlessly: I hope I am not too late?

There were two very important men dominating Sanaz's life at the time. The first was her brother. He was nineteen years old and had not yet finished high school and was the darling of their parents, who, after two girls, one of whom had died at the age of three, had finally been blessed with a son. He was spoiled, and his one obsession in life was Sanaz. He had taken to proving his masculinity by spying on her, listening to her phone conversations, driving her car around and monitoring her actions. Her parents had tried to appease Sanaz and begged her, as the older sister, to be patient and understanding, to use her motherly instincts to see him through this difficult period.

The other was her childhood sweetheart, a boy she had known since she was eleven. Their parents were best friends, and their families spent most of their time and vacations together. Sanaz and Ali seemed to have been in love forever. Their parents encouraged this union and called it a match made in heaven. When Ali went away to England six years ago, his mother took to calling Sanaz his bride. They wrote to each other, sent photographs, and recently, when the number of Sanaz's suitors increased, there were talks of engagement and a reunion in Turkey, where Iranians did not require entrance visas. Any day now it might happen, an event Sanaz looked forward to with some fear and trepidation.

I had never seen Sanaz without her uniform, and stood there almost transfixed as she took off her robe and scarf. She was wearing an orange T-shirt tucked into tight jeans and brown boots, yet the most radical transformation was the mass of shimmering dark brown hair that now framed her face. She shook her magnificent hair from side to side, a gesture that I later noticed was a habit with her; she would toss her head and run her fingers through her hair every once in a while, as if making sure that her most prized possession was still there. Her features looked softer and more radiant—the black scarf she wore in public made her small face look emaciated and almost hard.

I'm sorry I'm a little late, she said breathlessly, running her fingers through her hair. My brother insisted on driving me, and he refused to wake up on time. He never gets up before ten, but he wanted to know where I was going. I might be off on some secret tryst, you know, a date or something.

I have been worrying in case any of you would get into trouble for this class, I said, inviting them all to take their seats around the table in the living room. I hope your parents and spouses feel comfortable with our arrangement.

Nassrin, who was wandering around the room, inspecting the paintings as if seeing them for the first time, paused to say offhandedly, I mentioned the idea very casually to my father, just to test his reaction, and he vehemently disapproved.

How did you convince him to let you come? I asked. I lied, she said. You lied? What else can one do with a person who's so dictatorial he won't let his daughter, at *this age,* go to an all-female literature class? Besides, isn't this how we treat the regime? Can we tell the Revolutionary Guards the truth? We lie to them; we hide our satellite dishes. We tell them we don't have illegal books and alcohol in our houses. Even my venerable father lies to them when the safety of his family is at stake, Nassrin added defiantly.

What if he calls me to check on you? I said, half teasingly. He won't. I gave a brilliant alibi. I said Mahshid and I had volunteered to help translate Islamic texts into English. And he believed you? Well, he had no reason not to. I hadn't lied to him before—not really—and it was what he wanted to believe. And he trusts Mahshid completely.

So if he calls me, I should lie to him? I persisted. It's up to you, Nassrin said after a pause, looking down at her twisting hands. Do *you* think you should tell him? By now I could hear a note of desperation in her voice. Am I getting you into trouble?

Nassrin always acted so confident that sometimes I forgot how vulnerable she really was under that tough-girl act. Of course I would respect your confidence, I said more gently. As you said, you are a big girl. You know what you're doing.

I had settled into my usual chair, opposite the mirror, where the mountains had come to stay. It is strange to look into a mirror and see not yourself but a view so distant from you. Mahshid, after some hesitation, had taken the chair to my right. On the couch, Manna settled to the far right and Azin to the far left; they instinctively kept their distance. Sanaz and Mitra were perched on the love seat, their heads close together as they whispered and giggled.

At this point Yassi and Nassrin came in and looked around for seats. Azin patted the empty part of the couch, inviting Yassi with her hand. Yassi hesitated for a moment and then slid between Azin and Manna. She slumped into place and seemed to leave little room for her two companions, who sat upright and a little stiff in their respective corners. Without her robe, she looked a little overweight, as if she had not as yet lost her baby fat. Nassrin had gone to the dining room in search of a chair. We can squeeze you in here, said Manna. No, thank you, I actually prefer straight-backed chairs. When she returned, she placed her chair between the couch and Mahshid.

They kept that arrangement, faithfully, to the end. It became representative of their emotional boundaries and personal relations. And so began our first class.

5

"Upsilamba!" I heard Yassi exclaim as I entered the dining room with a tray of tea. Yassi loved playing with words. Once she told us that her obsession with words was pathological. As soon as I discover a new word, I have to use it, she said, like someone who buys an evening gown and is so eager that she wears it to the movies, or to lunch.

Let me pause and rewind the reel to retrace the events leading us to Yassi's exclamation. This was our first session. All of us had been nervous and inarticulate. We were used to meeting in public, mainly in classrooms and in lecture halls. The girls had their separate relationships with me, but except for Nassrin and Mahshid, who were intimate, and a certain friendship between Mitra and Sanaz, the rest were not close; in many cases, in fact, they would never have chosen to be friends. The collective intimacy made them uncomfortable.

I had explained to them the purpose of the class: to read, discuss and respond to works of fiction. Each would have a private diary, in which she should record her responses to the novels, as well as ways in which these works and their discussions related to her personal and social experiences. I explained that I had chosen them for this class because they seemed dedicated to the study of literature. I mentioned that one of the criteria for the books I had chosen was their authors' faith in the critical and almost magical power of literature, and reminded them of the nineteen-year-old Nabokov, who, during the Russian Revolution, would not allow himself to be diverted by the sound of bullets. He kept on writing his solitary poems while he heard the guns and saw the bloody fights from his window. Let us see, I said, whether seventy years later our disinterested faith will reward us by transforming the gloomy reality created of this other revolution.

The first work we discussed was *A Thousand and One Nights,* the familiar tale of the cuckolded king who slew successive virgin wives as revenge for his queen's betrayal, and whose murderous hand was finally stayed by the entrancing storyteller Scheherazade. I formulated certain general questions for them to consider, the most central of which was how these great works of imagination could help us in our present trapped situation as women. We were not looking for blueprints, for an easy solution, but we did hope to find a link between the open spaces the novels provided and the closed ones we were confined to. I remember reading to my girls Nabokov's claim that "readers were born free and ought to remain free."

What had most intrigued me about the frame story of *A Thousand and One Nights* were the three kinds of women it portrayed—all victims of a king's unreasonable rule. Before Scheherazade enters the scene, the women in the story are divided into those who betray and then are killed (the queen) and those who are killed before they have a chance to betray (the virgins). The virgins, who, unlike Scheherazade, have no voice in the story, are mostly ignored by the critics. Their silence, however, is significant. They surrender their virginity, and their lives, without resistance or protest. They do not quite exist, because they leave no trace in their anonymous death. The queen's infidelity does not rob the king of his absolute authority; it throws him off balance. Both types of women—the queen and the virgins—tacitly accept the king's public authority by acting within the confines of his domain and by accepting its arbitrary laws.

Scheherazade breaks the cycle of violence by choosing to embrace different terms of engagement. She fashions her universe not through physical force, as does the king, but through imagination and reflection. This gives her the courage to risk her life and sets her apart from the other characters in the tale.

Our edition of *A Thousand and One Nights* came in six volumes. I, luckily, had bought mine before it was banned and sold only on the black market, for exorbitant prices. I divided the volumes among the girls and asked them, for the next session, to classify the tales according to the types of women who played central roles in the stories.

Once I'd given them their assignment, I asked them each to tell the rest of us why they had chosen to spend their Thursday mornings here, discussing Nabokov and Jane Austen. Their answers were brief and forced. In order to break the ice, I suggested the calming distraction of cream puffs and tea.

This brings us to the moment when I enter the dining room with eight glasses of tea on an old and unpolished silver tray. Brewing and serving tea is an aesthetic ritual in Iran, performed several times a day. We serve tea in transparent glasses, small and shapely, the most popular of which is called slim-waisted: round and full at the top, narrow in the middle and round and full at the bottom. The color of the tea and its subtle aroma are an indication of the brewer's skill.

I step into the dining room with eight slim-waisted glasses whose honey-colored liquid trembles seductively. At this point, I hear Yassi shout triumphantly, "Upsilamba!" She throws the word at me like a ball, and I take a mental leap to catch it.

Upsilamba!—the word carries me back to the spring of 1994, when four of my girls and Nima were auditing a class I was teaching on the twentieth-century novel. The class's favorite book was Nabokov's *Invitation to a Beheading*. In this novel, Nabokov differentiates Cincinnatus C., his imaginative and lonely hero, from those around him through his originality in a society where uniformity is not only the norm but also the law. Even as a child, Nabokov tells us, Cincinnatus appreciated the freshness and beauty of language, while other children "understood each other at the first word, since they had no words that would end in an unexpected way, perhaps in some archaic letter, an upsilamba, becoming a bird or catapult with wondrous consequences."

No one in class had bothered to ask what the word meant. No one, that is, who was properly taking the class—for many of my old students just stayed on and sat in on my classes long after their graduation. Often, they were more interested and worked harder than my regular students, who were taking the class for credit. Thus it was that those who audited the class—including Nassrin, Manna, Nima, Mahshid and Yassi—had one day gathered in my office to discuss this and a number of other questions.

I decided to play a little game with the class, to test their curiosity. On the midterm exam, one of the questions was "Explain the significance of the word *upsilamba* in the context of *Invitation to a Beheading.* What does the word mean, and how does it relate to the main theme of the novel?" Except for four or five students, no one had any idea what I could possibly mean, a point I did not forget to remind them of every once in a while throughout the rest of that term.

The truth was that *upsilamba* was one of Nabokov's fanciful creations, possibly a word he invented out of *upsilon,* the twentieth letter in the Greek alphabet, and *lambda,* the eleventh. So that first day in our private class, we let our minds play again and invented new meanings of our own.

I said I associated *upsilamba* with the impossible joy of a suspended leap. Yassi, who seemed excited for no particular reason, cried out that she always thought it could be the name of a dance—you know, "C'mon, baby, do the Upsilamba with me." I proposed that for the next time, they each write a sentence or two explaining what the word meant to them.

Manna suggested that *upsilamba* evoked the image of small silver fish leaping in and out of a moonlit lake. Nima added in parentheses, Just so you won't forget me, although you have barred me from your class: an upsilamba to you too! For Azin it was a sound, a melody. Mahshid described an image of three girls jumping rope and shouting "Upsilamba!" with each leap. For Sanaz, the word was a small African boy's secret magical name. Mitra wasn't sure why the word reminded her of the paradox of a blissful sigh. And to Nassrin it was the magic code that opened the door to a secret cave filled with treasures.

Upsilamba become part of our increasing repository of coded words and expressions, a repository that grew over time until gradually we had created a secret language of our own. That word became a symbol, a sign of that vague sense of joy, the tingle in the spine Nabokov expected his readers to feel in the act of reading fiction; it was a sensation that separated the good readers, as he called them, from the ordinary ones. It also became the code word that opened the secret cave of remembrance.

6

In his foreword to the English edition of *Invitation to a Beheading* (1959), Nabokov reminds the reader that his novel does not offer "*tout pour tous.*" Nothing of the kind. "It is," he claims, "a violin in the void." And yet, he goes on to say, "I know . . . a few readers who will jump up, ruffling their hair." Well, absolutely. The original version, Nabokov tells us, was published in installments in 1935. Almost six decades later, in a world unknown and presumably unknowable to Nabokov, in a forlorn living room with windows looking out towards distant white-capped mountains, time and again I would stand witness to the unlikeliest of readers as they lost themselves in a madness of hair-ruffling.

Invitation to a Beheading begins with the announcement that its fragile hero, Cincinnatus C., has been sentenced to death for the crime of "gnostic turpitude": in a place where all citizens are required to be transparent, he is opaque. The principal characteristic of this world is its arbitrariness; the condemned man's only privilege is to know the time of his death—but the executioners keep even this from him, turning every day into a day of execution. As the story unfolds, the reader discovers with increasing discomfort the artificial texture of this strange place. The moon from the window is fake; so is the spider in the corner, which, according to convention, must become the prisoner's faithful companion. The director of the jail, the jailer and the defense lawyer are all the same man, and keep changing places. The most important character, the executioner, is first introduced to the prisoner under another name and as a fellow prisoner: M'sieur Pierre. The executioner and the condemned man must learn to love each other and cooperate in the act of execution, which will be celebrated in a gaudy feast. In this staged world, Cincinnatus's only window to another universe is his writing.

The world of the novel is one of empty rituals. Every act is bereft of substance and significance, and even death becomes a spectacle for which the good citizens buy tickets. It is only through these empty rituals that brutality becomes possible. In another Nabokov novel, *The Real Life of Sebastian Knight,* Sebastian's brother discovers two seemingly incongruous pictures in his dead brother's library: a pretty, curly-haired child playing with a dog and a Chinese man in the act of being beheaded. The two pictures remind us of the close relation between banality and brutality. Nabokov had a special Russian term for this: *poshlust.*

Poshlust, Nabokov explains, "is not only the obviously trashy but mainly the falsely important, the falsely beautiful, the falsely clever, the falsely attractive." Yes, there are many examples you can bring from everyday life, from the politicians' sugary speeches to certain writers' proclamations to chickens. Chickens? You know, the ones the street vendors sell nowadays—if you lived in Tehran, you couldn't possibly miss them. The ones they dip in paint—shocking pink, brilliant red or turquoise blue—in order to make them more attractive. Or the plastic flowers, the bright pink-and-blue artificial gladiolas carted out at the university both for mourning and for celebration.

What Nabokov creates for us in *Invitation to a Beheading* is not the actual physical pain and torture of a totalitarian regime but the nightmarish quality of living in an atmosphere of perpetual dread. Cincinnatus C. is frail, he is passive, he is a hero without knowing or acknowledging it: he fights with his instincts, and his acts of writing are his means of escape. He is a hero because he refuses to become like all the rest.

Unlike in other utopian novels, the forces of evil here are not omnipotent; Nabokov shows us their frailty as well. They are ridiculous and they can be defeated, and this does not lessen the tragedy— the waste. *Invitation to a Beheading* is written from the point of view of the victim, one who ultimately sees the absurd sham of his persecutors and who must retreat into himself in order to survive.

Those of us living in the Islamic Republic of Iran grasped both the tragedy and absurdity of the cruelty to which we were subjected. We had to poke fun at our own misery in order to survive. We also instinctively recognized poshlust—not just in others, but in ourselves. This was one reason that art and literature became so essential to our lives: they were not a luxury but a necessity. What Nabokov captured was the texture of life in a totalitarian society, where you are completely alone in an illusory world full of false promises, where you can no longer differentiate between your savior and your executioner.

We formed a special bond with Nabokov despite the difficulty of his prose. This went deeper than our identification with his themes. His novels are shaped around invisible trapdoors, sudden gaps that constantly pull the carpet from under the reader's feet. They are filled with mistrust of what we call everyday reality, an acute sense of that reality's fickleness and frailty.

There was something, both in his fiction and in his life, that we instinctively related to and grasped, the possibility of a boundless freedom when all options are taken away. I think that was what drove me to create the class. My main link with the outside world had been the university, and now that I had severed that link, there on the brink of the void, I could invent the violin or be devoured by the void.

7

The two photographs should be placed side by side. Both embody the "fragile unreality"—to quote Nabokov on his own state of exile—of our existence in the Islamic Republic of Iran. One cancels the other, and yet without one, the other is incomplete. In the first photograph, standing there in our black robes and scarves, we are as we had been shaped by someone else's dreams. In the second, we appear as we imagined ourselves. In neither could we feel completely at home.

The second photograph belonged to the world inside the living room. But outside, underneath the window that deceptively show-cased only the mountains and the tree outside our house, was the other world, where the bad witches and furies were waiting to transform us into the hooded creatures of the first.

The best way I can think of explaining this self-negating and paradoxical inferno is through an anecdote, one that, like similar anecdotes, defies fiction to become its own metaphor.

The chief film censor in Iran, up until 1994, was blind. Well, nearly blind. Before that, he was the censor for theater. One of my playwright friends once described how he would sit in the theater wearing thick glasses that seemed to hide more than they revealed. An assistant who sat by him would explain the action onstage, and he would dictate the parts that needed to be cut.

After 1994, this censor became the head of the new television channel. There, he perfected his methods and demanded that the scriptwriters give him their scripts on audiotape; they were forbidden to make them attractive or dramatize them in any way. He then made his judgments about the scripts based on the tapes. More interesting, however, is the fact that his successor, who was not blind—not physically, that is—nonetheless followed the same system.

Our world under the mullahs' rule was shaped by the colorless lenses of the blind censor. Not just our reality but also our fiction had taken on this curious coloration in a world where the censor was the poet's rival in rearranging and reshaping reality, where we simultaneously invented ourselves and were figments of someone else's imagination.

We lived in a culture that denied any merit to literary works, considering them important only when they were handmaidens to something seemingly more urgent—namely ideology. This was a country where all gestures, even the most private, were interpreted in political terms. The colors of my head scarf or my father's tie were symbols of Western decadence and imperialist tendencies. Not wearing a beard, shaking hands with members of the opposite sex, clapping or whistling in public meetings, were likewise considered Western and therefore decadent, part of the plot by imperialists to bring down our culture.

A few years ago some members of the Iranian Parliament set up an investigative committee to examine the content of national television. The committee issued a lengthy report in which it condemned the showing of *Billy Budd,* because, it claimed, the story promoted homosexuality. Ironically, the Iranian television programmers had mainly chosen that film because of its lack of female characters. The cartoon version of *Around the World in Eighty Days* was also castigated, because the main character—a lion—was British and the film ended in that bastion of imperialism, London.

Our class was shaped within this context, in an attempt to escape the gaze of the blind censor for a few hours each week. There, in that living room, we rediscovered that we were also living, breathing human beings; and no matter how repressive the state became, no matter how intimidated and frightened we were, like Lolita we tried to escape and to create our own little pockets of freedom. And like Lolita, we took every opportunity to flaunt our insubordination: by showing a little hair from under our scarves, insinuating a little color into the drab uniformity of our appearances, growing our nails, falling in love and listening to forbidden music.

An absurd fictionality ruled our lives. We tried to live in the open spaces, in the chinks created between that room, which had become our protective cocoon, and the censor's world of witches and goblins outside. Which of these two worlds was more real, and to which did we really belong? We no longer knew the answers. Perhaps one way of finding out the truth was to do what we did: to try to imaginatively articulate these two worlds and, through that process, give shape to our vision and identity.

8

How can I create this other world outside the room? I have no choice but to appeal once again to your imagination. Let's imagine one of the girls, say Sanaz, leaving my house and let us follow her from there to her final destination. She says her good-byes and puts on her black robe and scarf over her orange shirt and jeans, coiling her scarf around her neck to cover her huge gold earrings. She directs wayward strands of hair under the scarf, puts her notes into her large bag, straps it on over her shoulder and walks out into the hall. She pauses a moment on top of the stairs to put on thin lacy black gloves to hide her nail polish.

We follow Sanaz down the stairs, out the door and into the street. You might notice that her gait and her gestures have changed. It is in her best interest not to be seen, not be heard or noticed. She doesn't walk upright, but bends her head towards the ground and doesn't look at passersby. She walks quickly and with a sense of determination. The streets of Tehran and other Iranian cities are patrolled by militia, who ride in white Toyota patrols, four gun-carrying men and women, sometimes followed by a minibus. They are called the Blood of God. They patrol the streets to make sure that women like Sanaz wear their veils properly, do not wear makeup, do not walk in public with men who are not their fathers, brothers or husbands. She will pass slogans on the walls, quotations from Khomeini and a group

called the Party of God: MEN WHO WEAR TIES ARE U.S. LACKEYS. VEIL-
ING IS A WOMAN'S PROTECTION. Beside the slogan is a charcoal draw-
ing of a woman: her face is featureless and framed by a dark chador.
MY SISTER, GUARD YOUR VEIL. MY BROTHER, GUARD YOUR EYES.

If she gets on a bus, the seating is segregated. She must enter
through the rear door and sit in the back seats, allocated to women.
Yet in taxis, which accept as many as five passengers, men and women
are squeezed together like sardines, as the saying goes, and the same
goes with minibuses, where so many of my students complain of
being harassed by bearded and God-fearing men.

You might well ask, What is Sanaz thinking as she walks the streets
of Tehran? How much does this experience affect her? Most probably,
she tries to distance her mind as much as possible from her surroundings. Perhaps she is thinking of her brother, or of her distant
boyfriend and the time when she will meet him in Turkey. Does she
compare her own situation with her mother's when she was the same
age? Is she angry that women of her mother's generation could walk
the streets freely, enjoy the company of the opposite sex, join the police force, become pilots, live under laws that were among the most
progressive in the world regarding women? Docs she feel humiliated
by the new laws, by the fact that after the revolution, the age of marriage was lowered from eighteen to nine, that stoning became once
more the punishment for adultery and prostitution?

In the course of nearly two decades, the streets have been turned
into a war zone, where young women who disobey the rules are
hurled into patrol cars, taken to jail, flogged, fined, forced to wash the
toilets and humiliated, and as soon as they leave, they go back and do
the same thing. Is she aware, Sanaz, of her own power? Does she realize how dangerous she can be when her every stray gesture is a disturbance to public safety? Does she think how vulnerable the
Revolutionary Guards are who for over eighteen years have patrolled
the streets of Tehran and have had to endure young women like herself, and those of other generations, walking, talking, showing a strand
of hair just to remind them that they have not converted?

We have reached Sanaz's house, where we will leave her on her
doorstep, perhaps to confront her brother on the other side and to
think in her heart of her boyfriend.

These girls, my girls, had both a real history and a fabricated one.

Although they came from very different backgrounds, the regime that ruled them had tried to make their personal identities and histories irrelevant. They were never free of the regime's definition of them as Muslim women.

Whoever we were—and it was not really important what religion we belonged to, whether we wished to wear the veil or not, whether we observed certain religious norms or not—we had become the figment of someone else's dreams. A stern ayatollah, a self-proclaimed philosopher-king, had come to rule our land. He had come in the name of a past, a past that, he claimed, had been stolen from him. And he now wanted to re-create us in the image of that illusory past. Was it any consolation, and did we even wish to remember, that what he did to us was what we allowed him to do?

9

It is amazing how, when all possibilities seem to be taken away from you, the minutest opening can become a great freedom. We felt when we were together that we were almost absolutely free. This feeling was in the air that very first Thursday morning. I had a frame for the class, and had selected a number of books to read, but I was prepared to let the class shape me; I was prepared for the violin to fill the void, and alter it by its music.

Often I ask myself: did I choose my students for that class or did they choose me? It is true that I had some specific criteria in mind when I invited them to participate, yet it seems as if they were the ones who created the class, who through some invisible agency led me to the present configuration in my living room.

Take the youngest, Yassi. There she is, in the first photograph, with a wistful look on her face. She is bending her head to one side, unsure of what expression to choose. She is wearing a thin white-and-gray scarf, loosely tied at the throat—a perfunctory homage to her family's strict religious background. Yassi was a freshman who audited my graduate courses in my last year of teaching. She felt intimidated by the older students, who, she thought, by virtue of their seniority, were blessed not only with greater knowledge and a better command of English but also with more wisdom. Although she understood the most difficult texts better than many of the graduate students, and although she read the texts more dutifully and with more pleasure than most, she felt secure only in her terrible sense of insecurity.

About a month after I had decided privately to leave Allameh Tabatabai, Yassi and I were standing in front of the green gate at the entrance of the university. What I remember most distinctly about the university now is that green gate. I passed through it at least twice a day on weekdays for a number of years, but I still can't quite conjure it properly. In my memory the iron gate acquires an elastic quality and becomes a magic door, unsupported by walls, guarding the university grounds. Yet I do remember its boundaries. It opened on one side to a wide street that appeared to lead straight into the mountains. On the other side it faced a small garden that belonged to the Faculty of Persian and Foreign Languages and Literature, a garden with Persian roses and other native flowers around a small, cracked ornamental fountain, a broken statue standing in its waterless midst.

I owe my memory of the green gate to Yassi: she mentioned it in one of her poems. The poem is called "How Small Are the Things That I Like." In it, she describes her favorite objects—an orange backpack, a colorful coat, a bicycle just like her cousin's—and she also describes how much she likes to enter the university through the green gate. The gate appears in this poem, and in some of her other writings, as a magical entrance into the forbidden world of all the ordinary things she had been denied in life.

Yet that green gate was closed to her, and to all my girls. Next to the gate there was a small opening with a curtain hanging from it. It was an aberration that attracted attention, because it did not belong there: it gaped with the arrogant authority of an intruder. Through this opening all the female students, including my girls, went into a small, dark room to be inspected. Yassi would describe later, long after that first session, what was done to her in this room: "I would first be checked to see if I have the right clothes: the color of my coat, the length of my uniform, the thickness of my scarf, the form of my shoes, the objects in my bag, the visible traces of even the mildest makeup, the size of my rings and their level of attractiveness, all would be checked before I could enter the campus of the university, the same university in which men also study. And to them the main door, with its immense portals and emblems and flags, is generously open."

That small side opening was the source of endless tales of frustration, humiliation and sorrow. It was meant to make the girls ordinary and invisible. Instead, it brought them into focus and turned them into objects of curiosity.

Imagine Yassi standing with me in front of that green gate, laughing between conspiratorial whispers, our bodies close together. She was talking about the teacher who taught Islamic morality and translation. A Pillsbury Dough Boy personality, she said. Three months after his wife's death, he had married her younger sister, because a man—and here Yassi lowered her voice—*a man has his special needs.*

Then her voice took on a serious tone as she began to describe his recent lecture on the difference between Islam and Christianity. She now became this dough-faced little man standing by the blackboard, pink chalk in one hand, white chalk in the other. On one side he had written, in large white letters, MUSLIM GIRL, and drawn a vertical line in the middle of the board. On the other side, in large pink letters, he wrote CHRISTIAN GIRL. He had then asked the class if they knew the differences between the two. One was a virgin, he said at last, after an uncomfortable silence, white and pure, keeping herself for her husband and her husband only. Her power came from her modesty. The other, well, there was not much one could say about her except that she was not a virgin. To Yassi's surprise, the two girls behind her, both active members of the Muslim Students' Association, had started to giggle, whispering, *No wonder more and more Muslims are converting to Christianity.*

We were standing there in the middle of the wide street, laughing— one of the rare moments when I saw Yassi's lopsided and shy smile disappear and give way to the pure mischief hidden beneath it. I cannot see that laughter in most of her photographs, where she stands at some distance from the others, as if indicating that she, as the junior member of our class, knows her place.

Almost every day my students would recount such stories. We laughed over them, and later felt angry and sad, although we repeated them endlessly at parties and over cups of coffee, in bread-lines, in taxis. It was as if the sheer act of recounting these stories gave us some control over them; the deprecating tone we used, our gestures, even our hysterical laughter seemed to reduce their hold over our lives.

In the sunny intimacy of our encounter, I asked Yassi to have an ice cream with me. We went to a small shop, where, sitting opposite each other with two tall *cafés glacés* in between us, our mood changed. We became, if not somber, quite serious. Yassi came from an enlightened religious family that had been badly hurt by the revolution. They felt the Islamic Republic was a betrayal of Islam rather than its assertion. At the start of the revolution, Yassi's mother and older aunt joined a progressive Muslim women's group that, when the new government started to crack down on its former supporters, was forced to go underground. Yassi's mother and aunt went into hiding for a long time. This aunt had four daughters, all older than Yassi, all of whom in one way or another supported an opposition group that was popular with young religious Iranians. They were all but one arrested, tortured and jailed. When they were released, every one of them married within a year. They married almost haphazardly, as if to negate their former rebellious selves. Yassi felt that they had survived the jail but could not escape the bonds of traditional marriage.

To me, Yassi was the real rebel. She did not join any political group or organization. As a teenager she had defied family traditions and, in the face of strong opposition, had taken up music. Listening to any form of nonreligious music, even on the radio, was forbidden in her family, but Yassi forced her will. She was the little cinder girl, living in the shadows of an inaccessible palace, in love with the unseen prince, who would one day hear her music.

Her rebellion did not stop there: she did not marry the right suitor at the right time and instead insisted on leaving her hometown of Shiraz to go to college in Tehran. Now she lived partly with her older sister and husband and partly in the home of an uncle with fanatical religious leanings. The university, with its low academic standards, its shabby morality and ideological limitations, had been a disappointment to her. In one sense it was more limited than her home, where she was blessed with a loving and intellectual environment. The loss of that love and warmth had caused her many sleepless nights in Tehran. She missed her parents and family, and she felt guilty for the pain she had inflicted on them. Later, I discovered that her guilt caused her long hours of disabling migraine headaches.

What could she do? She did not believe in politics and did not want to marry, but she was curious about love. That day, sitting opposite me, playing with her spoon, she explained why all the normal acts of life had become small acts of rebellion and political insubordination to her and to other young people like her. All her life she was shielded. She was never let out of sight; she never had a private corner in which to think, to feel, to dream, to write. She was not allowed to meet any young men on her own. Her family not only instructed her on how to behave around men—they seemed to think they could tell her how she should feel about them as well. What seems natural to someone like you, she said, is so strange and unfamiliar to me.

Could she ever live the life of someone like me, live on her own, take long walks holding hands with someone she loved, even have a little dog perhaps? She did not know. It was like this veil that meant nothing to her anymore yet without which she would be lost. She had always worn the veil. Did she want to wear it or not? She did not know. I remember the movement of her hand as she said this—flitting in front of her face as if to ward off an invisible fly. She said she could not imagine a Yassi without a veil. What would she look like? Would it affect the way she walked or how she moved her hands? How would others look at her? Would she become a smarter or a dumber person? These were her obsessions, alongside her favorite novels by Austen, Nabokov and Flaubert.

Again she repeated that she would never get married, never ever. She said that for her a man always existed in books, that she would spend the rest of her life with Mr. Darcy—even in the books, there were few men for her. What was wrong with that? She wanted to go to America, like her uncles, like me. Her mother and her aunts had not been allowed to go, but her uncles were given the chance. Could she ever overcome all the obstacles and go to America? Should she go to America? She wanted me to advise her. They all did. But what could I offer her, she who wanted so much more from life than she had been given?

There was nothing in reality that I could give her, so I told her instead about Nabokov's "other world." I asked her if she had noticed how in most of Nabokov's novels—*Invitation to a Beheading, Bend Sinister, Ada, Pnin*—there was always the shadow of another world, one that was only attainable through fiction. It is this world that prevents his heroes and heroines from utter despair, that becomes their refuge in a life that is consistently brutal.

Take *Lolita*. This was the story of a twelve-year-old girl who had nowhere to go. Humbert had tried to turn her into his fantasy, into his dead love, and he had destroyed her. The desperate truth of *Lolita's* story is *not* the rape of a twelve-year-old by a dirty old man but *the confiscation of one individual's life by another*. We don't know what Lolita would have become if Humbert had not engulfed her. Yet the novel, the finished work, is hopeful, beautiful even, a defense not just of beauty but of life, ordinary everyday life, all the normal pleasures that Lolita, like Yassi, was deprived of.

Warming up and suddenly inspired, I added that in fact Nabokov had taken revenge against our own solipsizers; he had taken revenge on the Ayatollah Khomeini, on Yassi's last suitor, on the dough-faced teacher for that matter. They had tried to shape others according to their own dreams and desires, but Nabokov, through his portrayal of Humbert, had exposed all solipsists who take over other people's lives. She, Yassi, had much potential; she could be whatever she wanted to be—a good wife or a teacher and poet. What mattered was for her to know what she wanted.

I went on to tell her one of my favorite Nabokov stories, called "The Magician's Room." At first he had wanted to call it "The Underground Man." It was about a gifted writer and critic whose two great loves had been fiction and film. After the revolution, all that he had loved was forbidden, driven underground. So he decided to stop writing, to stop making a living for as long as the Communists were in power. He seldom left his small apartment. At times he was near starvation, and if not for his devoted friends and students and a little money left him by his parents, he would have starved.

I described his apartment in detail. It was bare and white— flagrantly white: the walls, the tiles, even the kitchen cabinets. The only decoration in the living room was a large painting on the otherwise empty wall facing the entrance. The painting was of trees, shades of thick textured green on green. There was no light, yet the trees were illuminated, as if reflecting a luminosity that came not from the sun but from within.

The furniture in the magician's living room consisted of one brown sofa, a small table and two matching chairs. A rocking chair seemed stranded in the space between the living and dining area. A small rug, the gift of an already forgotten lost love, was thrown in front of the rocking chair. In this room, on that sofa, the underground man received his carefully selected visitors. They were famous filmmakers, scriptwriters, painters, writers, critics, former students and friends. They all came to ask his advice about their films, books and lovers; they wanted to know how they could bypass the regulations, how they could cheat the censor or carry on their clandestine love affairs. He shaped their works and their lives for them. He spent hours talking through the structure of an idea or, in the cutting room, editing a film. He advised some friends on how to make up with their lovers. He advised others that if they wanted to write better, they should fall in love. He read almost all the publications in the Soviet Union and was somehow up-to-date on the latest or best films and books written abroad.

Many wished to be part of his hidden kingdom, but he picked only a few who passed his secret test. He made all the bids, accepting and rejecting them for reasons of his own. In return for his help, he asked that his friends never acknowledge or mention his name publicly. There were many whom he had cut from his life because they had gone against this demand. I remember one of his oft-repeated sentences: "I want to be forgotten; I am not a member of this club."

The look on Yassi's face encouraged me to shape and invent my story. She reminded me of what I must have looked like as a very small child when my father, at night and also in the early morning before he went to work, would sit by my bed and weave stories. When he was angry at something I had done, when he wanted me to do something, when he wished to appease me, all the mundane details of an everyday relationship he transformed into a tale that choked me with sudden thrills and tremors.

What I did not tell Yassi that day was that Nabokov's magician, the man who was as dangerous to the state as an armed rebel, did not exist—or, at least, not in fiction. He was real and lived less than fifteen minutes away from where she and I were sitting, aimlessly stirring our long spoons in the tall glasses.

That was how I chose to ask Yassi to participate in my class.

IO

I have asked you to imagine us, to imagine us in the act of reading *Lolita* in Tehran: a novel about a man who, in order to possess and captivate a twelve-year-old girl, indirectly causes the death of her mother, Charlotte, and keeps her as his little entrapped mistress for two years. Are you bewildered? Why *Lolita*? Why *Lolita* in Tehran?

I want to emphasize once more that *we* were *not* Lolita, the Ayatollah was *not* Humbert and this republic was *not* what Humbert called his princedom by the sea. *Lolita* was *not* a critique of the Islamic Republic, but it went against the grain of all totalitarian perspectives.

Let us go to the part when Humbert arrives at Lolita's summer camp to pick her up after her mother's death, of which she knows nothing. This scene is the prelude to two years of captivity, during which the unwitting Lolita drifts from one motel to another with her guardian-lover:

"Let me retain for a moment that scene in all its trivial and fateful detail: hag Holmes writing out a receipt, scratching her head, pulling a drawer out of her desk, pouring change into my impatient palm, then neatly spreading a banknote over it with a bright '. . . and five!'; photographs of girl-children; some gaudy moth or butterfly, still alive, safely pinned to the wall ('nature study'); the framed diploma of the camp's dietitian; my trembling hands; a card produced by efficient Holmes with a report of Dolly Haze's behavior for July ('fair to good; keen on swimming and boating'); a sound of trees and birds, and my pounding heart . . . I was standing with my back to the open door, and then I felt the blood rush to my head as I heard her respiration and voice behind me."

Although this is not one of the more spectacular scenes in *Lolita,* it demonstrates Nabokov's skill, and I believe it is at the heart of the novel. Nabokov called himself a painterly writer, and this scene gives a good indication of what he meant. The description is pregnant with the tension between what has gone on before (Charlotte's discovery of Humbert's treachery and their confrontation, leading to Charlotte's fatal accident) and the knowledge of more terrible things to come. Through the juxtaposition of insignificant objects (a framed diploma, photographs of girl-children), ordinary transactions ("fair to good; keen on swimming and boating") with personal feeling and emotions ("my impatient palm," "my trembling hands," "my pounding heart"), Nabokov foreshadows Humbert's terrible deeds and Lolita's orphaned future.

Ordinary objects in this seemingly descriptive scene are destabilized by emotions, revealing Humbert's guilty secret. From now on, Humbert's shiver and tremble will color every nuance of his narrative, imposing emotion onto landscape, time and incident, however seemingly marginal or insignificant. Did you, like my girls, feel that the evil implied in Humbert's actions and emotions is all the more terrifying because he parades as a normal husband, normal stepfather, normal human being?

Then there is the butterfly—or is it a moth? Humbert's inability to differentiate between the two, his indifference, implies a moral carelessness in other matters. This blind indifference echoes his callous attitude towards Charlotte's dead son and Lolita's nightly sobs. Those who tell us Lolita is a little vixen who deserved what she got should remember her nightly sobs in the arms of her rapist and jailer, because you see, as Humbert reminds us with a mixture of relish and pathos, "she had absolutely nowhere else to go."

This came to mind when we were discussing in our class Humbert's confiscation of Lolita's life. The first thing that struck us in reading *Lolita*—in fact it was on the very first page—was how Lolita was given to us as Humbert's creature. We only see her in passing glimpses. "What I had madly possessed," he informs us, "was not she, but my own creation, another fanciful Lolita—perhaps, more real than Lolita . . . having no will, no consciousness—indeed no real life of her own." Humbert pins Lolita by first naming her, a name that becomes the echo of his desires. There, on the very first page, he adumbrates her various names, names for different occasions, Lo, Lola and in his arms always Lolita. We are also informed of her "real" name, Dolores, the Spanish word for *pain*.

To reinvent her, Humbert must take from Lolita her own real history and replace it with his own, turning Lolita into a reincarnation of his lost, unfulfilled young love, Annabel Leigh. We know Lolita not directly but through Humbert, and not through her own past but through her narrator/molester's past or imaginary past. This is what

Humbert, a number of critics and in fact one of my students, Nima, called Humbert's solipsization of Lolita.

Yet she does have a past. Despite Humbert's attempts to orphan Lolita by robbing her of her history, that past is still given to us in glimpses. Nabokov's art makes these orphaned glimmers all the more poignant in contrast to Humbert's all-encompassing obsession with his own past. Lolita has a tragic past, with a dead father and a dead two-year-old brother. And now also a dead mother. Like my students, Lolita's past comes to her not so much as a loss but as a lack, and like my students, she becomes a figment in someone else's dream.

At some point, the truth of Iran's past became as immaterial to those who appropriated it as the truth of Lolita's is to Humbert. It became immaterial in the same way that Lolita's truth, her desires and life, must lose color before Humbert's one obsession, his desire to turn a twelve-year-old unruly child into his mistress.

When I think of Lolita, I think of that half-alive butterfly pinned to the wall. The butterfly is not an obvious symbol, but it does suggest that Humbert fixes Lolita in the same manner that the butterfly is fixed; he wants her, a living breathing human being, to become stationary, to give up her life for the still life he offers her in return. Lolita's image is forever associated in the minds of her readers with that of her jailer. Lolita on her own has no meaning; she can only come to life through her prison bars.

This is how I read *Lolita*. Again and again as we discussed *Lolita* in that class, our discussions were colored by my students' hidden personal sorrows and joys. Like tearstains on a letter, these forays into the hidden and the personal shaded all our discussions of Nabokov. And more and more I thought of that butterfly; what linked us so closely was this perverse intimacy of victim and jailer.

II

I used big diaries for my class notes. The pages of these diaries were almost all blank, except for Thursdays and sometimes spilling over to Fridays, Saturdays and Sundays. When I left Iran, the diaries were too heavy to take with me, so I tore out the relevant pages, and this is what

I have in front of me: torn and scarred pages of those unforgotten diaries. There are some scrawls and references that I can no longer decipher, but my notes for the first few months are tidy and clean. They mostly refer to insights I gained during our discussions.

In the first few weeks of class, we read and discussed the books I had assigned in an orderly, almost formal manner. I had prepared a set of questions for my students, modeled on those a friend had sent me from her women's-studies program, aimed at drawing them out. They answered the questions dutifully—What do you think of your mother? Name six personalities you admire most in life and six you dislike most. What two words would you use to describe yourself? . . . Their answers to these dull questions were dull; they wrote what was expected of them. I remember that Manna tried to personalize her responses. In answer to "What is your image of yourself?" she had written, "I am not ready for that question yet." They were not ready—not yet.

From the beginning, I took notes, as if of an experiment. As early as November, just over a month into the meetings, I wrote: "Mitra: other women say that having children is their destiny as if they are doomed." I added: "Some of my girls are more radical than I am in their resentment of men. All of them want to be independent. They think they cannot find men equal to them. They think they have grown and matured, but men in their lives have not, they have not bothered to think." November 23: "Manna: I am scared of myself, nothing I do or have is like that of others around me. Others scare me. I scare me." Throughout, from start to finish, I observe that they have no clear image of themselves; they can only see and shape themselves through other people's eyes—ironically, the very people they despise. I have underlined *love yourself, self-confidence.*

Where they opened up and became excited was in our discussion of the works. The novels were an escape from reality in the sense that we could marvel at their beauty and perfection, and leave aside our stories about the deans and the university and the morality squads in the streets. There was a certain innocence with which we read these books; we read them apart from our own history and expectations, like Alice running after the White Rabbit and jumping into the hole. This innocence paid off: I do not think that without it we could have understood our own inarticulateness. Curiously, the novels we escaped into led us finally to question and prod our own realities, about which we felt so helplessly speechless.

Unlike the generation of writers and intellectuals I was brought up with and now consorted with, this new generation, the one my girls belonged to, was not interested in ideologies or political positions. They had a genuine curiosity, a real thirst for the works of great writers, those condemned to obscure shadows by both the regime and the revolutionary intellectuals, most of their books banned and forbidden. Unlike in pre-revolutionary times, now the "non-Revolutionary writers," the bearers of the canon, were the ones celebrated by the young: James, Nabokov, Woolf, Bellow, Austen and Joyce were revered names, emissaries of that forbidden world which we would turn into something more pure and golden than it ever was or will be.

In one sense the desire for beauty, the instinctive urge to struggle with the "wrong shape of things," to borrow from Vadim, the narrator of Nabokov's last novel, *Look at the Harlequins!,* drove many from various ideological poles to what we generally label as culture. This was one domain where ideology played a relatively small part.

I would like to believe that all this eagerness meant something, that there was in the air, in Tehran, something not quite like spring but a breeze, an aura that promised spring was on its way. This is what I cling to, the faint whiff of a sustained and restrained excitement, reminding me of reading a book like *Lolita* in Tehran. I still find it in my former students' letters when, despite all their fears and anxieties for a future without jobs or security and a fragile and disloyal present, they write about their search for beauty.

12

I wonder if you can imagine us. We are sitting around the iron-and-glass table on a cloudy November day; the yellow and red leaves reflected in the dining room mirror are drenched in a haze. I and perhaps two others have copies of *Lolita* on our laps. The rest have a heavy Xerox. There is no easy access to these books—you cannot buy them in the bookstores anymore. First the censors banned most of them, then the government stopped them from being sold: most of the foreign-language bookstores were closed or had to rely on their pre-revolutionary stock. Some of these books could be found at secondhand bookstores, and a very few at the annual international book fair in Tehran. A book like *Lolita* was difficult to find, especially the annotated version that my girls wanted to have. We photocopied all three hundred pages for those without copies. In an hour when we take a break, we will have tea or coffee with pastry. I don't remember whose turn it is for pastry. We take turns; every week, one of us provides the pastry.

13

"Moppet," "little monster," "corrupt," "shallow," "brat"—these are some of the terms assigned to Lolita by her critics. Compared to these assaults, Humbert's similar attacks on Lolita and her mother seem almost mild. Then there are others—among them Lionel Trilling, no less—who see the story as a great love affair, and still others who condemn *Lolita* because they feel Nabokov turned the rape of a twelve-year-old into an aesthetic experience.

We in our class disagreed with all of these interpretations. We unanimously (I am rather proud to say) agreed with Véra Nabokov and sided with Lolita. "Lolita discussed by the papers from every possible point of view except one: that of its beauty and pathos," Véra wrote in her diary. "Critics prefer to look for moral symbols, justification, condemnation, or explanation of HH's predicament. . . . I wish, though, somebody would notice the tender description of the child's helplessness, her pathetic dependence on monstrous HH, and her heartrending courage all along culminating in that squalid but essentially pure and healthy marriage, and her letter, and her dog. And that terrible expression on her face when she had been cheated by HH out of some little pleasure that had been promised. They all miss the fact that the 'horrid little brat' Lolita is essentially very good indeed—or she would not have straightened out after being crushed so terribly, and found a decent life with poor Dick more to her liking than the other kind."

Humbert's narration is confessional, both in the usual sense of the term and in that he is literally writing a confession in jail, awaiting trial for the murder of the playwright Claire Quilty, with whom Lolita ran away to escape him and who cast her off after she refused to participate in his cruel sex games. Humbert appears to us both as narrator and seducer—not just of Lolita but also of us, his readers, whom throughout the book he addresses as "ladies and gentlemen of the jury" (sometimes as "Winged gentlemen of the jury"). As the story unfolds, a deeper crime, more serious than Quilty's murder, is revealed: the entrapment and rape of Lolita (you will notice that while Lolita's scenes are written with passion and tenderness, Quilty's murder is portrayed as farce). Humbert's prose, veering at times towards the shamelessly overwrought, aims at seducing the reader, especially the high-minded reader, who will be taken in by such erudite gymnastics. Lolita belongs to a category of victims who have no defense and are never given a chance to articulate their own story. As such, she becomes a double victim: not only her life but also her life story is taken from her. We told ourselves we were in that class to prevent ourselves from falling victim to this second crime.

Lolita and her mother are doomed before we see them: the Haze house, as Humbert calls it, more gray than white, is "the kind of place you know will have a rubber tube affixable to the tub faucet in lieu of shower." By the time we stand in the front hall (graced with door chimes and "that banal darling of arty middle class, van Gogh's 'Arlesienne' ") our smile has already turned smug and mocking. We glance at the staircase and hear Mrs. Haze's "contralto voice" before Charlotte ("a weak solution of Marlene Dietrich") descends into view. Sentence by sentence and word by word, Humbert destroys Charlotte even as he describes her: "She was obviously one of those women whose polished words may reflect a book club or a bridge club, or any other deadly conventionality, but never her soul."

She never has a chance, poor woman; nor does she improve on further acquaintance as the reader is regaled with descriptions of her superficiality, her sentimental and jealous passion for Humbert and her nastiness to her daughter. Through his beautiful language ("you can always trust a murderer for his fancy prose style"), Humbert focuses the reader's attention on the banalities and small cruelties of American consumerism, creating a sense of empathy and complicity with the reader, who is encouraged to conceive of as understandable his ruthless seduction of a lonely widow and his eventual marriage to her in order to seduce her daughter.

Nabokov's art is revealed in his ability to make us feel sympathy for Humbert's victims—at least for his two wives, Valeria and Charlotte—without our approving of them. We condemn Humbert's acts of cruelty towards them even as we substantiate his judgment of their banality. What we have here is the first lesson in democracy: all individuals, no matter how contemptible, have a right to life, liberty and the pursuit of happiness. In *Invitation to a Beheading* and *Bend Sinister,* Nabokov's villains are the vulgar and brutal totalitarian rulers trying to possess and control imaginative minds; in *Lolita,* the villain is the one with the imaginative mind. The reader could never be confused by Monsieur Pierre, but how is he to judge a Monsieur Humbert?

Humbert makes fullest use of his art and guile in setting the reader up for his most heinous crime: his first attempt at possessing Lolita. He prepares us for the ultimate scene of seduction with the same immaculate precision with which he prepares to dope Lolita and take advantage of her listless body. He tries to win us to his side by placing us in the same category as himself: as ardent critics of consumer culture. He describes Lolita as a vulgar vixen—"a disgustingly conventional little girl," he calls her. "And neither is she the fragile child of a feminine novel."

Like the best defense attorneys, who dazzle us with their rhetoric and appeal to our higher sense of morality, Humbert exonerates himself by implicating his victim—a method we were quite familiar with in the Islamic Republic of Iran. ("We are not against cinema," Ayatollah Khomeini had declared as his henchmen set fire to the movie houses, "we are against prostitution!") Addressing the "Frigid gentlewomen of the jury," Humbert informs us: "I am going to tell you something very strange: it was she who seduced me. . . . [N]ot a trace of modesty," he confides, "did I perceive in this beautiful badly formed young girl whom modern co-education, juvenile mores, the campfire racket and so forth had utterly and hopelessly depraved. She saw the stark act merely as part of a youngster's furtive world, unknown to others."

So far it would seem that Humbert the criminal, with the help of Humbert the poet, has succeeded in seducing both Lolita and the reader. Yet in fact he fails on both fronts. In the case of Lolita, he never succeeds in possessing her willingly, so that every act of lovemaking from then on becomes a crueler and more tainted act of rape; she evades him at every turn. And he fails to completely seduce the reader, or some readers at least. Again ironically, his ability as a poet, his own fancy prose style, exposes him for what he is.

You do see how Nabokov's prose provides trapdoors for the unsuspecting reader: the credibility of every one of Humbert's assertions is simultaneously challenged and exposed by the hidden truth implied by his descriptions. Thus another Lolita emerges that reaches beyond the caricature of the vulgar insensitive minx, although she is that, too. A hurt, lonely girl, deprived of her childhood, orphaned and with no refuge. Humbert's rare insights give us glimpses into Lolita's character, her vulnerability and aloneness. Were he to paint the murals in the Enchanted Hunters, the motel where he first raped her, he tells us, he would have painted a lake, an arbor in flames and finally there would have been "a fire opal dissolving within a ripple-ringed pool, a last throb, a last dab of color, stinging red, smarting pink, a sigh, a wincing child." (Child, please remember, ladies and gentlemen of the jury, although this child, had she lived in the Islamic Republic, would have been long ripe for marriage to men older than Humbert.)

As the story develops, Humbert's list of grievances grows. He calls her "the vile and beloved slut" and talks of her "obscene young legs," yet we soon discover what Humbert's complaints mean: she sits on his lap, picking her nose, engrossed in "the lighter section of a newspaper, indifferent to my ecstasy as if it were something she sat upon, a shoe, a doll, the handle of a tennis racket." Of course, all murderers and all oppressors have a long list of grievances against their victims, only most are not as eloquent as Humbert Humbert.

Nor is he always the gentle lover: her slightest attempt at independence brings on his most furious wrath: "I delivered a tremendous backhand cut that caught her smack on her hot hard little cheek bone. And then the remorse, the poignant sweetness of sobbing atonement, groveling love, the hopelessness of sensual reconciliation. In the velvet night, at Mirana Motel (Mirana!) I kissed the yellowish soles of her long-toed feet, I immolated myself . . . but it was all of no avail. Both doomed were we. And soon I was to enter a new cycle of persecution."

No fact is more touching than Lolita's utter helplessness. The very first morning after their painful (to Lo, putting on a brave show) and ecstatic (to Humbert) sexual encounter, she demands some money to call her mother. "Why can't I call my mother if I want to?" "Because," Humbert answers, "your mother is dead." That night at the hotel, Lo and Humbert have separate rooms, but "in the middle of the night she came sobbing into mine, and we made it up very gently. You see, she had absolutely nowhere else to go."

And this of course was the whole crux of the matter: she had nowhere else to go, and for two years, in dingy motels and byways, in his home or even in school, he forces her to consent to him. He prevents her from mixing with children her own age, watches over her so she never has boyfriends, frightens her into secrecy, bribes her with money for acts of sex, which he revokes when he has had his due.

Before the reader makes his judgment about either Humbert or our own blind censor, I must remind him that at some point Humbert addresses his audience as "Reader! *Bruder!*"—a reminder of a well-known line by Baudelaire, the preface to his book of poems *Les Fleurs du Mal:*—"*Hypocrite lecteur,—mon semblable,—mon frère!*"

14

Reaching for a pastry, Mitra says that something has been bothering her for some time. Why is it that stories like *Lolita* and *Madame Bovary*—stories that are so sad, so tragic—make us happy? Is it not sinful to feel pleasure when reading about something so terrible? Would we feel this way if we were to read about it in the newspapers or if it happened to us? If we were to write about our lives here in the Islamic Republic of Iran, should we make our readers happy?

That night, like many other nights, I took the class to bed with me. I felt I had not adequately answered Mitra's question, and was tempted to call my magician and talk to him about our discussion. It was one of those rare nights when I was kept awake not by my nightmares and anxieties but by something exciting and exhilarating. Most nights I lay awake waiting for some unexpected disaster to descend on our house or for a telephone call that would give us the bad news about a friend or a relative. I think I somehow felt that as long as I was conscious, nothing bad could happen, that bad things would come in the middle of my dreams.

I can trace my nightly tremors back to the time when, in my sophomore year, while studying at a horrible school in Switzerland, I was summoned in the middle of a history lesson with a stern American teacher to the principal's office. There I was told that they had just heard on the radio that my father, the youngest mayor in Tehran's history, had been jailed. Only three weeks earlier I had seen a large color photograph of him in *Paris Match,* standing by General de Gaulle. He was not with the Shah or any other dignitary—it was just Father and the General. Like the rest of my family, my father was a culture snob, who went into politics despising politicians and defying them almost at every turn. He was insolent to his superiors, at once popular and outspoken and on good terms with journalists. He wrote poetry and thought his real vocation should have been writing. I learned later that the General had taken a special liking to him after my father's welcoming speech, which was delivered in French and filled with allusions to great French writers such as Chateaubriand and Victor Hugo. De Gaulle chose to reward him with the Legion of Honor. This did not go over well with the Iranian elite, who had resented my father's insubordinate attitude before and were now jealous of the extra attentions paid him.

One small compensation for the bad news was that I did not have to continue my Swiss education. That Christmas I went back home with a special escort to take me to the airport. The reality of my father's imprisonment was established for me when I landed at the Tehran airport and did not find him waiting for me there. For the four years that they kept him in his "temporary" jail—in the jail's library, adjacent to the morgue—we were told alternately that he was going to be killed or that he would be set free almost at once. He was eventually exonerated of all charges except one, insubordination. This I always remember—insubordination: it became a way of life for me after that. Much later, when I read a sentence by Nabokov— "curiosity is insubordination in its purest form"—the verdict against my father came to my mind.

I never recovered from the shock of that moment when I was pulled out of the security of Mr. Holmes's—I think that was his name—stern classroom and told that my father, the mayor, was now in jail. Later, the Islamic Revolution took away whatever sense of security I had managed to re-establish after my father's release from jail.

Several months into the class, my girls and I discovered that almost every one of us had had at least one nightmare in some form or another in which we either had forgotten to wear our veil or had not worn it, and always in these dreams the dreamer was running, running away. In one, perhaps my own, the dreamer wanted to run but she couldn't: she was rooted to the ground, right outside her front door. She could not turn around, open the door and hide inside. The only one among us who claimed she had never experienced such fear was Nassrin. "I was always afraid of having to lie. You know what they say: to thine own self be true and all that. I believed in that sort of thing," she said with a shrug. "But I have improved," she added as an afterthought.

Later, Nima told us that the son of one of his friends, a ten-year-old, had awakened his parents in horror telling them he had been having an "illegal dream." He had been dreaming that he was at the seaside with some men and women who were kissing, and he did not know what to do. He kept repeating to his parents that he was having illegal dreams.

In *Invitation to a Beheading*, on the wall of Cincinnatus C.'s jail, which is decorated like a third-rate hotel, there are certain instructions for the prisoners, such as: "A prisoner's meekness is a prison's pride." Rule number six, one that lies at the heart of the novel, is: "It is desirable that the inmate should not have dreams at all, or if he does, should immediately himself suppress nocturnal dreams whose context might be incompatible with the condition and status of the prisoner, such as: resplendent landscapes, outings with friends, family dinners, as well as sexual intercourse with persons who in real life and in the waking state would not suffer said individual to come near, which individual will therefore be considered by the law to be guilty of rape."

In the daytime it was better. I felt brave. I answered the Revolutionary Guards, I argued with them, I was not afraid of following them to the Revolutionary Committees. I did not have time to think about all the dead relatives and friends, about our own narrow and lucky escapes. I paid for it at night, always at night, when I returned. What will happen now? Who will be killed? When will they come? I had internalized the fear, so that I did not think of it always consciously, but I had insomnia; I roamed the house and I read and fell asleep with my glasses on, often holding on to my book. With fear come the lies and the justifications that, no matter how convincing, lower our self-esteem, as Nassrin had painfully reminded us.

Certain things saved me: my family and a small group of friends, the ideas, the thoughts, the books that I discussed with my underground man when we took our afternoon walks. He worried constantly—if we were stopped, what excuse could we give? We were not married; we were not brother and sister. . . . He worried for me and for my family, and every time he worried, I became bolder, letting my scarf slip, laughing out loud. I could not do much to "them," but I could get angry at him or at my husband, at all the men who were so cautious, so worried about me, for "my sake."

After our first discussion of *Lolita,* I went to bed excited, thinking about Mitra's question. Why did *Lolita* or *Madame Bovary* fill us with so much joy? Was there something wrong with these novels, or with us?—were Flaubert and Nabokov unfeeling brutes? By the next Thursday, I had formulated my thoughts and could not wait to share them with the class.

Nabokov calls every great novel a fairy tale, I said. Well, I would agree. First, let me remind you that fairy tales abound with frightening witches who eat children and wicked stepmothers who poison their beautiful stepdaughters and weak fathers who leave their children behind in forests. But the magic comes from the power of good, that force which tells us we need not give in to the limitations and restrictions imposed on us by McFate, as Nabokov called it.

Every fairy tale offers the potential to surpass present limits, so in a sense the fairy tale offers you freedoms that reality denies. In all great works of fiction, regardless of the grim reality they present, there is an affirmation of life against the transience of that life, an essential defiance. This affirmation lies in the way the author takes control of reality by retelling it in his own way, thus creating a new world. Every great work of art, I would declare pompously, is a celebration, an act of insubordination against the betrayals, horrors and infidelities of life. The perfection and beauty of form rebels against the ugliness and shabbiness of the subject matter. This is why we love *Madame Bovary* and cry for Emma, why we greedily read *Lolita* as our heart breaks for its small, vulgar, poetic and defiant orphaned heroine.

15

Manna and Yassi had come in early. Somehow we got to talking about the definitions we had concocted for the members of the class. I told them I called Nassrin my Cheshire cat, because she was in the habit of appearing and disappearing at strange times. When Nassrin came in with Mahshid, we told her what we had been saying. Manna said, "If I had to come up with a definition for Nassrin, I would call her a contradiction in terms." This, for some reason, made Nassrin angry. She turned to Manna, almost accusingly: "You are the poet, Mitra the painter, and what am I—a contradiction in terms?"

There was a certain truth to Manna's half-ironic definition. The sun and clouds that defined Nassrin's infinite moods and temperaments were too intimate, too inseparable. She lived by startling statements that she blurted out in a most awkward manner. My girls all surprised me at one point or another, but she more than the rest.

One day Nassrin had stayed on after class, to help me sort out and file my lecture notes. We had talked randomly, about the university days and the hypocrisy of some officials and activists in various Muslim associations. She had gone on to tell me, as she calmly put sheets of paper in blue file folders and entered the date and subject for each file, that her youngest uncle, a very devoted and pious man, had sexually abused her when she was barely eleven years old. Nassrin recounted how he used to say that he wanted to keep himself chaste and pure for his future wife and refused friendships with women on that count. *Chaste and pure,* she mockingly repeated. He used to tutor Nassrin—a restless and unruly child—three times a week for over a year. He helped her with Arabic and sometimes with mathematics. During those sessions as they sat side by side at her desk, his hands had wandered over her legs, her whole body, as he repeated the Arabic tenses.

This was a memorable day in many ways. In class, we were discussing the concept of the villain in the novel. I had mentioned that Humbert was a villain because he lacked curiosity about other people and their lives, even about the person he loved most, Lolita. Humbert, like most dictators, was interested only in his own vision of other people. He had created the Lolita he desired, and would not budge from that image. I reminded them of Humbert's statement that he wished to stop time and keep Lolita forever on "an island of entranced time," a task undertaken only by Gods and poets.

I tried to explain how *Lolita* was a more complex novel than any of the previous ones we had read by Nabokov. On the surface of course *Lolita* is more realistic, but it also has the same trapdoors and unexpected twists and turns. I showed them a small photograph of Joshua Reynolds's painting *The Age of Innocence,* which I had found accidentally in an old graduate paper. We were discussing the scene in which Humbert, paying a visit to Lolita's school, finds her in a class-room. Reynolds's print of a young girl-child in white, with brown curly hair, hangs above the chalkboard. Lolita is sitting behind an-other "nymphet," an exquisite blonde with a "very naked porcelain-white neck" and "wonderful platinum hair." Humbert settles in beside Lolita, "just behind that neck and that hair," and unbuttons his overcoat and, for a bribe, forces Lolita to put her "inky, chalky, red-knuckled hand" under her desk to satisfy what in ordinary language is called his lust.

Let us pause for a moment on this casual description of Lolita's schoolgirl hands. The innocence of the description belies the action Lolita is forced to perform. The words "inky, chalky, red-knuckled" are enough to take us to the edge of tears. There is a pause. . . . Do I imagine it now?—was there a long pause after we discussed that scene?

"What bothers us most, of course," I said, "is not just the utter helplessness of Lolita but the fact that Humbert robs her of her child-hood." Sanaz picked up her Xerox of the novel and began. " 'And it struck me,' " she read, " 'as my automaton knees went up and down, that I simply didn't know a thing about my darling's mind and that quite possibly behind the awful juvenile clichés, there was in her a garden and a twilight, and a palace gate—dim adorable regions which happened to be lucidly and absolutely forbidden to me, in my pol-luted rags and miserable convulsions . . .' "

I tried to ignore the meaningful glances my girls exchanged among themselves.

"It is hard for me," Mahshid said at last, "to read the parts about Lolita's feelings. All she wants is to be a normal girl. Remember the scene when Avis's father comes to pick her up and Lolita notices the way the fat little daughter and father cling to each other? All she wants is to live a normal life."

"It is interesting," said Nassrin, "that Nabokov, who is so hard on poshlust, would make us pity the loss of the most conventional forms of life."

"Do you think Humbert changes when he sees her in the end," Yassi interrupted, "broken, pregnant and poor?"

The time for our break had come and gone, but we were too absorbed in our discussion to notice. Manna, who seemed engrossed by a passage in the book, raised her head. "It's strange," she said, "but some critics seem to treat the text the same way Humbert treats Lolita: they only see themselves and what they want to see." She turned to me and continued: "I mean, the censors, or some of our politicized critics, don't they do the same thing, cutting up books and re-creating them in their own image? What Ayatollah Khomeini tried to do to our lives, turning us, as you said, into figments of his imagination, he also did to our fiction. Look at Salman Rushdie's case."

Sanaz, playing with her long hair and rolling it around her finger, looked up and said, "Many people feel that Rushdie portrayed their religion in a distorted and irreverent manner. I mean, they don't object to his writing fiction but to his being offensive."

"Is it possible to write a reverent novel," said Nassrin, "and to have it be good? Besides, the contract with the reader is that this is not reality, it's an invented world. There must be some blasted space in life," she added crossly, "where we can be offensive, for God's sake."

Sanaz was a little startled by the vehemence of Nassrin's retort. Through most of this discussion, Nassrin had been drawing furious lines in her notebook, and after she had delivered her pronouncement, she went on with her drawing.

"The problem with the censors is that they are not malleable." We all looked at Yassi. She shrugged as if to say she couldn't help it, the word appealed to her. "Do you remember how on TV they cut Ophelia from the Russian version of *Hamlet*?"

"That would make a good title for a paper," I said. " 'Mourning Ophelia.' " Ever since I had started going abroad for talks and conferences in 1991, mainly to the United States and England, every subject immediately took on the shape of a title for a presentation or a paper.

"Everything is offensive to them," said Manna. "It's either politically or sexually incorrect." Looking at her short but stylish hairdo, her blue sweatshirt and jeans, I thought how misplaced she looked enveloped in the voluminous fabric of her veil.

Mahshid, who had been quiet until then, suddenly spoke up. "I have a problem with all of this," she said. "We keep talking about how Humbert is wrong, and I do think he is, but we are not talking about the issue of morality. Some things *are* offensive to some people." She paused, startled by her own vehemence. "I mean, my parents are very religious—is that a crime?" she asked, raising her eyes to me. "Do they not have a right to expect me to be like them? Why should I condemn Humbert but not the girl in *Loitering with Intent* and say it's okay to have an adulterous relationship? These are serious questions, and they become difficult when we apply them to our own lives," she said, lowering her gaze, as if looking for a response in the designs on the carpet.

"I think," Azin shot back, "that an adulterous woman is much better than a hypocritical one." Azin was very nervous that day. She had brought her three-year-old daughter (the nursery was closed; there was no one to look after her), and we'd had difficulty convincing her to leave her mother's side and watch cartoons in the hall with Tahereh Khanoom, who helped us with the housework.

Mahshid turned to Azin and said with quiet disdain: "No one was talking about making a choice between adultery and hypocrisy. The point is, do we have any morality at all? Do we consider that anything goes, that we have no responsibility towards others but only for satisfying our needs?"

"Well, that is the crux of the great novels," Manna added, "like *Madame Bovary* or *Anna Karenina,* or James's for that matter—the question of doing what is right or what we want to do."

"And what if we say that it is right to do what we want to do and not what society or some authority figure tells us to do?" said Nassrin, this time without bothering to lift her head from her notebook. There was something in the air that day that did not relate directly to the books we had read. Our discussion had plunged us into more personal and private arenas, and my girls found that they could not resolve their own dilemmas quite as neatly as they could in the case of Emma Bovary or Lolita.

Azin had bent forward, her long gold earrings playing hide-and-seek in the ringlets of her hair. "We need to be honest with ourselves," she said. "I mean, that is the first condition. As women, do we have the same right as men to enjoy sex? How many of us would say yes, we do have a right, we have an equal right to enjoy sex, and if our husbands don't satisfy us, then we have a right to seek satisfaction elsewhere." She tried to make her point as casually as possible, but she had managed to surprise us all.

Azin is the tallest one in our group, the one with the blond hair and milky skin. She would often bite the corner of her lower lip and launch into tirades about love, sex and men—like a child throwing a big stone into the pool; not just to make a splash, but to wet the adults in the bargain. Azin had been married three times, most recently to a good-looking and rich merchant from a traditional provincial bazaari family. I had seen her husband at many of my conferences and meetings, which were usually attended by my girls. He seemed very proud of her and always treated me with exaggerated deference. At every meeting, he made sure I was comfortable; if there was no water at the podium, he would see to it that the mistake was rectified; if extra chairs were needed, he would boss the staff around. Somehow at these meetings it seemed that he was the gracious host, who had granted us his space, his time, because that was all he had to give.

I was sure that Azin's assault had been partly directed against Mahshid, and perhaps indirectly against Manna, too. Their clashes were not only the result of their different backgrounds. Azin's outbursts, her seeming frankness about her personal life and desires, made Manna and Mahshid, both reserved by temperament, deeply uncomfortable. They disapproved of her, and Azin sensed that. Her efforts at friendship were rejected as hypocritical.

Mahshid's response, as usual, was silence. She drew into herself and refused to fill the void that Azin's question had left behind. Her silence extended to the others, and was broken finally by a short giggle from Yassi. I thought this was a good time for a break and went to the kitchen to bring in the tea.

When I returned, I heard Yassi laughing. Trying to lighten the mood, she was saying, "How could God be so cruel as to create a Muslim woman with so much flesh and so little sex appeal?" She turned towards Mahshid and stared at her in mock horror.

Mahshid look down and then shyly and royally lifted her head, her slanted eyes widening in an indulgent smile. "You don't need sex appeal," she told Yassi.

But Yassi would not give up. "Laugh, please, laugh," she implored Mahshid. "Dr. Nafisi, please command her to laugh." And Mahshid's attempt at laughter was drowned out by the others' less guarded hilarity.

There was a pause and a silence as I placed the tray of tea on the table. Nassrin suddenly said: "I know what it means to be caught between tradition and change. I've been in the middle of it all my life."

She seated herself on the arm of Mahshid's chair, while Mahshid did her best to drink her tea and keep it from coming into collision with Nassrin, whose expressive hands, moving in all directions, came precariously close to knocking the teacup over several times.

"I know it firsthand," Nassrin said. "My mother came from a wealthy, secular and modern family. She was the only daughter, had two brothers, both of whom had chosen a diplomatic career. My grandfather was very liberal and he wanted her to finish her education and go to college. He sent her to the American school." "The American school?" echoed Sanaz, her hand lovingly playing with her hair. "Yes, in those days most girls didn't even finish high school, never mind going to the American school, and my mother could speak English and French." Nassrin sounded rather pleased and proud of this fact.

"But then what did she do? She fell in love with my father, her tutor. She was terrible in math and science. It is ironic," said Nassrin, again lifting her left hand dangerously close to Mahshid's cup. "They thought my father, coming from a religious background, would be safe with a young girl like my mother, and anyway, who would have thought that a modern young woman like her would be interested in a stern young man who seldom smiled, never looked her in the eyes, and whose sisters and mother all wore the chador? But she fell for him, perhaps because he was so different, perhaps because for her, wearing the chador and caring for him seemed more romantic than going to some college and becoming a lady doctor or whatever.

"She said she never regretted it, her marriage, but she always talked about her American school, her old high school friends, whom she never saw again after her marriage. And she taught me English.

When I was a kid she used to teach me the ABCs and then she bought me English books. I never had trouble with English, thanks to her. Nor did my sister, who was much older than me, by nine years. Rather strange for a Muslim woman—I mean, she should have taught us Arabic, but she never learned the language. My sister married someone quote, unquote"—Nassrin made a large quotation mark with her hands—"'modern' and went to live in England. We only see them when they come home for vacations."

The time for break was over, but Nassrin's story had drawn us in, and even Azin and Mahshid seemed to have come to a temporary truce. When Mahshid stretched her hand to pick a cream puff, Azin handed the dish over to her with a friendly smile, forcing a gracious thank-you.

"My mother remained faithful to my dad. She changed her whole life for him, and never really complained," Nassrin continued. "His only concession was that he let her make us weird food, fancy French food my father would call it—all fancy food for him was French. Although we were brought up according to my dad's dictates, my mother's family and her past were always in the shadows, hinting at another way of life. It wasn't just that my mother could never get along with my father's family, who considered her uppity and an outsider. She's very lonely, my mother is. Sometimes I think I wish she would commit adultery or something."

Mahshid looked up at her, startled, and Nassrin got up and laughed. "Well," she said, "or something."

Nassrin's story, and the confrontation between Azin and Mahshid, had changed our mood too much for us to return to our class discussion. We ended up making desultory conversation, mainly gossiping about our experiences at the university, until we broke up.

When the girls left that afternoon, they left behind the aura of their unsolved problems and dilemmas. I felt exhausted. I chose the only way I knew to cope with problems: I went to the refrigerator, scooped up the coffee ice cream, poured some cold coffee over it, looked for walnuts, discovered we had none left, went after almonds, crushed them with my teeth and sprinkled them over my concoction.

I knew that Azin's outrageousness was partly defensive, that it was her way of overcoming Mahshid's and Manna's defenses. Mahshid thought Azin was dismissive of her traditional background, her thick, dark scarves, her old-maidenish ways; she didn't know how effective her own contemptuous silences could be. Small and dainty, with her cameo brooches—she did actually wear cameo brooches—her small earrings, pale blue blouses buttoned up to the neck and her pale smiles, Mahshid was a formidable enemy. Did she and Manna know how their obstinate silences, their cold, immaculate disapproval, affected Azin, made her defenseless?

In one of their confrontations, during the break, I had heard Mahshid telling Azin, "Yes, you have your sexual experiences and your admirers. You are not an old maid like me. Yes, old maid— I don't have a rich husband and I don't drive a car, but still you have no right, no right to disrespect me." When Azin complained, "But how? How was I disrespectful?", Mahshid had turned around and left her there, with a smile like cold leftovers. No amount of talk and discussion on my part, both in class and with each of them in private, had helped matters between them. Their only concession had been to try and leave each other alone inside the class. Not very malleable, as Yassi might say.

16

Is this how it all started? Was it the day we were sitting at his dining room table, greedily biting into our forbidden ham-and-cheese sandwich and calling it a croque monsieur? At some point we must have caught the same expression of ravenous, unadulterated pleasure in each other's eyes, because we started to laugh simultaneously. I raised my glass of water to him and said, Who would have thought that such a simple meal would appear to us like a kingly feast? and he said, We must thank the Islamic Republic for making us rediscover and even covet all these things we took for granted: one could write a paper on the pleasure of eating a ham sandwich. And I said, Oh, the things we have to be thankful for! And that memorable day was the beginning of our detailing our long list of debts to the Islamic Republic: parties, eating ice cream in public, falling in love, holding hands, wearing lipstick, laughing in public and reading *Lolita* in Tehran.

We sometimes met on a corner of the wide, leafy boulevard leading to the mountains for our afternoon walks. I used to wonder what the Revolutionary Committee would think of these meetings. Would they suspect us of political conspiracy or of a lovers' rendezvous? It was encouraging in a strange way that they would perhaps never guess the real purpose of our encounters. Was not life exciting when every simple act acquired the complexity of a dangerous secret mission? We always had something to exchange—books, articles, tapes, boxes of chocolates he received from Switzerland—for chocolates were expensive, especially ones from Switzerland. He brought me videos of rare films, which my children and I, and later my students and I, would watch: *A Night at the Opera, Casablanca, The Pirate, Johnny Guitar.*

My magician used to say he could tell a great deal about people from their photographs, especially the angle of their noses. After some hesitation, I brought him some photographs of my girls, anxiously awaiting his pronouncement. He would hold one in his hand, scrutinize it from different perspectives and issue a short statement.

I wanted him to read their writings and to look at their drawings, right there and then: I wanted to know what he thought. They are fine people, he said, looking at me with the ironic smile of an indulgent father. Fine? Fine people? I wanted him to say that they were geniuses, although I was glad to be assured of their fineness. Two of them, he thought, could make something of their writings. Shall I bring them to you? Will you meet with them? No, he was trying to get rid of people, not add to his acquaintances.

17

Cincinnatus C., the hero of *Invitation to a Beheading,* talks of a "rare kind of time . . . the pause, hiatus, when the heart is like a feather . . . part of my thoughts is always crowding around the invisible umbilical cord that joins this world to something—to what I shall not say yet." Cincinnatus's release by his jailers depends on his discovery of this invisible cord deep inside himself that joins him to another world, so that he can finally escape the staged and fake world of his executioners. In his preface to *Bend Sinister,* Nabokov describes a similar link to another world, a puddle that appears to Krug, his fictional hero, at various points in the novel: "a rent in his world leading to another world of tenderness, brightness and beauty."

I think in some ways our readings and discussions of the novels in that class became our moment of pause, our link to that other world of "tenderness, brightness and beauty." Only eventually, we were compelled to return.

During the break one morning, while we were enjoying our coffee and pastries, Mitra began to tell us how she felt as she climbed up the stairs every Thursday morning. She said that step by step she could feel herself gradually leaving reality behind her, leaving the dark, dank cell she lived in to surface for a few hours into open air and sunshine. Then, when it was over, she returned to her cell. At the time, I felt this was a point against the class, as if it should somehow guarantee open air and sunshine beyond its confines. Mitra's confession led to a debate about how we needed this pause from real life, in order to return to it refreshed and ready to confront it. Yet Mitra's point stayed with me: what about after the pause? Whether we wished it or not, our lives outside that living room made their claims.

But it was the fairy-tale atmosphere Mitra had alluded to that made it possible for all eight of us to share confidences and to share so much of our secret life with one another. This aura of magical affinity made it possible for Mahshid and Manna to find a way to peacefully coexist with Azin for a few hours every Thursday morning. It allowed us to defy the repressive reality outside the room—not only that, but to avenge ourselves on those who controlled our lives. For those few precious hours we felt free to discuss our pains and our joys, our personal hang-ups and weaknesses; for that suspended time we abdicated our responsibilities to our parents, relatives and friends, and to the Islamic Republic. We articulated all that happened to us in our own words and saw ourselves, for once, in our own image.

Our discussion of *Madame Bovary* continued way past the hour. It had happened before, but this time no one wanted to leave. The description of the dining table, the wind in Emma's hair, the face she sees before she dies—these details kept us going for hours. Initially our class hours were from nine to twelve, but gradually they were prolonged into the afternoon. I suggested that day that we continue with our discussion and that everyone stay for lunch. I think this is how we established lunches.

I remember all we had in the refrigerator were eggs and tomatoes, and we made a tomato omelette. Two weeks later we had a feast. Each one of my girls had cooked something special—rice and lamb, potato salad, dolmeh, saffron rice and a big round cake. My family joined us, and we all gathered around the table, joking and laughing. *Madame Bovary* had done what years of teaching at the university had not: it created a shared intimacy.

During the years they came to my house, they knew my family, my kitchen, my bedroom, the way I dressed and walked and talked at home. I had never set foot in their houses, I never met the traumatized mother, the delinquent brother, the shy sister. I could never place or locate their private narrative within a context, a locality. Yet I had met all of them in the magical space of my living room. They came to my house in a disembodied state of suspension, bringing to my living room their secrets, their pains and their gifts.

Gradually my life and family became part of the landscape, moving in and out of the living room during the breaks. Tahereh Khanoom would sometimes join in and tell us stories about her part of town, as she liked to call it. One day my daughter, Negar, burst in crying. She was hysterical. Between tears she kept saying she couldn't cry *there;* she didn't want to cry in front of *them.* Manna went into the kitchen and came back with Tahereh Khanoom and a glass of water. I went to Negar, held her in my arms and tried to calm her. Gently I took off her navy scarf and robe; under that thick scarf her hair was damp with sweat. Unbuttoning her uniform, I asked her to tell us what had happened.

That day in the middle of her last class—science—the principal and the morality teacher had barged in and told the girls to put their hands on their desks. The entire class had been escorted out of the classroom, without any explanation, their schoolbags searched for weapons and contraband: tapes, novels, friendship bracelets. Their bodies were searched, their nails inspected. One student, a girl who had returned from the United States the previous year with her family, was taken to the principal's office: her nails were too long. There, the principal herself had cut the girl's nails, so close that she had drawn blood. Negar had seen her classmate after they were dismissed, in the school yard, waiting to go home, nursing the guilty finger. The morality teacher stood beside her, discouraging other students from approaching. For Negar, the fact that she couldn't even go near and console her friend was as bad as the whole trauma of the search. She kept saying, Mom, she just doesn't know about our rules and regulations; you know, she just came back from America—how do you think she feels when they force us to trample on the American flag and shout, Death to America? I hate myself, I hate myself, she repeated as I rocked her back and forth and wiped the mixture of sweat and tears from her soft skin.

This of course diverted the whole class. Everyone tried to distract Negar by joking and telling her stories of their own, how once Nassrin had been sent to the disciplinary committee to have her eyelashes checked. Her lashes were long, and she was suspected of using mascara. That's nothing, said Manna, next to what happened to my sister's friends at the Amir Kabir Polytechnic University. During lunch three of the girls were in the yard eating apples. They were reprimanded by the guards: they were biting their apples too seductively! After a while Negar was laughing with them, and she finally went with Tahereh Khanoom to have her lunch.

18

Imagine you are walking down a leafy path. It is early spring before sundown, around six P.M. The sun is in the process of receding, and you are walking alone, caressed by the breezy light of the late afternoon. Then, suddenly, you feel a large drop on your right arm. Is it raining? You look up. The sky is still deceptively sunny: only a handful of clouds linger here and there. Seconds later, another drop. Then, with the sun still perched in the sky, you are drenched in a shower of rain. This is how memories invade me, abruptly and unexpectedly: drenched, I am suddenly left alone again on the sunny path, with a memory of the rain.

I have said that we were in that room to protect ourselves from the reality outside. I have also said that this reality imposed itself on us, like a petulant child who would not give his frustrated parents a moment to themselves. It created and shaped our intimacies, throwing us into unexpected complicity. Our relations became personal in many different ways. Not only did the most ordinary activities gain a new luminosity in the light of our secret, but everyday life sometimes took on the quality of make-believe or fiction. We had to reveal aspects of ourselves to one another that we didn't even know existed. I constantly felt I was being undressed in front of perfect strangers.

19

A few weeks ago, while driving down the George Washington Memorial Parkway, my children and I were reminiscing about Iran. I noticed with a sudden misgiving the alien tone they had adopted when talking about their own country. They kept repeating "they," "they over there." Over where? Where you buried your dead canary by a rosebush with your grandfather? Where your grandmother brought you chocolates we had forbidden you to eat? They did not remember many things. Some memories made them sad and nostalgic; others they dismissed. The names of my parents, Bijan's aunt and uncle, our close friends, they evoked like magic mantras joyfully taking shape and disappearing with each utterance.

What triggered our reminiscences? Was it the Doors CD that my children were so accustomed to hearing in Iran? They had bought it for me for Mother's Day, and we were listening to it in the car. Jim Morrison's seductively nonchalant voice purred from the stereo: "I'd like to have another kiss . . ." His voice stretched and curved and twisted while we talked and laughed. "She's a twentieth-century fox," he intoned. . . . Some memories bore them, some excite them, like when they make fun of their mother, dancing all over the place from the hall to the living room, singing, "C'mon baby light my fire . . ." They tell me they have already forgotten so much; so many faces have become dim. When I ask them, Do you remember this or that? most often they don't. Now Jim Morrison has moved to a song by Brecht: "Oh show me the way to the next whiskey bar," he sings, and we accompany him on the next line, "Oh, don't ask why. . . ." Even while we lived in Iran, they, like most kids their age, had little affection for Persian music. For them, Persian music was identified with political songs and military marches—for pleasure they turned somewhere else. I was shocked to realize that their childhood memories of songs and films in Iran would be the Doors, the Marx Brothers and Michael Jackson.

They liven up to one memory. This one is surprisingly clear; they fill in all the details I had forgotten. As it comes back to me and images form in my mind, their voices interrupting one another, Jim Morrison fades into the background. Yes, Yassi was there that day, wasn't she? They remember my whole class, but Yassi is the one they remember most, because at a certain point she became so much a part of our family. They all did: Azin, Nima, Manna, Mahshid and Nassrin were frequent visitors. They used to spoil my children, bringing them gifts, an act they performed despite my disapproval. My family had accepted these intruders as another one of my eccentricities, with tolerance and curiosity.

It happened in the summer of 1996, when my two children were home from school. It was a lazy morning. We had puttered about the house and prepared breakfast late. Yassi had stayed over the night before. She did that regularly now, so we came to expect her. She slept in a spare room next to the living room that was supposed to be my office, but it was too noisy for me; I had moved my office downstairs, to a basement room with windows opening onto the small garden.

It was an odds-and-ends room, with a desk and a very old laptop, some books, my winter clothes and Yassi's makeshift bed and lamp. Sometimes she spent hours in that room, with the lights turned off, because of her headaches. Almost every time she came from a visit to her hometown, she had these headaches. That morning she looked radiant, I remember. This is how I see her: in the kitchen or in the hall, standing or sitting. I imagine her mimicking some comical professor, doubling over with laughter.

That summer there were many days when Yassi would follow me around the house, telling me stories. Our place was mainly in the kitchen or the hall, and I enjoyed the fact that, unlike the grown-ups and like my own children, she actually liked my cooking. She loved my so-called pancakes and French toast, my concoctions of eggs, tomatoes and vegetables. Never once did she smile the indulgent smile that my grown-up friends gave me, as if to say, When will you learn? As I cooked or chopped, she would move with me and spin stories, mostly about her classes. Negar, who was eleven by then, would join us and the three of us would talk for hours.

That day Yassi was holding forth on her favorite subject: her uncles. She had five uncles and three aunts. One uncle had been killed by the Islamic Republic, and the rest lived in the United States or Europe. The women were the backbone of the family, the ones on whom everyone depended. They worked at home and they worked outside the home. Their marriages had been arranged, at a very young age, to much older men, and apart from one of the sisters—Yassi's mother—they all had to put up with spoiled, nagging husbands, inferior to them intellectually and in every other way.

It was the men, the uncles, who always held the promise of the future for Yassi. They were like Peter Pan, descending every once in a while from never-never land. When they came to her city, there were endless gatherings and celebrations. Everything the uncles said was enchanting. They had seen things no one else had seen, done things no one else had done. And they would bend down and play with her hair and say, Hey, little one, what have you been doing?

It was a quiet and peaceful morning. I was in my long housedress, curled on a chair in the living room, listening to Yassi's tale about a poem one of her uncles had sent her. Tahereh Khanoom was in the kitchen. From the open dining room door we could hear different noises, the sound of running tap water, the thin clink of pots and pans, half a sentence addressed to the children, who were in the hall by the kitchen, alternately laughing and quarreling. I remember yellow and white daffodils; the whole living room was filled with vases of daffodils. I had put the vases not on the tables but on the floor, beside a painting of yellow flowers in two blue vases, also on the floor.

We were waiting for my mother's Turkish coffee. My mother made fabulous Turkish coffee, thick, bittersweet, and this served as her excuse for periodic intrusions. At different intervals in the day, we would hear her calling us through the connecting door to our apartment. "Tahereh, Tahereh . . ." she would call, and she continued calling even when Tahereh and I answered her back in unison. Assured that we did indeed want our coffee, she disappeared, sometimes for over an hour.

This was my mother's way of communication for as long as I can remember. Curious about my class on Thursday mornings and too proud just to barge in, she used the coffee to gain admittance to our sanctuary. One morning she "accidentally" came upstairs and called me from the kitchen. "Do your guests want coffee?" she asked, glancing through the open door at my curious, smiling students. So another ritual was added to our Thursdays: my mother's coffee hour. She soon formed her favorites among my students and tried to create separate relations with them.

For as long as I can remember, she would ask perfect strangers to our house for coffee. One day we had to turn away an alarmingly athletic man in his late thirties, who had by mistake rung our bell asking for the lady who had told him to drop by and have coffee with her when he was in the neighborhood. The guards at the hospital opposite our house were her regular "customers." At first they would stand reverently, coffee cups in hands; later, at her insistence, they sat down uneasily on the edge of chairs as they related all the gossip about the neighbors and the goings-on at the hospital. This was how we later learned the details of what happened that day.

Yassi and I were waiting for our coffee, basking in the luxury of no special urgency, when the bell rang, sounding louder than usual because of the quiet of the street. As the bell rings one more time in my memory, I hear Tahereh Khanoom dragging her slippers along the floor, making her way to the front door of the apartment. I hear her footsteps fading as she slowly goes down the stairs to the street door. We hear a few words exchanged between her and a man.

She returned rather startled. There were two plainclothes officers at the door, she explained, men from the Revolutionary Committee. They wanted to raid the apartment of Mr. Colonel's tenant. Mr. Colonel was a new neighbor, whom my mother consistently ignored because of his newly rich ways and manners. He had destroyed a beautiful vacant garden next to our place and built an ugly, gray-stone three-story apartment. He lived on the second floor, his daughter was on the third and he rented out the first. Tahereh Khanoom explained that "they" wanted to arrest Mr. Colonel's tenant, but they couldn't gain admittance to the house. So they wanted to go into our yard and climb over our walls to get into the neighbor's house. We obviously, or perhaps not so obviously, wished to deny them this permission. As Tahereh Khanoom wisely put it, What good is a Committee official who doesn't have a search warrant and can only go into people's houses through their neighbors' yards? They needed no search warrant when it came to barging into decent people's houses at all times, so why were they so helpless when it came to this one particular crook? We had our differences with our neighbor, but we were not about to hand him over to the Committee.

As Tahereh Khanoom was relating all of this, there was a commotion in the street below. We heard the sounds of men talking hurriedly, feet running, a car engine starting. We hardly had time to wrap up our criticism of the Committee when there was another ring at the door. This time, it was more persistent. A few minutes later Tahereh Khanoom returned, accompanied by two young men in the khaki outfits that were then fashionable with the Revolutionary Guards. They explained that they no longer needed our garden wall to jump over to the neighbor's house: the culprit had now jumped into our garden and was armed and hiding there. They wanted to use our balcony, and the balcony of the third floor, to keep him busy by shooting at him while their colleagues sought to catch him. Our permission was not required, but they were considerate of "other people's wives and mothers," so they asked for it anyway. They let us know, by implication and gesture, that their prey was dangerous: not only was he an armed drug pusher, but he had other crimes to his name.

Three others, who proceeded to march upstairs, now accompanied our two intruders. What went through my mind then was, I later discovered, exactly the same thing that occupied Tahereh Khanoom's. Upstairs, on a corner of the big terrace, we had hidden our large and forbidden satellite dish. Later, we all wondered how it was that our concern was not so much for our lives or for the fact that five armed strangers were using our house for a shooting match with a neighbor who was also armed and hiding somewhere in our garden. We, like all normal Iranian citizens, were guilty and had something to hide: we were worried about our satellite dish. Tahereh Khanoom, who was more coolheaded than I and knew their language better, was assigned to go upstairs. Yassi was in charge of looking after my two bewildered children, and I accompanied the two men to our balcony, which opened into our bedroom and gave onto the garden below. I remember in the midst of all the confusion, at one point I thought, What a good story for Yassi's uncles. I bet even they can't top this.

The events of that day, even after my children and I thoroughly inspected every detail, are somewhat confused. As I remember it, I seem to be in all places simultaneously. Like the genie in the *Aladdin* cartoon, one moment I was on the balcony in the middle of cross fire, listening to the Committee men threatening the culprit while relating in bits and pieces his sinful history, intimating that he was supported by "people in high places," which explained why they had no official search warrant; next, I was upstairs, assured by Tahereh Khanoom that the guards were too busy to pay attention to our satellite dish. Later she told me that the guards had tried to use her as a shield, saying that this man would shoot at them but not her.

In between the shootings, my interpreters of these strange proceedings revealed that were they to succeed in their present enterprise, our neighbor would probably be released by his high-powered patrons. He warned me insistently about the evil nature of this criminal, who had now taken cover at the farthermost corner of our garden, under the generous shade of my favorite willow. With comical despair, they took to bewailing the hopeless nature of their mission to us—we, who considered both sides equally criminal and intrusive and wanted them both out of our lives as soon as possible.

The game now shifted to our other neighbor's house, as his two frightened children and their baby-sitter took refuge in the street. One of their windows was shattered by the gunfight. The culprit hid for some time in a small toolshed at the end of their garden by the swimming pool, but by now the guards had approached him from several sides. He threw his gun into the swimming pool—why, I cannot say—and the scene shifted to the street. We brought the neighbor's two sons into our house. The children—the neighbor's and mine—and Yassi and I leaned out the window to watch the Committee men as they dragged their prey into the back of a white Toyota patrol car, he shouting all the while, calling out to his wife and son and warning his wife that under no circumstances should she open the door to the house.

We did have our coffee in the end that day, as all the participants—Yassi, Tahereh Khanoom, the children and I—and the guards at the hospital all gathered in my mother's parlor to exchange stories. The guards gave us the inside scoop on Mr. Colonel's tenant. He was in his early thirties. His arrogance and rough manners had earned him the hatred and fear of the hospital staff. For the past six weeks, our street had been under observation by the Committee members who had just made their move.

We all agreed that this was a factional fight and that the culprit most likely worked for some high officials. That would explain how, at such a young age, he could afford the exorbitant rent, the opium and the antique cars in his garage. The hospital guards were told he was one of the terrorists responsible for some of the assassinations in Paris over the past ten years. It was predicted by our self-appointed investigative committee that he would soon be released. As it turned out, these predictions were correct: not only was he released, but he came to our door one day soon after his return and tried to persuade Tahereh Khanoom to lodge a complaint against the Revolutionary Committee members who had barged into our house to arrest him, something we did not do.

That night, as my husband and I were drinking tea at yet another meeting convened at our neighbor's house, the children, intrigued by the events of the day, decided to inspect all the scenes of the skirmish. In the process, they discovered in the toolshed a small tape recorder in the arrested man's black leather jacket, which he had hidden there. We were law-abiding citizens and, after listening to an incomprehensible conversation about some trucks, we handed the tape recorder and the jacket over to the Committee, despite passionate protests from the children.

This story was repeated many times, including the following Thursday, when Tahereh Khanoom and my children, who had by then lost their shy curiosity—and with it the necessary decorum to keep them off the premises during my class—re-enacted the scene to an eager and smiling audience. It was interesting to see that "they," the Committee men, were so helpless, so bungling and unprofessional. As Yassi pointed out, we had seen better action movies. Still, it was no consolation to learn that our lives were in the hands of bungling fools. Despite all the jokes and the power we felt then, the house became a little less secure after that, and for a long time we were startled by the sound of the doorbell.

In fact, the bell became like a warning from that other world we had tried to turn into a joke. It was only a few months later when the sound of another bell brought two more Committee members to our house. They were there to raid our house and to take our satellite dish away. This time there were no heroics: when they left, our house was in semi-mourning. My daughter, in response to my admonition about her spoiled attitude, asked me with bitter disdain how I could possibly understand her affliction. When I was her age, she said, was I punished for wearing colored shoelaces, for running in the school yard, for licking ice cream in public?

All this was discussed in my class the following Thursday, in detail. Again we skipped back and forth between our lives and novels: was it surprising that we so appreciated and responded to *Invitation to a Beheading*? We were all victims of the arbitrary nature of a totalitarian regime that constantly intruded into the most private corners of our lives and imposed its relentless fictions on us. Was this rule the rule of Islam? What memories were we creating for our children? This constant assault, this persistent lack of kindness, was what frightened me most.

20

A few months earlier, Manna and Nima had come to me for advice. They had saved some money and had to choose between buying some "necessities of life," as they put it, or a satellite dish. They had very little money and they had saved what little they had from private tutoring. After four years of marriage, like many other young couples, they could not afford to live on their own. They lived with Manna's mother and younger sister. I don't remember what advice I gave them that day, but I know that shortly afterward they bought a satellite dish. They were euphoric about their satellite dish, and every day after that I would hear about a new American classic they had watched the night before.

Satellite dishes were becoming the rage all over Iran. It was not merely people like me, or the educated classes, who craved them. Tahereh Khanoom informed us that in the poorer, more religious sections of Tehran, the family with a dish would rent out certain programs to their neighbors. I remember that when I was on a visit to the United States in 1996, David Hasselhoff, the star of *Baywatch,* bragged that his show was the most popular show in Iran.

Manna and Nima were never, strictly speaking, my students. Both were working towards their master's degree in English literature at the University of Tehran. They had read my articles and had heard about my classes from some friends, and one day they just appeared in class. They asked me afterward if they could audit my courses. After that, they attended every hour of every class I taught, as well as my talks and public lectures. I would see them at those lectures, mostly standing near the door, always with a smile. I felt their smiles were meant to encourage me to continue talking about Nabokov and Bellow and Fielding, that they were meant to tell me how crucial it was that I should go on doing so at all costs to myself or them.

They had met at the University of Shiraz and had fallen in love in large part because of their common interest in literature and their isolation from university life in general. Manna later explained how their attachment was based, more than anything else, on words. During their courtship they wrote letters and read poetry to each other. They became addicted to the secure world they created through words, a conspiratorial world in which everything that was hostile and uncontrollable became soft and articulated. She was writing her thesis on Virginia Woolf and the Impressionists; he, on Henry James.

Manna used to get excited in a very quiet way; her happiness seemed to come from some unknown depth inside of her. I can still remember the very first day I saw her and Nima in my class. They reminded me of my two children whenever they entered a conspiracy to make me happy. At first Nima was the more talkative of the two. He would walk beside me, and Manna followed a little behind him. Nima would talk and tell stories and I'd notice Manna peering past Nima to catch my reaction. Seldom did she ever volunteer herself to talk. It was only after several months, when at my insistence she showed me some of her poetry, that she was forced to talk to me directly and not through Nima.

I have chosen to give them rhyming names, although their names sound different in real life. Yet I was so used to seeing them together, voicing the same thoughts and feelings, that to me they were like two siblings who had just discovered something wondrous in their back garden, a doorway into a magic kingdom. I was the fairy godmother, the madwoman in whom they could confide.

While we sorted papers and reorganized my office at home, placing the novels side by side, arranging my notes in different files, they shared stories and gossip from the University of Tehran, where I had held a post years before. I knew many of the people they mentioned, including our favorite villain, Professor X, who nurtured a sophisticated and persistent hatred towards them both, Nima and Manna. He was one of the very few professors who had not resigned or been expelled since I had left that university. In the meantime, he thought they did not sufficiently respect him. He had developed an efficient way of solving all of the complicated problems of literary criticism: he put all matters of interpretation to a vote. Since the voting was performed by a show of hands, debates tended to be resolved in his favor.

His principal quarrel with Manna and Nima was sparked by a paper Manna wrote on Robert Frost. At the next session, he informed the class about his various disagreements with her thesis, and asked them to vote on the matter. All of the students except for Manna, Nima and one other person voted for the professor's views. After the vote, the professor turned to Nima and asked him why he was such a turncoat. Was it perhaps because his wife had brainwashed him? The more he questioned them and put their ideas to vote, the more obstinate they became. They brought him books by prominent critics that supported their ideas against his. In one outburst of anger, he expelled them from his class.

One of his students had decided to write his thesis on *Lolita*. He used no sources, had not read Nabokov, but his thesis fascinated the professor, who had a thing about young girls spoiling the lives of intellectual men. This student wanted to write about how Lolita had seduced Humbert, an "intellectual poet," and ruined his life. Professor X, with a look of thoughtful intensity, asked the student if he knew about Nabokov's own sexual perversions. Nima, with ripples of contempt in his voice, mimicked the professor, shaking his head sadly and saying how, in novel after novel, we find the lives of intellectual men being destroyed by flighty females. Manna swore that he kept throwing her poisonous glances as he embarked on his pet subject. Yet despite his views on Nabokov's flighty young vixens, when this man had been "looking" for a new wife, his main condition had been that her age should not exceed twenty-three. His second wife, duly recruited, was at least two decades younger than he.

21

One Thursday morning so hot that the heat seemed to have permeated the cool of our air-conditioned house, seven of us were talking aimlessly before the class began. We were talking about Sanaz. She had missed class the preceding week without calling to explain, and now we didn't know if she would come again. No one, not even Mitra, had heard from her. We were speculating that maybe the troublesome brother had hatched a new plot. Sanaz's brother was by now a constant topic of conversation, one of a series of male villains who resurfaced from week to week.

"Nima tells me we don't understand the difficulty men face here," said Manna with a hint of sarcasm. "They too don't know how to act. Sometimes they act like macho bullies because they feel vulnerable."

"Well, that's to an extent true," I said. "After all, it takes two to create a relationship, and when you make half the population invisible, the other half suffers as well."

"Can you imagine the kind of man who'd get sexually provoked just by looking at a strand of my hair?" said Nassrin. "Someone who goes crazy at the sight of a woman's toe . . . wow!" she continued, "My toe as a lethal weapon!"

"Women who cover themselves are aiding and abetting the regime," said Azin with a defiant flourish.

Mahshid remained silent, her eyes targeting the table's iron leg.

"And those whose trademark is painting their lips fiery red and flirting with male professors," said Manna with an icy stare. "I suppose they are doing all this to further the cause?" Azin turned red and said nothing.

"How about genitally mutilating men," Nassrin suggested coolly, "so as to curb their sexual appetites?" She had been reading Nawal al-Sadawi's book on brutality against women in some Muslim societies. Sadawi, a doctor, had gone to some lengths to explain the horrendous effects of genitally mutilating young girls in order to curb their sexual appetites. "I was working on this text for my translation project—"

"Your translation project?"

"Yes, don't you remember? I told my father I was translating Islamic texts into English to help Mahshid."

"But I thought that was just an excuse so that you could come here," I said.

"It was, but I decided to do these translations for at least three hours a week, sometimes more, for the extra lies. I reached a compromise with my conscience," she said with a smile.

"I have to tell you that the Ayatollah himself was no novice in sexual matters," Nassrin went on. "I've been translating his magnum opus, *The Political, Philosophical, Social and Religious Principles of Ayatollah Khomeini,* and he has some interesting points to make."

"But it's already been translated," said Manna. "What's the point?"

"Yes," said Nassrin, "parts of it have been translated, but after it became the butt of party jokes, ever since the embassies abroad found out that people were reading the book not for their edification but for fun, the translations have been very hard to find. And anyway, my translation is thorough—it has references and cross-references to works by other worthies. Did you know that one way to cure a man's sexual appetites is by having sex with animals? And then there's the problem of sex with chickens. You have to ask yourself if a man who has had sex with a chicken can then eat the chicken afterwards. Our leader has provided us with an answer: *No,* neither he nor his immediate family or next-door neighbors can eat of that chicken's meat, but it's okay for a neighbor who lives two doors away. My father would rather I spent my time on such texts than on Jane Austen or Nabokov?" she added, rather mischievously.

We were not startled by Nassrin's erudite allusions to the works of Ayatollah Khomeini. She was referring to a famous text by Khomeini, the equivalent of his dissertation—required to be written by all who reach the rank of ayatollah—aimed at responding to the questions and dilemmas that could be posed to them by their disciples. Many others before Khomeini had written in almost identical manner. What was disturbing was that these texts were taken seriously by people who ruled us and in whose hands lay our fate and the fate of our country. Every day on national television and radio these guardians of morality and culture would make similar statements and discuss such matters as if they were the most serious themes for contemplation and consideration.

It was in the middle of this scholarly discussion, peppered with loud laughter on Azin's part and increasing moroseness on Mahshid's, that we heard the sound of screeching brakes, and I knew that Sanaz was being deposited by her brother. A pause, a car door slamming, the doorbell and a few moments later Sanaz entered, the first words on her lips an apology. She seemed so distraught at being late and having missed the class that she was ready to burst into tears.

I tried to calm her down, and Yassi went into the kitchen to bring her tea. She held a big box of pastries in her hands. What's this for, Sanaz? It was my turn last week, she said lamely, so I brought it this week instead. I took the pastries from her hand—she was sweating— and she uncoiled her black robe and scarf. She had tied her hair tightly behind her ears with a rubber band. Her face looked naked and forlorn.

Finally she took her usual place, beside Mitra, with a big glass of ice water in her hand and her tea stationed in front of her on the table, and we all waited in silence to hear what she would say. Azin tried to break the silence with a joke. We all thought you'd gone to Turkey for your engagement party and forgot to invite us. Sanaz attempted a smile and took a sip of water instead of responding. She seemed to want to at once say something and reveal nothing. There were tears in her voice before they became visible in her eyes.

Her story was familiar. A fortnight earlier, Sanaz and five of her girlfriends had gone for a two-day vacation by the Caspian Sea. On their first day, they had decided to visit her friend's fiancé in an adjoining villa. Sanaz kept emphasizing that they were all properly dressed, with their scarves and long robes. They were all sitting outside, in the garden: six girls and one boy. There were no alcoholic beverages in the house, no undesirable tapes or CDs. She seemed to be suggesting that if there had been, they might have deserved the treatment they received at the hands of the Revolutionary Guards.

And then "they" came with their guns, the morality squads, surprising them by jumping over the low walls. They claimed to have received a report of illegal activities, and wanted to search the premises. Unable to find fault with their appearance, one of the guards sarcastically said that looking at them, with their Western attitudes. . . . What is a Western attitude? Nassrin interrupted. Sanaz looked at her and smiled. I'll ask him next time I run into him. The truth of the matter was that their search for alcoholic beverages, tapes and CDs had led to nothing, but they already had a search warrant and didn't want it to go to waste. The guards took all of them to a special jail for infractions in matters of morality. There, despite their protests, the girls were kept in a small, dark room, which they shared the first night with several prostitutes and a drug addict. Their jail wardens came into their room two or three times in the middle of the night to wake up those who might have dozed off, and hurled insults at them.

They were held in that room for forty-eight hours. Despite their repeated requests, they were denied the right to call their parents. Apart from brief excursions to the rest room at appointed times, they left the room twice—the first time to be led to a hospital, where they were given virginity tests by a woman gynecologist, who had her students observe the examinations. Not satisfied with her verdict, the guards took them to a private clinic for a second check.

On the third day, their anxious parents in Tehran, unable to locate them, were told by the concierge at their villa that their children might have been killed in a recent car accident. They set off at once to the resort town in search of their daughters, and finally found them. The girls were then given a summary trial, forced to sign a document confessing to sins they had not committed and subjected to twenty-five lashes.

Sanaz, who is very thin, was wearing a T-shirt under her robe. Her jailers jokingly suggested that since she was wearing an extra garment, she might not feel the pain, so they gave her more. For her, the physical pain had been more bearable than the indignity of the virginity tests and her self-loathing at having signed a forced confession. In some perverse way, the physical punishment was a source of satisfaction to her, a compensation for having yielded to those other humiliations.

When they were finally released and taken home by their parents, Sanaz had to deal with another indignity: her brother's admonitions. What did they expect? How could they let six unruly girls go on a trip without male supervision? Would nobody ever listen to him, just because he was a few years younger than his scatterbrained sister, who should have been married by now? Sanaz's parents, although sympathetic to her and her ordeal, did have to agree that perhaps it had not been such a good idea to let her go on the trip; not that they did not trust her, but conditions in the country were unsuitable for such indiscretions. On top of everything else, I am now the guilty party, she said. I've been deprived of the use of my car and am being chaperoned by my wise younger brother.

I cannot leave Sanaz and her story alone. Time and again I have gone back to it—I still do—re-creating it bit by bit: the garden fence, the six girls and one boy sitting on the veranda, perhaps telling jokes and laughing. And then "they" come. I remember this incident just as I remember so many others from my own life in Iran; I even remember the events people have written or told me about since I left. Strangely, they too have become my own memories.

Perhaps it is only now and from this distance, when I am able to speak of these experiences openly and without fear, that I can begin to understand them and overcome my own terrible sense of helplessness. In Iran a strange distance informed our relation to these daily experiences of brutality and humiliation. There, we spoke as if the events did not belong to us; like schizophrenic patients, we tried to keep ourselves away from that other self, at once intimate and alien.

22

In his memoir, *Speak, Memory,* Nabokov describes a watercolor that hung above his bed when he was a young child. It is a landscape, an image of a narrow path disappearing into a forest full of trees. His mother read a story to him about a boy who disappeared one day into the painting above his bed and this became young Vladimir's wish as he prayed every night. As you imagine us in that room, you must also understand our desire for this dangerous vanishing act. The more we withdrew into our sanctuary, the more we became alienated from our day-to-day life. When I walked down the streets, I asked myself, Are these my people, is this my hometown, am I who I am?

Neither Humbert nor the blind censor ever possesses his victims; they always elude him, just as objects of fantasy are always simultaneously within reach and inaccessible. No matter how they may be broken, the victims will not be forced into submission.

All this was on my mind one Thursday evening after class as I was looking at the diaries my girls had left behind, with their new essays and poems. At the start of our class, I had asked them to describe their image of themselves. They were not ready then to face that question, but every once in a while I returned to it and asked them again. Now, as I sat curled up on the love seat, I looked at dozens of pages of their recent responses.

I have one of these responses in front of me. It belongs to Sanaz, who handed it in shortly after her jail experience at the seaside. It is a simple drawing in black and white, of a naked girl, the white of her body caught in a black bubble. She is crouched in an almost fetal position, hugging one bent knee. Her other leg is stretched out behind her. Her long, straight hair follows the same curved line as the contour of her back, but her face is hidden. The bubble is lifted in the air by a giant bird with long black talons. What interests me is a small detail as opposed to the more obvious imagery of the girl, the bubble and the girl's hand that reaches out of the bubble and holds on to the talon. Her subservient nakedness is dependent on that talon, and she reaches out to it.

The drawing immediately brought to my mind Nabokov's statement in his famous afterword to *Lolita* about how the "first little throb of *Lolita*" went through him in 1939 or early 1940, when he was ill with a severe attack of intercostal neuralgia. He recalls that "the initial shiver of inspiration was somehow prompted by a newspaper story about an ape in the Jardin des Plantes, who, after months of coaxing by a scientist, produced the first drawing ever charcoaled by an animal: this sketch showed the bars of the poor creature's cage."

The two images, one from the novel and the other from reality, reveal a terrible truth. Its terribleness goes beyond the fact that in each case an act of violence has been committed. It goes beyond the bars, revealing the victim's proximity and intimacy with its jailer. Our focus in each is on the delicate spot where the prisoner touches the bar, on the invisible contact between flesh and cold metal.

Most of the others expressed themselves in words. Manna saw herself as fog, moving over concrete objects, taking on their form but never becoming concrete herself. Yassi described herself as a figment. Nassrin, in one response, gave me the Oxford English Dictionary's definition of the word *paradox*. Implicit in almost all their descriptions was the way they saw themselves in the context of an outside reality that prevented them from defining themselves clearly and separately.

Manna had once written about a pair of pink socks for which she was reprimanded by the Muslim Students' Association. When she complained to a favorite professor, he started teasing her about how she had already ensnared and trapped her man, Nima, and did not need the pink socks to entrap him further.

These students, like the rest of their generation, were different from my generation in one fundamental aspect. My generation complained of a loss, the void in our lives that was created when our past was stolen from us, making us exiles in our own country. Yet we had a past to compare with the present; we had memories and images of what had been taken away. But my girls spoke constantly of stolen kisses, films they had never seen and the wind they had never felt on their skin. This generation had no past. Their memory was of a half-articulated desire, something they had never had. It was this lack, their sense of longing for the ordinary, taken-for-granted aspects of life, that gave their words a certain luminous quality akin to poetry.

I wonder if right now, at this moment, I were to turn to the people sitting next to me in this café in a country that is not Iran and talk to them about life in Tehran, how they would react. Would they condemn the tortures, the executions and the extreme acts of aggression? I think they would. But what about the acts of transgression on our ordinary lives, like the desire to wear pink socks?

I had asked my students if they remember the dance scene in *Invitation to a Beheading:* the jailer invites Cincinnatus to a dance. They begin a waltz and move out into the hall. In a corner they run into a guard: "They described a circle near him and glided back into the cell, and now Cincinnatus regretted that the swoon's friendly embrace had been so brief." This movement in circles is the main movement of the novel. As long as he accepts the sham world the jailers impose upon him, Cincinnatus will remain their prisoner and will move within the circles of their creation. The worst crime committed by totalitarian mind-sets is that they force their citizens, including their victims, to become complicit in their crimes. Dancing with your jailer, participating in your own execution, that is an act of utmost brutality. My students witnessed it in show trials on television and enacted it every time they went out into the streets dressed as they were told to dress.

They had not become part of the crowd who watched the executions, but they did not have the power to protest them, either.

The only way to leave the circle, to stop dancing with the jailer, is to find a way to preserve one's individuality, that unique quality which evades description but differentiates one human being from the other. That is why, in their world, rituals—empty rituals—become so central. There was not much difference between our jailers and Cincinnatus's executioners. They invaded all private spaces and tried to shape every gesture, to force us to become one of them, and that in itself was another form of execution.

In the end, when Cincinnatus is led to the scaffold, and as he lays his head on the scaffold, in preparation for his execution, he repeats the magic mantra: "by myself." This constant reminder of his unique-ness, and his attempts to write, to articulate and create a language dif-ferent from the one imposed upon him by his jailers, saves him at the last moment, when he takes his head in his hands and walks away towards voices that beckon him from that other world, while the scaf-fold and all the sham world around him, along with his executioner, disintegrate.

PART II

Gatsby

I

A young woman stands alone in the midst of a crowd at the Tehran airport, backpack on her back, a large bag hanging from one shoulder, pushing an oversize carry-on with the tips of her toes. She knows that her husband of two years and her father must be somewhere out there with the suitcases. She stands in the customs area, teary-eyed, desperately looking for a sympathetic face, for someone she can cling to and say, Oh how happy, how glad, how absolutely happy I am to be back home. At long last, here to stay. But no one so much as smiles. The walls of the airport have dissolved into an alien spectacle, with giant posters of an ayatollah staring down reproachfully. Their mood is echoed in the black and bloodred slogans: DEATH TO AMERICA! DOWN WITH IMPERIALISM & ZIONISM! AMERICA IS OUR NUMBER-ONE ENEMY!

Not having registered as yet that the home she had left seventeen years before, at the age of thirteen, was not home anymore, she stands alone, filled with emotions wriggling this way and that, ready to burst at the slightest provocation. I try not to see her, not to bump into her, to pass by unnoticed. Yet there is no way I can avoid her.

This airport, the Tehran airport, has always brought out the worst in me. When I left it the first time, it was a hospitable and magical place, with a fine restaurant that hosted dances on Friday evenings and a coffee shop with big French windows opening onto a balcony. As children my brother and I stood transfixed by those windows, eating ice cream as we counted the planes. Always on arrival there was a particular moment of epiphany, when suddenly a blanket of lights signaled that we had arrived, that Tehran was lying in wait for us below. For seventeen years I dreamed of those lights, so beckoning and seductive. I dreamed of being submerged in them and of never having to leave again.

The dream had finally come true. I was home, but the mood in the airport was not welcoming. It was somber and slightly menacing, like the unsmiling portraits of Ayatollah Khomeini and his anointed successor, Ayatollah Montazeri, that covered the walls. It seemed as if a bad witch with her broomstick had flown over the building and in one sweep had taken away the restaurants, the children and the women in colorful clothes that I remembered. This feeling was confirmed when I noticed the cagey anxiety in the eyes of my mother and friends, who had come to the airport to welcome us home.

As we were leaving the customs area, a morose young man stopped us: he wanted to search me. We've already been searched, I reminded him. Not the carry-on bags, he said curtly. But why? This is my home, I wanted to say, as if this should have offered me protection against suspicion and scrutiny. He needed to search me for alcoholic beverages. I was taken to a corner. Bijan, my husband, observed me anxiously, not knowing whom to fear most, the morose guard or me. His face took on a smile that later became very familiar to me: complicit, reconciling, cynical. Do you argue with a mad dog? someone later asked me.

First they emptied my bag: lipstick, pens and pencils, my diary and glasses case. Then they attacked my backpack, from which they extracted my diploma, my marriage license, my books—*Ada, Jews Without Money, The Great Gatsby* . . . The guard picked them up disdainfully, as if handling someone else's dirty laundry. But he did not confiscate them—not then. That came sometime later.

2

During my first years abroad—when I was in school in England and Switzerland, and later, when I lived in America, I attempted to shape other places according to my concept of Iran. I tried to Persianize the landscape and even transferred for a term to a small college in New Mexico, mainly because it reminded me of home. *You see, Frank and Nancy, this little stream surrounded by trees, meandering its way through a parched land, is just like Iran. Just like Iran, just like home.* What impressed me most about Tehran, I told whoever cared to listen, were the mountains and its dry yet generous climate, the trees and flowers that bloomed and thrived on its parched soil and seemed to suck the light out of the sun.

When my father was jailed, I went back home and was allowed to stay for a year. Later, I was insecure enough to marry on the spur of a moment, before my eighteenth birthday. I married a man whose most important credential was that he wasn't like us—he offered a way of life which, in contrast to ours, seemed pragmatic and uncomplicated; and he was so sure of himself. He didn't value books ("the problem with you and your family is that you live more in books than in reality"), he was insanely jealous—jealousy was part of the image he had of himself as a man in command of his destiny and property—he was success-oriented ("When I have my own office, my chair will be higher than those of the visitors, so they'll always feel intimidated by my presence") and he admired Frank Sinatra. The day I said yes, I knew I was going to divorce him. There were no limits to my self-destructive urges and the risks I was prepared to take with my own life.

I moved with him to Norman, Oklahoma, where he was getting his master's in engineering at the University of Oklahoma, and in six months' time I had reached the conclusion that I would divorce him as soon as my father was out of jail. That took another three years. He refused to divorce me ("A woman enters her husband's home in her wedding gown and leaves it in her shroud"). He had underestimated me. He wanted his wife to dress smartly, do her nails, go to the hairdresser every week. I defied him with my long skirts and tattered jeans, wore my hair long and sat on the campus green with my American friends while his friends passing by threw sly glances in our direction.

My father was all in favor of divorce, and threatened to sue for alimony, a woman's only protection under Islamic law. My husband finally consented when I agreed not to sue for alimony and let him have the money in our bank account, the car and the carpets. He returned home while I stayed on in Norman, the only foreign student in the English Department. I shunned the company of the Iranian community, especially the men, who had numerous illusions about a young divorcée's availability.

These are my memories of Norman: red earth and fireflies, singing and demonstrating on the Oval, reading Melville, Poe, Lenin and Mao

Tse Tung, reading Ovid and Shakespeare on warm spring mornings with a favorite professor, of conservative political leaning, and accompanying another in the afternoons, singing revolutionary songs. At night watching new films by Bergman, Fellini, Godard and Pasolini. As I remember those days, the disparate sights and sounds mix and mingle in my memory: sad stills of Bergman's women merge into the soothing sound of David, my radical professor, singing on his guitar:

Long-haired preachers come out every night
And they tell you what's wrong and what's right
And when you ask them for something to eat
They tell you in voices so sweet:
You will eat by and by, in that glorious place in the sky
Work and pray, live on hay, you will get pie in sky when you die.
That's a lie!

We would demonstrate in the mornings, taking over the administration building, singing songs on the green in front of the English Department, called South Oval, watching as the occasional streakers ran across the green towards the redbrick building that was the library. I marched while the suffering ROTC students, in those days of protest against the Vietnam War, tried to ignore our presence on the grass. Later I would go to parties with my true love, who introduced me to Nabokov when he gave me *Ada,* in whose flyleaf he had written: *To Azar, my Ada, Ted.*

My family had always looked down on politics, with a certain rebellious condescension. They prided themselves on the fact that as far back as eight hundred years ago—*fourteen generations,* my mother would proudly emphasize—the Nafisis were known for their contributions to literature and science. The men were called *hakim*s, men of knowledge, and later, in this century, the Nafisi women had gone to universities and taught at a time when few women dared leave home. When my father became the mayor of Tehran, instead of celebration there was a sense of unease in the family. My younger uncles, who at the time were university students, refused to acknowledge my father as their brother. Later, when my father fell out of favor, my parents managed to make us feel more proud of his term in jail than we had ever been when he was mayor.

I joined the Iranian student movement reluctantly. My father's imprisonment and my family's vague nationalist sympathies had sensitized me towards politics, but I was more of a rebel than a political activist—though in those days there was not much difference between them. One attraction was the fact that the men in the movement didn't try to assault or seduce me. Instead, they held study groups in which we read and discussed Engels's *Origin of the Family, Private Property, and the State* and Marx's *The 18ᵗʰ Brumaire of Louis Bonaparte.* In the seventies, the mood—not just among Iranians, but among American and European students—was revolutionary. There was the Cuban example, and China of course. The revolutionary cant and romantic atmosphere were infectious, and the Iranian students were at the forefront of the struggle. They were active, and even confrontational, going to jail for occupying the Iranian consulate in San Francisco.

The Iranian student group at the University of Oklahoma was a chapter of the World Confederation of Iranian Students, which had members and chapters in most major cities in Europe and the United States. In Oklahoma, it was responsible for the introduction on campus of the RSB, the militant student branch of the Revolutionary Communist Party, and the creation of the Third World Committee Against Imperialism, composed of radical students from different nationalities. The confederation, fashioning itself after Lenin's democratic centralism, exerted a strong hold over its members' lifestyles and social activities. As time went by, the more militant and Marxist elements came to dominate the group, ousting or isolating those with more moderate and nationalist tendencies. Its members usually sported Che Guevara sports jackets and boots; the women usually cropped their hair short, seldom used makeup and wore Mao jackets and khakis.

I then began a schizophrenic period in my life in which I tried to reconcile my revolutionary aspirations with the lifestyle I most enjoyed. I never fully integrated into the movement. During the long and confrontational meetings between rival factions, I would often leave the room under different pretenses, and sometimes locked myself in the bathroom to escape. I insisted on wearing long dresses outside the meetings and refused to cut my hair. I never gave up the habit of reading and loving "counterrevolutionary" writers—T. S. Eliot,

Austen, Plath, Nabokov, Fitzgerald—but I spoke passionately at the rallies; inspired by phrases I had read in novels and poems, I would weave words together into sounds of revolution. My oppressive yearning for home was shaped into excited speeches against the tyrants back home and their American backers, and although I felt alienated from the movement itself, which was never a home to me at any point, I had found an ideological framework within which to justify this unbridled, unreflective passion.

The fall of 1977 was memorable for two events: my marriage in September and the Shah's last official and most dramatic visit to the United States in November. I had met Bijan Naderi two years earlier, at a meeting at Berkeley. He was the leader of the group I most sympathized with. I fell in love with him for all the wrong reasons: not because of his revolutionary rhetoric but because he possessed a sense of confidence in himself and his beliefs that went beyond the hysterics of the movement. He was loyal, passionately committed to whatever he undertook, be it his family, his job or the movement, but his loyalty never made him blind to what the movement would become. I admired him as much for this as for his refusal, later, to follow the revolutionary mandates.

In the many demonstrations in which I participated, shouting slogans against U.S. involvement in Iran, in the protest meetings during which we argued into the night, thinking we were talking about Iran but in reality more concerned with what had happened in China, the picture of home loomed large. It was mine and I could constantly conjure it, and relate to the world through its hazy image.

There were discrepancies, or essential paradoxes, in my idea of "home." There was the familiar Iran I felt nostalgic about, the place of parents and friends and summer nights by the Caspian Sea. Yet just as real was this other, reconstructed, Iran about which we talked in meeting after meeting, quarreling about what the masses in Iran wanted. Apparently, as the movement grew more radical in the seventies, the masses wanted us to serve no alcohol in our celebrations and not to dance or play "decadent" music: only folk and revolutionary music were allowed. They wanted the girls to cut their hair short or wear it in pigtails. They wanted us to avoid the bourgeois habits of studying.

3

Just over a month after we landed at the Tehran airport, I found myself standing in the English Department at the University of Tehran. As I arrived, I almost ran into a young man in a gray suit, curly-haired and friendly-looking. I later discovered he was another recent recruit, just back from the United States and, like me, filled with new and exciting ideas. The secretary, who radiated a certain saintliness despite her corpulent beauty, smiled at me and shuffled in through a door to the department head's office. She came back a moment later and nodded me into the room. Walking in, I tripped over a small wooden wedge between the two doors and lost my balance, nearly landing on the department head's desk.

I was greeted with a bemused smile and offered a seat. I had last been in this office two weeks before, when I had been interviewed by a different department head, a tall and friendly man who had asked me about various relatives, prominent writers and academicians. I was grateful to him for trying to put me at ease, but also worried that for the rest of my life I would live in competition with prominent family shadows.

This new man, Dr. A, was different. His smile was friendly but not intimate; it was more appraising. He invited me to a party at his house, that very night, yet his manner was distant. We talked about literature and not relatives. I tried to explain to him why I had changed my mind about my dissertation. You see, I told him, I wanted to do a comparative study of the literature of the twenties and thirties, the proletarians and the non-proletarians. The best person was Fitzgerald—for the twenties, I mean. This seemed obvious to him. But then I had difficulty choosing his counterpoint—should I choose Steinbeck, Farrell or Dos Passos? You didn't think any of them would measure up to Fitzgerald, did you? Well, not in a literary sense. What other sense is there? So, anyway, then I came across the real proletarians, whose spirit was best captured by Mike Gold. Who? Mike Gold: he was the editor of the radical popular literary journal *New Masses*. You may not believe it, but he was a big shot in his day. He was the first person to formulate the concept of proletarian art in the United States. Even writers like Hemingway took note of what he said—calling Hemingway a white-collar writer and Thornton Wilder "the Emily Post of culture."

Well, in the end I decided to leave Fitzgerald out of it. I was curious about Gold, and why he took over—for he did take over. In the thirties people like Fitzgerald were pushed out by this new breed, and I wanted to know why. Plus I was a revolutionary myself; I wanted to understand the passion that drove the likes of Mike Gold. You wanted passion, he asked, and you went from Fitzgerald to this other fellow? Our discussion was interesting, and I did accept his invitation to his party that evening.

The other one, the tall, friendly department head I had met on my first visit, I was informed, was now in jail. No one knew when he would be released, or even if he would be released at all. Many professors had been expelled by now, and others would soon follow suit. This is how things were in those first days of the revolution, when I innocently and with feelings utterly inappropriate to the circumstances started my teaching career as the youngest and newest member of the English Department at the Faculty of Persian and Foreign Languages and Literature at the University of Tehran. Had I been offered a similar position at Oxford or Harvard, I would not have felt more honored or intimidated.

The look in Dr. A's face as I tripped on the edge of his door was one with which many others, very different from him, would greet me over the years. It was a look of surprise tinged with leniency. A funny child, it seemed to say, who needs to be guided and sometimes put in her place. Later on, a different look would emerge, a look of frustration, as if I had not acted according to our initial contract: I had become a wayward and unruly child and could not be controlled.

4

All my memories of those first years revolve around the University of Tehran. It was the navel, the immovable center to which all political and social activities were tied. When in the U.S. we read or heard about the turmoil in Iran, the University of Tehran seemed to be the scene of the most important battles. All groups used the university to make their statements.

It was thus not surprising that the new Islamic government took over the university as the site of its weekly Friday prayers. This act gained added significance, because at all times, even after the revolution, the Muslim students, especially the more fanatical ones, were a minority overshadowed by the leftist and secular student groups. It seemed as if with this act, the Islamic faction asserted its victory over other political groups: like a victorious army it positioned itself on the most cherished site of the occupied land, at the heart of the vanquished territory. Every week, one of the most prominent clergymen would stand on the podium to address the thousands who occupied the university grounds, men on one side, women on the other. He would stand with a gun in one hand and offer the sermon of the week, preaching on the most important political issues of the day. Yet it seemed as if the grounds themselves rebelled against this occupation.

I felt in those days that there was a turf war going on between different political groups and that this struggle was being fought out mainly at the university. I did not know then that I would also have my own battle to fight. Looking back, I am glad I was unaware of my special vulnerability: with my small collection of books, I was like an emissary from a land that did not exist, with a stock of dreams, coming to reclaim this land as my home. Amid the talk of treason and changes in government, events that now in my mind have become confused and timeless, I sat whenever I had a chance with books and notes scattered around me, trying to shape my classes. I taught a very large seminar in that first semester, called Research, in which we focused on *The Adventures of Huckleberry Finn,* and a survey of twentieth-century fiction.

I tried to be somewhat fair politically. Side by side with *The Great Gatsby* and *A Farewell to Arms,* I would teach works by Maxim Gorky and Mike Gold. I spent most days browsing the bookstores lining the street opposite the university. That street, newly renamed Avenue of the Revolution, was the center for the most important bookstores and publishers in Tehran. It was such a pleasure to go from one store to another and to find an occasional seller or customer who would introduce you to a sudden gem, or startle you by knowing about an obscure English writer by the name of Henry Green.

In the midst of my feverish preparation, I would be summoned to the university for matters that had nothing to do with my classes and books. Almost every week, sometimes every day of the week, there were either demonstrations or meetings, and we were drawn to these like a magnet, independently of our will.

One memory curls itself wantonly and imperceptibly around me, teasing me seductively. With coffee in one hand and a pen and notebook in the other, I was preparing to go to the balcony to work on my class syllabus. The phone rang. It was the agitated and urgent voice of a friend. She wanted to know if I had heard: Ayatollah Taleghani, a very popular, controversial clergyman, one of the most important figures of the revolution, had died. He was relatively young and radical, and there were already rumors he had been killed. A procession had been scheduled for him beginning at the University of Tehran.

I cannot remember the distance between the phone call and my presence, almost an hour later, at the entrance of the university. There was a traffic jam. Bijan and I got out of the taxi in the vicinity of the university and started to walk. For some reason, after a while, as if pushed by some invisible source of energy, our pace quickened into a run. A huge crowd of mourners had gathered, blocking the streets that led to the university. There were reports of a fight having broken out between members of the Mujahideen, a radical religious organization that claimed to be Taleghani's spiritual and political heir, and those belonging to what was loosely called the Hizbollah, Party of Allah, mainly composed of fanatics and vigilantes determined to implement the laws of God on earth. The fight was over who should have the honor of carrying Taleghani's body. Many were crying, beating their chests and their heads, calling out: "Today is the day of mourning! Taleghani has gone to heaven today."

Over the next two decades, this particular chant would be used for many others, a symptom of the symbiosis between the revolution's founders and death. That was the first time I experienced the desperate, orgiastic pleasure of this form of public mourning: it was the one place where people mingled and touched bodies and shared emotions without restraint or guilt. There was a wild, sexually flavored frenzy in the air. Later, when I saw a slogan by Khomeini saying that the Islamic Republic survives through its mourning ceremonies, I could testify to its truth.

I met many people that day who appeared and disappeared like characters in a cartoon. Was it there that I saw Farideh? She belonged to an extremely radical leftist group—my brother, who knew some of her comrades, had introduced her to me, thinking she could help me settle in. I saw her for a vague second, busy as always, on the verge of attacking someone or something: I saw her and lost her.

I stood in the middle of the whirlpool, struggling to find a familiar face. Always in these demonstrations I would lose sight of those who'd come with me. Now I had lost my husband, and for a while I kept looking for him. The crowd pushed towards me. Voices appeared to be echoing out of different loudspeakers. Posters of Taleghani had mushroomed everywhere: on the walls, on the doors and windows of the bookshops, even on trees. The wide street in front of the university contracted and expanded to accommodate our movements and for a long time I moved senselessly, swaying to the beat of the crowd. Then I found myself beating my fists against a tree and crying, crying, as if the person closest to me had died and I was now all alone in the whole wide world.

5

Before the new term began in September 1979, I spent most of my time hunting for the books on my syllabus. In one bookstore, as I was rummaging through a few copies of *The Great Gatsby* and *A Farewell to Arms,* the owner approached me. "If you're interested in those, you'd better buy them now," he said, shaking his head sadly. I looked at him sympathetically and said smugly, "There's too much demand for them. They can't do anything about that—can they?"

He was right. In a few months' time, Fitzgerald and Hemingway were very difficult to find. The government could not remove all of the books from the stores, but gradually it closed down some of the most important foreign-language bookstores and blocked the distribution of foreign books in Iran.

The night before my first class I was very nervous, like a child on her first day of school. I had chosen my clothes with unusual care, and also went over my meager stock of books. I had left most of them in the U.S. with my sister-in-law, along with an antique mirror: my father's present. I thought I would bring them back later, not knowing that I would not return for another eleven years, by which time my sister-in-law had given away most of my books.

That first day, I went to the university armed with my trusty *Gatsby.* It was showing signs of wear: the dearer a book was to my heart, the more battered and bruised it became. *Huckleberry Finn* was still available in bookstores, and I bought a new copy in anticipation. After some hesitation, I also picked up *Ada,* which wasn't on the syllabus, and threw it in as a security blanket.

The university was built during the reign of Reza Shah, in the thirties. The main buildings on campus had very high ceilings, propped up by thick cement columns. They were always a little cold in winter and dank in summer. Memory has given them gargantuan proportions they probably didn't have in reality, but those expansive buildings of the thirties had a strange feel about them. They were made for crowds: you never felt quite at home.

On my way to the English Department, I absentmindedly registered the different stands set out in the big hall at the foot of the over-wide staircase. There were long tables—more than ten of them—filled with literature belonging to various revolutionary groups. Students were standing in clusters, talking and sometimes quarreling, ready to defend their territory at a moment's notice. There were no visible enemies, but a sense of menace lingered over the room.

Those were crucial days in Iranian history. A battle was being fought on all levels over the shape of the constitution and the soul of the new regime. The majority of people, among them important clerics, were in favor of a secular constitution. Powerful opposition groups—both secular and religious—were forming to protest the autocratic tendencies within the ruling elite. The strongest of the opposition groups were Ayatollah Shariatmadari's Muslim People's Republican Party and the National Democratic Front, made up of secular progressives who were at the forefront of the struggle to preserve democratic rights, including women's rights and freedom of the press. They were very popular at the time and drew about a million people on the twelfth anniversary of the death of the late nationalist hero Mossadegh to the village of Ahamad Abad, where Mossadegh was buried. They campaigned vigorously for a constituent assembly.

The closing down of the most popular and progressive paper, *Ayandegan,* had led to a series of large violent demonstrations, in which the demonstrators were attacked by the government-backed vigilantes. In those days it was normal to see these goons on their motorbikes carrying black flags and banners, at times led by a cleric riding in front of them in a bulletproof Mercedes-Benz. Despite these ominous signs, the Communist Tudeh Party and the Marxist Fedayin Organization supported the radical reactionaries against what they called the liberals, and continued to put pressure on Prime Minister Bazargan, whom they suspected of having American sympathies.

The opposition was greeted with brutal violence. "The clog-wearers and the turbaned have given you a chance," Khomeini warned. "After each revolution several thousands of the corrupt elements are executed in public and burned and the story is over. They are not allowed to publish newspapers." Citing the example of the October Revolution and the fact that the state still controlled the press, he went on to say, "We will close all parties except the one, or a few which will act in a proper manner . . . we all made mistakes. We thought we were dealing with human beings. It is evident we are not. We are dealing with wild animals. We will not tolerate them anymore."

It now seems amazing to me, as I relate the events of those years, how focused I was on my work. For I was as anxious about how my class would receive me as I was about the political upheavals.

My first class was in a long room with windows down one side. The room was full when I walked in, but as soon as I took my place behind the desk, my nervousness left me. The students were unusually quiet. My hands were loaded with all the books and Xeroxes I had brought for the class, an eclectic mix of revolutionary writers whose works had been translated into Persian and "elitists" such as Fitzgerald, Faulkner and Woolf.

That class went all right, and the ones after it became easier. I was enthusiastic, naïve and idealistic, and I was in love with my books. The students were curious about me and Dr. K, the curly-haired young man I had bumped into at Dr. A's office, strange new recruits at a time when most students were doing their best to expel their professors: they were all "anti-revolutionary," a term that covered a vast range—anything from working with the previous regime to using obscene language in class.

That first day I asked my students what they thought fiction should accomplish, why one should bother to read fiction at all. It was an odd way to start, but I did succeed in getting their attention. I explained that we would in the course of the semester read and discuss many different authors, but that one thing these authors all had in common was their subversiveness. Some, like Gorky or Gold, were overtly subversive in their political aims; others, like Fitzgerald and Mark Twain, were in my opinion more subversive, if less obviously so. I told them we would come back to this term, because my understanding of it was somewhat different from its usual definition. I wrote on the board one of my favorite lines from the German thinker Theodor Adorno: "The highest form of morality is not to feel at home in one's own home." I explained that most great works of the imagination were meant to make you feel like a stranger in your own home. The best fiction always forced us to question what we took for granted. It questioned traditions and expectations when they seemed too immutable. I told my students I wanted them in their readings to consider in what ways these works unsettled them, made them a little uneasy, made them look around and consider the world, like Alice in Wonderland, through different eyes.

At that time, students and faculty were differentiated mainly by their political affiliations. Gradually I matched names to faces, and learned to read them, to know who was with whom against whom and who belonged to what group. It is almost frightening how these images appear out of the void, like the faces of the dead come back to life to execute some unfulfilled task.

I can see Mr. Bahri in the middle row, playing with his pencil, his head down, writing. Is he writing my words, I wonder, or only pretending to do so? Every once in a while he lifts his head and gazes at me, as if trying to decipher a puzzle, and then he bends back down and continues with his writing.

In the second row, by the window, is a man whose face I remember well. He sits with both arms folded across his chest, listening defiantly, taking in every word, not so much because he wants or needs to learn but because, for reasons of his own, he has decided not to miss any of this. I will call him Mr. Nyazi.

My most radical students sit in the very back rows, with sardonic smiles. One face I remember well: Mahtab's. She sits self-consciously, looking straight at the blackboard, acutely aware of those sitting to her right and left. She is dark-skinned, with a simple face that seems to have retained its baby fat and resigned, sad eyes. I later discovered that she came from Abadan, an oil city in the south of Iran.

Then of course there is Zarrin, and her friend Vida. They caught my eye on that first day because they looked so different, as if they had no right to be in that class, or on the university grounds for that matter. They didn't fit any of the categories into which students in those days were so clearly divided. Leftists' mustaches covered their upper lips, to distinguish them from the Muslims, who carved out a razor-thin line between upper lip and mustache. Some Muslims also grew beards or what stubble they could muster. The leftist women wore khaki or dull green—large, loose shirts over loose trousers—and the Muslim girls scarves or chadors. In between these two immutable rivers stood the non-political students, who were all mechanically branded as monarchists. But not even the real monarchists stood out like Zarrin and Vida.

Zarrin had fair, fragile skin, eyes the color of melting honey and light brown hair, which she had gathered behind her ears. She and Vida were sitting in the first row, at the far right, near the door. Both were smiling. It seemed slightly rude of them to be there, looking like that, so pastel and serene. Even I, who had abdicated by now all revolutionary claims, was surprised by their appearance.

Vida was more sober, more conventionally academic, but with Zarrin there was always a danger of swerving, of losing control. Unlike many others, they were not defensive about their non-revolutionary attitude, nor did they seem to feel a need for justification. In those days the students canceled classes at the slightest provocation. Almost every day there were new debates, new events, and in the midst of all this Zarrin and her friend—more deliberately than dutifully—attended all classes, looking fresh and neat and immaculate.

I remember one day when my leftist students had canceled classes, protesting the fresh murder of three revolutionaries, I was walking downstairs when they caught up with me. In the previous session I had mentioned that they might have trouble finding copies of some of the books I had assigned. They wanted to tell me about a bookstore with the largest stock of English books in Tehran and eagerly volunteered that it still carried copies of *The Great Gatsby* and *Herzog*.

They had already read *Gatsby*. Were Fitzgerald's other books similar to this? We went on talking Fitzgerald as we walked down the wide staircase, past the various tables with their political goods for sale and the rather large crowd assembled in front of a wall plastered with newspapers. We walked onto the hot asphalt and sat on one of the benches by the stream running through the campus, and talked like children sharing coveted stolen cherries. I felt very young, and we laughed as we talked. Then we went our separate ways. We never became more intimate than that.

6

"Criminals should not be tried. The trial of a criminal is against human rights. Human rights demand that we should have killed them in the first place when it became known that they were criminals," proclaimed Ayatollah Khomeini, responding to protests by international human rights organizations of the wave of executions that followed the revolution. "They criticize us because we are executing the brutes." The jubilant mood of celebration and freedom that had followed the Shah's overthrow soon gave way to apprehension and fear as the regime continued to execute and murder "anti-revolutionaries" and a new vigilante justice emerged as bands of self-organized militants terrorized the streets.

NAME: Omid Gharib

SEX: male

DATE OF ARREST: 9 June 1980

PLACE OF ARREST: Tehran

PLACE OF DETENTION: Tehran, Qasr Prison

CHARGES: Being Westernized, brought up in a Westernized family; staying too long in Europe for his studies; smoking Winston cigarettes; displaying leftist tendencies.

SENTENCE: three years' imprisonment; death

TRIAL INFORMATION: The accused was tried behind closed doors. He was arrested after the authorities intercepted a letter he had sent to his friend in France. He was sentenced to three years' imprison-

ment in 1980. On 2 February 1982, while Omid Gharib was serving his prison term, his parents learned that he was executed. The
circumstances surrounding his execution are not known.

ADDITIONAL INFORMATION:

DATE OF EXECUTION: 31 January 1982

PLACE OF EXECUTION: Tehran

SOURCE: Amnesty International Newsletter, July 1982, volume XII,
number 7.

In those days we were all passersby in the crowded streets of a
metropolitan city, faces buried deep in our collars, preoccupied with
our own problems. I felt a certain distance from most of my students.
When in the States we had shouted Death to this or that, those deaths
seemed to be more symbolic, more abstract, as if we were encouraged
by the impossibility of our slogans to insist upon them even more.
But in Tehran in 1979, these slogans were turning into reality with
macabre precision. I felt helpless: all the dreams and slogans were
coming true, and there was no escaping them.

By mid-October, we were almost three weeks into classes and I
was getting used to the irregular beat of my days at the university.
There was seldom a day when our routine was not interrupted by a
death or assassination. Meetings and demonstrations were constantly
staged at the university for various reasons; almost every week classes
were either boycotted or canceled on the smallest pretext. The only
way I could give rhyme or rhythm to my life was to read my books
and work up my confused classes, which, surprisingly amid all the
turmoil, formed fairly regularly and were attended by the majority of
the students.

On a mild day in October, I tried to make my way through a
crowd that had gathered in front of our building around a well-
known leftist professor from the History Department. I stopped impulsively to listen to her. I do not remember much of what she said,
but part of my mind picked up some of her words and hid them in a
safe corner. She was telling the crowd that for the sake of independence, she was willing to wear the veil. She would wear the veil to
fight U.S. imperialists, to show them . . . To show them what?

I hastily made my way up the stairs to the conference room of the
English Department, where I had an appointment with a student, Mr.

Bahri. Ours was a formal relationship—I was so used to calling and thinking of him by his last name that I have completely forgotten his first name. At any rate, it is irrelevant. What is relevant perhaps, in a roundabout way, are his light complexion and dark hair, the stubborn silence that remained even when he spoke and his seemingly permanent lopsided grin. This grin colored everything he said, giving the impression that what he did not say, what he so blatantly hid and denied his listeners, put him in a superior position.

Mr. Bahri wrote one of the best student papers I had ever read on *The Adventures of Huckleberry Finn*, and ever since that day, for as long as I stayed at the University of Tehran, he somehow appeared beside or behind me all through the agitated meetings. He literally became my shadow, casting the weight of his lopsided silence upon me.

He wanted to inform me that he liked my classes and that "they" approved of my teaching methods. When I had assigned too much reading, the students at first reacted by considering a boycott of the class, but on later consideration they voted against it. He had come to ask or instruct me to add more revolutionary material, to teach more revolutionary writers. A stimulating discussion on the implications of the words *literature, radical, bourgeois* and *revolutionary* ensued, which proceeded, as I recall, with great emotion and intensity, though little substantial progress was made on the simple matter of definitions. All through this rather heated conversation, we were both standing at the end of a long table surrounded by empty chairs.

At the end of our talk, I was so excited I reached out to him in a gesture of goodwill and friendship. He silently, deliberately, withdrew both his hands behind his back, as if to remove them from even the possibility of a handshake. I was too bewildered, too much of a stranger to the newness of revolutionary ways, to take this gesture in stride. I recounted it later to a colleague, who, with a mocking smile, reminded me that no Muslim man would or should touch a *namahram* woman—a woman other than his wife, mother or sister. He turned to me in disbelief and said, "You really did not know that?"

My experiences, especially my teaching experiences, in Iran have been framed by the feel and touch of that aborted handshake, as much as by that first approach and the glow of our naïve, excited conversation. The image of my student's oblique smile has remained, brilliant yet opaque, while the room, the walls, the chairs and the long conference table have been covered over by layers and layers of what usually in works of fiction is called dust.

7

The first few weeks of classes were spent in a frenzy of meetings. We had department meetings and faculty meetings and meetings with students; we went to meetings in support of women, of workers, of militant Kurdish or Turkmen minorities. In those days I formed alliances and friendships with the head of the department, my brilliant and radical colleague Farideh and others from the departments of psychology, German and linguistics. We would all go to our favorite restaurant near the university for lunch and exchange the latest news and jokes. Already our carefree mood seemed a little out of place, but we had not yet given up hope.

During these luncheons we spent a great deal of time joking with or about one of our colleagues, who was worried he'd lose his job: the Muslim students had threatened to expel him for his use of "obscenities" in the classroom. The truth was that this man loved to worry about himself. He had just divorced his wife and had to maintain her, plus his home and swimming pool. We heard endlessly about this swimming pool. Somehow, inappropriately, he kept comparing himself to Gatsby, calling himself Little Great Gatsby. The only similarity, so far as I could see, was the swimming pool. This vanity colored his grasp of all great works of imagination. As it turned out, he was not expelled. He outstayed us all, gradually becoming intolerant of his brightest students, as I discovered years later when two of them, Nima and Manna, paid a high price for disagreeing with his viewpoints. As far as I know, he still teaches and repeats the same material to new students year after year. Little has changed, only he did marry a new and much younger wife.

In between these lunches we went to the Film Club, which had not yet been closed down, and watched Mel Brooks and Antonioni movies, marched off to exhibitions and still believed that the Khomeini crowd could not succeed, that the war was not yet over. Dr. A took us to a photo exhibition of protests and demonstrations during the Shah's time. He walked ahead of us, pointing to various pictures from the first year, saying, "Show me how many mullahs you see demonstrating, show me how many of these sons of . . . were out in the streets shouting for the Islamic Republic." Meanwhile, plots were being hatched, assassinations carried out, some through the novel approach of suicide bombings. The secularists and liberals were being ousted, and Ayatollah Khomeini's rhetoric against the Great Satan and its domestic agents was growing more virulent every day.

It is amazing how everything can fall into a routine. I seemed not to notice the unexpected and breathless quality of everyday life that belied every form of stability. After a while even the revolution found its rhythm: the violence, the executions, public confessions to crimes that had never been committed, judges who coolly talked about amputating a thief's hand or legs and killing political prisoners because there was not enough room for them now in jail. One day I sat watching the television, mesmerized by the image of a mother and son. The son belonged to one of the Marxist organizations. His mother was telling him that he deserved to die because he had betrayed the revolution and his faith, and he agreed with her. They both sat there on what seemed to be an empty stage except for their two chairs. They sat opposite each other, talking as they might have of arrangements for his forthcoming marriage. Only they were casually agreeing that his crimes were so heinous that the only way he could atone for them and save his family's honor was to embrace death.

In the mornings, with *The Adventures of Huckleberry Finn* under my arm, I would make my way through the wide, leafy streets leading to the university. As I approached the campus, the number of slogans on the walls and the violence of their demands increased. Never once was there a protest against the killings: the demands were almost always punctually for more blood. I, like others, went about my business. It was only at night and in my diary that my growing desperation, my nightmares, poured out uninhibited.

As I look over the pages of my diary, written in different colored inks in a notebook with a black plastic cover, I find the despair that never impinged upon the surface of my life. In that diary I have registered the deaths, which we seldom talked about, though they dominated the newspapers and the television.

One night at home I went to the kitchen for a glass of water and saw on television the battered and bruised face of the former head of the dreaded Ministry of National Security and Information, a general known for his cruelty. He had been one of the officials involved in framing and imprisoning my father. It must have been a rerun of his confession scene, for he had been killed a few months before. I can still remember, when my father was in jail, the number of times my mother would curse this general and his fellow conspirators. And now here he was, in civilian clothes, pleading for forgiveness from judges whose stern brutality even he could not fathom. There was not a shred of humanity in his expression. It was as if he had been forced to negate his former self and in the process he had abdicated his place alongside other men. I felt strangely connected to him, as if the complete surrender of his dignity had also diminished me. How many times had I dreamt of revenge on this particular man? Was this how one's dreams were to be fulfilled?

The government dailies published his and several other pictures after the next round of executions. These photographs were also published in a cheap pamphlet with yellowing pages sold by street vendors, alongside others on the secrets of health and beauty. I bought one of these poison pamphlets: I wanted to remember everything. Their faces, despite their terrible last moments, were forced to assume the peaceful indifference of death. But what amount of helplessness and desperation did those awful calm faces inspire in us, the survivors?

In the later months and years, every once in a while Bijan and I would be shocked to see the show trials of our old comrades in the U.S. on television. They eagerly denounced their past actions, their old comrades, their old selves, and confessed that they were indeed the enemies of Islam. We would watch these scenes in silence. Bijan was calmer than me, and would rarely show any emotion. He'd sit on the couch, his eyes glued to the television screen, seldom moving a muscle, while I fidgeted and got up to fetch a glass of water or change places. I felt I needed something to hold on to, and would dig harder into the armchair. When I turned to look at Bijan, I would encounter his placid expression; sometimes a whirling of resentment would well up inside of me. How could he be so composed? Once I moved and sat on the floor by his couch. I don't think I have ever felt such utter loneliness. After a few minutes, he rested a hand on my shoulder.

I turned around and asked Bijan, Did you ever dream that this could happen to us? He said, No I didn't, but I should have. After we all helped create this mess, we were not doomed to have the Islamic Republic. And in a sense, he was right. There was a very brief period, between the time the Shah left on January 16, 1979, and Khomeini's return to Iran on February 1, when one of the nationalist leaders, Dr. Shahpour Bakhtiar, had become the prime minister. Bakhtiar was perhaps the most democratic-minded and farsighted of the opposition leaders of that time, who, rather than rallying to his side, had fought against him and joined up with Khomeini. He had immediately disbanded Iran's secret police and set the political prisoners free. In rejecting Bakhtiar and helping to replace the Pahlavi dynasty with a far more reactionary and despotic regime, both the Iranian people and the intellectual elites had shown at best a serious error in judgment. I remember at the time that Bijan's was one lone voice in support of Bakhtiar, while all others, including mine, were only demanding destruction of the old, without much thought to the consequences.

One day, opening the morning paper, I saw pictures of Ali and Faramarz and other friends from the student movement. I knew instantly they had been killed. Unlike the generals, these were not photographs taken after the executions. They were old pictures, passport photos and student I.D.'s. In these insidiously innocent photos they smiled, with a conscious pose for the camera. I tore out the pages and for months hid them in my closet, using them as shoe trees, taking them out almost daily to look again at those faces I had last seen in another country that appeared to me now only in my dreams.

8

Mr. Bahri, who was at first reserved and reluctant to talk in class, began after our meeting to make insightful remarks. He spoke slowly, as if forming his ideas in the process of expressing them, pausing between words and sentences. Sometimes he seemed to me like a child just beginning to walk, testing the ground and discovering unknown potentials within himself. He was also at this time becoming increasingly immersed in politics. He had become an active member of the student group supported by the government—the Muslim Students' Association—and more and more often I would find him in the hallways immersed in arguments. His movements had gained an urgency, his eyes purpose and determination.

As I got to know him better, I noticed he was not as arrogant as I had thought him to be. Or perhaps I grew more accustomed to his special kind of arrogance, that of a naturally shy and reserved young man who had discovered an absolutist refuge called Islam. It was his doggedness, his newfound certainty, that gave him this arrogance. At times he could be very gentle, and when he talked, he would not look you in the eyes—not just because a Muslim man should not look a woman in the eyes, but because he was too timid. It was this mixture of arrogance and shyness that aroused my curiosity.

When we spoke, we always seemed to be in some private conference. We almost never agreed, but it seemed necessary that we argue out our differences and persuade each other of the rightness of our position. The more irrelevant I became, the more powerful he grew, and slowly and imperceptibly our roles reversed. He was not an agitator—he did not give fine, passionate speeches—but he worked his way up doggedly, with patience and dedication. By the time I was expelled from the university, he had become the head of the Muslim Students' Association.

When the radical students canceled classes, he was among the few who showed up, with evident disapproval. During these canceled classes, we usually talked about the various events unfolding at the university or the political issues of the day. He cautiously tried to make me understand what political Islam meant, and I rebuffed him, because it was exactly Islam as a political entity that I rejected. I told him about my grandmother, who was the most devout Muslim I had ever known, even more than you, Mr. Bahri, and still she shunned politics. She resented the fact that her veil, which to her was a symbol of her sacred relationship to God, had now become an instrument of power, turning the women who wore them into political signs and symbols. Where do your loyalties lie, Mr. Bahri, with Islam or the state?

I was not unfond of Mr. Bahri, and yet I developed a habit of blaming him and holding him responsible for everything that went wrong. He was baffled by Hemingway, felt ambivalent about Fitzgerald, loved Twain and thought we should have a national writer like him. I loved and admired Twain but thought all writers were national writers and that there was no such thing as a National Writer.

9

I do not remember what I was doing or where I was on that Sunday when I first heard the news that the American embassy had been occupied by a ragtag group of students. It is strange, but the only thing I remember was that it was sunny and mild, and the news did not sink in until the next day, when Ahmad, Khomeini's son, announced his father's support of the students and issued a defiant statement: "If they do not give us the criminals," he said, referring to the Shah and Bakhtiar, "then we will do whatever is necessary." Two days later, on November 6, Prime Minister Bazargan, who was being increasingly attacked by the religious hard-liners and the left as liberal and pro-Western, resigned.

Soon the walls of the embassy were covered with new slogans: AMERICA CAN'T DO A DAMN THING AGAINST US! THIS IS NOT A STRUGGLE BETWEEN THE U.S. AND IRAN, IT'S A STRUGGLE BETWEEN ISLAM AND BLASPHEMY. THE MORE WE DIE, THE STRONGER WE WILL BECOME. A tent was raised on the sidewalk and filled with propaganda against America, exposing its crimes around the world and proclaiming the necessity to export the revolution. At the university, the mood was both jubilant and apprehensive. Some of my students, Bahri and Nyazi among them, had disappeared and were presumably active on the front lines of this new struggle. Tense discussions and excited whispers replaced regular classes.

Both the religious and leftist organizations, especially the Mujahideen and the Marxist Fedayin, supported the hostage-taking. I remember one heated debate where one of the students who was mocked as a liberal kept saying, What's the point of taking them hostage? Haven't we already kicked them out? And one of my students unreasonably reasoned that no, not yet, that American influence was still everywhere. We wouldn't be free until the Voice of America was shut down.

By now the American embassy was no longer known as the American embassy—it was "the nest of spies." When taxi drivers asked us where we wanted to go, we would say, Please take us to the nest of spies. People were bused in daily from the provinces and villages who didn't even know where America was, and sometimes thought they were actually being taken to America. They were given food and money, and they could stay and joke and picnic with their families in front of the nest of spies—in exchange, they were asked to demonstrate, to shout, "Death to America," and every now and then to burn the American flag.

Three men sit in a semicircle talking eagerly, while a little farther on two women in black chadors, with three or four small children hovering around them, are making sandwiches and handing them over to the men. A festival? A picnic? An Islamic Woodstock? If you move a little closer to this small group, you can hear their conversation. Their accents indicate that they come from the province of Isfahan. One of them has heard that the Americans are becoming Muslims by the thousands and that Jimmy Carter is really scared. He should be scared, another one says as he bites into his sandwich. I hear the American police are confiscating all portraits of the Imam. Truth is mixed with wild rumors, rumors of the Shah's mistreatment by his former Western allies, of the imminent Islamic revolution in America. Will America hand him over?

Farther down, you can hear sharper and more clipped cadences. "But this isn't democratic centralism . . . religious tyranny . . . long-term allies . . ." and, more than any other word, *liberals*. Four or five students with books and pamphlets under their arms are deep in discussion. I recognize one of my leftist students, who sees me, smiles and comes towards me. Hello, Professor. I see you've joined us. Who is us? I ask him. The masses, the real people, he says quite seriously. But this is not your demonstration, I say. You're wrong there. We have to be present every day, to keep the fire going, to prevent the liberals from striking a deal, he says.

The loudspeakers interrupt us. "Neither East, nor West; we want the Islamic Republic!" "America can't do a damn thing!" "We will fight, we will die, we won't compromise!"

I could never accept this air of festivity, the jovial arrogance that dominated the crowds in front of the embassy. Two streets away, a completely different reality was unfolding. Sometimes it seemed to me that the government operated in its own separate universe: it created a big circus, put on a big act, while people went about their business.

The fact was that America, the place I knew and had lived in for so many years, had suddenly been turned into a never-never land by the Islamic Revolution. The America of my past was fast fading in my mind, overtaken by all the clamor of new definitions. That was when the myth of America started to take hold of Iran. Even those who wished its death were obsessed by it. America had become both the land of Satan and Paradise Lost. A sly curiosity about America had been kindled that in time would turn the hostage-takers into its hostages.

10

In my diary for the year 1980 I have a small note: "*Gatsby* from Jeff." Jeff was an American reporter from New York with whom I roamed the streets of Tehran for a few months. At the time I didn't understand why I had become so dependent on these rambles. Some people take up alcohol during periods of stress, and I took up Jeff. I needed desperately to describe what I had witnessed to that other part of the world I had now left behind, seemingly forever. I took up writing letters to my American friends, giving minute and detailed accounts of life in Iran, but most of those letters were never sent.

It was obvious that Jeff was lonely, and, despite his obsessive love for his job, for which he had been greatly acknowledged, he needed to talk to someone who could speak his language and share a few memories. I discovered to my surprise that I was afflicted by the same predicament. I had just returned to my home, where I could speak at last in my mother tongue, and here I was longing to talk to someone who spoke English, preferably with a New York accent, someone who was intelligent and appreciated *Gatsby* and Häagen-Dazs and knew about Mike Gold's Lower East Side.

I had started having nightmares and sometimes woke up screaming, mainly because I felt I would never again be able to leave the country. This was partly based on fact, since the first two times I tried to leave I was turned down at the airport and once I was even escorted back to the headquarters of the Revolutionary Court. In the end, I did not leave Iran for eleven years: even after I was confident that they would give me permission, I could not perform the simple act of going to the passport office and asking for a passport. I felt impotent and paralyzed.

II

Art is no longer snobbish or cowardly. It teaches peasants to use tractors, gives lyrics to young soldiers, designs textiles for factory women's dresses, writes burlesque for factory theatres, does a hundred other useful tasks. Art is useful as bread.

This rather long statement, which comes from an essay by Mike Gold, "Toward Proletarian Art," was written in 1929 in the radical *New Masses.* The essay in its time attracted a great deal of attention and gave birth to a new term in the annals of American literature: the *proletarian writer.* The fact that it could be influential and taken seriously by serious authors was a sign of changing times. *The Great Gatsby* was published in 1925 and *Tender Is the Night* in 1934. In between the publication of these two great novels, many things happened in the United States and Europe that made Gold influential for a while and diminished Fitzgerald's importance, making him almost irrelevant to the social and literary scene. There was the Depression, the increasing threat of fascism and the growing influence of Soviet Marxism.

Before I started teaching *The Great Gatsby,* we had discussed in class some short stories by Maxim Gorky and Mike Gold. Gorky was very popular at the time—many of his stories and his novel *The Mother* had been translated into Persian, and he was read widely by the revolutionaries, both old and young. This made *Gatsby* seem oddly irrelevant, a strange choice to teach at a university where almost all the students were burning with revolutionary zeal. Now, in retrospect, I see that *Gatsby* was the right choice. Only later did I come to realize how the values shaping that novel were the exact opposite of those of the revolution. Ironically, as time went by, it was the values inherent in *Gatsby* that would triumph, but at the time we had not yet realized just how far we had betrayed our dreams.

We started reading *Gatsby* in November, but couldn't finish it until January, because of the constant interruptions. I was taking some risks in teaching such a book at such a time, when certain books had been banned as morally harmful. Most revolutionary groups were in agreement with the government on the subject of individual freedoms, which they condescendingly called "bourgeois" and "decadent." This made it easier for the new ruling elite to pass some of the most reactionary laws, going so far as to outlaw certain gestures and expression of emotions, including love. Before it established a new constitution or parliament, the new regime had annulled the marriage-protection law. It banned ballet and dancing and told ballerinas they had a choice between acting or singing. Later women were banned from singing, because a woman's voice, like her hair, was sexually provocative and should be kept hidden.

My choice of *Gatsby* was not based on the political climate of the time but on the fact that it was a great novel. I had been asked to teach a course on twentieth-century fiction, and this seemed to me a reasonable principle for inclusion. And beyond that, it would give my students a glimpse of that other world that was now receding from us, lost in a clamor of denunciations. Would my students feel the same sympathy as Nick for Gatsby's fatal love for the beautiful and faithless Daisy Fay? I read and reread *Gatsby* with greedy wonder. I could not wait to share the book with my class, yet I was held back by a strange feeling that I did not want to share it with anyone.

My students were slightly baffled by *Gatsby*. The story of an idealistic guy, so much in love with this beautiful rich girl who betrays him, could not be satisfying to those for whom sacrifice was defined by words such as *masses, revolution* and *Islam*. Passion and betrayal were for them political emotions, and love far removed from the stirrings of Jay Gatsby for Mrs. Tom Buchanan. Adultery in Tehran was one of so many other crimes, and the law dealt with it accordingly: public stoning.

I told them this novel was an American classic, in many ways the quintessential American novel. There were other contenders: *The Adventures of Huckleberry Finn, Moby-Dick, The Scarlet Letter.* Some cite its subject matter, the American dream, to justify this distinction. We in ancient countries have our past—we obsess over the past. They, the Americans, have a dream: they feel nostalgia about the promise of the future.

I told them that although the novel was specifically about Gatsby and the American dream, its author wanted it to transcend its own time and place. I read to them Fitzgerald's favorite passage from Conrad's preface to *The Nigger of the "Narcissus,"* about how the artist "appeals to our capacity for delight and wonder, to the sense of mystery surrounding our lives; to our sense of pity, and beauty and pain . . . and to the subtle but invincible conviction of solidarity that knits together the loneliness of innumerable hearts, to the solidarity in dreams, in joy, in sorrow, in aspirations, in illusions, in hope, in fear which binds men to each other, which binds together all humanity— the dead to the living and the living to the unborn."

I tried to explain to my students that Mike Gold and F. Scott Fitzgerald had written about the same subject: dreams or, more specifically, the American dream. What Gold had only dreamed of had been realized in this faraway country, now with an alien name, the Islamic Republic of Iran. "The old ideals must die . . ." he wrote. "Let us fling all we are into the cauldron of the Revolution. For out of our death shall arise glories." Such sentences could have come out of any newspaper in Iran. The revolution Gold desired was a Marxist one and ours was Islamic, but they had a great deal in common, in that they were both ideological and totalitarian. The Islamic Revolution, as it turned out, did more damage to Islam by using it as an instrument of oppression than any alien ever could have done.

Don't go chasing after the grand theme, the idea, I told my students, as if it is separate from the story itself. The idea or ideas behind the story must come to you through the experience of the novel and not as something tacked on to it. Let's pick a scene to demonstrate this point. Please turn to page 125. You will remember Gatsby is visiting Daisy and Tom Buchanan's house for the first time. Mr. Bahri, could you please read the few lines beginning with "Who wants to . . ."?

"Who wants to go to town?" demanded Daisy insistently. Gatsby's eyes floated toward her. "Ah," she cried, "you look so cool."

Their eyes met, and they stared together at each other, alone in space. With an effort she glanced down at the table.

"You always look so cool," she repeated.

She had told him that she loved him, and Tom Buchanan saw. He was astounded. His mouth opened a little, and he looked at Gatsby, and then back at Daisy as if he had just recognized her as some one he knew a long time ago.

On one level, Daisy is simply telling Gatsby he looks cool and Fitzgerald is telling us that she still loves him, but he doesn't want to just say so. He wants to put us there in the room. Let's look at what he's done to give this scene the texture of a real experience. First he creates a tension between Gatsby and Daisy, and then he complicates it with Tom's sudden insight into their relationship. This moment, suspended in mid-air, is far more effective than if Nick had simply reported that Daisy tried to tell Gatsby that she loved him.

"Yes," cut in Mr. Farzan, "because he is in love with the money and not with Daisy. She is only a symbol."

No, she is Daisy, and he is in love with her. There is money too, but that is not all; that is not even the point. Fitzgerald does not tell you—he takes you inside the room and re-creates the sensual experience of that hot summer day so many decades ago, and we, the readers, draw our breath along with Tom as we realize what has just happened between Gatsby and Daisy.

"But what use is love in this world we live in?" said a voice from the back of the room.

"What kind of a world do you think is suitable for love?" I asked.

Mr. Nyazi's hand darted up. "We don't have time for love right now," he said. "We are committed to a higher, more sacred love."

Zarrin turned around and said sardonically, "Why else do you fight a revolution?"

Mr. Nyazi turned very red, bowed his head and after a short pause took up his pen and started to write furiously.

In retrospect it appears strange to me only now, as I write about it, that as I was standing there in that classroom talking about the American dream, we could hear from outside, beneath the window, the loudspeakers broadcasting songs whose refrain was "*Marg bar Amrika!*"—"Death to America!"

A novel is not an allegory, I said as the period was about to come to an end. It is the sensual experience of another world. If you don't enter that world, hold your breath with the characters and become involved in their destiny, you won't be able to empathize, and empathy is at the heart of the novel. This is how you read a novel: you inhale the experience. So start breathing. I just want you to remember this. That is all; class dismissed.

12

Throughout that year, between the fall of 1979 and the summer of 1980, many events happened that changed the course of the revolution and of our lives. Battles were being fought and lost. One of the most significant of these was over women's rights: from the very start, the government had waged a war against women, and the most important battles were being fought then.

One day, I think it was in early November, I announced to my students, after the last straggler had drifted in, that they had canceled class many times for their own reasons and I in principle did not agree with this, but on that day I would be forced to go against my own principles and cancel class. I told them I was going to a protest meeting, to oppose the government's attempts to impose the veil on women and its curtailment of women's rights. I had missed some of the large demonstrations against the revolutionary government's policies against women, and I was determined not to miss any more.

Unconsciously, I was developing two different ways of life. Publicly, I was involved in what I considered to be a defense of myself as a person. This was very different from my political activities during my student days, made in behalf of an unknown entity called the "oppressed masses." This was more personal. At the same time, a more private rebellion began to manifest itself in certain tendencies, like incessant reading, or the Herzog-like passion of writing letters to friends in the States that were never sent. I felt a silent defiance that may also have shaped my public desire to defend a vague and amorphous entity I thought of as myself.

From the beginning of the revolution there had been many aborted attempts to impose the veil on women; these attempts failed because of persistent and militant resistance put up mainly by Iranian women. In many important ways the veil had gained a symbolic significance for the regime. Its reimposition would signify the complete victory of the Islamic aspect of the revolution, which in those first years was not a foregone conclusion. The unveiling of women mandated by Reza Shah in 1936 had been a controversial symbol of modernization, a powerful sign of the reduction of the clergy's power. It was important for the ruling clerics to reassert that power. All this I can explain now, with the advantage of hindsight, but it was far from clear then.

Mr. Bahri's body stiffened as he focused on my words. Zarrin kept her usual smile, and Vida whispered to her conspiratorially. I did not pay much attention to their reactions: I was very angry, and this anger was a new feeling for me.

Mr. Bahri lingered on after I dismissed the class, hovering for a while near the cluster of students who had gathered around me—but he made no attempt to come closer. I had returned my notes and books to my bag, except my *Gatsby,* which I held absentmindedly in one hand.

I did not want to enter a debate with Mahtab and her friends, whose Marxist organization had tacitly taken sides with the government, denouncing the protesters as deviant, divisive and ultimately acting in the service of the imperialists. Somehow I found myself arguing not with Mr. Bahri but with them, the ostensibly progressive ones. They claimed that there were bigger fish to fry, that the imperialists and their lackeys needed to be dealt with first. Focusing on women's rights was individualistic and bourgeois and played into their hands. What imperialists, which lackeys? Do you mean those battered and bruised faces shown on nightly television confessing to their crimes? Do you mean the prostitutes they recently stoned to death or my former school principal, Mrs. Parsa, who, like the prostitutes, was accused of "corruption on earth," "sexual offenses" and "violation of decency and morality," for having been the minister of education? For which alleged offenses she was put in a sack and either stoned or shot to death? Are those the lackeys you are talking about, and is it in order to wipe these people out that we have to defer and not protest? I am familiar with your line of arguments, I shot back—after all, I was in the same business not so long ago.

Arguing with my leftist students, I had a funny feeling that I was talking to a younger version of myself, and the gleam I saw in that familiar stranger's face frightened me. My students were more respectful, less aggressive than I had been when I argued a point—they were talking to their professor, after all, with whom they sort of sympathized, to a fellow traveler who might be saved.

As I write about them in the opaque glow of hindsight, Mahtab's face slowly fades and is transformed into the image of another girl, also young, in Norman, Oklahoma.

13

At the time I lived in Oklahoma, one of our rival factions in the student movement, the most radical group within the Confederation of Iranian Students, convened a conference in Oklahoma City. I missed the conference, having gone to another meeting in Texas. When I returned I noticed an unusual air of excitement among both "our" people and "theirs." Apparently one of their members, a former running champion, was suspected of being an agent of the Iranian secret police, SAVAK. Some zealous members had decided to "extract" the truth from him. They had lured him into a room at the Holiday Inn and tried to get him to confess by means of torture, including burning his fingers with a cigarette. When they had left the room and were in the parking lot, their victim managed to escape.

The next day the door flew open in the middle of the conference, admitting several FBI agents with dogs and the "culprit," who was told to identify his assailants. One of our friends, who had previously admonished me for my anti-revolutionary clothes, her voice breaking with excitement, related to me what had happened, boasting about "the power of the masses." By "masses" she meant the participants in the conference who had stood aside, creating an avenue for the agents, their dogs and the hapless culprit to walk through. As he passed by, they muttered threats in Persian. When he finally reached one of the leaders of that faction, the most popular in fact, a short, intense-looking guy who like many of his comrades had dropped out of college to become a full-time revolutionary and who usually sported a cap and coat in imitation of Lenin, he broke down and started crying and asked him in Persian why he had treated him so cruelly. The self-proclaimed Lenin of the Iranian revolution looked at him triumphantly, daring him to "spill" to the FBI. He could not bring himself to expose his tormentors and left with the agents, once more proving the justness of the oppressed masses.

The following day, there was a short report in *The Oklahoma Daily*. More than the report, it was the way so many students reacted that frightened me. In the coffee shops, in the student union, even in the sunny streets of Norman, whenever the political Iranian students met they carried on heated discussions. Many quoted Comrade Stalin approvingly, spouting lines from a fashionable book, *A Brief History of the Bolshevik Party* or some such, about the need to destroy once and for all the Trotskyites, the White Guards, the termites and poisonous rats who were bent on destroying the revolution.

Sitting in the student union drinking coffee or Coke, our comrades, disturbing the next table's flirtations, flared up and defended the right of the masses to torture and physically eliminate their oppressors. I still remember one of them, a chubby guy with a soft, boyish face, the outlines of his round belly protruding from under his navy blue woolen sweater. He refused to sit down and, towering over our table, swinging a glass of Coke precariously in one hand, he argued that there were two kinds of torture, two kinds of killing—those committed by the enemy and those by the friends of the people. It was okay to murder enemies.

I could tell Mr. Bahri, now eternally bending towards me in some urgent argument: listen, be careful what you wish for. Be careful with your dreams; one day they may just come true. I could have told him to learn from Gatsby, from the lonely, isolated Gatsby, who also tried to retrieve his past and give flesh and blood to a fancy, a dream that was never meant to be more than a dream. He was killed, left at the bottom of the swimming pool, as lonely in death as in life. I know you most probably have not read the book to the end, you have been so busy with your political activities, but let me tell you the ending anyway—you seem to be in need of knowing. Gatsby is killed. He is killed for a crime Daisy committed, running over Tom's mistress in Gatsby's yellow car. Tom fingered Gatsby to the bereaved husband, who killed Gatsby as he lay floating in his swimming pool waiting for Daisy to call. Could my former comrades have predicted that one day they would be tried in a Revolutionary Court, tortured and killed as traitors and spies? Could they, Mr. Bahri? I can tell you with complete confidence that they could not. Not in their wildest dreams.

14

I left Mahtab and her friends, but those memories could not easily be left behind: they pursued me like mischievous beggars to the protest meeting. Two distinct and hostile groups had formed among the protesters, eyeing each other suspiciously. The first, smaller group consisted mainly of government workers and housewives. They were there instinctively, because their interests were at stake. They were clearly not used to demonstrations: they stood together in a huddle, uncertain and resentful. Then there were the intellectuals like myself, who did know a thing or two about demonstrations, and the usual hecklers, shouting obscenities and brandishing slogans. Two of them took photographs of the crowd, jumping menacingly from side to side. We covered our faces and shouted back.

Soon the number of vigilantes increased. They gathered in small groups and began moving towards us. The police fired a few perfunctory shots into the air while men with knives, clubs and stones approached us. Instead of protecting the women, the police started to disperse us, pushing some with the butt of their guns and ordering the "sisters" to make no trouble and go home. There was a feeling of desperate anger in the air, thick with taunting jeers. The meeting continued despite the provocations.

A few nights later, another protest was convened at the Polytechnic University. A huge crowd had gathered in the auditorium by the time I arrived, laughing and talking. As one of the speakers—a tall, stately woman wearing a long, sturdy skirt, her long hair tied back behind her ears—moved towards the podium, the electricity was turned off. There were murmurs of protest, but no one moved. The speaker stood stiffly and defiantly with the text in front of her and two people held a candle and a flashlight for her to read by. All we could see was her disembodied face and the white paper in her hands, illuminated by the light behind her. Only the cadence of her voice and that light have remained with me. We were not listening to the words: we were there to support and to bear witness to the act, to preserve the image of her flickering in the candlelight.

That woman and I were destined to meet mainly at public events. The last time I saw her was in the fall of 1999 in New York, when, as Iran's foremost feminist publisher, she was invited to a talk at Columbia University. After the meeting, we reminisced over coffee. I hadn't seen her since the Tehran book fair in 1993, when she had invited me to give a talk on the modern novel. The talk was held on the second floor of an open cafeteria in the main building of the book fair. As I spoke, I became more and more excited about my theme and my scarf kept slipping back from my hair. The number of people in the audience grew until there was no room to sit or stand. As soon as the talk ended, this woman was summoned by security and reprimanded for my improper veil and inflammatory talk. The fact that I had spoken about works of fiction was inconsequential to them. After that, her lecture series was banned.

We were smiling over these memories, sitting in a dark corner of a restaurant, secure in the busy indifference of a mild New York evening. For a moment I felt that she had not changed at all since she had given that talk years earlier: she was still wearing a long, sturdy skirt, and her long hair was still gathered behind her ears. Only her smile had changed: it was a smile of desperation. A few months later she was arrested with a number of prominent activists, journalists, writers and student leaders. These arrests were part of a new wave of repression, during which over twenty-five publications were closed down and many dissenters arrested or jailed. Hearing the news as I sat in my office in Washington, D.C., a feeling I had not experienced for a long time came over me: a sense of utter helplessness, of inarticulate anger tinged with vague but persistent guilt.

15

It was around this time, mid-fall, that I spoke again with Mr. Bahri. He said, Well, Professor, they most probably deserve it: the students are very angry. We were talking about three faculty members who were being threatened with expulsion, one of whom had been singled out mainly because he was Armenian. The other was my colleague who described himself as Little Great Gatsby: both had been accused of using obscene language in class. A third was accused of being a CIA agent. Dr. A, who was still head of the department, had refused to accept their expulsion.

Dr. A himself was rapidly falling out of favor. In the early days of the revolution, he had been put on trial by the students at Tehran University for defending a prison guard. Eighteen years after the event, I read about it in an homage that one of his former students, herself a well-known translator, paid him in a magazine. She described how one day she had been watching the trial of a secret-police agent on television when a familiar voice, Dr. A's, attracted her attention. He had come to testify in favor of his former student, whom he believed to be a compassionate individual, a man who often helped out his less fortunate classmates. Dr. A told the Revolutionary Court: "I believe it is my duty as a human being to acquaint you with this aspect of the accused's personality." Such an action, during those initial black-and-white days of the revolution, was unheard of and very dangerous.

The accused, who had been enrolled in the university's night classes, was a prison guard who had apparently been charged with beating and torturing political prisoners. It was said that mainly because of Dr. A's testimony in his favor, he got off easy, with only a two-year jail sentence. None of my friends and acquaintances knew what happened to him later.

Dr. A's student regrets in her account that she participated in his trial without voicing a protest. She goes on to conclude that Dr. A's action was a manifestation of the principles he had taught in his literature classes. "Such an act," she explains, "can only be accomplished by someone who is engrossed in literature, has learned that every individual has different dimensions to his personality. . . . Those who judge must take all aspects of an individual's personality into account. It is only through literature that one can put oneself in someone else's shoes and understand the other's different and contradictory sides and refrain from becoming too ruthless. Outside the sphere of literature only one aspect of individuals is revealed. But if you understand their different dimensions you cannot easily murder them. . . . If we had learned this one lesson from Dr. A our society would have been in a much better shape today."

The threats of expulsion were an extension of the purges that continued throughout that year, and have never really ceased, up to this day. After a meeting with Dr. A and two other colleagues about this matter, I stormed down the hall and came across Mr. Bahri. He was standing at the corner of the long corridor talking to the president of the Islamic Association of University Staff. The two were leaning towards each other in the attitude of men who are involved in deeply serious matters, matters of life and death. I called Mr. Bahri, who walked towards me with respect, gracefully dissimulating any irritation he might have felt at this disruption. I questioned him about trying the faculty members and dismissing them illegally.

His expression changed into one of alarm mixed with determination. He explained that I had to understand that things had changed. What does this mean, I said, that things have changed? It means that morality is important to our students; it means that the faculty is answerable to the students. Did this make it all right, then, to put a responsible and dedicated teacher like Dr. A on trial?

Mr. Bahri said that he himself had not participated in that trial. Of course Dr. A is too Western in his attitudes, he added. He is flirtatious and loose.

So is this our new definition of the word *Western,* I shot back—are we now officially living in the Soviet Union or China? And should Dr. A now be tried for his flirtations? No, but he should understand certain things. You cannot go and support a spy, a lackey, someone who is responsible for the deaths of so many. He went on to tell me that he thought there were far more important people than Dr. A to be tried. There were CIA spies, such as our own Professor Z, who were free to come and go as they pleased.

I told him they had no proof that the gentleman in question was a CIA agent, and in any case I doubted the CIA would be foolish enough to employ someone like him. But even those whom he called the functionaries of the old regime, regardless of their guilt, shouldn't be treated this way. I could not understand why the Islamic government had to gloat over these people's deaths, brandishing their photographs after they had been tortured and executed. Why did they show us these pictures? Why did our students every day shout slogans demanding new death sentences?

Mr. Bahri did not respond at first. He stood still, his head bent, his hands linked in front of him. Then he started to speak, slowly and with tense precision. Well, they have to pay, he said. They are on trial for their past deeds. The Iranian nation will not tolerate their crimes. And these new crimes? I asked as soon as he had uttered his last word. Should they be tolerated in silence? Everyone nowadays is an enemy of God—former ministers and educators, prostitutes, leftist revolutionaries: they are murdered daily. What had these people done to deserve such treatment?

His face had become hard, and the shadow of obstinacy had colored his eyes. He repeated that people had to pay for their past crimes. This is not a game, he said. It is a revolution. I asked him if I too was on trial for my past. But he was right in a sense: we all have to pay in the end. There were no innocents in the game of life, that was for sure. We all had to pay, but not for the crimes we were accused of. There were other scores to settle. I did not know then that I had already begun to pay, that what was happening was part of the payment. It was much later that these feelings would be clarified.

16

It was late; I had been at the library. I was spending a great deal of time there now, as it was becoming more and more difficult to find "imperialist" novels in bookstores. I was emerging from the library with a few books under my arm when I noticed him standing by the door. His two hands were joined in front of him in an expression of reverence for me, his teacher, but in his strained grimace I could feel his sense of power. I remember Mr. Nyazi always with a white shirt, buttoned up to the neck—he never tucked it in. He was stocky and had blue eyes, very closely cropped light brown hair and a thick, pinkish neck. It seemed as if his neck were made of soft clay; it literally sat on his shirt collar. He was always very polite.

"Ma'am, may I talk to you for a second?" Although we were in the middle of the semester, I had not as yet been assigned an office, so we stood in the hall and I listened. His complaint was about Gatsby. He said he was telling me this for my own good. For my own good? What an odd expression to use. He said surely I must know how much he respected me, otherwise he would not be there talking to me. He had a complaint. Against whom, and why me? It was against Gatsby. I asked him jokingly if he had filed any official complaints against Mr. Gatsby. And I reminded him that any such action would in any case be useless as the gentleman was already dead.

But he was serious. No, Professor, not against Mr. Gatsby himself but against the novel. The novel was immoral. It taught the youth the wrong stuff; it poisoned their minds—surely I could see? I could not. I reminded him that Gatsby was a work of fiction and not a how-to manual. Surely I could see, he insisted, that these novels and their characters became our models in real life? Maybe Mr. Gatsby was all right for the Americans, but not for our revolutionary youth. For some reason the idea that this man could be tempted to become Gatsby-like was very appealing to me.

There was, for Mr. Nyazi, no difference between the fiction of Fitzgerald and the facts of his own life. *The Great Gatsby* was representative of things American, and America was poison for us; it certainly was. We should teach Iranian students to fight against American immorality, he said. He looked earnest; he had come to me in all goodwill.

Suddenly a mischievous notion got hold of me. I suggested, in these days of public prosecutions, that we put *Gatsby* on trial: Mr. Nyazi would be the prosecutor, and he should also write a paper offering his evidence. I told him that when Fitzgerald's books were published in the States, there were many who felt just as he did. They may have expressed themselves differently, but they were saying more or less the same thing. So he need not feel lonely in expressing his views.

The next day I presented this plan to the class. We could not have a proper trial, of course, but we could have a prosecutor, a lawyer for the defense and a defendant; the rest of the class would be the jury. Mr. Nyazi would be the prosecutor. We needed a judge, a defendant and a defense attorney.

After a great deal of argument, because no one volunteered for any of the posts, we finally persuaded one of the leftist students to be the judge. But then Mr. Nyazi and his friends objected: this student was biased against the prosecution. After further deliberation, we agreed upon Mr. Farzan, a meek and studious fellow, rather pompous and, fortunately, shy. No one wanted to be the defense. It was emphasized that since I had chosen the book, I should defend it. I argued that in that case, I should be not the defense but the defendant and promised to cooperate closely with my lawyer and to talk in my own defense. Finally, Zarrin, who was holding her own conference in whispers with Vida, after a few persuasive nudges, volunteered. Zarrin wanted to know if I was Fitzgerald or the book itself. We decided that I would be the book: Fitzgerald may have had or lacked qualities that we could detect in the book. It was agreed that in this trial the rest of the class could at any point interrupt the defense or the prosecution with their own comments and questions.

I felt it was wrong for me to be the defendant, that this put the prosecutor in an awkward position. At any rate, it would have been more interesting if one of the students had chosen to participate. But no one wanted to speak for *Gatsby*. There was something so obstinately arrogant about Mr. Nyazi, so inflexible, that in the end I persuaded myself I should have no fear of intimidating him.

A few days later, Mr. Bahri came to see me. We had not met for what seemed like a long time. He was a little outraged. I enjoyed the fact that for the first time, he seemed agitated and had forgotten to talk in his precise and leisurely manner. Was it necessary to put this book on trial? I was somewhat taken aback. Did he want me to throw the book aside without so much as a word in its defense? Anyway, this is a good time for trials, I said, is it not?

17

All through the week before the trial, whatever I did, whether talking to friends and family or preparing for classes, part of my mind was constantly occupied on shaping my arguments for the trial. This after all was not merely a defense of *Gatsby* but of a whole way of looking at and appraising literature—and reality, for that matter. Bijan, who seemed quite amused by all of this, told me one day that I was studying *Gatsby* with the same intensity as a lawyer scrutinizing a textbook on law. I turned to him and said, You don't take this seriously, do you? He said, Of course I take it seriously. You have put yourself in a vulnerable position in relation to your students. You have allowed them—no, not just that; you have forced them into questioning your judgment as a teacher. So you have to win this case. This is very important for a junior member of the faculty in her first semester of teaching. But if you are asking for sympathy, you won't get it from me. You're loving it, admit it—you love this sort of drama and anxiety. Next thing you know, you'll be trying to convince me that the whole revolution depends on this.

But it does—don't you see? I implored. He shrugged and said, Don't tell me. I suggest you put your ideas to Ayatollah Khomeini.

On the day of the trial, I left for school early and roamed the leafy avenues before heading to class. As I entered the Faculty of Persian and Foreign Languages and Literature, I saw Mahtab standing by the door with another girl. She wore a peculiar grin that day, like a lazy kid who has just gotten an A. She said, Professor, I wondered if you would mind if Nassrin sits in on the class today. I looked from her to her young companion; she couldn't have been more than thirteen or fourteen years old. She was very pretty, despite her own best efforts to hide it. Her looks clashed with her solemn expression, which was neutral and adamantly impenetrable. Only her body seemed to express something: she kept leaning on one leg and then the other as her right hand gripped and released the thick strap of her heavy shoulder bag.

Mahtab, with more animation than usual, told me that Nassrin's English was better than most college kids', and when she'd told her about *Gatsby*'s trial, she was so curious that she'd read the whole book. I turned to Nassrin and asked, What did you think of *Gatsby*? She paused and then said quietly, I can't tell. I said, Do you mean you don't know or you can't tell me? She said, I don't know, but maybe I just can't tell you.

That was the beginning of it all. After the trial, Nassrin asked permission to continue attending my classes whenever she could. Mahtab told me that Nassrin was her neighbor. She belonged to a Muslim organization but was a very interesting kid, and Mahtab was working on her—an expression the leftists used to describe someone they were trying to recruit.

I told Nassrin she could come to my class on one condition: at the end of term, she would have to write a fifteen-page paper on *Gatsby*. She paused as she always did, as if she didn't quite have sufficient words at her command. Her responses were always reluctant and forced; one felt almost guilty for making her talk. Nassrin demurred at first, and then she said: I'm not that good. You don't need to be good, I said. And I'm sure you are—after all, you're spending your free time here. I don't want a scholarly paper; I want you to write your own impressions. Tell me in your own words what *Gatsby* means to you. She was looking at the tip of her shoes, and she muttered that she would try.

From then on, every time I came to class I would look for Nassrin, who usually followed Mahtab and sat beside her. She would be busy taking notes all through the session, and she even came a few times when Mahtab did not show up. Then suddenly she stopped coming, until the last class, when I saw her sitting in a corner, busying herself with the notes she scribbled.

Once I had agreed to accept my young intruder, I left them both and continued. I needed to stop by the department office before class to pick up a book Dr. A had left for me. When I entered the classroom that afternoon, I felt a charged silence follow me in. The room was full; only one or two students were absent—and Mr. Bahri, whose activities, or disapproval, had kept him away. Zarrin was laughing and swapping notes with Vida, and Mr. Nyazi stood in a corner talking to two other Muslim students, who repaired to their seats when they caught sight of me. Mahtab was sitting beside her new recruit, whispering to her conspiratorially.

I spoke briefly about the next week's assignment and proceeded to set the trial in motion. First I called forth Mr. Farzan, the judge, and asked him to take his seat in my usual chair, behind the desk. He sauntered up to the front of the class with an ill-disguised air of self-satisfaction. A chair was placed near the judge for the witnesses. I sat beside Zarrin on the left side of the room, by the large window, and Mr. Nyazi sat with some of his friends on the other side, by the wall. The judge called the session to order. And so began the case of the Islamic Republic of Iran versus *The Great Gatsby.*

Mr. Nyazi was called to state his case against the defendant. Instead of standing, he moved his chair to the center of the room and started to read in a monotonous voice from his paper. The judge sat uncomfortably behind my desk and appeared to be mesmerized by Mr. Nyazi. Every once in a while he blinked rather violently.

A few months ago, I was finally cleaning up my old files and I came across Mr. Nyazi's paper, written by hand in immaculate handwriting. It began with "In the Name of God," words that later became mandatory on all official letterheads and in all public talks. Mr. Nyazi picked up the pages of his paper one by one, gripping rather than holding them, as if afraid that they might try to escape his hold. "Islam is the only religion in the world that has assigned a special sacred role to literature in guiding man to a godly life," he intoned. "This becomes clear when we consider that the Koran, God's own word, is the Prophet's miracle. Through the Word you can heal or you can destroy. You can guide or you can corrupt. That is why the Word can belong to Satan or to God.

"Imam Khomeini has relegated a great task to our poets and writers," he droned on triumphantly, laying down one page and picking up another. "He has given them a sacred mission, *much* more exalted than that of the materialistic writers in the West. If our Imam is the shepherd who guides the flock to its pasture, then the writers are the faithful watchdogs who must lead according to the shepherd's dictates."

A giggle could be heard from the back of the class. I glanced around behind me and caught Zarrin and Vida whispering. Nassrin was staring intently at Mr. Nyazi and absentmindedly chewing her pencil. Mr. Farzan seemed to be preoccupied with an invisible fly, and blinked exaggeratedly at intervals. When I turned my attention back to Mr. Nyazi, he was saying, "Ask yourself which you would prefer: the guardianship of a sacred and holy task or the materialistic reward of money and position that has corrupted—" and here he paused, without taking his eyes off his paper, seeming to drag the sapless words to the surface—"that has *corrupted,*" he repeated, "the Western writers and deprived their work of spirituality and purpose. *That* is why our Imam says that the pen is mightier than the sword."

The whispers and titters in the back rows had become more audible. Mr. Farzan was too inept a judge to pay attention, but one of Mr. Nyazi's friends cried out: "Your Honor, could you please instruct the gentlemen and ladies in the back to respect the court and the prosecutor?"

"So be it," said Mr. Farzan, irrelevantly.

"Our poets and writers in this battle against the Great Satan," Nyazi continued, "play the same role as our faithful soldiers, and they will be accorded the same reward in heaven. We students, as the future guardians of culture, have a heavy task ahead of us. Today we have planted Islam's flag of victory inside the nest of spies on our own soil. Our task, as our Imam has stated, is to purge the country of the decadent Western culture and . . ."

At this point Zarrin stood up. "Objection, Your Honor!" she cried out.

Mr. Farzan looked at her in some surprise. "What do you object to?"

"This is supposed to be about *The Great Gatsby,*" said Zarrin. "The prosecutor has taken up fifteen precious minutes of our time without saying a single word about the defendant. Where is this all going?"

For a few seconds both Mr. Farzan and Mr. Nyazi looked at her in wonder. Then Mr. Nyazi said, without looking at Zarrin, "This is an Islamic court, not *Perry Mason.* I can present my case the way I want to, and I am setting the context. I want to say that as a Muslim I cannot accept *Gatsby.*"

Mr. Farzan, attempting to rise up to his role, said, "Well, please move on then."

Zarrin's interruptions had upset Mr. Nyazi, who after a short pause lifted his head from his paper and said with some excitement, "You are right, it is not worth it . . ."

We were left to wonder what was not worth it for a few seconds, until he continued. "I don't have to read from a paper, and I don't need to talk about Islam. I have enough evidence—every page, *every single page*," he cried out, "of this book is its own condemnation." He turned to Zarrin and one look at her indifferent expression was enough to transform him. "All through this revolution we have talked about the fact that the West is our enemy, it is the Great Satan, not because of its military might, not because of its economic power, but because of, because of"—another pause—"because of its sinister assault on the very roots of our culture. What our Imam calls cultural aggression. This I would call a rape of our culture," Mr. Nyazi stated, using a term that later became the hallmark of the Islamic Republic's critique of the West. "And if you want to see cultural rape, you need go no further than this very book." He picked his *Gatsby* up from beneath the pile of papers and started waving it in our direction.

Zarrin rose again to her feet. "Your Honor," she said with barely disguised contempt, "these are all baseless allegations, falsehoods . . ."

Mr. Nyazi did not allow his honor to respond. He half rose from his seat and cried out: "Will you let me finish? You will get your turn! I will tell you why, I will tell you why . . ." And then he turned to me and in a softer voice said, "Ma'am, no offense meant to you."

I, who had by now begun to enjoy the game, said, "Go ahead, please, and remember I am here in the role of the book. I will have my say in the end."

"Maybe during the reign of the corrupt Pahlavi regime," Nyazi continued, "adultery was the accepted norm."

Zarrin was not one to let go. "I object!" she cried out. "There is no factual basis to this statement."

"Okay," he conceded, "but the values were such that adultery went unpunished. This book preaches illicit relations between a man and woman. First we have Tom and his mistress, the scene in her apartment—even the narrator, Nick, is implicated. He doesn't like their lies, but he has no objection to their fornicating and sitting on each other's laps, and, and, those parties at Gatsby's . . . remember, ladies and gentlemen, this Gatsby is the hero of the book—and who is he? He is a charlatan, he is an adulterer, he is a liar . . . this is the man Nick celebrates and feels sorry for, this man, this destroyer of homes!" Mr. Nyazi was clearly agitated as he conjured the fornicators, liars and adulterers roaming freely in Fitzgerald's luminous world, immune from his wrath and from prosecution. "The only sympathetic person here is the cuckolded husband, Mr. Wilson," Mr. Nyazi boomed. "When he kills Gatsby, it is the hand of God. He is the only victim. He is the genuine symbol of the oppressed, in the land of, of, of the Great Satan!"

The trouble with Mr. Nyazi was that even when he became excited and did not read from his paper, his delivery was monotonous. Now he mainly shouted and cried out from his semi-stationary position.

"The one good thing about this book," he said, waving the culprit in one hand, "is that it exposes the immorality and decadence of American society, but we have fought to rid ourselves of this trash and it is high time that such books be banned." He kept calling Gatsby "this Mr. Gatsby" and could not bring himself to name Daisy, whom he referred to as "that woman." According to Nyazi, there was not a single virtuous woman in the whole novel. "What kind of model are we setting for our innocent and modest sisters," he asked his captive audience, "by giving them such a book to read?"

As he continued, he became increasingly animated, yet he refused throughout to budge from his chair. "Gatsby is dishonest," he cried out, his voice now shrill. "He earns his money by illegal means and tries to buy the love of a married woman. This book is supposed to be about the American dream, but what sort of a dream is this? Does the author mean to suggest that we should all be adulterers and bandits? Americans are decadent and in decline because this is their dream. They are going down! This is the last hiccup of a dead culture!" he concluded triumphantly, proving that Zarrin was not the only one to have watched *Perry Mason*.

"Perhaps our honorable prosecutor should not be so harsh," Vida said once it was clear that Nyazi had at last exhausted his argument. "Gatsby dies, after all, so one could say that he gets his just deserts."

But Mr. Nyazi was not convinced. "Is it just Gatsby who deserves to die?" he said with evident scorn. "*No!* The whole of American society deserves the same fate. What kind of a dream is it to steal a man's wife, to preach sex, to cheat and swindle and to . . . and then that guy, the narrator, Nick, he claims to be moral!"

Mr. Nyazi proceeded in this vein at some length, until he came to a sudden halt, as if he had choked on his own words. Even then he did not budge. Somehow it did not occur to any of us to suggest that he return to his original seat as the trial proceeded.

18

Zarrin was summoned next to defend her case. She stood up to face the class, elegant and professional in her navy blue pleated skirt and woolen jacket with gold buttons, white cuffs peering out from under its sleeves. Her hair was tied back with a ribbon in a low ponytail and the only ornament she wore was a pair of gold earrings. She circled slowly around Mr. Nyazi, every once in a while making a small sudden turn to emphasize a point. She had few notes and rarely looked at them as she addressed the class.

As she spoke, she kept pacing the room, her ponytail, in harmony with her movements, shifting from side to side, gently caressing the back of her neck, and each time she turned she was confronted with Mr. Nyazi, sitting hard as rock on that chair. She began with a passage I had read from one of Fitzgerald's short stories. "Our dear prosecutor has committed the fallacy of getting too close to the amusement park," she said. "He can no longer distinguish fiction from reality."

She smiled, turning sweetly towards "our prosecutor," trapped in his chair. "He leaves no space, no breathing room, between the two worlds. He has demonstrated his own weakness: an inability to read a novel on its own terms. All he knows is judgment, crude and simplistic exaltation of right and wrong." Mr. Nyazi raised his head at these words, turning a deep red, but he said nothing. "But is a novel good," continued Zarrin, addressing the class, "because the heroine is virtuous? Is it bad if its character strays from the moral Mr. Nyazi insists on imposing not only on us but on all fiction?"

Mr. Farzan suddenly leapt up from his chair. "Ma'am," he said, addressing me. "My being a judge, does it mean I cannot say anything?"

"Of course not," I said, after which he proceeded to deliver a long and garbled tirade about the valley of the ashes and the decadence of Gatsby's parties. He concluded that Fitzgerald's main failure was his inability to surpass his own greed: he wrote cheap stories for money, and he ran after the rich. "You know," he said at last, by this point exhausted by his own efforts, "Fitzgerald said that the rich are different."

Mr. Nyazi nodded his head in fervent agreement. "Yes," he broke in, with smug self-importance, clearly pleased with the impact of his own performance. "And our revolution is opposed to the materialism preached by Mr. Fitzgerald. We do not need Western materialisms, or American goods." He paused to take a breath, but he wasn't finished. "If anything, we *could* use their technical know-how, but we *must* reject their morals."

Zarrin looked on, composed and indifferent. She waited a few seconds after Mr. Nyazi's outburst before saying calmly, "I seem to be confronting two prosecutors. Now, if you please, may I resume?" She threw a dismissive glance towards Mr. Farzan's corner. "I would like to remind the prosecutor and the jury of the quotation we were given at our first discussion of this book from Diderot's *Jacques le Fataliste:* 'To me the freedom of [the author's] style is almost the guarantee of the purity of his morals.' We also discussed that a novel is not moral in the usual sense of the word. It can be called moral when it shakes us out of our stupor and makes us confront the absolutes we believe in. If that is true, then *Gatsby* has succeeded brilliantly. This is the first time in class that a book has created such controversy.

"*Gatsby* is being put on trial because it disturbs us—at least some of us," she added, triggering a few giggles. "This is not the first time a novel—a non-political novel—has been put on trial by a state." She turned, her ponytail turning with her. "Remember the famous trials of *Madame Bovary, Ulysses, Lady Chatterley's Lover* and *Lolita*? In each case the novel won. But let me focus on a point that seems to trouble his honor the judge as well as the prosecutor: the lure of money and its role in the novel.

"It is true that Gatsby recognizes that money is one of Daisy's attractions. He is in fact the one who draws Nick's attention to the fact that in the charm of her voice is the jingle of money. But this novel is *not* about a poor young charlatan's love of money." She paused here for emphasis. "Whoever claims this has not done his homework." She turned, almost imperceptibly, to the stationary prosecutor to her left, then walked to her desk and picked up her copy of *Gatsby*. Holding it up, she addressed Mr. Farzan, turning her back on Nyazi, and said, "No, Your Honor, this novel is not about 'the rich are different from you and me,' although they are: so are the poor, and so are you, in fact, different from me. It is about wealth but not about the vulgar materialism that you and Mr. Nyazi keep focusing on."

"You tell them!" a voice said from the back row. I turned around. There were giggles and murmurs. Zarrin paused, smiling. The judge, rather startled, cried out, "Silence! Who said that?" Not even he expected an answer.

"Mr. Nyazi, our esteemed prosecutor," Zarrin said mockingly, "seems to be in need of no witnesses. He apparently is both witness and prosecution, but let us bring our witnesses from the book itself. Let us call some of the characters to the stand. I will now call to the stand our most important witness.

"Mr. Nyazi has offered himself to us as a judge of Fitzgerald's characters, but Fitzgerald had another plan. He gave us his own judge. So perhaps we should listen to him. Which character deserves to be our judge?" Zarrin said, turning towards the class. "Nick, of course, and you remember how he describes himself: 'Everyone suspects himself of at least one of the cardinal virtues, and this is mine: I am one of the few honest people that I have ever known.' If there is a judge in this novel, it is Nick. In a sense he is the least colorful character, because he acts as a mirror.

"The other characters are ultimately judged in term of their honesty. And the representatives of wealth turn out to be the most dishonest. Exhibit A: Jordan Baker, with whom Nick is romantically involved. There is a scandal about Jordan that Nick cannot at first remember. She had lied about a match, just as she would lie about a car she had borrowed and then left out in the rain with the top down. 'She was incurably dishonest,' Nick tells us. 'She wasn't able to endure being at a disadvantage, and given this unwillingness I suppose she had begun dealing in subterfuges when she was very young in order to keep that cool insolent smile turned to the world and yet satisfy the demands of her hard jaunty body.'

"Exhibit B is Tom Buchanan. His dishonesty is more obvious: he cheats on his wife, he covers up her crime and he feels no guilt. Daisy's case is more complicated because, like everything else about her, her insincerity creates a certain enchantment: she makes others feel they are complicit in her lies, because they are seduced by them. And then, of course, there is Meyer Wolfshiem, Gatsby's shady business partner. He fixes the World Cup. 'It never occurred to me that one man could start to play with the faith of fifty million people— with the single-mindedness of a burglar blowing a safe.' So the question of honesty and dishonesty, the way people are and the way they present themselves to the world, is a sub-theme that colors all the main events in the novel. And who are the most dishonest people in this novel?" she asked, again focusing on the jury. "The rich, of course," she said, making a sudden turn towards Mr. Nyazi. "The very people our prosecutor claims Fitzgerald approves of.

"But that's not all. We are not done with the rich." Zarrin picked up her book and opened it to a marked page. "With Mr. Carraway's permission," she said, "I should like to quote him on the subject of the rich." Then she began to read: " 'They were careless people, Tom and Daisy—they smashed up things and creatures and then retreated back into their money or their vast carelessness, or whatever it was that kept them together, and let other people clean up the mess they had made . . .'

"So you see," said Zarrin, turning again to Mr. Farzan, "this is the judgment the most reliable character in the novel makes about the rich. The rich in this book, represented primarily by Tom and Daisy and to a lesser extent Jordan Baker, are careless people. After all, it is Daisy who runs over Myrtle and lets Gatsby take the blame for it, without even sending a flower to his funeral." Zarrin paused, making a detour around the chair, seemingly oblivious to the judge, the prosecutor and the jury.

"The word *careless* is the key here," she said. "Remember when Nick reproaches Jordan for her careless driving and she responds lightly that even if she is careless, she counts on other people being careful? *Careless* is the first adjective that comes to mind when describing the rich in this novel. The dream they embody is an alloyed dream that destroys whoever tries to get close to it. So you see, Mr. Nyazi, this book is no less a condemnation of your wealthy upper classes than any of the revolutionary books we have read." She suddenly turned to me and said with a smile, "I am not sure how one should address a book. Would you agree that your aim is not a defense of the wealthy classes?"

I was startled by Zarrin's sudden question but appreciated this opportunity to focus on a point that had been central to my own discussions about fiction in general. "If a critique of carelessness is a fault," I said, somewhat self-consciously, "then at least I'm in good company. This carelessness, a lack of empathy, appears in Jane Austen's negative characters: in Lady Catherine, in Mrs. Norris, in Mr. Collins or the Crawfords. The theme recurs in Henry James's stories and in Nabokov's monster heroes: Humbert, Kinbote, Van and Ada Veen. Imagination in these works is equated with empathy; we can't experience all that others have gone through, but we can understand even the most monstrous individuals in works of fiction. A good novel is one that shows the complexity of individuals, and creates enough space for all these characters to have a voice; in this way a novel is called democratic—not that it advocates democracy but that by nature it is so. Empathy lies at the heart of *Gatsby,* like so many other great novels—the biggest sin is to be blind to others' problems and pains. Not seeing them means denying their existence." I said all this in one breath, rather astonished at my own fervor.

"Yes," said Zarrin, interrupting me now. "Could one not say in fact that this blindness or carelessness towards others is a reminder of another brand of careless people?" She threw a momentary glance at Nyazi as she added, "Those who see the world in black and white, drunk on the righteousness of their own fictions.

"And if," she continued with some warmth, "Mr. Farzan, in real life Fitzgerald was obsessed with the rich and with wealth; in his fiction he brings out the corrupt and decaying power of wealth on basically decent people, like Gatsby, or creative and lively people, like Dick Diver in *Tender Is the Night.* In his failure to understand this, Mr. Nyazi misses the whole point of the novel."

Nyazi, who for some time now had been insistently scrutinizing the floor, suddenly jumped up and said, "I object!"

"To what, exactly, do you object?" said Zarrin with mock politeness.

"Carelessness is not enough!" he shot back. "It doesn't make the novel more moral. I ask you about the sin of adultery, about lies and cheating, and you talk about carelessness?"

Zarrin paused and then turned to me again. "I would now like to call the defendant to the stand." She then turned to Mr. Nyazi and, with a mischievous gleam in her eyes, said, "Would you like to examine the defendant?" Nyazi murmured a defiant no. "Fine. Ma'am, could you please take the stand?" I got up, rather startled, and looked around me. There was no chair. Mr. Farzan, for once alert, jumped up and offered me his. "You heard the prosecutor's remarks," Zarrin said, addressing me. "Do you have anything to say in your defense?"

I felt uncomfortable, even shy, and reluctant to talk. Zarrin had been doing a great job, and it seemed to me there was no need for my pontifications. But the class was waiting, and there was no way I could back down now.

I sat awkwardly on the chair offered me by Mr. Farzan. During the course of my preparations for the trial, I had found that no matter how hard I tried, I could not articulate in words the thoughts and emotions that made me so excited about *Gatsby*. I kept going back to Fitzgerald's own explanation of the novel: "That's the whole burden of this novel," he had said, "the loss of those illusions that give such color to the world so that you don't care whether things are true or false as long as they partake of the magical glory." I wanted to tell them that this book is not about adultery but about the loss of dreams. For me it had become of vital importance that my students accept *Gatsby* on its own terms, celebrate and love it because of its amazing and anguished beauty, but what I had to say in this class had to be more concrete and practical.

"You don't read *Gatsby*," I said, "to learn whether adultery is good or bad but to learn about how complicated issues such as adultery and fidelity and marriage are. A great novel heightens your senses and sensitivity to the complexities of life and of individuals, and prevents you from the self-righteousness that sees morality in fixed formulas about good and evil . . ."

"But, ma'am," Mr. Nyazin interrupted me. "There is nothing complicated about having an affair with another man's wife. Why doesn't Mr. Gatsby get his own wife?" he added sulkily.

"Why don't you write your own novel?" a muffled voice cracked from some indefinable place in the middle row. Mr. Nyazi looked even more startled. From this point on, I hardly managed to get a word in. It seemed as if all of a sudden everyone had discovered that they needed to get in on the discussion.

At my suggestion, Mr. Farzan called for a ten-minute recess. I left the room and went outside, along with a few students who felt the need for fresh air. In the hall I found Mahtab and Nassrin deep in conversation. I joined them and asked them what they thought of the trial.

Nassrin was furious that Nyazi seemed to think he had a monopoly on morality. She said she didn't say she'd approve of Gatsby, but at least he was prepared to die for his love. The three of us began walking down the hallway. Most of the students had gathered around Zarrin and Nyazi, who were in the midst of a heated argument. Zarrin was accusing Nyazi of calling her a prostitute. He was almost blue in the face with anger and indignation, and was accusing her in turn of being a liar and a fool.

"What am I to think of your slogans claiming that women who don't wear the veil are prostitutes and agents of Satan? You call this morality?" she shouted. "What about Christian women who don't believe in wearing veils? Are they all—every single one of them—decadent floozies?"

"But this is an Islamic country," Nyazi shouted vehemently. "And this is the law, and whoever . . ."

"The law?" Vida interrupted him. "You guys came in and changed the laws. Is it the law? So was wearing the yellow star in Nazi Germany. Should all the Jews have worn the star because it was the blasted law?"

"Oh," Zarrin said mockingly, "don't even try to talk to him about that. He would call them all Zionists who deserved what they got." Mr. Nyazi seemed ready to jump up and slap her across the face.

"I think it's about time I used my authority," I whispered to Nassrin, who was standing by, transfixed. I asked them all to calm down and return to their seats. When the shouts had died down and the accusations and counteraccusations had more or less subsided, I suggested that we open the floor to discussion. We wouldn't vote on the outcome of the trial, but we should hear from the jury. They could give us their verdict in the form of their opinions.

A few of the leftist activists defended the novel. I felt they did so partly because the Muslim activists were so dead set against it. In essence, their defense was not so different from Nyazi's condemnation. They said that we needed to read fiction like *The Great Gatsby* because we needed to know about the immorality of American culture.

They felt we should read more revolutionary material, but that we should read books like this as well, to understand the enemy.

One of them mentioned a famous statement by Comrade Lenin about how listening to "Moonlight Sonata" made him soft. He said it made him want to pat people on the back when we needed to club them, or some such. At any rate, my radical students' main objection to the novel was that it distracted them from their duties as revolutionaries.

Despite, or perhaps because of, the heated arguments, many of my students were silent, although many gathered around Zarrin and Vida, murmuring words of encouragement and praise. I discovered later that most students had supported Zarrin, but very few were prepared to risk voicing their views, mainly because they lacked enough self-confidence to articulate their points as "eloquently," I was told, as the defense and the prosecutor. Some claimed in private that they personally liked the book. Then why didn't they say so? Everyone else was so certain and emphatic in their position, and they couldn't really say why they liked it—they just did.

Just before the bell rang, Zarrin, who had been silent ever since the recess, suddenly got up. Although she spoke in a low voice, she appeared agitated. She said sometimes she wondered why people bothered to claim to be literature majors. Did it mean anything? she wondered. As for the book, she had nothing more to say in its defense. The novel was its own defense. Perhaps we had a few things to learn from it, from Mr. Fitzgerald. She had not learned from reading it that adultery was good or that we should all become shysters. Did people all go on strike or head west after reading Steinbeck? Did they go whaling after reading Melville? Are people not a little more complex than that? And are revolutionaries devoid of personal feelings and emotions? Do they never fall in love, or enjoy beauty? This is an amazing book, she said quietly. It teaches you to value your dreams but to be wary of them also, to look for integrity in unusual places. Anyway, she enjoyed reading it, and that counts too, can't you see?

In her "can't you see?" there was a genuine note of concern that went beyond her disdain and hatred of Mr. Nyazi, a desire that even *he* should see, definitely see. She paused a moment and cast a look around the room at her classmates. The class was silent for a while after that. Not even Mr. Nyazi had anything to say.

I felt rather good after class that day. When the bell rang, many had not even noticed it. There had been no formal verdict cast, but the excitement most students now showed was the best verdict as far as I was concerned. They were all arguing as I left them outside the class—and they were arguing not over the hostages or the recent demonstrations or Rajavi and Khomeini, but over Gatsby and his alloyed dream.

19

Our discussions of *Gatsby* for a short while seemed as electric and important as the ideological conflicts raging over the country. In fact, as time went by, different versions of this debate did dominate the political and ideological scene. Fires were set to publishing houses and bookstores for disseminating immoral works of fiction. One woman novelist was jailed for her writings and charged with spreading prostitution. Reporters were jailed, magazines and newspapers closed and some of our best classical poets, like Rumi and Omar Khayyam, were censored or banned.

Like all other ideologues before them, the Islamic revolutionaries seemed to believe that writers were the guardians of morality. This displaced view of writers, ironically, gave them a sacred place, and at the same time it paralyzed them. The price they had to pay for their new pre-eminence was a kind of aesthetic impotence.

Personally, the *Gatsby* "trial" had opened a window into my own feelings and desires. Never before—not during all my revolutionary activities—did I feel so fervently as I did now about my work and about literature. I wanted to spread this spirit of goodwill, so I made a point the next day of asking Zarrin to stay after class, to let her know how much I had appreciated her defense. I'm afraid it fell on deaf ears, she said somewhat despondently. Don't be so sure, I told her.

A colleague, passing me two days later in the hall, said: I heard shouts coming from the direction of your class the other day. Imagine my surprise when instead of Lenin versus the Imam I heard it was Fitzgerald versus Islam. By the way, you should be thankful to your young protégé. Which one? I asked him with a laugh. Mr. Bahri—he seems to have become your knight in shining armor. I hear he quieted down the voices of outrage and somehow convinced the Islamic association that you had put America on trial.

The university was going through many rapid changes in those days, and bouts between the radical and Muslim students became more frequent and more apparent. "How is it that you have sat idle and allowed a handful of Communists to take control of the university?" Khomeini reprimanded a group of Muslim students. "Are you less than them? Challenge them, argue with them, stand up to them and express yourselves." He went on to tell a story, as he so often did—a parable of sorts. Khomeini had asked a leading political cleric, Modaress, what he should do when an official in his town decided to call his two dogs Sheikh and Seyyed, a clear insult to clerics. Modaress's advice, according to Khomeini, had been brief and to the point: "Kill him." Khomeini concluded by quoting Modaress: "You hit first and let others complain. Don't be the victim, and don't complain."

20

A few days after the *Gatsby* trial, I hastily gathered my notes and books and left the classroom somewhat preoccupied. The aura of the trial still dominated the class. Some students had waylaid me in the halls to talk about *Gatsby* and present their views. There were even two or three papers written voluntarily on the subject. Stepping outside into the gentle light of the late afternoon sun, I paused on the steps, drawn by a heated argument between a handful of Muslim students and their Marxist and secular opponents. They were gesticulating and shouting. I noticed Nassrin standing a little apart from the crowd, listening to their arguments.

Soon Zarrin, Vida and a friend of theirs from another class joined me. We were all standing there idly, observing the show, making desultory comments, when Mr. Bahri came out the door with a purposeful frown. He paused for a moment, hovering beside me on the wide steps. His gaze followed mine to the intersection of the argument. He turned to me with a smile and said, "Nothing unusual. They are just having a bit of fun," and left. I stood there somewhat stupefied with Zarrin and her friends.

As the crowd dispersed, Nassrin remained alone and hesitant, and I beckoned for her to join us. She walked shyly towards our group. It was a mild afternoon; the trees and their shadows seemed to be engaged in a flirtatious dance. Somehow my students got me talking about my own student days. I was telling them about American students' idea of protest: boys with long hair streaking across the quad.

After I finished my stories, there was some laughter, followed by silence as we returned to the scene in front of us. I told them that perhaps my best memories were of my professors. In fact, I laughed, four of my very favorites were Dr. Yoch, who was conservative, the revolutionary Dr. Gross and Dr. Veile and Dr. Elconin, both liberals. Someone said, "Oh, Professor"—they called me Professor; it sounded even stranger to me then than it does now—"you would have liked Professor R, who taught in our department until very recently."

One or two students had not heard of him, some knew of him and one had been to his classes a few times. He was a professor at the Faculty of Fine Arts, a well-known and controversial film and theater critic and writer of short stories. He was what one would call a trendsetter: at twenty-one, he had become the literary editor of a magazine, and in a short time he and a few of his friends had made many enemies and admirers among the literary set. It seemed that now, in his late thirties, he had announced his retirement. Rumors were circulating that he was writing a novel.

One of the students said that he was moody and unpredictable. Zarrin's friend corrected him: he was not moody, just different. Another, with a flash of insight, turned to me and said, "You know, Professor, he is one of those people who have a knack for becoming legendary. I mean, they cannot be ignored."

The legend was that he set no time limits for his classes, that a class could start at three in the afternoon and continue for five or six hours. The students had to stay for as long as it continued. Soon his reputation spread, especially among those interested in film. Many from other universities, despite the threat of penalization, sneaked out of their classes to attend his. They were not allowed into the University of Tehran without a student I.D. card, but by now participating in his classes had become a challenge. The most dedicated and rebellious jumped over the fences to escape the guards at the entrance. His lectures were always crowded; students sometimes had to stand for hours just to get in.

He taught drama and film—Greek theater, Shakespeare, Ibsen and Stoppard, as well as Laurel and Hardy and the Marx Brothers. He loved Vincente Minnelli, John Ford and Howard Hawks. I registered these stories unconsciously and put them aside for later. Years later, when he gave me as a birthday present videotapes of *The Pirate, Johnny Guitar* and *A Night at the Opera,* I would remember that day on the steps of the university.

Vida asked me if I had heard about his latest stunt before he was expelled. He left before he could be expelled, another student corrected her. I had not heard anything about his departure, I said, including this stunt, as she put it. But after I heard the story for the first time, I was always eager to repeat it to any sympathetic listener. When I knew him—my magician—much later, I forced him to tell and retell it to me many times.

One day the radical students and faculty members in the Drama Department at the Faculty of Fine Arts convened to change the student curriculum. They felt certain courses were too bourgeois and were not needed anymore, and they wanted to add new, revolutionary courses. Heated debates had ensued in that packed meeting as drama students demanded that Aeschylus, Shakespeare and Racine be replaced with Brecht and Gorky, as well as some Marx and Engels— revolutionary theory was more important than plays. The faculty had all sat on the platform in the hall, except for this particular professor, who stood at the back by the door.

In a nod to democracy, it was asked if anyone disapproved of the new proposal. From the back of the room, a voice said quietly, "I disagree." A silence fell over the room. The voice gave as his reason his conviction that as far as he was concerned, there was no one, and he meant no one, certainly no revolutionary leader or political hero, more important than Racine. What he could teach was Racine. If they did not want to know about Racine, that was up to them. Whenever they decided they wanted to run a proper university and reinstate Racine, then he would be happy to come back and teach. Heads turned abruptly towards the voice in disbelief. It was the impertinent magician. Some started to attack him and his "formalist" and "decadent" views. They claimed his ideas were old-fashioned and that he should get with the times. A girl rose and tried to calm the cries of indignation. She said this professor always had the students' best interests at heart and that he should be given a chance to defend himself.

Later, when I told him the story as I had heard it, he corrected me: he had started to talk from the back but was asked to go to the podium. He had walked to the podium in the silence that had already put him on trial.

When he spoke again, it was to say that he felt one single film by Laurel and Hardy was worth more than all their revolutionary tracts, including those of Marx and Lenin. What they called passion was not passion, not even madness; it was some coarse emotion not worthy of true literature. He said that if they changed the curriculum, he would refuse to teach. True to his word, he never did go back, although he participated in the vigils against the closing of the universities. He wanted his students to know that his withdrawal that day was not out of fear of government reprisal.

I was told that he almost imprisoned himself in his apartment, meeting with a select group of friends and disciples. "I bet he'd see you, Professor," one of my students said eagerly. I was not so sure.

21

The last day we gave to *Gatsby* was in January; heavy snow had covered the streets. There were two images I wanted my students to discuss. I no longer have my battered *Gatsby* with me, the one with cryptic notes in the margins and at the end of book. When I left Iran, I left my precious books behind. This *Gatsby* is new, published in 1993. The cover is unfamiliar and I don't know how to treat it.

I would like to begin with a quote from Fitzgerald that is central to our understanding, not just of *Gatsby* but of Fitzgerald's whole body of work, I began. We have been talking about what *Gatsby* is all about and we've mentioned some themes, but there is an overall undercurrent to the novel which I think determines its essence and that is the question of loss, the loss of an illusion. Nick disapproves of all the people with whom Gatsby is in one way or another involved, but he does not pass the same judgment on Gatsby. Why? Because Gatsby possesses what Fitzgerald, in his story "Absolution," calls the "honesty of imagination."

At this point, Mr. Nyazi's hand shot up. "But Gatsby is even more dishonest than all the others," he squealed. "He earns his money through unlawful activities and he consorts with criminals."

In a sense you are right, I said. Gatsby fakes everything, even his own name. All the other characters in the novel have more stable positions and identities. Gatsby is constantly being made and remade by others. At all of his parties, most of his guests speculate in conspiratorial whispers about who he is and the fabulous or awful deeds he has committed. Tom sets out to investigate his true identity and Nick himself is curious about the mysterious Jay Gatsby. Yet what Gatsby inspires is curiosity tinged with awe. The reality of Gatsby's life is that he is a charlatan. But the truth is that he is a romantic and tragic dreamer, who becomes heroic because of his belief in his own romantic delusion.

Gatsby cannot tolerate the shabbiness of his life. He has an "extraordinary gift for hope, a romantic readiness," and "some heightened sensitivity to the promises of life." He cannot change the world, so he re-creates himself according to his dream. Let's see how Nick explains this: "Jay Gatsby of West Egg, Long Island, sprang from his Platonic conception of himself. He was a son of God—a phrase which, if it means anything, means just that—and he must be about His Father's business, the service of a vast, vulgar, and meretricious beauty. So he invented just the sort of Jay Gatsby that a seventeen-year-old boy would be likely to invent, and to this conception he was faithful to the end."

Gatsby's loyalty was to his reinvented self, which saw its fulfillment in Daisy's voice. It was to the promises of that self that he remained faithful, to the green light at the end of the dock, not a shabby dream of wealth and prosperity. Thus the "colossal illusion" is born for which he sacrifices his life. As Fitzgerald puts it, "No amount of fire or freshness can challenge what a man will store up in his ghostly heart."

Gatsby's loyalty to Daisy is linked to his loyalty to his imagined idea of himself. "He talked a lot about the past, and I gathered that he wanted to recover something, some idea of himself perhaps, that had gone into loving Daisy. His life had been confused and disordered since then, but if he could once return to a certain starting place and go over it all slowly, he could find out what that thing was. . . ."

The dream, however, remains incorruptible and it extends beyond Gatsby and his personal life. It exists in a broader sense in the city, in New York itself, and the East, the harbor that once became the dream of hundreds of thousands of immigrants and is now the mecca of Midwesterners, who came to it in search of a new life and thrills. While the city evokes enchanted dreams and half-promises, in reality it harbors shabby love affairs and relationships such as Tom and Myrtle's. The city, like Daisy, has in it a promise, a mirage that when reached becomes debased and corrupted. The city is the link between Gatsby's dream and the American dream. The dream is not about money but what he imagines he can become. It is not a comment on America as a materialistic country but as an *idealistic* one, one that has turned money into a means of retrieving a dream. There is nothing crass here, or the crassness is so mingled with the dream that it becomes very difficult to differentiate between the two. In the end, the best ideals and the most sordid of realities all come together. Could you please turn to the last page. You remember that this is Nick's last good-bye to Gatsby's house. Mr. Bahri, I see you have honored us with your presence today. Could you kindly read the passage, third line in the paragraph beginning with "Most of the big shore places . . ."

" 'And as the moon rose higher the inessential houses began to melt away until gradually I became aware of the old island here that flowered once for Dutch sailors' eyes—a fresh, green breast of the new world. Its vanished trees, the trees that had made way for Gatsby's house, had once pandered in whispers to the last and greatest of all human dreams; for a transitory enchanted moment man must have held his breath in the presence of this continent, compelled into an aesthetic contemplation he neither understood nor desired, face to face for the last time in history with something commensurate to his capacity for wonder.' "

Shall I read on? Please continue until the end of the next paragraph.

" 'And as I sat there brooding on the old, unknown world, I thought of Gatsby's wonder when he first picked out the green light at the end of Daisy's dock. He had come a long way to this blue lawn, and his dream must have seemed so close that he could hardly fail to grasp it. He did not know that it was already behind him, somewhere back in that vast obscurity beyond the city, where the dark fields of the republic rolled on under the night.' "

He could be dishonest in life and he could lie about himself, but one thing he could not do was to betray his own imagination. Gatsby is ultimately betrayed by the "honesty of his imagination." He dies, for in reality no such person can survive.

We, the readers, like Nick, both approve and disapprove of Gatsby. We are more certain of what we disapprove of than of what we admire, for, like Nick, we are caught in the romantic implications of his dream. His story reverberates with the tales of the pioneers who came to the shores of America in search of a new land and a new future and of their dream, already tainted with the violence that had gone into making it real.

Gatsby never should have tried to possess his dream, I explained. Even Daisy knows this; she is as much in love with him as she can ever be and yet she cannot go against her own nature and not betray him.

One autumn night they stop at a place where "the sidewalk was white with moonlight. . . . Out of the corner of his eye Gatsby saw that the blocks of the sidewalk really formed a ladder and mounted to a secret place above the trees—he could climb to it, if he climbed alone, and once there he could suck on the pap of life, gulp down the incomparable milk of wonder. His heart beat faster and faster as Daisy's white face came up to his own. He knew that when he kissed this girl, and forever wed his unutterable visions to her perishable breath, his mind would never romp again like the mind of God."

Now, could you kindly turn to page 8, read from "No— Gatsby . . ."

" 'No—Gatsby turned out all right at the end; it is what preyed on Gatsby, what foul dust floated in the wake of his dreams that temporarily closed out my interest in the abortive sorrows and short-winded elations of men.' "

For Gatsby, access to wealth is a means to an end; it is a means to the possession of his dream. That dream removes from him the power to differentiate between imagination and reality—of "foul dust" he tries to create a fairyland. His reveries for a while "provided an outlet for his imagination; they were a satisfactory hint of the unreality of reality, a promise that the rock of the world was founded securely on a fairy's wing."

So now, let us review all the points we have discussed. Yes, the novel is about concrete living relationships, a man's love for a woman, a woman's betrayal of that love. But it is also about wealth, its great attraction as well as its destructive power, the carelessness that comes with it, and, yes, it is about the American dream, a dream of power and wealth, the beguiling light of Daisy's house and the port of entry to America. It is also about loss, about the perishability of dreams once they are transformed into hard reality. It is the longing, its immateriality, that makes the dream pure.

What we in Iran had in common with Fitzgerald was this dream that became our obsession and took over our reality, this terrible, beautiful dream, impossible in its actualization, for which any amount of violence might be justified or forgiven. This was what we had in common, although we were not aware of it then.

Dreams, Mr. Nyazi, are perfect ideals, complete in themselves. How can you impose them on a constantly changing, imperfect, incomplete reality? You would become a Humbert, destroying the object of your dream; or a Gatsby, destroying yourself.

When I left the class that day, I did not tell them what I myself was just beginning to discover: how similar our own fate was becoming to Gatsby's. He wanted to fulfill his dream by repeating the past, and in the end he discovered that the past was dead, the present a sham, and there was no future. Was this not similar to our revolution, which had come in the name of our collective past and had wrecked our lives in the name of a dream?

22

After the class I felt exhausted. I tried to leave quickly, pretending I had some important business at hand. In fact, I had nothing to do. I put on my coat and hat and gloves and left. I had nowhere to go. It snowed heavily that afternoon, and then the sun came out over piles of clean, fresh white snow. I had a friend, a childhood friend I loved a great deal—she was older than me—when I was very young, before I was sent to England. She and I would sometimes walk in the snow for a long time. We would walk to our favorite pastry shop, where they had amazing cream puffs, made with real cream. We bought the cream puffs and went back out into the snow, in whose protective gleam we ate them as we talked nonsense and walked and walked.

I left the university and started to walk past the book-lined street. The street vendors selling tapes had turned up the volume, and they hopped from one foot to the other to keep warm, their woolen hats pulled low over their ears, steam escaping from their mouths and appearing to rise with the sound of the music, rising and disappearing into the blue sky. I walked down the street until the bookstores gave way to other shops, and to a movie house where we used to go as children that was now closed. So many movie houses were burned down during those jubilant days of the revolution! I continued down the street until I came to a square called Ferdowsi, named after our greatest epic poet, and paused. Was it on this spot that my friend and I had stopped to laugh that day as we licked our cream puffs?

As the years went by, the snow became polluted with the increasing pollution of Tehran; my friend was now in exile, and I had come home. Until then home had been amorphous and elusive: it presented itself in tantalizing glimpses, with the impersonal familiarity of old family photographs. But all of these feelings belonged to the past. Home was constantly changing before my eyes.

I had a feeling that day that I was losing something, that I was mourning a death that had not yet occurred. I felt as if all things personal were being crushed like small wildflowers to make way for a more ornate garden, where everything would be tame and organized. I had never felt this sense of loss when I was a student in the States. In all those years, my yearning was tied to the certainty that home was mine for the having, that I could go back anytime I wished. It was not until I had reached home that I realized the true meaning of exile. As I walked those dearly beloved, dearly remembered streets, I felt I was squashing the memories that lay underfoot.

23

The spring semester started ominously. From the very beginning, there were few classes. For the past year the government had been preoccupied with suppressing political opposition groups, closing down the progressive newspapers and magazines, punishing former government functionaries and carrying on a war against the minorities, especially the Kurds. Now it turned its attention towards the universities, hotbeds of dissent, where the Muslim revolutionaries did not hold power. The universities played the role of the now-banned newspapers in protesting the suppression of progressive forces. Almost daily a protest meeting, talk or demonstration was organized at one of the universities, especially the University of Tehran.

One morning as I entered the department building, I could sense that something was wrong. An enlarged photograph of Hashemi Rafsanjani, who at the time was the speaker of the Parliament, was pasted to the wall opposite the entrance. Beside it was a flyer alerting students to a "conspiracy" to shut down the universities. Beneath the photograph and the warning, a large half-circle of students had formed, which seemed to contain smaller half-circles within it. As I drew closer, the students, some of whom I recognized as my own, made way and opened a space for me, in the middle of which I found Mr. Nyazi, arguing heatedly with one of the leaders of a leftist student organization.

Mr. Nyazi was vehemently denying that the government had any intention of closing down the universities. The other student pointed to Mr. Rafsanjani's speech at Mashad University about the need to purify the educational system and to trigger a cultural revolution in the universities. They went back and forth for some time, encouraged by murmurs from the crowd surrounding them. I did not stay to the end of the arguments; it seemed clear that there wouldn't be any. In those days the secular and leftist forces dominated the universities, and certain developments were not yet conceivable to some of us. To think that the universities could be closed down seemed as farfetched as the possibility that women would finally succumb to wearing the veil.

It did not take long, however, for the government to announce its intention to suspend classes and to form a committee for the implementation of the cultural revolution. This committee was given the power to reconstruct the universities in such a way as to make them acceptable to the leaders of the Islamic Republic. What they wanted was not very clear, but they had no doubt as to what they didn't want. They were given the power to expel undesirable faculty, staff and students, to create a new set of rules and a new curriculum. It was the first organized effort to purge Iran of what was called decadent Western culture. The majority of students and faculty did not give in to this dictate, and once more the University of Tehran became the scene of a battle.

Going to classes became more impossible every day. We were all frantically shuffling from one meeting to another, as if by force of sheer movement we would be able to stop them. The faculty marched, and the students marched. There were many disagreements between the various student organizations.

The students convened demonstrations and sit-ins. I went to these demonstrations, although I felt no affinity at this point towards any particular organization. If the leftists had come to power, they would have done the same thing. This, of course, was not the point: the point was to save the university, which, like Iran, we had all had a hand in destroying.

24

And so began a new cycle of violent demonstrations. We would start marching, usually in front of the University of Tehran, and as we moved, the crowd would increase. We marched towards the poorer areas, and, usually at a narrow alley or a particular intersection, "they" would come, attacking us with knives and clubs. The demonstrators would disperse, only to reorganize quietly farther up the street. We walked the meandering streets and unpaved winding alleys and suddenly "they" would come again and attack us at the point of another intersection, with their knives drawn, and we would run again, and again we would meet at some other point a few blocks away.

I remember one day particularly well. I had left home early with Bijan; he dropped me off near the university on his way to work. A few blocks before the university, I noticed a group, mainly young people, carrying signs and walking towards campus. I noticed Nassrin, whom I had not seen for a few weeks. She had some leaflets in her hand and was walking in the front row. At a certain street corner, she and another girl separated from the group and turned into the street. I suddenly remembered that Nassrin had never given me her promised paper on *Gatsby;* she had dropped out of my life as suddenly as she had entered it. I wondered if I would ever see her again.

I found myself walking with a group of chanting students who had appeared magically. Suddenly, we heard the sound of bullets, which seemed to be coming out of nowhere. The bullets were real. One moment we were standing in front of the wide iron gate of the university and then I found myself running towards the bookstores, most of which had closed because of the unrest. I took cover under the awning of one that was still open. Nearby, a music vendor had left his tape deck running; some singer's mournful voice lamenting his love's betrayal.

That whole day was one long nightmare. I had no sense of time or place and felt myself joining groups that sooner or later dispersed, drifting from one street to another. In the afternoon a large demonstration was convened. It soon became the bloodiest confrontation between students and the government. The government had bused workers in from different factories, in addition to its usual goons and thugs and militia, arming them with batons and knives to stage a counterdemonstration against the students. The workers were chosen because of the leftists' idealization of the proletariat as their natural allies.

Once the guns started to fire, we all ran in different directions. I remember at one point I ran into a former classmate of mine, my best friend from sixth grade, in fact. In the midst of gunshots and chants we hugged, and chatted about the almost two decades since we had last seen each other. She told me everyone was moving towards the hospital near the University of Tehran, where the bodies of murdered and wounded students were supposedly being kept.

Somehow, I lost her in the crowd and found myself alone on the grounds of the large hospital whose name had recently been changed from Pahlavi, the name of the last shah, to Imam Khomeini. The rumor now was that the police and guards had stolen the bodies of murdered students in order to prevent the news of their death from getting out. The students wanted to storm the hospital to stop the transfer of bodies.

I walked towards the main building, and now in my memory I seem to be forever walking towards that building, never quite reaching it: I was walking in a trance, with people running towards me as well as in the opposite direction. Everyone seemed to have a purpose, some destination in mind—except me; I was walking alone. Suddenly, coming towards me, I saw a familiar face: it was Mahtab.

At that moment as I looked at her, paralyzed and frozen, she looked more than anything like a lost animal in danger. Perhaps it was shock that forced her to walk in a straight line, almost mechanically, and not swerve to the left or right, keeping near perfect balance. Imagine Mahtab walking towards me. Two girls block my view, and then she appears, wearing a loose beige shirt over jeans: she moves into my line of vision and our eyes meet. She was prepared to pass me by, but she stopped for a short second. So there we were, the two of us, sharing a moment in our ghastly search. She paused to inform me that "they" had managed to hijack the bodies from the hospital morgues. No one knew where the bodies had been transferred. She said this and disappeared, and I did not see her for another seven years.

As I stood there alone on the hospital grounds, with people rushing around me, I had a strange experience: I felt as if my heart had been torn from my body and had landed with a thump in an empty space, a vast void that I did not know existed. I felt tired and frightened. The fear was not of bullets: they were too immediate. I was scared of some lack, as if the future were receding from me.

25

The students kept a vigil on the grounds of the university, to prevent it from closing down. They kept their vigil until, in what almost amounted to a bloody battle—although the government forces were the only ones with guns—they were evacuated and the militia, the

Revolutionary Guards and the police conquered the university grounds.

It was during one of these vigils that I saw Mr. Bahri. The night was filled with anxiety, as well as the false coziness of such events, as we sat on the ground in close proximity, exchanging jokes, information or stories, sometimes arguing away the pleasantly warm nights. He was standing alone in a dark corner, leaning against a tree. So what do you think of this? I asked him. He smiled a precocious smile and said, No, ma'am, what do *you* think? Mr. Bahri, I said slowly. What I think is becoming increasingly irrelevant. So irrelevant, in fact, that I think I will go home, grab a good book and try to get some sleep.

I knew I had startled him, but I had also startled myself. All of a sudden I felt as if this was not my fight. For most of those present, the excitement of the battle meant almost everything, and I was not excited, not in that way. Did it matter to me who closed the university down, whether it was my leftist students or the Islamic ones? What mattered was that the university should not be closed at all, that it should be allowed to function as a university and not become a battleground for different political forces. But it took me a long time, in fact seventeen more years, to finally digest and formulate this understanding. For the time being, I went home.

Soon after that, the government managed to shut down the universities. They purged the faculty, students and staff. Some students were killed or jailed; others simply disappeared. The University of Tehran had become the seat of too much disappointment, too much sorrow and hurt. Never again would I rush so innocently, so eagerly, to a class as I did in those days at the dawn of the revolution.

26

One day in the spring of 1981—I can still feel the sun and the morning breeze on my cheeks—I became irrelevant. Just over a year after I had returned to my country, my city, my home, I discovered that the same decree that had transformed the single word *Iran* into the *Islamic Republic of Iran* had made me and all that I had been irrelevant. The fact that I shared this fate with many others did not help much.

In fact, I had become irrelevant sometime before then. After the so-called cultural revolution that led to the closing down of universities, I was essentially out of a job. We went to the university, but we had nothing much to do. I took to writing a diary and reading Agatha Christie. I roamed the streets with my American reporter, talking about Mike Gold's Lower East Side and Fitzgerald's West Egg. Instead of classes, we were summoned to endless meetings. The administration wanted us to stop working and at the same time to pretend that nothing had changed. Although the universities were closed, the faculty was required to be present and to offer projects to the Committee on the Cultural Revolution.

These were idle days, whose only enduring feature was the lasting friendships we formed with colleagues in our own and other departments. I was the youngest and newest addition to the group and had a great deal to learn. They told me about the pre-revolutionary days, about excitement and hope; they talked about some of their colleagues who had never returned.

The newly elected committee for the implementation of the cultural revolution visited the Faculty of Law and Political Sciences and the Faculty of Persian and Foreign Languages and Literature at the auditorium in the School of Law. Despite the formal and informal instructions to the female faculty and staff on the issue of the veil, until that day most women at our university had not obeyed the new rules. That meeting was the first I had attended at which all the female participants wore head scarves. All, that is, except three: Farideh, Laleh and me. We were independent and considered eccentric, so the three of us went to that meeting unveiled.

The three members of the Committee on the Cultural Revolution sat rather uncomfortably on the very high stage. Their expressions were by turns haughty, nervous and defiant. That meeting was the last at the University of Tehran in which the faculty openly criticized the government and its policies regarding higher education. Most were rewarded for their impertinence by being expelled.

Farideh, Laleh and I sat together conspicuously, like naughty children. We whispered, we consulted one another, we kept thrusting our hands up to talk. Farideh took the committee to task for using the university grounds to torture and intimidate the students. I told the Revolutionary Committee that my integrity as a teacher and a woman was being compromised by its insistence that I wear the veil under false pretenses for a few thousand tumans a month. The issue was not so much the veil itself as freedom of choice. My grandmother had refused to leave the house for three months when she was forced to unveil. I would be similarly adamant in my own refusal. Little did I know that I would soon be given the choice of either veiling or being jailed, flogged and perhaps killed if I disobeyed.

After that meeting, one of my more pragmatic colleagues, a "modern" woman, who decided to take up the veil and stayed there for another seventeen years after I was gone, told me with a hint of sarcasm in her voice, "You are fighting a losing battle. Why lose your job over an issue like this? In another couple of weeks you will be forced to wear the veil in the grocery stores."

The simplest answer, of course, was that the university was not a grocery store. But she was right. Soon we would be forced to wear it everywhere. And the morality squads, with their guns and Toyota patrols, would guard the streets to ensure our adherence. On that sunny day, however, when my colleagues and I made our protest known, these incidents did not seem to be preordained. So much of the faculty protested, we thought we might yet win.

We left the meeting with a feeling of jubilance. The committee had clearly been defeated: their responses had been lame, and as the meeting progressed, they became more incoherent and defensive. When we emerged from the assembly hall, Mr. Bahri was waiting for me with a friend. He did not talk to my other colleagues but directed all his comments towards me. He did not understand it: how could I do this? Were we not friends? Yes, we were friends, but this really wasn't personal—not in that way. Don't you see, you are unconsciously helping the enemy, the imperialists? he said mournfully. Is it too much to ask you to comply with a few rules to save the revolution? I could have asked him whose revolution, but I didn't. Farideh, Laleh and I were too euphoric, and we were going out to lunch to celebrate.

A few months after that, committees were established that led to the purging of some of the best faculty and students. Dr. A would resign and leave for the United States. Farideh would be expelled and later would go to Europe. The bright young professor whom I had met that first day in Dr. A's office was also expelled in due time—

I met him eleven years later, at a conference in Austin, Texas. Of the old group, only Laleh and I would remain, and soon we too would be expelled. The government would make the veil mandatory and put more students and faculty members on trial. I went to one more demonstration, called by the Mujahideen but supported by all the opposition forces, except the Communist Tudeh Party and the Fedayin Organization. By then, the first president of the Republic was in hiding and would soon flee the country. Over half a million participated in what turned out to be one of the bloodiest battles of the revolution. Over a thousand people were arrested, many, including teenagers, executed on the spot. Eight days later, on June 28, the Islamic Republic Party's headquarters were bombed, and over eighty of its members and top leaders in the government were killed. The government took revenge by executing and arresting individuals almost randomly.

Oddly, when the university administration began the process of my dismissal, it was not secular colleagues but Mr. Bahri and his friends—former students who almost all got F's that semester for not attending classes—who defended me and delayed my expulsion for as long as they could.

The feelings I thought I had left behind returned when, almost nineteen years later, the Islamic regime would once again turn against its students. This time it would open fire on those it had admitted to the universities, those who were its own children, the children of the revolution. Once more my students would go to the hospitals in search of the murdered bodies that were stolen by the guards and vigilantes and try to prevent them from stealing the wounded. Only this time I was walking those grounds in my imagination as I read faxes and e-mails in my office in Washington, D.C., from my former students in Iran, trying to decipher something beyond the hysteria of their words.

I would like to know where Mr. Bahri is right now, at this moment, and to ask him: how did it all turn out, Mr. Bahri—was this your dream, your dream of the revolution? Who will pay for all those ghosts in my memory? Who will pay for the snapshots of the murdered and the executed that we hid in our shoes and closets as we moved on to other things? Tell me, Mr. Bahri—or, to use that odd expression of Gatsby's, Tell me, old sport—what shall we do with all these corpses on our hands?

PART III

James

I

The war came one morning, suddenly and unexpectedly. It was announced on September 23, 1980, the day before the opening of schools and universities: we were in the car returning to Tehran from a trip to the Caspian Sea when we heard about the Iraqi attack on the radio. It all started very simply. The newscaster announced it matter-of-factly, the way people announce a birth or a death, and we accepted it as an irrevocable fact that would permeate all other considerations and gradually insinuate itself into the four corners of our lives. How many events go into that unexpected and decisive moment when you wake up one morning and discover that your life has forever been changed by forces beyond your control?

What triggered the war? Was it the arrogance of the new Islamic revolutionaries, who kept provoking what they deemed to be reactionary and heretical regimes in the Middle East and inciting the people of those countries to revolutionary uprisings? Was it the fact that the new regime held a special animosity towards Saddam Hussein, who had expelled the exiled Ayatollah Khomeini from Iraq after reportedly making a deal with the Shah? Was it the old hostility between Iraq and Iran and the fact that the Iraqis, with promises of support from a West hostile to Iran's new revolutionary government, dreamed of a swift and sweet victory?

In retrospect, when historical events are gathered up, analyzed and categorized into articles and books, their messiness disappears and they gain a certain logic and clarity that one never feels at the time. For me, as for millions of ordinary Iranians, the war came out of nowhere one mild fall morning: unexpected, unwelcome and utterly senseless.

All through that fall I took long walks around the wide, leafy alleys near our home, surrounded by scented gardens and meandering streams, and thought of my own ambivalence towards the war, for my anger was mixed with feelings of love and a desire to protect my home and country. One September evening—it was that twilight moment between seasons, when for a very short time the air is filled with a mixture of summer and fall—I was diverted from my thoughts by the colors of a magnificent sunset unfolding in front of me. I happened to catch the play of fading light between the thin branches of a creeper on a nearby clump of trees. I stood there watching the diaphanous reflection of the sunset until two passersby, walking from the opposite direction, distracted me and I continued on my way.

Down the slope of the street, on the wall to my right, in big black letters, was a quotation from Ayatollah Khomeini: THIS WAR IS A GREAT BLESSING FOR US! I registered the slogan in anger. A great blessing for whom?

2

The war with Iraq began that September and did not end until late July 1988. Everything that happened to us during those eight years of war, and the direction our lives took afterward, was in some way shaped by this conflict. It was not the worst war in the world, although it left over a million dead and injured. At first the war seemed to pull the divided country together: we were all Iranian and the enemy had attacked our homeland. But even in this, many were not allowed to participate fully. From the regime's point of view, the enemy had attacked not just Iran; it had attacked the Islamic Republic, and it had attacked Islam.

The polarization created by the regime confused every aspect of life. Not only were the forces of God fighting an emissary of Satan, Iraq's Saddam Hussein, but they were also fighting agents of Satan inside the country. At all times, from the very beginning of the revolution and all through the war and after, the Islamic regime never forgot its holy battle against its internal enemies. All forms of criticism were now considered Iraqi-inspired and dangerous to national security. Those groups and individuals without a sense of loyalty to the regime's brand of Islam were excluded from the war effort. They could be killed or sent to the front, but they could not voice their social or political preferences. There were only two forces in the world, the army of God and that of Satan.

Thus every event, every social gesture, also embodied a symbolic allegiance. The new regime had reached far beyond the romantic symbolism more or less prevalent in every political system to inhabit a realm of pure myth, with devastating consequences. The Islamic Republic was not merely modeled on the order established by the Prophet Muhammad during his reign over Arabia; it was the Prophet's rule itself. Iran's war with Iraq was the same as the war carried on by the third and most militant imam, Imam Hussein, against the infidels, and the Iranians were going to conquer Karballa, the holy city in Iraq where Imam Hussein's shrine was located. The Iranian battalions were named after the Prophet or the Twelve Shiite Saints; they were the army of Ali, Hussein and Mahdy, the twelfth imam, whose arrival the Shia Muslims awaited, and the military assaults against Iraq were invariably code-named after Muhammad's celebrated battles. Ayatollah Khomeini was not a religious or political leader but an imam in his own right.

In those days, I had become an avid and insatiable collector. I saved pictures of martyrs, young men, some mere children, published in the daily papers beside the wills they had made before going to the front. I cut out Ayatollah Khomeini's praise of the thirteen-year-old boy who had thrown himself in front of an enemy tank and collected accounts of young men who were given keys to heaven to wear around their neck as they were sent off to the front: they were told that when they were martyred, they would go straight to heaven. What had begun with an impulse to record events in my diary turned gradually into a greedy and feverish act of hoarding, as if through such actions I could place a jinx on forces beyond my control and impose upon them my own rhyme and reason.

It took us a while to understand what the war really meant, although the radio, television and papers were filled with it. They encouraged people to take advantage of the blackouts and used a system of alarms to instruct us: after the red siren a voice would say, "Attention! Attention! This is the alarm. Please go to your shelters . . ." Shelters? What shelters? Never once during the eight years of war did the government create a cohesive program for the safety and security of its citizens. Shelters meant the basements or the lower levels of apartment houses that sometimes buried you beneath them. Yet most of us did not realize our own vulnerability until later, when Tehran was also hit, like the other cities.

Our ambivalent attitude towards the war mainly stemmed from our ambivalence towards the regime. In those first air raids against Tehran, a house in the affluent part of the city was hit. It was rumored that its basement had been occupied by anti-government guerrillas. Hashemi Rafsanjani, then speaker of the Parliament, in an effort to appease the frightened population, claimed in a Friday prayer ceremony that the bombing so far had done no real harm, as its victims were the "arrogant rich and subversives," who probably would have been executed sooner or later anyway. He also recommended that women dress properly when sleeping, so that if their houses were hit, they would not be "indecently exposed to strangers' eyes."

3

"Let's celebrate!" my friend Laleh cried before sitting down at a table in our favorite restaurant, where I had been waiting for her. This was a few weeks after our encounter with the Committee on the Cultural Revolution, and by now we knew it was only a matter of time before we would either have to comply with the rules or be expelled. Since the government had recently made the veil mandatory at the workplace, I did not see much reason for her exuberance. Celebrate what? I wanted to know. "Today"—she paused and took an excited breath— "after nine years—eight and a half, to be exact—I was formally expelled from the university. I am now officially irrelevant, as you would put it, so lunch is on me! Since we can't drink publicly to my newly acquired status, let's eat ourselves to death," she added in a brave effort to make light of a development that would leave her penniless and, more important, force her to give up a job she loved and was good at. Stiff upper lip, I believe they call it. Well, this stiff upper lip was becoming quite a trend among friends and colleagues.

She had gone to the university that day to discuss her situation with the head of the Psychology Department, where she had been teaching since her return from Germany a few years earlier, and she had not worn a head scarf, of course. Of course! The guard at the gate had called out to her from inside his cage. As I imagine it now, the guard's post is literally a cage, a large protrusion of bars, but it may have been more of an outpost; made of metal perhaps? Or cement? With a window and a side door? I could pick up the phone and call Laleh, who two years ago finally moved to the U.S. and now lives in Los Angeles. I could ask her; she, unlike me, has a very precise memory.

Have you come across that new guard? she asked me, a limp captive lettuce leaf dangling from the end of her fork. The clumsy one with a mournful countenance. The very big one . . . She was trying to avoid using the word *fat*. No, I had not had the pleasure of meeting the aforementioned guard. Anyhow, he is of Oliver Hardy dimensions. Bigger, she said, chewing now on her lettuce with ferocious determination. But the resemblance ends there. I mean, this guy was flabby but not jovial, one of those dour, mirthless overweight men who don't even enjoy their food—you know the type.

Could you please lay off the guard of the mournful countenance, I pleaded with her, and get on with your story? She attacked a small cherry tomato that kept slipping from under her fork and did not begin again until she had finally speared it. He came out of his cage, Laleh at last continued, and said, Ma'am, your I.D. please. So I took out my I.D. and waved it in his face and started walking, but then he called me again. Ma'am, you know you can't go in like this? I said, I've been going in through this gate *like this* for the past eight years. No, ma'am, you have to have a head cover—new orders. That's my problem, I said, not yours. But he wouldn't let it rest. I am authorized to stop any woman who—at this point I interrupted him. I am not *any woman!* I said with all the authority I could muster.

It's right here, he protested, a written order signed by the president himself, that no girl, he corrected himself—no woman—is to pass in your condition. He said *in your condition*? I asked. Yep, that's what he said. I took another step; he blocked my way. I took a step to the right; he took a step to the right. I stopped; he stopped. For a few seconds we stood there looking at each other, and then he said, If you go through in that condition I will be held responsible. In *what* condition? I asked him. The last time I checked, I was the *only* person responsible for my condition, so don't you go around claiming responsibility for me. I don't know what perversion made me argue with this poor guy, said Laleh, her hand now trembling in excitement, and to tell him things he couldn't possibly understand. For a few minutes we just stood there, and then, on a sudden impulse, I looked over his shoulder to the left and, as he turned around, I ducked and started to run. To run? Yes, I ran.

At this point we were served our veal scallopini and mashed potatoes. Laleh began to search for some hidden treasure in her potatoes, making investigative circles with her inquisitive fork. I thought he'd give up, she said at last. I mean, all he had to do was take the bloody phone and call the higher authorities. But no, not him. I stopped for a second to look back to see if he had fallen off, but there he was, and I swear, he pulled his belt up and swung his hips from side to side. *He swung his hips?* Honestly, he did. She made a swinging movement with her fork inside the mashed potatoes. And then he started to run after me, she said.

Laleh and the fat guard had sprinted across the wide, leafy avenues of the university. Every once in a while Laleh would look back to see if he was still at it, but she swore that every time she stopped, rather than trying to catch up with her, he'd come to a halt, as if pushing invisible brakes to a sudden stop, then he'd pull his belt up, do the thing with his hips, and continue the chase. He reminded me, she said, of a panting, clumsy giant fish.

Laleh ran by three startled students, made it down the short steps leading to the Faculty of Persian and Foreign Languages and Literature, nearly toppled herself as her heel caught in a crack, passed the wide open area in front of the building, ran up past the open door into the cool, dark hall and up the wide flights of stairs to the second floor, where she came to a sudden halt at the entrance to the Department of Psychology and nearly fell into the arms of her department head, who was standing in the doorway talking to a colleague. He tried to cover his embarrassment by exclaiming, What's the matter, Professor Nassri, has there been an uprising? A few moments later the dutiful guard, sweat trickling down his cheeks like tears of desperation, his cap in his hand, came to a grinding halt by the door. There he made his explanations and the department head, not knowing whether to laugh or frown, dismissed him, promising to make a proper report to the proper authorities. An hour later Laleh had emerged from the door of the department, walked back to the entrance gate and, without so much as glancing at the guard, had marched out, a free woman.

A free woman? Yes, I was given a choice, to immediately comply with the rules or be sacked. I chose not to comply, so now I am a free woman. What will you do? I asked, as if I were not myself in exactly the same position. I don't know. She shrugged. I guess I will go back to sewing or baking cakes.

This was the astonishing thing about Laleh. She looked like the last person in the world to bake a cake, but she was an accomplished tailor, and a fantastic cook. The first time I met her, she struck me as everything that I was not: tidy and rather dry, the kind of person you would call correct. Her German education added to this illusion. I used to tease her that the word *immaculate* had been created for her. When I got to know her better, I came to see that all this orderliness was a camouflage for a passionate nature matched by insatiable desires.

Her hair was thick and obstinately unmanageable: it would not succumb to comb, brush, gels, even perms. Yet she tamed it through hours of painstaking straightening and styling, giving her the appearance of an exacting and foreboding matron. I have to either shave my head or do it this way, she would tell me, her voice tainted with exasperation. Only her big black eyes, flickering with mischievous designs, belied her otherwise conservative appearance. Later, when she would climb the trees with my three-year-old daughter, I could see the amount of discipline it must have taken for her to control her wayward longings.

As it happened, she was forced to make a living from her sewing for almost two years. She was not granted a license to practice child psychology, her specialty, and she had refused to teach with the veil. So she took up sewing, a task she abhorred, and for a while I and our other friends would go around wearing pretty chintz skirts with beautiful flower patterns, until a friend asked her to work at her school.

Our appetites that day seemed insatiable: Laleh ordered a crème caramel and I two scoops of ice cream, vanilla and coffee, with Turkish coffee and a side of walnuts. I sprinkled my walnuts thoughtfully over the coffee-drenched ice cream. We brooded over the fact that in our department, Farideh had been expelled, and Dr. A had left for the

States. Our more cautious colleagues, who had managed to remain unscathed, said that Farideh's expulsion was more a result of her headstrong resistance, a certain mulishness as one colleague creatively put it, than the administration's efforts.

4

A few days later I went to the University of Tehran for one more meeting with Mr. Bahri. He had asked for this meeting, hoping to convince me to comply with the new rules. I was fully prepared for a running contest at the gate, but to my surprise I was not accorded the same treatment as Laleh. The morose guard on duty was not the one she had described. He was neither lean nor fat; he did not even ask for my I.D. He simply pretended not to see me. I had my suspicions that Mr. Bahri had warned him not to interfere.

The conference room looked and felt just as it had when I first met Mr. Bahri to discuss the role of literature and revolution: large, cool and bare, with a dusty feel to it, although, except for the long table and twelve chairs, there were no surfaces to collect dust. Mr. Bahri and his friend were already sitting near the middle of the table, facing the door. They both stood up when I entered, and waited until I had taken a seat before settling back down. I chose to position myself opposite them.

Mr. Bahri did not take long to get to the point. He mentioned Laleh's escapade and the administration's admirable patience with "this sort of behavior." All through the meeting his eyes appeared to be glued to a black fountain pen, which he kept turning around and around in his hands like a curious object whose mystery he was hoping to fathom. He and his friends were well aware that before the revolution, whenever Professor Nassri went to the poorer, more traditional areas of town, she wore a scarf. Yes, she did this out of respect for those people's faith, I said coldly, and not because it was mandatory. All through this talk, Mr. Bahri's friend remained almost completely silent.

Mr. Bahri could not understand why we were making such a fuss over a piece of cloth. Did we not see that there were more important issues to think about, that the whole life of the revolution was at stake? What was more important, to fight against the satanic influence of Western imperialists or to obstinately hold on to a personal preference that created division among the ranks of the revolutionaries? These might not have been his exact words, but they were the gist of his language. In those days, people really talked that way. One had a feeling, in revolutionary and intellectual circles, that they spoke from a script, playing characters from an Islamized version of a Soviet novel.

It was ironic that Mr. Bahri, the defender of the faith, described the veil as a piece of cloth. I had to remind him that we had to have more respect for that "piece of cloth" than to force it on reluctant people. What did he imagine our students would think of us if they saw us wearing the veil when we had sworn never to do so? Would they not say that we had sold out our beliefs for a few thousand tumans a month? What would you think, Mr. Bahri?

What could he think? A stern ayatollah, a blind and improbable philosopher-king, had decided to impose his dream on a country and a people and to re-create us in his own myopic vision. So he had formulated an ideal of me as a Muslim woman, as a Muslim woman teacher, and wanted me to look, act and in short live according to that ideal. Laleh and I, in refusing to accept that ideal, were taking not a political stance but an existential one. No, I could tell Mr. Bahri, it was not that piece of cloth that I rejected, it was the transformation being imposed upon me that made me look in the mirror and hate the stranger I had become.

I think that day I realized how futile it was to "discuss" my views with Mr. Bahri. How could one argue against the representative of God on earth? Mr. Bahri, for the time being at least, derived his energy from the undeniable fact that he was on the side of Right; I was at best a stray sinner. For a few months I had seen it coming, but I think it was that day, after I left Mr. Bahri and his friend, that it first hit me how irrelevant I had become.

When I left the room, I did not make the mistake of trying to shake his hand. Mr. Bahri walked with me like a polite host seeing an honored guest to the door, his hands firmly clasped behind his back. I kept repeating, Please don't bother, and almost toppled down the stairs in my eagerness to get away. When I had nearly reached the first floor, I looked back. He was still standing there, in his frayed brown suit, his Mao shirt buttoned up to the neck, hands behind his back, gazing down at me with a look of perplexity. A lover's good-bye, Laleh would later mischievously say as I told her my story over another dish of ice cream, this time in the cool of her living room.

When I left Mr. Bahri that afternoon, I walked for about forty-five minutes and stopped by my favorite English bookstore. I went in there on a sudden inspiration, fearful that I might not have the opportunity to do so in the near future. And I was right: only a few months later, the Revolutionary Guards raided the bookstore and closed it down. The big iron bolt and chain they installed on the door signified the finality of their action.

I started picking books up with a greedy urgency. I went after the paperbacks, collecting almost all the Jameses and all six novels by Austen. I picked up *Howards End* and *A Room with a View*. Then I went after ones I had not read, four novels by Heinrich Böll, and some I had read a long time ago—*Vanity Fair* and *The Adventures of Roderick Random, Humboldt's Gift* and *Henderson the Rain King*. I picked up a bilingual selection of Rilke's poems and Nabokov's *Speak, Memory*. I even lingered for a while debating over an unexpurgated copy of *Fanny Hill*. Then I went after the mysteries. I picked up some Dorothy Sayers and, to my utter delight, found *Trent's Last Case,* two or three new Agatha Christies, a selection of Ross Macdonalds, all of Raymond Chandler and two Dashiell Hammetts.

I didn't have enough money to pay for them all. I took the few I could afford and refused the bookstore owner's very gallant offer to take the rest on credit. As he placed the books I had put on hold in two large paper bags, he smiled with amusement and told me, Don't worry; no one is going to take these away from you. No one knows who they are anymore. Besides, who wants to read them now, at this time?

Who indeed? People like me seemed as irrelevant as Fitzgerald was to Mike Gold, or Nabokov to Stalin's Soviet Union, or James to the Fabian Society, or Austen to the revolutionaries of her time. In the taxi, I took out the few books I had paid for and surveyed their covers, caressing their glossy surfaces, so giving to the touch. I knew that my meeting with Mr. Bahri meant it would only be a matter of time before I was expelled. I decided I would stop going to the university until they expelled me. Now that I would have a great deal of time on my hands, I could read without any feelings of guilt.

5

The government didn't take long to pass new regulations restricting women's clothing in public and forcing us to wear either a chador or a long robe and scarf. Experience had proven that the only way these regulations would be heeded was if they were implemented by force. Because of women's overwhelming objection to the laws, the government enforced the new rule first in the workplaces and later in shops, which were forbidden from transacting with unveiled women. Disobedience was punished by monetary fines, up to seventy-six lashes and jail terms. Later, the government created the notorious morality squads: four armed men and women in white Toyota patrols, monitoring the streets, ensuring the enforcement of the laws.

As I try now to piece together the disjointed and incoherent events of that period, I notice how my growing sense that I was descending into an abyss or void was accompanied by two momentous events that happened simultaneously: the war and the loss of my teaching job. I had not realized how far the routines of one's life create the illusion of stability. Now that I could not call myself a teacher, a writer, now that I could not wear what I would normally wear, walk in the streets to the beat of my own body, shout if I wanted to or pat a male colleague on the back on the spur of the moment, now that all this was illegal, I felt light and fictional, as if I were walking on air, as if I had been written into being and then erased in one quick swipe.

This new feeling of unreality led me to invent new games, survival games I would now call them. My constant obsession with the veil had made me buy a very wide black robe that covered me down to my ankles, with kimonolike sleeves, wide and long. I had gotten into the habit of withdrawing my hands into the sleeves and pretending that I had no hands. Gradually, I pretended that when I wore the robe, my whole body disappeared: my arms, breasts, stomach and legs melted and disappeared and what was left was a piece of cloth the shape of my body that moved here and there, guided by some invisible force.

The beginning of this game I can trace back quite specifically to the day I went to the Ministry of Higher Education with a friend who wanted to have her diploma validated. They searched us from head to foot and of the many sexual molestations I have had to suffer in my life, this was among the worst. The female guard told me to hold my hands up, up and up, she said, as she started to search me meticulously, going over every part of my body. She objected to the fact that I seemed to be wearing almost nothing under the robe. I explained to her that what I wore under my robe was none of her business. She took a tissue and told me to rub my cheeks clean of the muck I was wearing. I explained that I wore no muck. Then she took the tissue herself and rubbed it against my cheeks, and since she did not achieve the desired results, because I had not worn any makeup, as I had told her, she rubbed it even harder, until I thought she might be trying to rub my skin off.

My face was burning and I felt dirty—I felt like my whole body was a soiled, sweaty T-shirt that had to be cast off. That was when the idea of this game came to me: I decided to make my body invisible. The woman's coarse hands were reverse X rays that left only the surface intact and made the inside invisible. By the time she had finished inspecting me, I had become as light as the wind, a fleshless, boneless being. The trick to this magic act was that in order to remain invisible, I had to refrain from coming into contact with other hard surfaces, especially with human beings: my invisibility was in direct ratio to the degree to which I could make other people not notice me. Then, of course, from time to time I would make part of me return, like when I wished to defy an obstructionist figure of authority and I would leave a few strands of hair out and make my eyes reappear, to stare at them uncomfortably.

Sometimes, almost unconsciously, I would withdraw my hands into my wide sleeves and start touching my legs or my stomach. Do they exist? Do I exist? This stomach, this leg, these hands? Unfortunately, the Revolutionary Guards and the guardians of our morality did not see the world with the same eyes as me. They saw hands, faces and pink lipstick; they saw strands of hair and unruly socks where I saw some ethereal being drifting soundlessly down the street.

This was when I went around repeating to myself, and to anyone who cared to listen, that people like myself had become irrelevant. This pathological disorder was not limited to me; many others felt they had lost their place in the world. I wrote, rather dramatically, to an American friend: "You ask me what it means to be irrelevant? The feeling is akin to visiting your old house as a wandering ghost with unfinished business. Imagine going back: the structure is familiar, but the door is now metal instead of wood, the walls have been painted a garish pink, the easy chair you loved so much is gone. Your office is now the family room and your beloved bookcases have been replaced by a brand-new television set. This is your house, and it is not. And you are no longer relevant to this house, to its walls and doors and floors; you are not seen."

What do people who are made irrelevant do? They will sometimes escape, I mean physically, and if that is not possible, they will try to make a comeback, to become a part of the game by assimilating the characteristics of their conquerors. Or they will escape inwardly and, like Claire in *The American,* turn their small corner into a sanctuary: the essential part of their life goes underground.

My growing irrelevance, this void I felt within me, made me resent my husband's peace and happiness, his apparent disregard for what I, as a woman and an academic, was going through. At the same time, I depended on him for the sense of security he created for all of us. As everything crumbled around us, he calmly went about his business and tried to create a normal and quiet life for us. Being a very private person, he focused his energies on safeguarding his life at home, with family and friends and on work. He was a partner in an architectural and engineering firm. He loved his partners, who, like him, were dedicated to their work. Since their job was not directly related to culture or politics, and the firm was private, they were left in relative peace. Being a good architect or dedicated civil engineer did not threaten the regime, and Bijan was excited by the great projects they were given: a park in Isfahan, a factory in Borüjerd, a university in Ghazvin. He felt creative and he felt wanted, and, in the very best sense of the term, he felt he was of some service to his country. He was of the opinion that we had to serve our country, regardless of who ruled it. The problem for me was that I had lost all concept of terms such as *home, service* and *country.*

I became again the child I had been when I would indiscriminately and waywardly pick up books, slouch in the nearest available corner, and read and read. I picked up *Murder on the Orient Express, Sense and Sensibility, The Master and Margarita, Herzog, The Gift, The Count of Monte Cristo, Smiley's People*—any book I could get my hands on in my father's library, in secondhand bookstores, in the still-unravaged libraries in friends' houses—and read them all, an alcoholic drowning her inarticulate sorrows.

If I turned towards books, it was because they were the only sanctuary I knew, one I needed in order to survive, to protect some aspect of myself that was now in constant retreat. My other sanctuary, what helped restore some sense of sanity and relevance to my life, was of a more intimate and personal nature. On April 23, 1982, my niece Sanam was born, prematurely. From the moment I saw her, small and curled under a machine that was there to keep her alive, I felt a bond, a warmth; I knew she would be good for me and good to me. On January 26, 1984, my daughter, Negar, was born, and on September 15, 1985, my son, Dara. I have to be precise in terms of the day, month and year of their births, details that twinkle and tease every time I think of their blessed births, and have no compunction in becoming sentimental over their coming into this world. This blessing, like other blessings, was mixed. For one thing, I became more anxious. Until then I had worried for the safety of my parents, husband, brother and friends, but my anxiety for my children overshadowed all. When my daughter was born I felt I was given a gift, a gift that in some mysterious way preserved my sanity. And so it was with the birth of my son. Yet it was a source of constant regret and sorrow to me that their childhood memories of home, unlike my own, were so tainted.

My daughter, Negar, blushes every time I tell her that her particular brand of obstinacy, her passionate defense of what she considers to be justice, comes from her mother's reading too many nineteenth-century novels when she was pregnant with her. Negar has a way of throwing her head to the right and back in one move and pursing her lips just a little in defiance of whatever authority she is protesting at the moment. I embarrass her, and she wants to know, Why do I say such impossible things? Well, don't they say that what a mother eats during her pregnancy, as well as her moods and emotions, all have an effect on the child? While I was pregnant with you, I read too much Jane Austen, too much of the Brontës, George Eliot and Henry James. Look at your two favorite novels of all time: *Pride and Prejudice* and *Wuthering Heights*. But *you*, I add with glee, *you* are pure Daisy Miller. I don't know who this Daisy or Maisie or whatever of yours is, she tells me, pursing her lips, and I won't like James, I *know*. Yet she *is* like Daisy: a mixture of vulnerability and courage that accounts for these gestures of defiance, her way of throwing her head back which I first noticed when she was barely four, in the waiting room of a dentist's office of all places.

And when Dara jokingly asks, What about me? What did you do when you were pregnant with me? I tell him, Just to defy me, you turned out to be all that I imagined you would not be. And the moment I say this, I begin to believe it. Even in the womb, he took upon himself the task of proving my nightmarish anxieties wrong. While I was pregnant with him, Tehran was the object of continual bombings and I had become hysterical. There were stories about how pregnant women gave birth to crippled children, how their mother's anxiety had affected the unborn fetus in irremediable ways, and I imagined mine to be infected with all those maladies—that is, if we were spared and lived to see the birth of this child. How could I know that instead of my protecting him, he was coming into the world to protect me?

6

For a long time, I wallowed in the afterglow of my irrelevance. While doing so, I was also unconsciously examining my options. Should I give in to this non-existence imposed upon me by a force I did not respect? Should I pretend to comply and then cheat the regime in secret? Should I leave the country, as so many of my friends had done or had been forced to do? Should I withdraw from my job in silence the way some of my most honorable colleagues had done? Was there any other option?

It was during this period that I joined a small group who came together to read and study classical Persian literature. Once a week, on Sunday nights, we gathered at one of the participants' houses and for hours we studied text after text. Sunday nights—sometimes during the blackouts by candlelight—in different houses, belonging to the different members of the group, we would gather year after year. Even when our personal and political differences alienated us from one another, the magical texts held us together. Like a group of conspirators, we would gather around the dining room table and read poetry and prose from Rumi, Hafez, Sa'adi, Khayyam, Nezami, Ferdowsi, Attar, Beyhaghi.

We would take turns reading passages aloud, and words literally rose up in the air and descended upon us like a fine mist, touching all five senses. There was such a teasing, playful quality to their words, such joy in the power of language to delight and astonish. I kept wondering: when did we lose that quality, that ability to tease and make light of life through our poetry? At what precise moment was this lost? What we had now, this saccharine rhetoric, putrid and deceptive hyperbole, reeked of too much cheap rosewater.

I was reminded of a story I had heard and reheard about the Arab conquest of Persia, a conquest that brought Islam into Iran. By this account, when the Arabs attacked Iran, they won because the Persians themselves, perhaps tired of tyranny, had betrayed their king and opened the doors to their enemies. But after the invasion, when their books were burned, their places of worship destroyed and their language overtaken, the Persians took revenge by re-creating their burned and plundered history through myth and language. Our great epic poet Ferdowsi had rewritten the confiscated myths of Persian kings and heroes in a pure and sacred language. My father, who all through my childhood would read me Ferdowsi and Rumi, sometimes used to say that our true home, our true history, was in our poetry. The story came back to me then because, in a sense, we had done it again. This time we had opened the gates not to foreign invaders but to domestic ones, to those who had come to us in the name of our own past but who had now distorted every inch of it and robbed us of Ferdowsi and Hafez.

Gradually, I started to take on projects with this group. I used the material culled from my dissertation on Mike Gold and proletarian writers of the thirties in America to write my first article in Persian. I persuaded a friend from the group to translate a small book by Richard Wright, *The American Hunger,* and I wrote the introduction. It covered Wright's Communist experiences, his trials and ordeals and his final break with the Party. Later I encouraged my friend to translate Nabokov's *Lectures on Russian Literature*. I translated poems by Langston Hughes. A member of our group, a well-known Iranian writer, encouraged me to write a series of articles on modern Persian fiction for a literary magazine he edited and, later, to participate in weekly literary discussions with young Iranian writers.

This was the beginning of my writing career, which has stretched over almost two decades to the present. I created a protective shell around myself and started not thinking but writing, mainly literary criticism. I flung my diaries into the corner of my closet and forgot about them. I wrote without ever going back to them.

My articles gained recognition, yet I seldom felt complete satisfaction with them. I thought most were too tidy and rather pompous and learned. I felt passionate about the subjects I wrote about, but there were conventions and rules to follow and I missed the impulsiveness and enthusiasm I could bring to my classes. In class, I felt I was having an exciting dialogue with my students; in my articles I became a rather dry teacher. My articles succeeded for the exact reasons that I disliked them; their learned claims won me respect and admiration.

7

There should be a clear and logical reason why one day out of the blue I picked up the phone and called my magician. It is true that I had begun to brood too much over my unsatisfactory intellectual life, true that I missed my classes and felt restless and desperate, but still I don't know why on this particular day, and not the day before or after, I decided to call him.

There were so many myths around him—that he saw only a select few, that at night if the light in one of his rooms facing the street was on, it was a sign that he would see visitors; otherwise they should not bother him. These stories did not impress me; in fact, they were the one reason I hesitated to call him. He had created such an elaborate fiction out of his relationship with the world that the more he claimed to be detached, the more he seemed to be actually involved. The myths were his cocoon; in that land people created cocoons, elaborate lies to protect themselves. Like the veil.

So, we will settle for the fact that I called him impulsively for no very good reason. One afternoon I was alone at home, reading all day instead of working. Every once in a while I would look at my watch and say, I will start work in half an hour, in one hour; I'll quit as soon as I've reached the end of the chapter. Then I'd go to the refrigerator and make myself a sandwich, which I ate as I continued to read my book. I think it was after I had finished the sandwich that I got up and dialed his number.

Two rings and I heard a voice on the third: Hello? Mr. R? Yes? I am Azar; a pause. Azar Nafisi. Oh yes, yes. Can I see you? But of course. When would you like to come? When is best for you? How about the day after tomorrow, at five? Later, he explained that the size of his apartment was such that he could answer the phone from anywhere in his apartment on the third ring; otherwise, it meant that he either was out or did not wish to answer.

No matter how intimate we became, I always saw myself the way we were in that first meeting. I sat opposite him on the lonely chair, and he on the hard brown sofa. Both of us had our hands on our knees, he because it was customary with him, me because I was nervous and had unconsciously adopted a schoolkid's pose in front of a much respected teacher. Between us on the table he had set a tray with two dark green mugs of tea and a box of chocolates, immaculate squares of red with black lettering: Lindt, a rare luxury, all the more so because they could not be found in the shops where foreign chocolates were sold at exorbitant prices. The chocolates were the only luxury he treated himself and his visitors to. There must have been days when he went almost hungry, but he did have a store of chocolates in that half-empty refrigerator, which he did not eat much of himself but reserved for friends and visitors. I forgot to add: it was a cloudy, snowy day; and would it matter if I told you that I wore a yellow sweater, gray pants and black boots and he a brown sweater and jeans?

Unlike me, he appeared very confident. He acted as if I had come to ask for help and our task was to set up an elaborate rescue plan. And in a sense it was true. He talked as if he knew me, as if he knew not only the known facts but also the unknown mysteries, thus creating a formal intimacy, a shared strangeness between us. It seemed from that first meeting that, like Tom Sawyer and Huck Finn, we entered into a conspiracy—not a political one, but one cooked up by children to protect them against the grown-up world.

He finished my sentences for me, articulated my wishes and demands, and by the time I left, we already had a plan. This was what was good about him: people who went to see him somehow ended up with some plan or another, whether it was how to behave towards a lover or how to start a new project or structure a talk. I don't remember too clearly the exact nature of the plan I went home with, but he does, I am sure, for he seldom forgets. I had not finished my tea, and did not eat my chocolate, but I did go home giddy and satiated. We had talked about my present life, the intellectual state of affairs and then about James and Rumi all in one breath. Without intending to, we had strayed into a long and pointless discussion that had sent him to his immaculate library, and I left with a few books under my arm.

That first day colored our relationship—in my mind at least—until the day I left Iran. I stopped growing up in relation to him because it suited and even pleased me to do so, absolving me of certain responsibilities. While he had created around himself the illusion of a master, of someone always in control, he may not have been quite so much in control as I thought him to be—and I was not quite such a helpless novice.

I usually went to see him twice a week, once for lunch and once in the early evening. Later we added evening walks, around my house or his, during which we exchanged news, discussed projects, gossiped. Sometimes we went to a favorite coffee shop or restaurant with an intimate friend of his. Apart from that friend, we had two other friends in common who owned a bookstore that had become a meeting place of writers, intellectuals and young people. With them we enjoyed occasional lunches and excursions to the mountains. He never visited my house but often sent my family tokens of his regards, a box of chocolates, which they had come to identify with him, and even expect, on certain days of the week, videos, books and, sometimes, ice cream.

He called me "lady professor"—a term less odd and more often used in Iran than here. He said later that when friends asked him after our first meeting, What is the lady professor like?, he had said, She's okay. She is very American—like an American version of Alice in

Wonderland. Was this a compliment? Not particularly; it was merely a fact. Have I already mentioned that his favorite actress was Jean Arthur and that he liked Renoir and Minnelli? And that he wanted to be a novelist?

8

Turning points always seem so sudden and absolute, as if they have come bolt out of the blue. That is not true, of course. A whole slow process goes into their making. When I look back, I cannot trace the exact process that suddenly led me back into the classroom, against my own will almost, wearing the veil I had vowed never to wear.

The signs coalesced in all sorts of small events, like the sudden phone calls from various universities, including the University of Tehran, asking me to teach. When I refused, they would always say, Well, how about one or two classes, just to get a feel for how things are right now? Many would try to convince me that things had changed, that people like me were in demand, the atmosphere had become more "relaxed." I did teach a course or two at the Free Islamic University and the former National University, but I never accepted to return as a full-time faculty member.

By the mid-eighties a new brand of Islamists were gradually coming into being. They had begun to sense that all was not right with the direction their revolution was taking, and decided it was time to intercede. The lack of progress in the war with Iraq was taking its toll. Those who had been ardent revolutionaries at the start of the revolution—people now in their late teens and early twenties—and the younger generation, who were coming of age, were discovering the cynicism and corruption of the leaders who had taken power. The government also had discovered that it needed the cadre it had so casually expelled from the universities to meet the growing demands of the student body.

Some within the government and some former revolutionaries had finally realized that there was no way the Islamic regime could make us intellectuals vanish. In forcing us underground, it had also made us more appealing, more dangerous and, in a strange way, more powerful. It had made us scarce and, because of this, also in demand. So they decided to have us back, perhaps partly to be more certain of their control, and they started to contact people like me, who had once been branded as decadent and Westernized.

Mrs. Rezvan, an ambitious teacher in the Department of English at the Allameh Tabatabai University, was one of the intermediaries between the more progressive Islamic revolutionaries and the alienated secular intellectuals. Her husband had been a Muslim radical at the start of the revolution, and she had connections with the progressive revolutionaries and the secularists—with the insiders and outsiders; she was determined to use both to her advantage.

This Mrs. Rezvan seemed to have cropped up out of nowhere, bent on changing the course of my life through the sheer force of her will. I remember our first meeting well, partly because it was during one of those periods known in the history of the war as "the war of the cities." Sporadically, the two sides carried out ferocious attacks for a sustained period on certain key cities, such as Tehran, Isfahan and Tabriz in Iran and Baghdad and Mosul in Iraq. Usually, the fighting relaxed for a time after that, until the next bombing attack, which could sometimes last as long as a year.

It was mid-morning in the winter of 1987. My daughter, who was now three, and my one-and-a-half-year-old son and I were alone at home. Tehran had been hit by two rocket attacks earlier that morning, and I was trying to divert my children's attention by playing a favorite song involving a rooster and a fox on a small tape recorder—I was encouraging my daughter to sing along. It sounds too much like a sentimental movie: brave mother, brave children. I did not feel brave at all; the seeming tranquillity was due to an anxiety so paralyzing that it translated itself into calm. After the attacks we went to the kitchen, and I made them lunch. We then moved to the hall, where we felt more secure, because there were fewer windows. I built for them houses of cards that they destroyed with a touch of their small hands.

Right after lunch, the phone rang. It was a friend who had been one of my graduate students the previous year. She wanted to know if I could come to her place on Wednesday night. Mrs. Rezvan, a colleague of hers, really wanted to meet me. She liked me, had read all of my articles. Anyway, my friend concluded, Mrs. Rezvan is a phenomenon in her own right: if she didn't exist, we would have to invent her. So could you come, please?

A few nights later, in the midst of another blackout, I set off to my friend's house. When I got there, it was already dark. As I entered the large hall, from the depth of darkness I could see, flickering in the light of a kerosene lamp, a short, stocky woman dressed in blue. Her physical appearance is perfectly clear and alive in my mind. I can see her plain face, the sharp nose, short neck and dark cropped hair. But none of this captures the woman who, at the height of our intimacy, after we had visited each other's houses, once our children had become almost friends and our husbands got to know each other, remained always Mrs. Rezvan. What I cannot describe is her energy, which seemed to be caged inside her body. She appeared to be in constant motion, pacing her small office, my living room, the halls of the university.

She always seemed determined: determined not only to do certain things herself, but to make others, whom she targeted carefully, perform specific tasks that she had outlined for them. I have seldom met anyone whose will was so physically imposing. It was not the plainness of her features but the determination, the will and the half-ironic tone of her voice that remained with you.

Sometimes she would come to my house unexpectedly, in such an anxious state that I would think some disaster had befallen her. Yet it would only be to inform me that it was my duty to participate in some meeting or another. She always framed these requests as matters of life and death. Some of these "duties" I am grateful for, like forcing me to meet with a handful of progressive religious journalists—who are now fashionably called the "reformists"—and to write for their journals. They were fascinated by Western literature and philosophy and I discovered, to my surprise, that there were many points on which we could agree.

It is such a privilege to meet you, she told me that evening, the first time we met. I want to become your student. She said this with a perfectly serious expression, without a trace of humor or irony. This threw me off balance so violently that I immediately disliked her; I became shy and could not respond.

That night she did most of the talking. She had read my articles; she knew about me from certain friends and students. No, she was not trying to flatter me; she really wanted to learn. At any rate, I must teach at their university, the only liberal university in Iran, which still had some of the best minds. The head of the department, you will like him, not a man of literature, but a serious scholar. The state of literature in this country could not be any worse, and the state of English literature is most hopeless of all. We, those of us who care, must do something about this; we should leave our differences aside and work together.

After our first meeting, she pressured me through various intermediaries to accept her offer to teach at Allameh Tabatabai University on a regular basis. She called me incessantly, evoking God, students, my duty to the homeland, to literature: it was my task in life to teach at that university. She made promises; she promised to talk to the president of the university, to whomever I wished her to talk to.

I told her I did not want to wear the veil in the classroom. Did I not wear the veil, she asked, whenever I went out? Did I not wear it in the grocery store and walking down the street? It seemed I constantly had to remind people that the university was not a grocery store. What is more important, she countered, the veil or the thousands of young people eager to learn? What about the freedom to teach what I wanted? What about it? she asked conspiratorially. Haven't they banned any discussion of relations between men and women, drinking, politics, religion—what is there left to talk about? For you, she said, they would make an exception. Anyway, things are much freer now. They have all had a taste of good things; they want to get there too. Why not teach them James or Fielding or whoever—why not?

9

The meeting with Mrs. Rezvan had thrown me off balance. She was like an intermediary pleading on behalf of an unfaithful and unforgotten lover, pledging complete loyalty in return for my affections. Bijan thought I should return; he felt that is what I really wanted to do, if only I would admit it to myself. Most of my friends merely confused me by posing the dilemma back to me: is it better to help the young people who might otherwise not have a chance to learn or to refuse categorically to comply with this regime? Both sides were absolute in their position: some thought I would be a traitor if I neglected the young and left them to the teachings of the corrupt ideologies; others insisted I would be betraying everything I stood for if I worked for a regime responsible for ruining the lives of so many of our colleagues and students. Both were right.

I called the magician one morning in panicked confusion. Another urgent meeting was set up, for late afternoon in a favorite coffee shop. It was a tiny place, a bar in its pre-revolution days, now reincarnated as a café. It belonged to an Armenian, and forever shall I see on the glass door next to the name of the restaurant, which was in small letters, the compulsory sign in large black letters: RELIGIOUS MINORITY. All restaurants run by non-Muslims had to carry this sign on their doors so that good Muslims, who considered all non-Muslims dirty and did not eat from the same dishes, would be forewarned.

The space inside was narrow and shaped like a wide curve, with seven or eight stools on one side of the bar and, on the other, next to the wall-length mirror, another set of stools. When I went in, he was already seated at the far end of the bar. He got up and with an imperceptible mock curtsy, bent down, saying, Here I am, your servant at your service, m'lady, as he drew a stool for me to sit.

We ordered and I said breathlessly, This is an emergency. So I gathered. I have been asked to teach again. Is this new? he asked. No, but this time I'm wavering; I don't know what to do. Then somehow I managed to divert my own emergency meeting into a discussion of the book I was immersed in at the moment, Dashiell Hammett's *The Continental Op,* and Steve Marcus's marvelous essay on Hammett in which he cited a line from Nietzsche that struck me as pertinent to our situation. "Whoever fights monsters," Nietzsche had said, "should see to it that in the process he does not become a monster. And when you look long into an abyss, the abyss also looks into you." I had an amazing talent for subverting my own agendas, and we got so involved in our discussion that I completely forgot about the real purpose of the visit.

Suddenly, he said, Aren't you going to be late? I should have known how late it was by the changing colors of the window and the pale, withdrawing light. I went to telephone Bijan and shamefacedly informed him that I would be late. When I got back my magician was paying the bill. But we haven't finished yet, I feebly protested. We still need to discuss the main business we came here for. I thought all we had been discussing was the main business—your rediscovery of your love for Mr. Hammett and Co. You're lucky I've given up on life and am not trying to seduce you. All I would have to do is to let you go on about Hammett and the shameful disrespect for the detective story in Iran and other matters that apparently turn you on. No, I said with some embarrassment—I mean, about my teaching again. Oh that, he said dismissively. Well, obviously you must teach.

But I was not one to let go that easily. I was in love with the idea of moral imperatives and taking a stand and all that. So I relentlessly pursued my argument about the morality of returning to a job I had sworn I would never take up again so long as I was forced to wear the veil. He raised an eyebrow with an indulgent smile: Lady, he said at last, will you *please* wise up to where you live? As for your qualms about submitting to the regime, none of us can drink a single glass of water without the grace of the moral guardians of the Islamic Republic. You love the work, so go on, indulge yourself and accept the facts. We intellectuals, more than ordinary citizens, either play scrupulously into their hands and call it constructive dialogue or withdraw from life completely in the name of fighting the regime. So many people have made their name through their opposition to the regime, yet they too can't get along without it. You don't want to take up arms against the regime, do you?

No, I conceded, but I don't want to make deals with them, either. Anyway, how can *you* give me such advice? I asked him. Look at you. What about me? Didn't you refuse to teach, to write, to do anything under this regime? Aren't you saying through your actions that we should all withdraw? No, I am not saying that. You are still making the mistake of using me as a model. I am not a model. In many ways I might even be called a coward. I don't belong to their club, but I am also paying a big price. I don't lose, and I don't win. In fact, I don't exist. You see, I have withdrawn not just from the Islamic Republic but from life as such, but *you* can't do that—you have no desire to do that.

I tried to turn the tables, and reminded him that he had become a sort of role model for his friends and even for his foes. He disagreed.

No, the reason I am so popular is that I give others back what they need to find in themselves. You need me not because I tell you what I want you to do but because I articulate and justify what you want to do. That is why you like me—a man without qualities. That's what yours truly is all about. What about what you want? I asked. I've given that up, but I make it possible for you to do what you want. But you are going to pay the price, he told me. Remember that quote you read me about the abyss? It is impossible not to be touched by the abyss. I know how you want to have your cake and eat it too, I know all about that innocence, that Alice in Wonderland persona you want to preserve.

You love teaching. All of us, including me, we're all substitutes for your teaching. You enjoy it, so why not go ahead and teach? Teach them your Hammetts and your Austens—go on, enjoy yourself. Well, we are not talking about pleasure here, I shot back righteously. But of course, he mocked me, the lady who constantly boasts about her love for Nabokov and Hammett is now telling me we should not do what we love! That is what I call immoral. So now you *too* have joined the crowd, he said more seriously—what you've absorbed from this culture is that anything that gives pleasure is bad, and is immoral. You are more moral by sitting at home and twiddling your thumbs. If you want me to tell you it's your duty to teach, you've come to the wrong person. I won't do it. I say teach because you enjoy teaching: you will nag less at home, you will be a better person and probably your students will also have fun and maybe even learn something.

When we were in the taxi on our way home, he turned to me again and broke the silence that had descended between us. Seriously, he said, go back and teach. It isn't forever. You can always get out if you want. Make your deals, but go only as far as you can without compromising the fundamentals. And don't worry about what we, your colleagues and friends, might say behind your back. We'll talk behind your back no matter what you do. If you returned, we'd say, She's caved in; if you didn't, we'd say, She's scared of taking up the challenge. So I did what he advised, and they did talk behind my back just as they saw fit.

10

Less than a week after our emergency session, Mrs. Rezvan called me at home. She wanted me to meet with the head of the department, a nice man. You'll see things are different now, she insisted. They have become more liberal; they realize the value of good academics. What she forgot to mention was that "they" wanted the impossible: good academics who would preach their ideals and conform to their demands. She was right, however, about the head of the department. He was a first-rate linguist, a graduate of one of the best universities in the U.S. He was religious, but not ideological and not a sycophant. And, unlike most, he was genuinely interested in academic standards.

After that first meeting with the head of the department came a less pleasant meeting with the pious and less flexible president of the faculty. After the usual preliminaries, he took on a serious expression, as if to say, Enough about such trivial matters as philosophy and literature—now let's get down to the basics. He began by expressing some concern about my "background," especially my defiance of the veil. I told him that this was now the law of the land, that I could no longer appear anywhere in public without the veil and that therefore I would wear it. But I would not compromise on my classes: I would teach what I wanted to teach as I saw fit to teach it. He was surprised, but decided to accede, at least in principle, to my requirement for freedom.

All during the meeting, as befitted a truly Muslim man, he did not look me in the eyes. Most of the time he kept his head down like a shy eighteen-year-old. He focused on the design of the carpet, or targeted the wall. Sometimes he would play with his pen, looking at it intently, reminding me of my last meeting with Mr. Bahri. I had by now become something of an expert in the manners of pious men. They showed their opinion of you by the manner in which they avoided looking at you. Some made an aggressive point of averting their gaze. Once, a high functionary for whose organization I had prepared an evaluation report at the request of a male colleague, pointedly looked the other way throughout the thirty minutes of my report, and later addressed his points and questions to my male colleague, who I felt was literally sweating with shame. After a while I decided to address myself also solely to my colleague, refusing to acknowledge the high personage's presence—and foolishly, I refused the money the organization paid me for my pains.

But this dean seemed to avert his gaze out of genuine modesty and piety; I did not particularly appreciate his manner, but I could not feel hostile towards him. Had we not lived in the Islamic Republic, I might have shown some sense of humor about our awkward situation, for it was obvious that it was more embarrassing and painful to him than it was to me; and it was clear that he was curious and eager to discuss with me matters of which he knew little, like English literature, and just as eager to show off his knowledge of Plato and Aristotle.

When Mrs. Rezvan heard a report of our conversation she told me with a laugh that I was not the only one afraid of being "compromised." The university officials were also worried about me. In asking me to join the faculty, they had taken certain risks.

The next thing I knew, I was preparing for my first class. In my first semester I was loaded with three undergraduate introductory courses, ranging from introduction to the novel to drama and criticism, and two graduate courses, one on eighteenth-century fiction and the other a survey of literary criticism. My undergraduate classes each had between thirty and forty students, and the graduate seminars were crowded, some of them with more than thirty students. When I complained about the workload, I was reminded of the fact that some of the faculty taught over twenty hours a week. For the administrators, the quality of the work was of little consequence. They called my expectations unrealistic and idealistic. I called their indifference criminal.

As it turned out, neither one of us kept our promises. I always wore my veil improperly, and that became their prime excuse for constantly harassing me. And they never gave up on trying to force me to teach and act more acceptably. But for a long time we lived under a sort of truce. Mrs. Rezvan became a buffer between the administration and me, trying to smooth things over like a mediator in a bad marriage. Like all mediators, she did not forget her own advantages—persuading people like me into more active participation gave her leverage with the university officials—and for as long as she remained at the university, for better and for worse, the marriage somehow lasted.

She would tell me in that ironic tone of hers how we should mount a united front to save literature from the clutches of ignoramuses in the faculty who had no knowledge of literature. Did you know that the woman who taught the twentieth-century novel before you assigned only Steinbeck's *The Pearl* and one Persian novel? Or that a professor at Alzahrah University thought that *Great Expectations* was written by Joseph Conrad?

II

"Attention, attention! The siren you hear is the danger signal. Red alert! Leave at once and repair to your shelters!" I wonder at what point in my life, and after how many years, the echo of the red siren— like a screeching violin that plays mercilessly all over one's body— would cease in my mind. I cannot separate the eight years of war from that shrill voice that several times a day, at the most unexpected hours, would intrude into our lives. Three levels of danger had been established, but I never managed to differentiate between the red (danger), yellow (possibility of danger) and white (danger has stopped) sirens. Somehow, in the sound of the white siren, menace still lurked. Usually the red siren sounded too late, after the bomb had already been dropped, and in any case, even at the university we had no real shelters to repair to.

The air raids over Tehran were memorable for so many different reasons, not least for the sudden friendships and intimacies they inspired. Acquaintances who came to dinner would have no choice but to stay the night, sometimes over a dozen of them, and by morning it was as if they had known you all their lives. And those sleepless nights! In our house I was the one who slept least. I wanted to sleep close to my children so that if anything happened, it would happen to all of us. My husband slept or tried to sleep through the raids, but I would take two pillows, a few candles and my book to a small hall that separated the children's bedroom from ours and station myself by their doorway. I seemed to think that somehow, by keeping awake, I might throw a jinx and divert the bomb from harming our house.

One night I awoke suddenly at three or four in the morning and discovered that the house was in complete darkness. I knew at once there had been another blackout, because the small light in the hall was out. I looked out the window and saw that the streetlights were also gone. I turned on the flashlight; it cut a small circle of light from the darkness around me. A few minutes later I was ready with my pillows up against the wall, two lit candles and my book. I heard a sudden explosion. My heart heaved up and down and my hand went involuntarily to my stomach, just as it had during similar raids when I was pregnant. My eyes pretended nothing had happened, and rested on a page of *Daisy Miller.*

It was during this time that, while reading certain writers, I unconsciously took up pencil and paper again. I had never wholly given up my pleasurable undergraduate habit of underlining passages and taking notes. Most of my notes on *Pride and Prejudice, Washington Square, Wuthering Heights, Madame Bovary* and *Tom Jones* were made on these sleepless nights, when oddly enough my concentration was high, fueled perhaps by the effort to ignore the all-engrossing threat of bombs and rockets.

I had just begun *Daisy Miller* and was reading about that Europeanized young American, Winterbourne, who meets in Switzerland the enchanting and enigmatic Miss Daisy Miller. Winterbourne is fascinated by this beautiful—to some, shallow and vulgar; to others, innocent and fresh—young American woman, but he cannot decide if she is a "flirt" or a "nice" girl. The plot centers on Winterbourne's vacillations between Daisy, with her defiance of the rules of nicety, and his aristocratic aunt and her community of snobbish Americans, who decide to ignore her. The scene I was reading takes place after Daisy asks Winterbourne to introduce her to his aunt. Winterbourne tries to inform her, as delicately as he can, that his aunt will not see her. "Miss Daisy Miller stopped, and stood looking at him. Her prettiness was still visible in the darkness; she was opening and closing her enormous fan. 'She doesn't want to know me!' she said suddenly. 'Why don't you say so?' "

I heard the sound of another explosion. I felt thirsty, but could not make myself get up and get a drink. Then two more explosions. I read on, my eyes sometimes drifting from the book to the darkened hall. I am afraid of the dark, but the war and its explosions had made that fear insignificant. And in a scene I will always remember—not only because of that night—Daisy tells Winterbourne: " 'You needn't be afraid. I am not afraid!' And she gave a little laugh. Winterbourne fancied there was a tremor in her voice; he was touched, shocked, mortified by it. 'My dear young lady,' he protested, 'she knows no one. It's her wretched health.' The young girl walked on a few steps, laughing still. 'You needn't be afraid,' she repeated."

There is so much courage in that sentence, and irony in the fact that what Winterbourne was afraid of was not his aunt but Miss Daisy Miller's charms. For a moment I believe I really was diverted from the explosions, and I did manage to draw a line around the words *You needn't be afraid.*

As I continued to read, three things happened almost simultaneously. My daughter called me from her room, the phone rang and I heard a knock at the hall door. I picked up one candle and moved towards the phone, telling Negar I would be with her in a second. At that moment, the hall door opened and my mother, holding a candle, entered, saying, Are you okay? Don't be afraid! Almost every night after the explosions, my mother came in with her candle; her action had taken on the form of a ritual. She went to my daughter's room and I answered the phone. It was a friend; she also wanted to know if we were okay. It sounded to them as if the explosions had come from our part of the city. This had also become a ritual, to call friends and family to make sure they were safe, knowing that your own relief implied somcone else's death.

During these nights of interchanging red and white sirens, I unconsciously mapped out my future career. Throughout these endless nights of reading I concentrated only on fiction, and when I started to teach again, I found I had already prepared my two courses on the novel. Over the next decade and a half, more than anything else, I thought, wrote about and taught fiction. These readings made me curious about the origins of the novel and what I came to understand as its basically democratic structure. And I became curious as to why the realistic novel was never truly successful in our country. If a sound can be preserved in the same manner as a leaf or a butterfly, I would say that within the pages of my *Pride and Prejudice,* that most poly-

phonic of all novels, and my *Daisy Miller* is hidden like an autumn leaf
the sound of the red siren.

12

There were the sirens and the mechanical voice that commanded you
to attention, the sandbags in the streets and bombs usually early in the
morning or after midnight; there were long or short periods of calm
in between the bombings and their resumption, and there were
Austen and James and the different classrooms on the fourth floor of
the building that housed the Faculty of Persian and Foreign Languages and Literature. Two rows of classrooms were situated on
either side of the long and narrow hall. On one side they opened to a
view of the not so distant mountains, and on the other to the rather
sad and lovely garden, always a little neglected, with a small ornamental pool and a chipped statue in the middle. Around the pool were
circles and squares of shrubs and flowers, surrounded by trees. The
flowers appeared to have grown randomly: beautiful roses, large
dahlias and daffodils. Always it seemed to me that the garden belonged not to the university but to the pages of a Hawthorne novel.

I developed a ritual in preparation for my public appearance. I was
careful not to wear any makeup. The contours and lines of my body
would disappear as I slipped on my T-shirt and baggy black trousers,
a comfortable half-size too big for me, and over them my long black
robe and the black scarf that coiled around my neck. Last, I put my
books and notes in my bag. I would stuff my bag with far too many
books and notes, most of them unnecessary, but I took them with me
anyway, like a safety net.

Somehow the distance between my home and the university has
become hazy in my memory. Suddenly and magically, without passing the green gate and the guard, without passing the glass entrance
door to the building with signs denouncing Western culture, I am inside the Faculty of Persian and Foreign Languages and Literature,
standing at the bottom of the stairs.

As I walk up the stairs, I try to ignore the posters and notices
pasted haphazardly on the walls. They are mainly black-and-white

photographs of the war with Iraq, and slogans denouncing the Great Satan, namely America, and the emissaries of that Satan. Quotations from Ayatollah Khomeini—WHETHER WE KILL OR ARE KILLED WE SHALL BE VICTORIOUS! OUR UNIVERSITIES MUST BE ISLAMIZED! THIS WAR HAS BEEN A DIVINE BLESSING FOR US!—accompany the pictures.

I could never get over my resentment of those faded photographs, hanging neglected and forlorn on the cream-colored walls. Somehow these shabby posters and their slogans interfered with my work; they made me forget that I was at the university to teach literature. There were reprimands posted about the color of our uniforms, codes of conduct, but never a notice about a talk, a film or a book.

13

About two weeks into my second semester of teaching at Allameh, as soon as I opened the door to my office, I noticed on the floor an envelope that had been pushed under the door. I still have both the envelope and the yellowing piece of paper I found inside, folded once to fit. My name and address at the university is typed, but on the piece of paper there is only one line, childish and as obscene as its message: **The adulterous Nafisi should be expelled.** This was the welcoming gift I received on my formal return to academia.

Later that day, I spoke to the head of the department. The president had also received a note, with a similar message. I wondered why they told me this. I knew and they knew that the word *adulterous,* like all other words confiscated by the regime, had lost its meaning. It was merely an insult, intended to make you feel dirty and disqualified. I also knew that this could happen anywhere: the world is full of angry, pathological individuals pushing pieces of paper with obscene messages under doors.

What hurt, and still hurts, is that this mentality ultimately ruled our lives. This was the same language that the official papers, the radio and television and the clerics from their pulpits used to discredit and demolish their foes. And most of them succeeded at their task. What made me feel cheap, and in some way complicit, was the knowledge that so many people had been deprived of their livelihood on the basis of similar charges—because they had laughed loudly in public, because they had shaken hands with a member of the opposite sex. Should I just thank my lucky stars that I escaped with no more than one line scrawled on a cheap piece of paper?

I understood then what it meant when I was told that this university and my department in particular were more "liberal." It did not mean that they would take action to prevent such incidents: it meant that they would not take action against me on account of them. The administration did not understand my anger; they attributed it to a "feminine" outburst, as they would become accustomed to calling my protests in the years to come. They gave me to understand that they were prepared to put up with my antics, my informal addresses to my students, my jokes, my constantly slipping scarf, my *Tom Jones* and *Daisy Miller*. This was called tolerance. And the strange thing is that in some crooked way it was tolerance, and in some way I had to be grateful to them.

14

Whenever I picture myself, it is going up the stairs; I never see myself coming down. But I did go down that day, as I did every other day. I went down almost as soon as I had reached my office, disposed of the extra books and papers and picked up my notes for my first class. I descended at a more leisurely pace to the fourth floor, turned left and, near the end of the long hall, entered the classroom. The class was Introduction to the Novel II. The author under discussion was Henry James, and the novel, *Daisy Miller*.

As in my memory I once again open my book and spread out my notes, I glance over the forty-odd faces that stare back at me, seemingly ready at my command. Certain faces I have become accustomed to take consolation from. In the third row, on the girls' side, sits Mahshid, with Nassrin.

The first day of class the previous semester, I had been shocked to see Nassrin sitting there. My glance had traveled over students' faces casually and then reverted back to Nassrin, who was looking at me and smiling, as if to say, Yes, it's me. You have not made a mistake.

Over seven years had passed since I had seen little Nassrin with a bunch of leaflets under her arm disappearing into a sunny street near the University of Tehran. I had sometimes wondered what had become of her—was she perhaps married now? And there she was sitting beside Mahshid, with a bolder expression on her face, softened by a pale blush. The last time I had seen her she was wearing a navy scarf and a flowing robe, but now she was dressed in a thick black chador from head to foot. She looked even smaller in the chador, her whole body hidden behind the bulk of the dark, shapeless cloth. Another transformation was her posture: she used to sit bolt upright on the edge of the chair, as if prepared to run at a moment's notice; now she slumped almost lethargically, looking dreamy and absentminded, writing in slow motion.

After that class, Nassrin had stayed behind. I noticed that some of her old familiar gestures were still with her, like the restless movement of her hands and her constant shifting from one foot to the other. I asked her as I picked up my book and notes, Where have you been? Do you remember that you still owe me a paper on *Gatsby*? She smiled and said, Don't worry, I've got a good excuse. In this country, we are not short of good excuses.

She was brief in recounting the seven missing years of her life. In the barest outline, which I never dared ask her to detail, she informed me that soon after that day when I had last seen her, she and a few of her comrades had been arrested while distributing leaflets in the streets. You remember those days the regime went crazy attacking the Mujahideen—I was really very lucky. They executed so many of my friends, but initially gave me only ten years. Ten years was lucky? Well, yes. Do you remember that story of the twelve-year-old girl who was shot as she was running around the prison grounds asking for her mom? Well, I was there, and I did want to shout for my mother, too. They killed so many teenagers, I could've been any one of them. But this time, my father's religious credentials paid off. He had friends in the committee—in fact, one of the haj aghas had been his student. They spared me because of my dad. I got preferential treatment. After a while my ten years were reduced to three and I got off. Then for a while they wouldn't let me pursue my education and I was, still am, under probation. I was only allowed finally to enroll in college last year. So here I am. Welcome back, I said, but remember—

you still owe me a paper. I tried awkwardly to take her story as lightly as she intended me to.

I can still see Mahshid smiling her placid porcelain smile. Nassrin has a lethargic look about her—I always got the feeling she had not had a good night's sleep—but she will turn out to be one of my best and sharpest students.

To their right, by the wall, are the two members of the Muslim Students' Association. I have forgotten their names and they will have to endure the unpleasantness of being renamed: Miss Hatef and Miss Ruhi. They are all negative attention. Every once in a while, from beneath their black chadors, which reveal no more than a sharp nose on one and a small, upturned one on the other, they whisper; sometimes they even smile.

There is something peculiar about the way they wear their chadors. I have noticed it in many other women, especially the younger ones. For there is in them, in their gestures and movements, none of the shy withdrawal of my grandmother, whose every gesture begged and commanded the beholder to ignore her, to bypass her and leave her alone. All through my childhood and early youth, my grandmother's chador had a special meaning to me. It was a shelter, a world apart from the rest of the world. I remember the way she wrapped her chador around her body and the way she walked around her yard when the pomegranates were in bloom. Now the chador was forever marred by the political significance it had gained. It had become cold and menacing, worn by women like Miss Hatef and Miss Ruhi with defiance.

I will return to the beautiful girl with the too-sweet face in the fourth row. She is Mitra, who always gets the highest grades. She is quiet, barely says a word in class, and when she does, she expresses herself so calmly that sometimes I miss her point. I discover Mitra in her exam papers and, later, in her class journal.

Across the room, on the men's side, is Hamid, who will soon marry Mitra and go into computers. He is clean-shaven, handsome and intelligent, his smile carefree as he talks to his friends on either side of him. Just behind Hamid is Mr. Forsati. I see him always in a light brown coat and dark trousers. He too is smiling, but I discover that his smile is part of his physique. He has a beard, but it is trimmed and not full. He belongs to a new brand of Islamic students—very different from Mr. Bahri, with his fierce faith in revolutionary principles. Mr. Forsati is a Muslim, but he is not particularly devoted to the religious ideals that shaped the first generation of Islamic students. His interest, first and foremost, is in getting ahead. He doesn't seem close to anyone in the class, yet he is probably the most powerful person there, because he is the head of Islamic Jihad, one of the two lawful student organizations in Iran. The other, the Muslim Students' Association, is more revolutionary and Islamic in its practices. I soon discover that if I want to show a video in class or to organize a speakers' series, I will have to convince Mr. Forsati to lobby on my behalf, which he usually does with pleasure.

As I talk, my gaze involuntarily shifts to the last chair by the wall in the last row. Since the beginning of the semester, I have been both irritated and amused by the antics emerging from this corner of the room. Usually, midway through the lecture, the tall, lanky occupant of that chair—let us call him Mr. Ghomi—would lift himself up halfway, and, without waiting to rise fully or for me to give him permission to speak, begin to enumerate his objections. It was always objections—of this I could be certain.

Sitting beside Mr. Ghomi is an older student, Mr. Nahvi. He was more composed than his friend. He spoke calmly, mainly because he was always very certain. There were no doubts in him that might emerge in the form of an occasional outburst. He spoke clearly and monotonously, as if he could see each word forming in front of his eyes. He often followed me to my office and lectured me, mostly about Western decadence and how the absence of "the absolute" had been the cause of the downfall of Western civilization. He discussed these matters with assured finality, as facts that could not be argued. When I spoke, he paused respectfully, and as soon as I finished, he would go on in the same monotonous way and continue exactly where he had left off.

This was the second time Mr. Ghomi was taking my class. The first time, my first semester at Allameh, he hardly ever attended, under the pretext that he was in the militia and involved in the war effort. His war efforts always remained vague: he had not enlisted and had never been to the front. The war had become a good excuse for some of the Islamic activists to force undeserved privileges from the faculty. Mr. Ghomi flunked the finals and missed most of the tests, but he resented me nonetheless for failing him. I never quite knew if the lie about the war had become so much a part of his life that he had begun to believe in it, but he seemed to be genuinely hurt and for no good reason I felt almost guilty every time I encountered him. Now he came to the class regularly—more or less. Whenever I confronted students like him, I missed Mr. Bahri, who had had enough respect for the university never to abuse his position.

Mr. Ghomi came fairly regularly to class the second time around, and every time he did, he created some sort of commotion. He decided to turn Henry James into the biggest issue between us. He thrust his hand up at every opportunity and asked, or rather stated, his strident objections. James was his favorite target. He never questioned me directly—he did so obliquely, by insulting James, as if he bore a personal grudge against him.

15

When I picked *Daisy Miller* and *Washington Square* for my class, I never thought that Miss Daisy Miller and Miss Catherine Sloper would become such controversial and obsessive subjects of discussion. I had chosen the two novels because I felt they were more accessible than some of James's longer later works. Before James, we had read *Wuthering Heights.*

My emphasis in my introductory course was on the ways in which the novel, as a new narrative form, radically transformed basic concepts about the essential relationships between individuals, thereby changing traditional attitudes towards people's relationship to society, their tasks and duties. Nowhere is this developing change so apparent as in relations between men and women. Ever since Clarissa Harlow and Sophia Western—two modest and seemingly obedient daughters—refused to marry men they did not love, they changed the course of narrative and laid open to question the most basic institutions of their times, beginning with marriage.

Daisy and Catherine have little in common, yet both defy the conventions of their time; both refuse to be dictated to. They come from a long line of defiant heroines, including Elizabeth Bennet,

Catherine Earnshaw and Jane Eyre. These women create the main complications of the plot, through their refusal to comply. They are more complicated than the later, more obviously revolutionary, heroines of the twentieth century, because they make no claims to be radical.

Catherine and Daisy seemed too exacting to many of my students, who were more practical and did not understand what the fuss was all about. Why did Catherine defy both her father and her suitor? And why did Daisy tease Winterbourne so? What was it that these two difficult women wanted of their bewildered men? From the very first moment she appears with her parasol and her white muslin dress, Daisy creates some excitement, and some unrest, in Winterbourne's heart and mind. She presents herself to him as a puzzle, a dazzling mystery at once too difficult and too easy to solve.

Somewhere around this point, as I begin to move into a more detailed discussion of Daisy Miller, Mr. Ghomi raises his hand. His tone is one of protest, and immediately it puts me on the defensive and irritates me. What is it, he asks, that makes these women so revolutionary? Daisy Miller is obviously a bad girl; she is reactionary and decadent. We live in a revolutionary society and our revolutionary women are those who defy the decadence of Western culture by being modest. They do not make eyes at men. He continues almost breathlessly, with a sort of venom that is uncalled-for in relation to a work of fiction. He blurts out that Daisy is evil and deserves to die. He wants to know why Miss F in the third row felt that death was not her just reward.

Mr. Ghomi makes this little speech and sits down triumphantly, looking around him to see if anyone will challenge him. No one does. Except me, of course; they all expect me to perform the task. Mr. Ghomi always managed to divert the class from its course. At first I would get angry with him, but in time I came to see that sometimes he articulated sentiments that others did not dare express.

When I ask the class what they think of this, no one speaks. Mr. Ghomi, encouraged by this silence, raises his hand once more. We are more moral, because we've experienced real evil; we are in a war against evil, he says, a war both at home and abroad. At this point Mahshid decides to speak. If you remember, she says quietly, James experienced two terrible wars. When he was young, there was a civil war in America, and before he died he had witnessed the First World War. Mr. Ghomi's response was an imperceptible shrug; perhaps he felt those wars were not the righteous ones.

I see myself sitting in my chair in silence. The silence seems deliberate. After the class I continue to sit in my chair, caught in a vacuum of light coming from the large curtainless windows that cover one side of the room. Three of my female students come and hover by my desk. "We want you to know that the majority of this class disagrees with those guys," one of them says. "People are afraid to talk. This is a controversial subject. If we tell the truth, we're afraid he will report us. If we say what he wants to hear, we are afraid of you. We all appreciate your class."

Yes, I thought as I walked home that evening and, long after that, whenever this conversation returned to mind. You appreciate the class, but do you appreciate *Daisy Miller*? Well, do you?

16

If Mr. Ghomi had strong opinions about the Daisy Millers of the world, the class vacillated with the novel's hero, Winterbourne. With the exception of *A Doll's House,* there was no other work to which they responded so passionately. Their passion came from their bewilderment, their doubts. Daisy unhinged them, made them not know what was right and what was wrong.

One day at the end of class, a timid girl who sat in the front row but somehow managed to create the impression that she was hiding somewhere in the shadow of the last row hesitated shyly by my desk. She wanted to know if Daisy was a bad girl. "What do you think?" she asked me simply. What did I think? And why did her simple question irritate me so? I am now positive that my hedging and hesitation, my avoidance of a straight answer, my insistence on the fact that ambiguity was central to the structure of the Jamesian novel, badly disappointed her and that from then on I lost some of my authority with her.

We opened the book to the crucial scene at the Colosseum. Daisy, defying all caution and decorum, has gone to watch the moonlight with Mr. Giovanelli, an unscrupulous Italian who follows her every-where, to the chagrin of her correct countrymen and -women. Win-terbourne discovers them, and his response says more about his character than hers: "Winterbourne stopped, with a sort of horror; and, it must be added, with a sort of relief. It was as if a sudden illu-mination had been flashed upon the ambiguity of Daisy's behavior and the riddle had become easy to read. She was a young lady whom a gentleman need no longer be at pains to respect."

Daisy's night at the Colosseum is fatal to her in more ways than one: she catches the Roman fever that night from which she will die. But her death is almost predetermined by Winterbourne's reaction. He has just declared his indifference, and when she returns to the car-riage to leave, he recommends that she take her pills against Roman fever. " 'I don't care,' said Daisy, in a strange little tone, 'whether I have Roman fever or not.' " We all agreed in class that, symbolically, the young man's attitude towards Daisy determines her fate. He is the only one whose good opinion she desires. She is constantly asking him what he thinks about her actions. Without ever telling him, she poignantly and defiantly desires that he prove his devotion to her not by preaching, but by approving of her as she is, without any precon-ditions. It is ironic that ultimately Daisy is the one who really cares, and proves her devotion by dying.

Winterbourne was not the only one to feel relief on discovering the answer to Daisy's riddle. Many of my students shared his relief. Miss Ruhi asked why the novel did not end with Daisy's death. Did that not seem the best place to stop? Daisy's death seemed like a nice ending for all parties concerned. Mr. Ghomi could gloat over the fact that she had paid for her sins with her life, and most others in the class could now sympathize with her without any feeling of guilt.

But this is not the end. The novel ends just as it started, not with Daisy but with Winterbourne. At the beginning of the story, his aunt warned him that he was in danger of making a grave mistake about Daisy. She had meant that he could be duped by her. Now, after Daisy's death, Winterbourne ironically reminds his aunt, " 'You were right in that remark that you made last summer. I was booked to make a mistake. I have lived too long in foreign parts.' " He had underesti-mated Daisy.

At the beginning of the novel, the narrator tells us of a rumor that

Winterbourne is attached to a foreign woman. The novel ends, bringing us around full circle, with this same statement: "Nevertheless, he went back to live at Geneva, whence there continue to come the most contradictory accounts of his motives of sojourn: a report that he is 'studying' hard—an intimation that he is much interested in a very clever foreign lady."

The reader, who has identified with the hero until that moment, is left out in the cold. We are left to believe that Daisy, like the flower she is named after, is a beautiful and brief interruption. But this conclusion also is not wholly true. The narrator's tone at the end leads us to doubt if Winterbourne could ever see life the way he saw it before. Nothing will really be the same again, either for Winterbourne or for the unsuspecting reader—as I had occasion to find out much later, when my former students went back to their "mistakes" about Daisy in their writings and conversations.

17

In *The Tragic Muse,* James explains that his goal in writing is to produce "art as a human complication and social stumbling block," my friend Mina reminded me. This is what made James so difficult. Mina was a scholar of James and I had told her about my students' difficulties with *Daisy Miller.* Mina added, a little anxiously, I hope you are not thinking of dropping him because he is too difficult. I assured her that I had no such intention; anyway, it was not that he was too difficult for them, it was that he made them uncomfortable.

I told her my problem was not so much students like Ghomi, who were themselves so bluntly opposed to ambiguity, but my other students, who were victims of Ghomi's unambiguous attitude towards them. You see, I have a feeling that people like Ghomi always attack, because they are afraid of what they don't understand. What they say is we don't need James, but what they really mean is we are afraid of this fellow James—he baffles us, he confuses us, he makes us a little uneasy.

Mina told me that when she wanted to explain the concept of ambiguity in the novel, she always used her chair trick. In the next session I started the class by picking up a chair and placing it in front of me. What do you see? I asked the class. A chair. Then I placed the chair upside down. Now what do you see? Still a chair. Then I straightened the chair and asked a few students to stand in different places around the room, and asked both those standing and those sitting to describe the same chair. You see this is a chair, but when you come to describe it, you do so from where you are positioned, and from your own perspective, and so you cannot say there is only one way of seeing a chair, can you? No, obviously not. If you cannot say this about so simple an object as a chair, how can you possibly pass an absolute judgment on any given individual?

In order to encourage the silent majority in my classes to openly discuss their ideas, I asked my students to write their impressions of the works we were reading in diary form in a notebook. In their diaries, they were free to write about other matters related to the class or their experiences, but writing about the works was mandatory. Miss Ruhi always described the plot, which at least demonstrated that she had read the books I had assigned, and that she even, in some cases, had not only read them but also read about them. But she seldom expressed her own opinions. In one instance she mentioned that she had objected to *Wuthering Heights*'s immorality until she read somewhere about its mystical aspects, but in James's case there seemed to be no mysticism involved—he was very earthy, if at times too idealistic.

Her notebooks were always neat. At the top of each assignment she wrote in beautiful handwriting: "In the name of Allah, the Compassionate, the Merciful." She wrote that Daisy was not merely immoral, she was "unreasonable." Yet it was good to know that even in a decadent society like America there were still some norms, some standards according to which people were judged. She also quoted another teacher, lamenting the fact that certain writers made their unreasonable and immoral characters so attractive that readers instinctively sympathized with them. She lamented the fact that the right-thinking Mrs. Costello or Mrs. Walker was cast in such a negative light. This to her demonstrated a writer's satanic as well as godly powers. A writer like James, according to her, was like Satan: he had infinite powers, but he used them to do evil, to create sympathy for a sinner like Daisy and distaste for more virtuous people like Mrs.

Walker. Miss Ruhi had imbibed the same dregs as Mr. Nyazi and so many others.

Mr. Ghomi was true to his role. He rarely showed any indication of having read the novels. He ranted and raved about immorality and evil. He got into the habit of "educating" me by writing quotations from Imam Khomeini and other worthies about the duty of literature, about the decadence of the West, about Salman Rushdie. He also took to pasting in his notebook newspaper clippings reporting murder and corruption in the United States. One week he got so desperate that he resorted to quoting the slogans posted out in the streets. One such slogan I particularly liked: A WOMAN IN A VEIL IS PROTECTED LIKE A PEARL IN AN OYSTER SHELL. This slogan, when it appeared, was usually accompanied by a drawing of a predatory half-open oyster shell revealing a glossy pearl inside.

Mr. Nahvi, his silent older friend, wrote neat philosophical treatises on the dangers of doubt and uncertainty. He asked whether the uncertainty James made such a fuss over was not the reason for Western civilization's downfall. Like many others, Mr. Nahvi took certain things for granted, among them the decay of the West. He talked and wrote as if this downfall were a fact that even Western infidels did not protest. Every once in a while he handed his notes in, along with a pamphlet or a book on "Literature and Commitment," "The Concept of Islamic Literature" or some such.

Years later, when Mahshid and Mitra were in my secret Thursday class and we returned to *Daisy Miller*, they both lamented their own silence back then. Mitra confessed that she envied Daisy's courage. It was so strange and poignant to hear them talk about Daisy as if they had erred in regard to a real person—a friend or a relative.

One day, leaving class, I saw Mrs. Rezvan walking back to her office. She approached me and said, "I keep hearing interesting reports about your classes"—she did have reporters in every nook and cranny. "I hope you believe me now when I tell about the need to put something into these kids' heads. The revolution has emptied their heads of any form or thought, and our own intelligentsia, the cream of the crop, is no better."

I told her I was still not convinced that the best way of going about this was through the universities. I thought perhaps we could address it better through a united front with intellectuals outside the university. She gave me a sidelong glance and said, Yes, you could do that as well, but what makes you think you will have more success? After all, our intellectual elite has not acted any better than the clerics. Haven't you heard about the conversation between Mr. Davaii, our foremost novelist, and the translator of *Daisy Miller*? One day they were introduced. The novelist says, Your name is familiar—aren't you the translator of Henry Miller? No, *Daisy Miller*. Right, didn't James Joyce write that? No. Henry James. Oh yes, of course, Henry James. By the way what's Henry James doing nowadays? He's dead—been dead since 1916.

18

I told my magician that I could best describe my friend Mina with a phrase Lambert Strether, the protagonist of James's *The Ambassadors*, uses to describe himself to his "soul mate," Maria Gostrey. He tells her, "I'm a perfectly equipped failure." A perfectly equipped failure? he asked. Yes, and you know how she responds?

"Thank goodness you're a failure—it's why I so distinguish you! Anything else to-day is too hideous. Look about you—look at the successes. Would you be one, on your honour? Look, moreover," she continued, "at me."

For a little accordingly their eyes met. "I see," Strether returned. "You too are out of it."

"The superiority you discern in me," she concurred, "announces my futility. If you knew," she sighed, "the dreams of youth! But our realities are what has brought us together. We're beaten brothers in arms."

I told him, One day I will write an essay called "Perfectly Equipped Failures." It will be about their importance in works of fiction, especially modern fiction. I think of this particular brand as semi-tragic—sometimes comic and sometimes pathetic, or both. Don Quixote comes to mind, but this character is essentially modern, born and created at a time when failure itself was obliquely celebrated. Let us see, Pnin is one, and Herzog, and Gatsby perhaps, but perhaps not—he does not choose failure, after all. Most of James's and Bellow's favorite characters belong to this category. These are people who consciously choose failure in order to preserve their own sense of integrity. They are more elitist than mere snobs, because of their high standards. James, I believe, felt that in many ways he was one, with his misunderstood novels and his tenacity in keeping to the kind of fiction he felt was right, and so is my friend Mina, and your friend Reza, and of course you are one, most definitely, but you are not fictional, or are you? And he said, Well, right now I seem to be a figment of your imagination.

I believe I had picked Mina as a perfectly equipped failure when I first met her after the revolution, during one of my last department meetings at the University of Tehran. I was late and as I entered the room I saw, sitting opposite the door, to the right of the department head, a woman dressed in black. Her eyes and short, thick hair were also jet-black, and she appeared indifferent to the hostile arguments flying around her. She looked not so much composed as drawn inward. She was one of those people who are irrevocably, incurably honest and therefore both inflexible and vulnerable at the same time. This is what I remember about her: a shabby gentility, an air of "better days" clinging to all she wore. From that very first glance to our last meeting many years later, I was always oppressed by two sets of emotions when I met her: intense respect and sorrow. There was a sense of fatalism about her, about what she had accepted as her lot, that I could not bear.

Farideh and Dr. A had talked a great deal about Mina—her knowledge, her commitment to literature and to her work. There was a generosity to Farideh, which, despite her dogged commitment to what she called revolution, opened her up to certain people even when they were ideological opponents. She had an instinct for picking out the rebels, the genuine ones who, like Dr. A or Mina or Laleh, disagreed with her political principles. So it was that she instinctively sympathized with Mina and tried to console her, although she disagreed with her on almost all counts.

Mina had been recalled from a two-year sabbatical at Boston University, where she'd gone to write her book. She was given an ultimatum, and she, in my opinion, had made a mistake in returning to Iran.

Her book was on Henry James. She had studied under Leon Edel, and when I first saw her, it was difficult for her, quite an effort, to utter the simplest sentence. She of course never taught again: she came back to be expelled. She refused to wear the veil or to compromise; her only compromise had been to return. And maybe that was not a compromise but a necessity.

Mina's father had been the poet laureate—her family was cultured and well-off. Our families had gone on weekend outings together when we were young. She was older than me and never really talked to me during these family gatherings, but I remembered her vaguely. She is in some of the old photographs from my childhood, standing behind her father in their garden, with one of her uncles and my father and a young man I cannot identify. She looks solemn, with the shadow of a conditional smile.

Farideh and I tried to tell Mina how much we appreciated her, how outraged we were that the university did not. She listened impassively but seemed to enjoy our esteem. Her favorite brother, the president of a large company, had been arrested at the start of the revolution. Unlike most, he refused to put up with the new regime. Although he was not politically active, he supported the monarchy and like his sister he spoke his mind, even in jail. He had been insolent and that was enough. He was executed. Mina nowadays always dressed in black. Almost all her time in those days seemed to be devoted to her brother's widow and children.

Mina lived alone with her mother in a ridiculously large mansion. The day Farideh and I went to visit her, each carrying a large bouquet of flowers, was a sunny day clipped short as soon as we entered the mausoleum of her front hall. Her mother opened the door. She knew my parents and spent some time talking to me about them and then abruptly but politely left us as soon as her daughter descended the winding staircase. We were standing at the bottom of the steps with our colorful bouquets and pastel dresses, looking too breezy and light in the face of the somber gravity of that house, which seemed to pull all things into its shadows.

Mina's joys, the way she expressed her appreciation, were solemn. Yet she was very happy to see us and she led us into the huge semicircle of her living room. The room seemed to have complaints of its own, like a widow appearing for the first time in public without her husband. It was sparsely furnished; there were empty spaces where there should have been chairs, tables and a piano.

Mina's mother, a dignified woman in her late sixties, served us tea on a silver tray, with dainty glass teacups in silver filigree containers. Her mother was a wonderful cook, so going to her house was always a feast. But it was a mournful feast, because no amount of good food could bring cheer to that deserted mansion. Our hostesses' gracious hospitality, their efforts to make us feel welcomed, only made their well-concealed loss more emphatic.

Realism in fiction was Mina's obsession, and James her passion. What she knew, she knew thoroughly. We complemented each other, because my knowledge was impulsive and untidy, and hers meticulous and absolute. We could talk for hours on end. Before Farideh went into hiding and then joined her revolutionary group, escaping to Kurdistan and then to Sweden, the three of us used to talk about fiction and politics for hours, sometimes deep into the night.

Farideh and Mina were polar opposites when it came to politics— one was a dedicated Marxist and the other a determined monarchist. What they shared was their unconditional hatred for the present regime. When I think of how their talents were wasted, my resentment grows for a system that either physically eliminated the brightest and most dedicated or forced them to lay waste to the best in themselves, transforming them into ardent revolutionaries, like Farideh, or hermits, like Mina and my magician. They withdrew and simmered in their dashed dreams. For what good could Mina be without her James?

19

The air attacks on Tehran were resumed after a long period of calm in the late winter and early spring of 1988. I cannot think of those months and of the 168 missile attacks on Tehran without thinking of the spring, of its peculiar gentleness. It was a Saturday when Iraq hit the Tehran oil refinery. The news triggered the old fears and anxieties that had been lurking for over a year, since the last bombs had hit the city. The Iranian government responded with an attack on Baghdad, and on Monday, Iraq started its first round of missile attacks on Tehran. The intensity of what followed transformed that event into a symbol of all that I had experienced over the past nine years, like a perfect poem.

Soon after the first attacks, we decided to stick adhesive tape to our windows. We moved the children first to our own room, covering the windows in addition with thick blankets and shawls, and then, later, into the tiny windowless hall outside our bedrooms, the scene of my sleepless assignations with James and Nabokov. A few times we thought seriously of leaving Tehran, and once, in a frenzy, cleaned a small room that was later turned into my office near the garage, fortifying its windows; then we moved back up to sleep in our own bedrooms. I, who had been most frightened during the first round of attacks on Tehran, now seemed the calmest, as if to compensate for my former behavior.

On the first night of the missile attacks we watched with a few friends a German TV documentary commemorating the life of the late exiled Russian director Andrei Tarkovsky. In an attempt to appease the intellectuals, the annual Fajr (formerly Tehran) Film Festival presented a special screening of Tarkovsky's films. Although the films were censored and shown in the original Russian with no subtitles, there were lines outside the cinema hours before the box office opened. Tickets were sold on the black market at many times the actual price, and fights broke out over admittance, especially among those who had traveled from the provinces for the occasion.

Mr. Forsati came to see me after one class to inform me that he had obtained two extra tickets to a showing of Tarkovsky's *The Sacrifice,* a film I had expressed some desire to see. Since Mr. Forsati was the head of Islamic Jihad, one of the two Muslim students' associations at the university, he had access to the coveted tickets. He said the Tarkovsky mania was so pervasive that even the oil minister and his family had gone to a screening. People were starved for films. He told me laughingly that the less they understood, the more they treated it with respect. I said if that is the case, then they must love James. He responded, shrewdly, That is different; they respect Joyce the way they respect Tarkovsky. With James, they think they understand him, or that they should understand him, so they just get angry. They have more problems with James than with the more obviously difficult writers, like Joyce. I asked Mr. Forsati if he was going to see Tarkovsky. He said, If I do go, it is only to be a Roman in Rome; otherwise, I much prefer Tom Hanks.

The afternoon I went to see *The Sacrifice* was a fine winter day: not really winter, a mixture of winter and spring. Yet the most amazing feature of the day was not the heavenly weather, not even the movie itself, but the crowd in front of the movie house. It looked like a protest rally. There were intellectuals, office workers, housewives, some with their small children in tow, a young mullah standing uncomfortably to the side—the kind of mix of people you would never have found at any other gathering in Tehran.

Inside, the sudden burst of luminous colors on the screen brought a hushed silence over the audience. I had not been inside a movie theater for five years: all you could see in those days were old revolutionary movies from Eastern Europe, or Iranian propaganda films. I cannot honestly say what I thought of the film—the experience of sitting in a movie house, ensconced in the deep, cool leather, with a full-size screen in front of me, was too amazing. Knowing that I could not understand the words and that if I thought about the censorship I would be too angry to watch, I surrendered to the magic of colors and images.

Looking back on that time it seems to me that such rapture over Tarkovsky by an audience most of whom would not have known how to spell his name, and who would under normal circumstances have ignored or even disliked his work, arose from our intense sensory deprivation. We were thirsty for some form of beauty, even in an incomprehensible, overintellectual, abstract film with no subtitles and censored out of recognition. There was a sense of wonder at being in a public place for the first time in years without fear or anger, being in a place with a crowd of strangers that was not a demonstration, a protest rally, a breadline or a public execution.

The film itself was about war, and about its hero's vow never to speak again if his family was spared from the ravages of war. It concentrated on the hidden menace behind the seemingly calm flow of everyday life and the lush beauty of nature: the way war made itself felt by the rattle of the furniture caused by the bomber planes, and the terrible sacrifice required to confront this menace. For a brief time we experienced collectively the kind of awful beauty that can only be grasped through extreme anguish and expressed through art.

20

In a period of twenty-four hours, fourteen missiles hit Tehran. Since we had moved the children back to their room again, that night I pulled a small couch into their room and stayed awake reading until three in the morning. I read a thick Dorothy Sayers mystery, safe and secure with Lord Peter Wimsey, his faithful manservant and his scholarly beloved. My daughter and I were woken up at dawn with the sound of a nearby explosion.

It was not just the very loud noise—if one could call it a noise—of the explosion: more than the sound, we *felt* the explosion, like the fall of a massive weight on the house. The house shook, and the glass trembled in the window frames. After this last explosion I got up and went upstairs to the terrace. The sky was blue and pink, the mountains capped with snow; at a distance the smoke curled upwards from the fire where the missile had landed.

From that day on, we resumed the routine that had been imposed on our daily lives during the bombing and missile attacks. After each explosion there would be numerous phone calls to and from friends and relatives to find out if they were still alive. A savage relief, one of which I always felt a little ashamed, was inevitably triggered by the sound of familiar greetings. The general reaction in those days was a mixture of panic, anger and helplessness. After eight years of war, the Iranian government had done virtually nothing other than expand its propaganda effort to protect the city. It could only boast of the Iranian people's eagerness for martyrdom.

After the first attack, the notoriously overpopulated and polluted city of Tehran had become a ghost town. Most people fled to safer places. I recently read in an account that over a quarter of the population, including many government officials, had deserted the city. A new joke making the rounds was that this was the government's most effective policy yet to deal with Tehran's pollution and population problems. To me, the city had suddenly gained a new pathos, as if, under the attacks and the desertions, it had shed its vulgar veil to reveal a decent, humane face. Tehran looked the way most of its remaining citizens must have felt: sad, forlorn and defenseless, yet not without a certain dignity. The adhesive tape pasted on the window-panes to prevent the implosion of shattered glass told the story of its suffering, a suffering made more poignant because of its newly recovered beauty, the fresh green of trees, washed by spring showers, the blossoms and the rising snowcapped mountains now so near, as if pasted against the sky.

Two years into the war, Iran liberated the city of Khorramshahr, which had been captured by the Iraqis. In the context of other noticeable defeats, Saddam Hussein, encouraged by his worried Arab neighbors, had shown serious signs of reconciliation. But Ayatollah Khomeini and some within the ruling elite refused to sign a truce. They were determined now to capture the holy city of Karballa, in Iraq, the site of martyrdom of Imam Hussein. Any and all methods were used to achieve their purposes, including what became known as "human wave" attacks, where thousands of Iranian soldiers, mainly very young boys ranging in age from ten to sixteen and middle-aged and old men, cleared the minefields by walking over them. The very young were caught up in the government propaganda that offered them a heroic and adventurous life at the front and encouraged them to join the militia, even against their parents' wishes.

My vigils at night with Dashiell Hammett and others resumed. The result was that four years later I added a new section to my class—the mystery tale, beginning with Edgar Allan Poe.

21

With the resumption of the bombing, we moved our classes to the second floor. Every time there was an attack, people impulsively ran to the door and down the stairs; it was safer to move the classes downstairs. The new emergency had emptied the classrooms, so most were now half-full. Many students went back to their hometowns or to towns and cities that were not under attack; some simply stayed home.

The renewal of bombing had made people like Mr. Ghomi more important. They came and went after this with a new sense of urgency. The Islamic associations used every opportunity to disrupt the classes, playing military marches to announce a new victory, or to mourn for a member of the university community who had been martyred in the war. Midway through a passage from *Washington Square* or *Great Expectations,* suddenly the sound of the military march would take over, and after that, no matter how hard we tried to continue, all attempts at discussion were conquered by the march.

This boisterous cacophony was in marked contrast to the silence of the majority of the students and staff. I was actually surprised that more students didn't use these events as an excuse to cut classes or to refrain from doing their homework. Their seeming docility reflected a larger mood of resignation in the city itself. As the war raged on, with no victories, into the eighth year, signs of exhaustion were apparent even among the most zealous. By now, in the streets and in public places, people expressed anti-war sentiments or cursed the perpetrators of the war, while on television and radio the regime's ideal continued to play itself out undeterred. The recurrent image in those days was that of an elderly, bearded, turbaned man calling for unceasing jihad to an audience of adolescent boys with red "martyrs' " bands stretched across their foreheads. These were the dwindling remainders of a once vast group of young people who had been mobilized by the excitement of carrying real guns and the promise of keys to a heaven where they could finally enjoy all the pleasures from which they had abstained in life. Theirs was a world in which defeat was impossible, hence compromise meaningless.

The mullahs would regale us with stories of the unequal battles in which the Shiite saints had been martyred by infidels, while at times breaking into hysterical sobs, whipping their audience into a frenzy, welcoming martyrdom for the sake of God and the Imam. In contrast, the world of the viewers was one of silent defiance, a defiance that was meaningful only in the context of the raucous commitment demanded by the ruling hierarchy, but otherwise permeated, inevitably and historically, by resignation.

Life in death, the death wish of the regime and the obliging missiles of Iraq, could only be tolerated when one knew that the missile would deliver the final message at a moment exactly predetermined and that there was no point in trying to escape it. It was during these days that I realized what this silent resignation meant. It reflected the much maligned mysticism that we all held responsible, at least in part, for our country's historical failures. I understood then that this resignation was perhaps, under the circumstances, the only form of dignified resistance to tyranny. We could not openly articulate what we wished, but we could by our silence show our indifference to the regime's demands.

22

I can still hear the mourning and victory marches that disrupted so many classes to announce the death of a student or staff member in the line of duty or some victory of the army of Islam over its heathen foe. No one bothered to point out that the heathen foe in this warfare were fellow Muslims. The day I have in mind, the march was playing to commemorate the death of one of the leaders of the Muslim Students' Association. After class, I joined a few of my girls who were standing together outside in the yard. They were making fun of the dead student and laughing. They joked that his death was a marriage made in heaven—didn't he and his comrades say that their only beloved was God? This was an allusion to the last wills and testaments made by the martyrs of the war, which were given a great deal of publicity. Almost all claimed that death by martyrdom was their highest desire, because it promised them ultimate union with their true "Beloved."

"Oh yeah, sure, God." The girls were laughing. "God in the guise of all the women he devoured with his eyes before he filed complaints against them for indecency. This was how he got his kicks! They are all sexual perverts, the whole lot of them!"

Nassrin started to tell a story about a teacher of religion in her twelve-year-old cousin's school. This teacher instructed her students to cover themselves and promised them that in paradise they would get their just reward. There, in paradise, they would find streams running with wine and would be wooed by strong, muscular young men. Her fat lips seemed to be drooling when she spoke about the muscular young men that, like prize lamb, she could already see cooked to perfection.

I think something in my rather shocked expression stopped the flow of their mirth. I had not known the young martyr, and if I had, I would most likely not have been fond of him, but this air of jubilation was still shocking.

They felt some explanation was necessary. You don't know him, Mojgan told me. Next to him, Mr. Ghomi is an absolute angel. He was sick, sexually sick. You know, he got a friend expelled because he said the white patch of skin just barely visible under her scarf sexually provoked him. They were like hounds. Then Nassrin jumped in with a screed about one of the female guards. Her searches were like sexual assaults, she insisted. One day she squeezed and fondled Niloofar until she became hysterical. They expel us for laughing out loud, but you know what they did to this woman when she was discovered? She was reprimanded, expelled for a semester and then she was back at her job.

Later, I told Nassrin that as I watched them mocking the dead student, a poem by Bertolt Brecht kept running through my mind. I don't remember it well: "Indeed we live in dark ages, where to speak of trees is a sort of a crime," it went. I wish I could remember the poem better, but there is a line towards the end, something like "Alas, we who wanted kindness, could not be kind ourselves."

Nassrin was quiet for a moment after that. "You don't know what we have suffered," she said at last. "Last week they dropped a bomb near our house. It fell on an apartment building. The neighbors said that in one of the flats there was a birthday party and some twenty-odd children were killed.

"Immediately after the bombs fell and before the ambulances came, six or seven motorcycles arrived from out of nowhere and started circling the area. The riders all wore black, with red headbands across their foreheads. They started shouting slogans: *Death to America! Death to Saddam! Long live Khomeini!* People were very quiet. They just watched them with hatred. Some tried to go forward to help the wounded, but the thugs wouldn't let anyone go near the place. They kept shouting, 'War! War! Until victory!' How do you think we all felt as we stood there watching them?"

This was a ritual: after the bombings, these emissaries of death would prevent any sign of mourning or protest. When two of my cousins were killed by the Islamic regime, some of my relatives who were now on the side of the government called my uncle to congratulate him on the death of his son and daughter-in-law.

We exchanged stories as we walked that day. Nassrin told me more about her time in jail. The whole thing was an accident. I remember how young she had been, still in high school. You're worried about our brutal thoughts against "them," she said, but you know most of the stories you hear about the jails are true. The worst was when they called people's names in the middle of the night. We knew they had been picked for execution. They would say good-bye, and soon after that, we would hear the sound of bullets. We would know the number of people killed on any given night by counting the single bullets that inevitably came after the initial barrage. There was one girl there—her only sin had been her amazing beauty. They brought her in on some trumped-up immorality charge. They kept her for over a month and repeatedly raped her. They passed her from one guard to another. That story got around jail very fast, because the girl wasn't even political; she wasn't with the political prisoners. They married the virgins off to the guards, who would later execute them. The philosophy behind this act was that if they were killed as virgins, they would go to heaven. You talk of betrayals. Mostly they forced those who had "converted" to Islam to empty the last round into the heads of their comrades as tokens of their new loyalty to the regime. If I were not privileged, she said with rancor, if I were not *blessed* with a father who shared their faith, God knows where I would be now— in hell with all the other molested virgins or with those who put a gun to someone's head to prove their loyalty to Islam.

23

On August 4, 1914, Henry James added an entry to his journal: "Everything blackened over for the time blighted by the hideous Public situation. This is (Monday) the August Bank Holiday but with horrible suspense and the worst possibilities in the air." In his last two years of life, Henry James was radically transformed by his intense involvement in the First World War. For the first time, he became socially and politically active, a man who all his life had done his best to keep aloof from the actual passions of existence. His critics, like H. G. Wells, blamed him for his mandarin attitude towards life, which prevented him from any involvement with the social and political issues of the day. He wrote about his experience of World War I that it "almost killed me. I loathed so having lived on and on into anything so hideous and horrible."

When still very young, James had witnessed the Civil War in America. Physically, he was prevented from participating in a war in which his two younger brothers fought with courage and honor by a mysterious backache, acquired on a mission to rescue a burning barn. Psychologically, he kept the war at bay by writing and reading. Perhaps his frenetic activities to support and aid the British in World War I were partly to compensate for his earlier inactivity. It is also true that the war that had evoked his horror mesmerized him. He wrote to a friend, "But I have an imagination of disaster—and see life as ferocious and sinister."

In his youth, James wrote to his father that he was convinced of the "transitory organization of the actual social body. The only respectable state of mind is to constantly express one's perfect dissatisfaction with it." And in his best works of fiction this is what he did. In almost all of his novels the struggle for power is central to the way the plot moves and is resolved. This struggle for power is rooted in the central character's resistance to socially acceptable norms and in his desire for integrity and recognition. In *Daisy Miller,* the tension between the old and the new leads to Daisy's death. In *The Ambassadors,* it is Mrs. Newsome's almost awesome power and pressure over her ambassador and her family that creates the central tension in the plot. It is interesting to note that in this struggle the antagonist always represents worldly concerns, while the protagonist's desire is to preserve a sense of personal integrity in the face of outside aggression.

During the Civil War, when James was discovering his own powers, he wrote in part to compensate for his inability to participate in the war. Now, at the end of his life, he complained about the impotence of words in the face of such inhumanity. In an interview on March 21, 1915, with *The New York Times,* he said: "The war has used up words; they have weakened, they have deteriorated like motor car tires; they have, like millions of other things, been more overstrained and knocked about and voided of the happy semblance during the last six months than in all the long ages before, and we are now confronted with a depreciation of all our terms, or, otherwise speaking, with a loss of expression through increase of limpness, that may well make us wonder what ghosts will be left to walk."

Despite his despair, he turned to words again, this time to write not fiction but war pamphlets, appeals to America to join the war and not to remain indifferent to the suffering and atrocities in Europe. He also wrote poignant letters. In some he expressed his horror at events; in others he consoled friends who had lost a son or a husband in the war.

He fell into a round of activities, visiting wounded Belgian soldiers, and later British soldiers, in hospitals, raising money for Belgian refugees and the wounded and writing war propaganda from the fall of 1914 until December 1915. He also accepted the post of honorary head of the American Volunteer Motor-Ambulance Corps and joined the Chelsea Fund for Belgian refugees. All these were whirlwind activities for a shy and reclusive writer whose most ardent pursuits and passions had previously been reserved for his fiction. As his biographer Leon Edel would later say: ". . . the world seemed to find too much comfort in him and he had to often protect himself against its weeping too profusely on his shoulders." While visiting the hospitals, James likened himself to Whitman visiting the wounded during the Civil War. He said it made him feel less "finished and doddering when I go on certain days and try to pull the conversational cart uphill for them." What inner horror and fascination drove this man, who all his life had shied away from public activity, to become so actively involved in the war effort?

One reason for his involvement was the carnage, the death of so many young men, and the dislocation and destruction. While he mourned the mutilation of existence, he had endless admiration for the simple courage he encountered, both in the many young men who went to war and in those they left behind. In September, James moved to London. "I can hear and see and have informational contact," he wrote; "I eat my heart out alone." He lobbied the U.S. ambassador to Britain and other high American officials and reproached them for their neutrality. And he wrote pamphlets in defense of Britain and her allies.

James emphasized in his many letters one important resource to counter the senselessness of the war. He was aware, as many were not, of the toll such cruelty takes on emotions and of the resistance to compassion that such events engender. In fact, this insensitivity becomes a way of survival. As in his novels, he insisted on the most important of all human attributes—feeling—and railed against "the paralysis of my own powers to do anything but increasingly and inordinately feel."

Years later, on a pink index card I carried across the oceans from Tehran to Washington, D.C., I found two quotations about James's wartime experiences. I had written them out for Nassrin, but I never showed them to her. The first was from a letter he wrote to Clare Sheridan, a friend whose husband—they were newly married—had gone to war and been killed. "I am incapable of telling you not to repine and rebel," he wrote, "because I have so, to my cost, the imagination of all things, and because I am incapable of telling you not to feel. Feel, feel, I say—feel for all you're worth, and even if it half kills you, for that is the only way to live, especially to live at this terrible pressure, and the only way to honour and celebrate these admirable beings who are our pride and our inspiration." In letters to friends, again and again he urges them to feel. Feeling would stir up empathy and would remind them that life was worth living.

One of the peculiarities of James's reaction to the war was the fact that his feelings and emotions were not aroused for patriotic reasons. His own country, America, was not at war. Britain, the country where he had lived for forty years, was, but in all those forty years he had not asked for British citizenship. Now, he finally did. In June 1915, a few months before his death, Henry James was granted British nationality. He had written to his nephew Harry that he wished to make his civil status compatible with his moral and material status. "Hadn't it been for the War, I should certainly have gone on as I was, taking it as the simplest and easiest and even friendliest thing; but the circumstances are utterly altered now."

His more immediate reason for this sudden reversal was that, because of wartime conditions, he had been categorized as a "friendly alien" and needed police permission every time he traveled from London to his home in Sussex. But the more important and symbolic reason was his disenchantment with America's distance from the war. He wrote to a friend, Lilly Perry, that "the immediate presence of the Enemy transforms it from head to foot when one's own nationality does nothing for one that keeps pace with transformation."

The truth is that James, like many other great writers and artists, had chosen his own loyalties and nationality. His true country, his home, was that of the imagination. "Black and hideous to me is the tragedy that gathers," he wrote to his old friend Rhoda Broughton, "and I am sick beyond cure to have lived to see it. You and I, the ornaments of our generation, should have been spared this wreck of our belief that these long years we had seen civilization grow and the worst became possible." He had written to Edith Wharton of "this crash of civilization. The only gleam in the blackness, to me, is the action and the absolute unanimity of this country." James's idea of home was bound up with the idea of civilization. In Sussex, during the war, he had found it difficult to read and impossible to work. He described himself as living under "the funeral spell of our murdered civilization."

When, in September 1914, the Germans attacked and destroyed the Rheims cathedral in France, James wrote: "But no words fill the abyss of it—nor touch it, nor relieve one's heart, nor light by a spark the blackness; the ache of one's heart and the anguish of one's execution aren't mitigated by a shade, even as one brands it as the most hideous crime ever perpetuated against the mind of man."

All his life had been a struggle for power—not political power, which he disdained, but the power of culture. For him culture and civilization were everything. He had said that the greatest freedom of man was his "independence of thought," which enabled the artist to enjoy the "aggression of infinite modes of being." Yet in the face of so much carnage and destruction he felt helpless and impotent. His affinity with England, and with Europe in general, came from that sense of civilization, a tradition of culture and humaneness. But now he had also seen Europe's depravity, its fatigue with its own past, its predatory, cynical nature. It is no wonder he used all his powers, not least the power of words, to help those he believed to be in the right. He was not insensitive to their curative potential, and wrote to a friend, Lucy Clifford, "We must for dear life make our own counter-realities."

24

A few days after my talk with Nassrin, I found two girls standing outside my office just before class. One was Nassrin, with her usual pale smile. The other was dressed in a black chador that covered her from head to foot. After staring at this apparition for a while, I suddenly recognized my old student Mahtab.

For a second all three of us stood there, frozen in place. Nassrin seemed almost detached; detachment had become her defense against unpleasant memories and uncontrollable realities. It took me a few moments to digest this new Mahtab, to make a shift in my mind and transform that Mahtab, the leftist student in her trademark khaki pants whom I had last seen on the grounds of a hospital hunting for her murdered comrades, to this Mahtab, standing with a rueful smile and begging recognition outside my office. I made an uncertain gesture as if to embrace her, but then checked myself and asked her how she had been all these years. Only then did I remember to invite them into my office. I had very little time before my next class.

Mahtab had kept in touch with Nassrin, and when she'd heard I was teaching again at Allameh, she'd plucked up the courage to come and visit. Could she attend my class? And then perhaps after class, if I had time, if it wasn't a problem, she could tell me a little about herself. Of course, I said, she should absolutely come to class.

During the two hours of my lecture on James's *Washington Square,* my eyes often strayed to Mahtab in her black chador, sitting very straight, listening with a sort of alert nervousness I had never seen in her before. After class she followed me to my office, with Nassrin trailing in after her. I asked them to sit down and offered them some tea, which they both refused. Ignoring their refusal, I left to order tea and came back and closed the door, to ensure our privacy. Mahtab sat on the edge of a chair, while Nassrin stood beside her staring at the opposite wall. I told Nassrin to take a seat because she was making me nervous and turned to Mahtab and asked her, in as casual a tone as I could muster, what she had been doing all these years.

She looked at me at first with docile resignation, as if she had not understood my question. Then she fiddled with her fingers, half hidden under the folds of her chador, and said, Well, I have been where Nassrin was. Shortly after the day I saw you at the demonstrations, I was arrested. They gave me only five years, which was lucky—they knew I was no big shot in our organization. And then I was let off early. I got out after two and a half years, for good behavior. She left me to guess what good behavior meant to the kind of people who had put her in jail. There was a knock at the door, and Mr. Latif entered with the tea. We all paused until he had left the room.

I did think of you and of our classes, she said after he had left. After the initial interrogations, she had been assigned to a cell with fifteen others. There, she had met another student of mine, Razieh. Balancing the small cup of tea I had offered her in one hand, without letting her chador slip, she said, "Razieh told me about your classes on Hemingway and James at Alzahrah, and I told her about the *Gatsby* trial. We laughed a lot. You know, she was executed. I was lucky, she said. Less than a year after she was released from prison, Mahtab had married and had a baby; she was expecting another one. Three months pregnant. It doesn't show from under the chador, she said, pointing shyly to her stomach.

There was nothing I could ask her about my murdered student. I did not want to know how they had lived in their cell, what other memories they had shared. I felt that if she told me, I might do something foolish and would not make it to my afternoon class. I asked her about her baby's age but not about her husband. Could I ask her my favorite question: Did you two fall in love? I had heard about so many girls who had married soon after their release from jail, married because they could appease the suspicions of their jailers, who somehow thought of marriage as an antidote to political activities, or to prove to their parents that they were "good" girls now, or simply because there was nothing else for them to do.

"You know, I always thought *Gatsby* was so beautiful," Mahtab told me as she was getting up to go. "And the scene you read to us about that day when Daisy meets Gatsby again for the first time in five years, her face wet under the rain. And the other scene, when she tells him he looks so cool and she means to say that she loves him. We had fun at *Gatsby*'s trial, you know?" Yes, I knew. The fact that they remembered *Gatsby* and even remembered having fun with him would have been gratifying under different circumstances, but then, I was thinking among other thoughts, how the joy of reading *Gatsby* would now be forever marred by being linked in my memory with Mahtab's time in jail and Razieh's execution.

I felt I had to open the window, to let the air in after they were gone. From my office I could see the yard, where snow almost caressed the trees. There was a heaviness Mahtab had left behind, a tangible atmosphere of pain and resignation. Was she the lucky one, the one who was released and got married to some guy, the one who reported to the prison guards every month, the one with a hometown in ruins and a two-year-old child? She was lucky and Razieh was dead. Nassrin had also called herself lucky; my students had developed a strange concept of fortune.

The other quotation from James on the pink index card records his reaction to the death of Rupert Brooke, the beautiful young English poet who died of blood poisoning during the war. "I confess that I have no philosophy, nor piety, nor patience, no art of reflection," he wrote, "no theory of compensation to meet things so hideous, so cruel, and so mad, they are just unspeakably horrible and irremediable to me and I stare at them with angry and almost blighted eyes."

Next to the last words, I added at some later point in pencil: *Razieh.*

25

What strange places my students met, from what dark corners did they bring me news! I could not travel, I cannot travel even now to those places, no matter how many times I hear about them. Yet there must have been something cheerful about Razieh and Mahtab in their cell, not knowing if they will live or die, talking about James and Fitzgerald. Perhaps *cheerful* is not the right word. I mention this because it is not where I had imagined they would take my favorite novels, my golden emissaries from that other world. I think of Razieh in that jail, and of Razieh facing the firing squad on some night, perhaps the same night I was reading *The Long Goodbye* or *The Bostonians.*

I remember now, as I did then, that one of the most surprising things about Razieh was her love of James. I remember the class I taught at Alzahrah University and all its frustrations. The distinguishing feature of this so-called university was that it was the only all-girls college in Iran. It had a small campus with a beautiful and leafy garden and I taught two courses there while also teaching at the University of Tehran, in the first year after my return. I was shocked when, grading the midterm exams, I noticed that most of the class, rather than respond to the questions, had simply repeated my classroom lectures. In four cases this repetition was amazing. They had transcribed seemingly word for word what I had said about *A Farewell to Arms,* including my "you know"s and my digressions about Hemingway's personal life. Reading these exam papers, I felt I had been given a bizarre parody of my own lectures.

I thought they had cheated; it was inconceivable to me that they could have re-created my lectures so precisely without notes. My colleagues, however, informed me that this was regular practice: the students memorized everything their teachers said and gave it back to them without changing a word.

At the next class after that exam, I was furious. It was one of the only times in my teaching career that I got angry and showed it in class. I was young and inexperienced, and I thought certain standards were expected and understood. I remember I told them it would have been better if they had cheated—at least cheating required a certain ingenuity—but to repeat my lecture word for word, to include not so much as a glimmer of themselves in their response . . . I went on and on, and as I continued, I became more righteous in my indignation. It was the sort of anger one gets high on, the kind one takes home to show off to family and friends.

They were all silent, even those who had not committed the sins I had attributed to them. I dismissed the class early, although the culprits and a few others stayed behind to plead their case. They were docile even in their pleas: they wanted to be forgiven, they did not know any better, this was what most professors expected. Two were in tears. What could they do? They had never learned any better. From the first day they had set foot in elementary school, they had been told to memorize. They had been told that their own opinions counted for nothing.

Razieh stayed until they had all left. Then she told me she wanted to talk to me. "It isn't their fault," she said. "I mean, it is in a way, but

I always thought you were one of those who cared." The echo of reproach in her voice startled me. Would I have been so angry if I didn't care? "Yes, that is the easy way," she said quietly. "But you must think about where we are coming from. Most of these girls have never had anyone praise them for anything. They have never been told that they are any good or that they should think independently. Now you come in and confront them, accusing them of betraying principles they have never been taught to value. You should've known better."

There she was, this small girl, my student, lecturing me. She couldn't have been more than twenty, but somehow she managed to look authoritative without being impertinent. They love this class, she said. They even learned to love Catherine Sloper, though she isn't pretty and lacks everything they look for in a heroine. I said, In these revolutionary times it's hardly surprising that students wouldn't care much about the trials and tribulations of a plain, rich American girl at the end of the nineteenth century. But she protested vehemently. In these revolutionary times, she said, they care even more. I don't know why people who are better off always think that those less fortunate than themselves don't want to have the good things—that they don't want to listen to good music, eat good food or read Henry James.

She was a slight girl, slight and dark. Her seriousness must have been a burden to her fragile frame. Even so, she was not frail; how a person this fragile looking could give an impression of such solidity I do not know. Razieh. I don't remember her last name, but her first name I can use without having to worry about security, because she is dead. It seems ironic that I should only be able to use the real names of dead people. She had the respect of her classmates and, in those deeply ideological times, was listened to by girls from both ideological extremes. She was an active member of the Mujahideen, but this didn't keep her from being suspicious of their cant. She had no father, and her mother earned her living as a cleaning woman. Both Razieh and her mother were deeply religious, and it was her religious belief that attracted her to the Mujahideen: she felt contempt for the Islamists who had usurped power.

Razieh had an amazing capacity for beauty. She said, You know, all my life I have lived in poverty. I had to steal books and sneak into movie houses—but, God, I loved those books! I don't think any rich kid has ever cherished *Rebecca* or *Gone with the Wind* the way I did when I borrowed the translations from houses where my mother worked. But James—he is so different from any other writer I have ever read. I think I am in love, she added, laughing.

Razieh was such a strange mixture of contradictory passions. She was bitter and determined, stern and tough, and yet she loved novels and writing with a real passion. She said she did not wish to write but to teach. She was an inarticulate writer. She said, We envy people like you and we want to be you; we can't, so we destroy you. After I left that college, I saw her only once. I think she felt that by leaving their small college to teach at the University of Tehran I had abandoned them. I asked her to come to my classes, to keep in touch. But she never did.

A few months after the bloody demonstration in the summer of 1981, I was walking down a wide, sunny street near the University of Tehran when, coming from the opposite direction, I saw a figure wrapped in a black chador, a small figure. The only reason I paid attention to her at all was that she paused for a second, startled. It was Razieh. She did not say hello, and in her look I could see a denial, a plea not to be recognized. We glanced at each other and passed. I will never forget that glance on that day, and her so very thin small body, her narrow face and large eyes, like an owl's, or an imp's in some invented tale.

26

In memory of my student Razieh, I will now digress and talk about her favorite book. I shall consider this an in memoriam.

What was it about *Washington Square* that had so intrigued Razieh? True, there had been identification—she did see something of herself in its hapless heroine—but it was not that simple.

Washington Square seems straightforward enough, yet the characters cheat you: they act contrary to expectation, beginning with Catherine Sloper, the heroine. Catherine is trapped by her clever and materially successful father, who ignores her with contempt. He never forgives his devoted and shy daughter for the loss of his beloved wife, who died in childbirth. Moreover, he cannot get over his disappointment at Catherine's failure to be brilliant and beautiful. Catherine is also entrapped by her love of Morris Townsend, the "beautiful" (her word) young spendthrift who woos and courts her for her money. Mrs. Penniman, her shallow, sentimental and meddling widowed aunt, who tries to appease Catherine's romantic aspirations by proxy through matchmaking, completes the evil triumvirate.

Catherine is an exceptional heroine, even for James. She is the inverse of our ideas of what a heroine should be: hefty, healthy, plain, dull, literal and honest. She is squeezed in between three colorful, clever, egocentric characters, who abuse and underestimate her while she remains loyal and good. One by one, James strips away from Catherine the qualities that make a heroine attractive; what he takes away from her he distributes among the other three characters. To Morris Townsend he bestows "beauty" and brilliance; to Mrs. Penniman, a Machiavellian love of intrigue; and to Dr. Sloper, he gives irony and judgment. But at the same time he deprives them of the single quality that distinguishes his heroine: compassion.

Like many heroines, Catherine is wrong; she has a gift for self-deception. She believes that Morris loves her, and refuses to believe her father's protestations to the contrary. James did not like his heroes and heroines to be infallible. In fact, they all make mistakes, harmful mostly to themselves. Their mistakes, like the tragic flaw in a classical tragedy, become essential to their development and maturity.

Dr. Sloper, the most villainous of the three, is also the most correct. He is correct in his professional and in his private life and he makes all the right prognostications about his daughter, or almost all. He correctly, and with his usual touch of irony, predicts that Mrs. Penniman will try to persuade his daughter that some "young man with a moustache is in love with her. It will be quite untrue; no young man with a moustache or without will ever be in love with Catherine." From the beginning, Dr. Sloper doubts Morris Townsend's honorable intentions towards his daughter, and does his best to prevent their marriage. But what he can never penetrate is his daughter's heart. She constantly surprises him, because he does not really know her. He underestimates Catherine, but he does something worse: his failure is a failure of the heart. For Catherine's heart must be broken twice, once by her alleged lover, and then by her father. He is guilty of the same crime of which he accuses Morris, namely, lack of love for his daughter. Thinking of Dr. Sloper, we are reminded of one of Flaubert's insights: "You should have a heart in order to feel other people's hearts." And I was immediately reminded of poor Mr. Ghomi, who missed all these subtleties—or, rather, fortunate Mr. Ghomi, for whom no such scruples existed: in his book, a daughter must obey her father, and that was the end of the story.

Dr. Sloper never sees his daughter's needs. He complains about her lack of accomplishment yet never observes her hidden yearnings for music and theater. He sees her foolishness but misses her intense longing to be loved. It is not an accident that in her first meeting with Morris Townsend, at her cousin's wedding, Catherine, who has "suddenly developed a lively taste for dress," wears a red satin dress. The narrator informs us that "her great indulgence" was "really the desire of a rather inarticulate nature to manifest itself; she sought to be eloquent in her garments, and to make up for her diffidence of speech by a fine frankness of costume." The dress is a disaster; the color does not suit her, and makes her look ten years older. It is also the subject of her father's wittiest remarks. That same night, Catherine meets Morris and falls in love. Twice, her father misses his chance to understand and help her.

Thus, Dr. Sloper commits the most unforgivable crime in fiction—blindness. Pity is the password, says the poet John Shade in Nabokov's *Pale Fire*. This respect for others, empathy, lies at the heart of the novel. It is the quality that links Austen to Flaubert and James to Nabokov and Bellow. This, I believe, is how the villain in modern fiction is born: a creature without compassion, without empathy. The personalized version of good and evil usurps and individualizes the more archetypal concepts, such as courage or heroism, that shaped the epic or romance. A hero becomes one who safeguards his or her individual integrity at almost any cost.

I think most of my students would have agreed with this definition of evil, because it was so close to their own experience. Lack of empathy was to my mind the central sin of the regime, from which all the others flowed. My generation had tasted individual freedom and lost it; no matter how painful the loss, the recollection was there to protect us from the desert of the present. But what did this new generation have to safeguard them? Like Catherine's, their desires, their yearnings, their urges to express themselves, were manifested in bizarre ways.

As she is shunned by her father, manipulated by her aunt and finally deserted by her suitor, Catherine Sloper learns, painfully, to stand up to each and every one of them—not in their way but in her own, quietly and humbly. In all respects, she maintains her own style of dealing with events and with people. She defies her father even on his deathbed by refusing to promise that she will never marry Morris, although she has no intention by now of doing so. She refuses to "open her heart" to her aunt and appease her sentimental curiosity, and in the last pages of the book, in a quietly magnificent scene, she refuses the hand her fickle lover has now extended to her after twenty years. She surprises them with her every act. In each of these instances her actions arise not from a desire for revenge but from a sense of propriety and dignity, to use two outmoded terms much favored by Jamesian protagonists.

Only Catherine has the capacity to change and mature, although here, as in so many of James's novels, our heroine pays a dear price for this change. And she does take a form of revenge on both her father and her suitor: she refuses to give in to them. In the end, she has her triumph.

If we can call it that. One can believe James's claim to an "imagination of disaster"; so many of his protagonists are unhappy in the end, and yet he gives them an aura of victory. It is because these characters depend to such a high degree on their own sense of integrity that for them, victory has nothing to do with happiness. It has more to do with a settling within oneself, a movement inward that makes them whole. Their reward is not *happiness*—a word that is central in Austen's novels but is seldom used in James's universe. What James's characters gain is self-respect. And we become convinced that this must be the hardest thing in the world when, as we come to the end of the last page of *Washington Square,* after Catherine's exasperated suitor leaves, we learn that: "Catherine, meanwhile, in the parlour, picking up her morsel of fancy-work, had seated herself with it again—for life, as it were."

27

I rang the bell to his apartment one more time, but again there was no response. I stepped back from the door and looked at the window of his living room: the curtains were closed; all was cream-colored and quiet. I had an appointment with him that afternoon, after which Bijan would pick me up and take me to a friend's house for dinner. I was thinking of finding a phone to call him when a neighbor with a bag of fruit appeared, opened the front door and invited me in with a welcoming smile. I thanked him and ran up the stairs. The door to his apartment was open, but there was no response to my repeated calls, so I went in.

The apartment was in tip-top shape, everything in its place: the rocking chair, the kilim, the day's newspapers neatly folded on the table, the bed made. I wandered from room to room looking for some sign of disorder, some clue to this break in the routine. The door was open. He must have gone out for something—say, coffee or milk— and left the door open for me. What else could explain his absence? What else could it be? Could they have come to get him? Could they have taken him away? Once that idea entered my mind, it refused to leave. It kept reverberating like a mantra: they've taken him away, they've taken him away, they've . . . It was not unknown—they'd done it before to others. Once, a writer's apartment was found unlocked. His friends had found on the kitchen table the remnants of his breakfast, the yolk of an egg streaming across the plate, a piece of toast, butter, some strawberry jam, a half-empty glass of tea. Every room seemed to describe an unfinished act: in the bedroom, an unmade bed; in the office, piles of books scattered on the floor and over the big stuffed chair; on the desk, an open book, a pair of glasses. Two weeks later they discovered that he had been whisked away by the secret police, for questioning. These questionings were part of our everyday lives.

But why? Why should they take him? He had no political affiliations, wrote no inflammatory articles. But then, he has so many friends. . . . How do I know he isn't secretly involved in some political group, an underground guerrilla leader? The thought seemed absurd, but any explanation was better than none at all: I had to find a reason for the sudden absence of a man bound to routines, conscious of his obligations, always exactly five minutes early to his appointments, a man, I suddenly realized, who had deliberately created an image of himself out of his routines, bread crumbs for us to follow.

I went to the phone by the couch in the living room. Should I call Reza, his best friend? But then I'd worry him too—better wait for a while; maybe he'd return. And what if they come back and find me here? Shut up, *shut up*! Just wait, he'll be back any minute. I glanced at my watch. He's only forty-five minutes late. Only? I'll wait for another half hour, then I will decide.

I went to the library and scanned the rows of books, all organized by subject and title. I picked up a novel, put it back. I picked up a book of criticism and then I noticed Eliot's *Four Quartets*. Yes, not a bad idea. I opened it the way we used to open Hafez, closing our eyes, asking our question and letting our finger rest somewhere at random. It opened to the page in the middle of "Burnt Norton," beginning with the lines "At the still point of the turning world. Neither flesh nor/fleshless;/Neither from nor towards; at the still point, there the dance/is."

I closed the book, moved back to the couch and felt exhausted.

The phone rang. If it's a friend, he'll hang up after the third ring. And if not? What if it's him? He left the door open, he called my home and found no one there, he's calling me here. But then why no note? If it had been me, I probably would have forgotten to leave a note, I with my untidy mind, but not him—he'd remember. But what if he didn't have time to write, or *couldn't* write? If they had come to take him away, would he say, Wait, let me write a note to this friend, whom you can come and pick up later: Dear Azar, Sorry, couldn't wait for you. Stay where you are; they'll be back for you soon.

Suddenly I panicked. I have to call Reza, I thought. Better call him than die of anxiety. Two heads are better than one and all that. I called Reza and explained the situation. His voice was soothing, but did I sense a sudden panic rimmed around his soothing words? He said, Give me a half hour and I'll be there.

As soon as I put the receiver down, I regretted having called him. If something bad is going to happen, why involve someone else, and if he is okay. . . . I went back to *Four Quartets,* and this time turned to the beginning, the lines I used to read aloud to myself when I first studied Eliot in college:

> Time present and time past
> Are both perhaps present in time future,
> And time future contained in time past.
> If all time is eternally present
> All time is unredeemable.

How had I missed that point about the unredeemability of the present when I had read it so many times before? I started to read aloud, walking in circles around the room:

> What might have been is an abstraction
> Remaining a perpetual possibility
> Only in a world of speculation.
> What might have been and what has been
> Point to one end, which is always present.

Now I came to a favorite part, and felt myself on the edge of tears:

> Footfalls echo in the memory
> Down the passage which we did not take
> Towards the door we never opened
> Into the rose-garden. My words echo
> Thus, in your mind.
>   But to what purpose
> Disturbing the dust on a bowl of rose-leaves
> I do not know.

I repeated the last two lines, feeling tears, to my dismay, running down my cheeks. His friend finally arrived. I let him in, and immediately received his comfort and transferred to him my anxiety and fear. He held my hand and patted me on the back. Don't worry, he said. He's nuts—maybe he had to go to an emergency editing session. He's been known to disappear on one of those assignments for days. But when he makes an appointment the day before? Couldn't he have left a note? After a while we both sat down on the couch, holding hands, feeling forsaken and intimate with our doubts and fears.

We didn't notice the door open, we heard a key in the lock. He had forgotten he'd left the door unlocked. He came in and his first words were, I'm so sorry. I was out with the Kid. He looked very pale and, if arched eyebrows could sag, I would say that his had sagged. Fatigue fought with regret, with his realization of the anxiety he had put us through. Well, the least you could have done is get yourself arrested or come in with your interrogators, I said feebly. You say you were out with the Kid?

The Kid was his name for a grown-up man, eighteen and a high school senior when he first met him in one of his classes that year of the revolution. My magician had a special affection for the Kid, who wanted to go to medical school but was fascinated by his talk of Aeschylus and Chaplin. He passed the entrance exam with a first, only to be denied a place because he admitted to being a Baha'i. During the Shah's reign, the Baha'is were protected and flourished—one sin for which the Shah was never forgiven. After the revolution, their property was confiscated and their leaders murdered. Baha'is had no civic rights under the new Islamic constitution and were barred from schools, universities and workplaces.

The Kid could easily have taken an ad in the paper, like so many others did, denying that he belonged to the decadent and imperialist sect, disowning his parents—who, luckily, were out of harm's way in Europe—and claiming to have been converted by some ayatollah. That's all it would have taken and the doors would have been opened to him. Instead, he had admitted to being a Baha'i, although he was not even a practicing Baha'i and had no religious inclinations, denying himself in the process a brilliant career in medicine, for there was no doubt that he would have been a brilliant doctor.

Now he lived with his old grandmother and did odd jobs—he couldn't hold any one of them for long. He was currently working at a pharmacy, the nearest he would ever come to being a doctor. I had never met him, but I'd heard of him, of his devastating good looks, his love for a Muslim girl, who would soon forsake him to marry a rich older man and would later try to make up with him as a married woman.

The Kid had called just before lunch. His grandmother, who had been ill for a long time, had died and he was calling from the hospital, half-choked. He kept repeating he didn't know what to do. So my magician had left in a hurry. He thought he'd be back soon, long before my visit.

He'd found him standing in front of the hospital, beside a soft and boneless woman: the aunt. The Kid had almost cried, but crying in front of a godlike mentor was impossible, so he had been grown-up, his dry eyes worse than tears. There were no burial places for Baha'is; the regime had destroyed the Baha'i cemetery in the first years of the revolution, demolishing the graves with a bulldozer. There were rumors that the cemetery had been turned into a park or a playground. Later, I found out it had become a cultural center, called Bakhtaran. What were you supposed to do when your grandmother died if there was no cemetery?

I got up and started pacing around the room. You sit down, he said, pointing to a spot on the couch beside him. Sit here and be quiet. Don't fidget—that's a good girl. I said, Before you start up again, let me make a phone call. I rang up Bijan and told him to go to the party without me, I would join him later. When I returned, I heard Reza saying, It's amazing, this obsession with taking possession not just of the living but also of the dead. At the start of the revolution, the revolutionary prosecutor bulldozed Reza Shah's grave, destroying the monument and creating a public toilet in its place—which he inaugurated by pissing in it. I interrupted their conversation and asked if they wanted coffee. I brought out three mismatched mugs and set them on the table with a pot of boiling water and some instant coffee. He got up, went to the refrigerator and brought us a box of chocolates; always the perfect gentleman.

So the Kid had borrowed a car from a friend and was standing there with his sniffling aunt. He couldn't imagine leaving him with the aunt to take care of the corpse and decided to go with them, despite the Kid's strong protestations. He had thought of me and called my house, but there was no answer. No, he had not thought of calling Reza or any other friend. He had gotten into the car with the Kid.

They drove to the back of the hospital, and there, the corpse, already wrapped in a white shroud, was given to them. They each took hold of one end and put the corpse in the trunk of the car. They then proceeded to drive to a garden he had heard of outside Tehran for the burial. They worried they might be stopped—what would they tell the militia? How would they prevent them from opening the trunk? The Kid worried about the car. After all, it belonged to his friend and he didn't want to drag innocent people into this. Innocent people! my magician cried out. Can you imagine feeling guilty about trying to bury your grandmother, to give her any kind of burial, never mind a decent one?

I wanted to touch him, but the experience had put him outside of our reach: he was still there in that car, driving towards the garden. There were many such instances, when expressions of sympathy could not be exchanged. What do you say to someone who is telling you about the rape and murder of virgins—I'm sorry, I feel your pain? My magician and Nassrin were of the type who did not want sympathy; they expected us to understand and to tailor our empathy to the shape of their grief. Of course, with him it was worse: he felt guilt and anger.

They drove down the same highway they had taken so many times, towards the Caspian Sea. The land, the trees, the mountains, slipped by and the aunt did not say a word; she just sat in the back, and from time to time they heard her sniffles and snorts. The men could not talk about anything real; they made halfhearted small talk about last year's Oscars.

The garden looked like any other garden; behind the mud-brick walls, he could see the tall trees inside. They honked. An old man opened the gate and they were led inside. They were shown a few plots with headstones; two freshly dug plots were ready. Families of the dead had to perform the final ritual of washing the corpse and putting it in the shroud. The Kid and his aunt went into a small building, and my magician sat there holding a small bouquet of daffodils and narcissus he had bought along the way. The rest went by quickly, like a dream: placing the body in the ground, throwing earth over it, standing by the freshly dug grave for a few moments and leaving the flowers behind. The Kid paid the old man. They got back into the car and drove straight to his apartment, and now here I am, at your service. Looking at me, a sudden kindness blossomed in his eyes. And I apologize, he said. How thoughtless of me not to have thought of what you would feel.

We sat there for a little while longer. If we talked, I don't remember. Then I got up and said, Could you call me a taxi please, and he did. When the doorbell rang, it took me a while to put on my robe and then the scarf and to find my bag and say good-bye. We had not talked about the object of my visit—it all seemed rather pointless. Of course, there would be tomorrow and I would call again and arrange another visit and we would talk. For now, I kissed both of them on the cheek, thanked Reza and hurried down the stairs to the waiting car.

28

Two nights before the announcement of the first cease-fire in the war of cities, a few friends came over to watch John Ford's *Mogambo*. Mr. Forsati by now was in the habit of bringing me videos. One day, out of the blue, he followed me to my office, carrying a small parcel in his hands. It turned out to be a video of *Big*. From then on, he brought me films, mostly second- or third-rate American releases. It was said that the Islamists procured them from the sailors on duty in the Gulf, who were allowed to watch forbidden films, and smuggled them on-shore. After a while, I began to make requests. I asked for classics, like *Jules and Jim* and *Modern Times,* or films by Howard Hawks, John Ford, Buñuel or Fellini. These names were new to him, and at first it was more difficult for him to find them, perhaps because they were of little interest to sailors. One day he brought me *Mogambo*. He said it was a gift. He never thought he'd fall in love with an old film, but there it was: he had, and he had a hunch I'd like it.

That night there was a blackout for several hours, obliterating the whole city. We sat by candlelight and talked and drank Vishnovka, a homemade cherry vodka, a few fairly distant explosions interrupting the otherwise calm flow of conversation. The next night it was an-nounced that Iraq would accept a cease-fire if it could fire the last mis-sile. It was like a game played between two children—what mattered most was who would get the last word.

The cease-fire lasted only two days. Many people, believing it would hold, had returned to Tehran. The shops were open late and the streets were overcrowded with people catching up on their New Year's shopping. A few hours before the cease-fire was broken, I made a bet with a friend about how long it would last. These wagers had become a regular habit. We would bet on when, where and how many missiles would hit the city. It helped reduce the tension, however lugubrious some of our victories may have seemed.

The attacks were resumed on Monday at 10:30 P.M. By early Tuesday morning, six missiles had hit Tehran. Many who had just arrived back began almost immediately to leave again. The sudden hush that fell over the city was intermittently broken by military marches blasting out into the streets from mosques, government offices, Revolutionary Committee buildings and private houses. They were interrupted by "important announcements" about missile attacks on Baghdad and new victories over the "imperialist-Zionist enemy." We were to rejoice over these victories of "light over darkness" and console ourselves with the thought that the Iraqis were suffering the same fate.

29

The universities were closed down before the Iranian New Year on March 21, 1988, and remained closed until the cease-fire. People were tired and seemed not to care about the government's edicts anymore. Weddings and parties went on, heedless of the militia and the Revolutionary Guards. The black-clad men on motorcycles—death's cupbearers, as they were called by some—disappeared from the scenes of bombings, where people increasingly shouted out their despair and anger, cursing both Saddam and our own regime. Much of daily life came to a standstill in those days, and we sought ever more active means of escape. Going on climbs in the mountains circling Tehran or taking long walks became a daily fixture, through which we struck many new, if rarely lasting, friendships.

The Iraqi dictator was by now a household name, almost as familiar as Khomeini, for he had nearly as much control over our lives. His tremendous power over our destiny had turned him into an intrusive presence. No key decision could be arrived at without taking him and his future moves into consideration. His name was mentioned frequently and casually. A major character in children's games, his every move, past, present and future, was a favorite topic of conversation.

Because of Iraq's continual and concentrated bombing of major cities, especially Tehran, the regime was forced to relax its reign. For the first time, the Revolutionary Guards and Committees became less visible; the vice squads were almost totally withdrawn from the streets. At a time when Tehran was in deepest mourning, it was able to put on its gayest face. Women, in growing numbers, shunned the prescribed dark colors to put on their brightest scarves; many wore makeup, and their nylon stockings became more visible under their robes. Parties featuring music and alcohol were thrown without much concern for the raiding squads, without having to bribe the local committees.

The place where the regime tried to keep its hold, ironically, was in the realm of our imagination. Television was saturated with documentaries on the two world wars. As the now almost empty streets of Tehran became livelier and more colorful, on television we saw Londoners searching for food in garbage cans or huddled together in underground shelters. We were told about how the people of Stalingrad and Leningrad had survived the harsh siege of their cities on a diet of their comrades' flesh. This was not only to justify an increasingly unpopular and desperate war, whose end the regime had refused to contemplate until it had "liberated" the whole of Iraq. It was also aimed at intimidating and controlling a restive population, by holding up the prospect of even greater misfortune, and by reminding us that all had once not been so well on the Western front.

We had come to believe in rumors. A new one began to spread that spring: Iraq had in its possession new and far more powerful missiles that could land on any part of the city without any prior warning whatsoever. So we told ourselves to be content with the ordinary bombs, and prayed to be spared the missiles. Finally, in April, we were attacked by the dreaded missiles. Soon after that, the Iraqi chemical bombing of a Kurdish town inside Iraq heralded an even more horrifying prospect. The newest rumors were that Iraq planned to use chemical bombs against Tehran and other major cities. The regime used the news to create a massive panic. The daily papers came out with extras on how to combat a chemical attack; a new alarm signal—green this time—was introduced. A few green-signal practices, apart from causing general panic, also convinced us that nobody would escape the paralyzing effects of the new threat. A special "Combat the

Chemical Bomb Day" was announced, during which the Revolutionary Guards paraded up and down the streets with their own gas masks
and vehicles, bringing the traffic in much of the city to a standstill.

Soon after this, a missile hit a bakery in a crowded section of
Tehran. People who were gathered at the scene began to see clouds of
flour rising in the air. Someone shouted, "Chemical bomb!" In the
ensuing scramble, many were injured as people and cars crashed into
each other. And to be sure, the Revolutionary Guards, with their gas
masks, arrived sometime later, to the rescue.

By now, most districts carried some inescapable sign of having
been hit by missile attacks, which continued unabated. Rows of ordinary houses and shops gave way to broken windows; then a few
houses where the damage was more extensive; then the ruins of a
house or two, where only the barest structure could be discerned in
the rubble. Going to visit a friend or a shop or supermarket, we drove
past these sights as if moving along a symmetrical curve. We would
begin our ride on the rising side of the curve of devastation until we
reach the ruined peak, followed by a gradual return to familiar sites
and, finally, our intended destination.

30

I had not seen Mina for a long time, and the festivities surrounding
the Iranian New Year offered a good excuse to renew our relations. I
remember the day I went to her house well, because it coincided with
two important events: a former colleague was getting married, and
Tehran was hit with seven missiles. The first explosion sounded as I
came out of a flower shop. A worker from the shop, some passersby
and I stood to watch the cloud rising on the western horizon of the
city. It looked white and innocent enough, like a child who has just
committed a murder.

Mina was happy to see me. In many ways, I was by then her only
contact with academia. Her family had sold their mansion and moved
to a new house, a smaller, ghostly version of their old home. Mina was
still dressed in black. She seemed faded and unhappy. She told me she
kept going through bouts of depression and was on medication.

I asked her, with a certain persistence, about her unfinished book on James. I had the simplistic and wishful notion that once she started to work on the book, everything would fall into place. She said she would never resume her work. She needed time to breathe, she added later, to enable her to concentrate on her work again. In the meantime, she had translated Leon Edel's *The Modern Psychological Novel* and was in the process of translating Ian Watt's *The Rise of the Novel*. She said, Of course, these books aren't so fashionable these days. Everyone has gone postmodern. They can't even read the text in the original—they're so dependent on some pseudo-philosopher to tell them what it says. I told her not to worry, that nobody taught James anymore either, that he too was unfashionable, which was a sign that we must be doing something right.

Mina was a meticulous and literal translator. This created difficulties with her publisher, who wanted her to make the text "accessible" to the public. She was contemptuous of the existing translations of Virginia Woolf. She refused to use the Iranian translation of *Mrs. Dalloway* for the quotations in the Edel book, and this had caused her more trouble.

She asked me about my classes. I told her my students and I were having a hard time with James, especially with his prose. She smiled. Then your students are in good company, she said. Some of the best-known critics and writers have complained about it. Yes, but here our problem is different, you know. I assigned them more obviously difficult novelists—Nabokov and Joyce—but somehow they're having a harder time with James. The surface realism gives them the illusion that he should be easier to understand, and baffles them all the more. Look here, I said. What's the deal with this word *fuliginous*? He uses it in *The Bostonians*—"fuliginous eyes"—and in *The Ambassadors,* to describe Waymarsh's face. What does the blasted word mean? You know it cannot be found in the American Heritage Dictionary?

Mina could not let me continue; her loyalties would not allow it. She, like Catherine Sloper, had an "undiverted heart" and, despite her brilliant mind, sometimes took things awfully literally. She said, with evident emotion, How else but by giving volume to his words could he create the illusion of life? Are you thinking of dropping him?

She had asked me this question a long time ago, and every once in a while that anxiety returned to her. I said, No, of course not. How could I drop a novelist who in describing a brilliant woman says not dazzling or incandescent but "unobscured Miss B"? I wish I could steal his intricacies of language. But give my kids a break—remember, most of them were fed on Steinbeck's *The Pearl*.

I told her what fun we had the day we chose our best and worst passages. Mahshid pointed to the "bird haunted trees," and Nassrin read a passage from *The Ambassadors* describing a lunch by the waterside: "—the mere way Madame de Vionnet, opposite him over their intensely white table-linen, their omelette aux tomates, their bottle of straw-coloured Chablis, thanked him for everything almost with the smile of a child, while her grey eyes moved in and out of their talk, back to the quarter of the warm spring air, in which early summer had already begun to throb, and then back again to his face and their human questions."

These talks with Mina, seemingly so irrelevant to the events around us, were a great source of satisfaction to us both. It is only now, when I try to gather up the morsels of those days, that I discover how little, if ever, we talked about our personal lives—about love and marriage and how it felt to have children, or not to. It seemed as if, apart from literature, the political had devoured us, eliminating the personal or private.

31

One of the last missiles to land before the cease-fire hit a nearby house, in an alley where two of our friends, a couple and their youngest daughter, lived. They had a publishing house and bookstore not far from their home, where many Iranian writers and intellectuals gathered and where debates raged late into the evening. The night before, a few of my friends, including Laleh, had stayed with us watching films until almost dawn. In the cozy confusion of a sleepover, we fixed a breakfast of bread, fresh cream, homemade jam and coffee. I was in the kitchen when I felt the house go down with a shudder. It had been too close. Soon we discovered just how close.

After the bomb, many people ran towards the site, while dozens, mostly women and children, bleeding, shouting, crying and cursing, were running in the opposite direction. When the Revolutionary Guards and the ambulances arrived, the cries became louder. Timidly, the guards set out to inspect the area. In the yard of the house where the missile had landed, two children were lying senseless. The guards dragged out two dead women from under the rubble; one was very young, wearing a colorful housedress. The other was middle-aged and fat; her skirt clung to her thighs.

The next evening, we went over to console our friends. It was raining gently; the air scattered the smell of fresh earth and spring blossoms. A small crowd had gathered near the devastated houses. Our hostess led us inside and, gracious as ever, served us fragrant tea and small, delicious pastries. She had somehow managed to fill the kitchen with big bowls of lilacs.

The windows were shattered. Shards of glass had pierced their valuable paintings, and they had spent the previous night removing glass from various parts of the house. Smiling, she took us to the rooftop. Behind us rose my beloved mountains and in front of us were the three demolished houses. In the least damaged one, a man and a woman seemed to be searching for things to salvage from what must have been the second floor of the building. The house in the middle was now mostly rubble.

32

The war ended the way it had started, suddenly and quietly. At least that is how it seemed to us. The effects of the war would stay with us for a long time, perhaps forever. At first we felt bewildered, and wondered how to go back to what had passed for ordinary life before the war. The Islamic regime had reluctantly accepted peace because of its inability to ward off Iraq's attacks. Constant defeats on the battle-ground had left many within the militia and Revolutionary Guards in a disposition of despair and disillusion. The mood among the regime's adherents was low. Ayatollah Khomeini declared that peace, for him, had meant "drinking the cup of poison." This mood was re-flected in the universities, especially among the militia, the veterans of the war and their affiliates: for them, peace meant defeat.

The war with the external enemy was over, but the war with the domestic one was not. Shortly after the signing of the peace agreement, Ayatollah Khomeini set up a three-man commission in the Iranian jails to decide on the political prisoners' loyalty to the regime. Several thousand, including some who were in jail for years waiting for a trial and some who had served their terms and were to be freed, were executed summarily and in secret. The victims of this mass execution were murdered twice, the second time by the silence and anonymity surrounding their executions, which robbed them of a meaningful and acknowledged death and thus, to paraphrase Hannah Arendt, set a seal on the fact that they had never really existed.

When classes resumed at last, we picked up almost exactly where we had left off. A few of the desks had been moved and there were several mysterious absences and curious new recruits, but otherwise there was almost no indication that the university had been closed for over two months. There was no air of jubilation, only a general sense of weary relief.

This was the beginning of disillusion and disenchantment. The war was lost, the economy was in shambles and there were few jobs to be had. Those who had gone to the front with no real skills had to depend on the compensations promised to them as war veterans. But even those were not handed out evenly. Most of the Islamic foundations created in the name of martyrs of the war had degenerated into sources of wealth for their corrupt leaders. Later, these children of the revolution would expose the degree of this corruption and revolt against it. Those in the Islamic associations had tasted power and things Western; they used their power principally to gain privileges denied to others.

After the war, Islamic Jihad, the student association that Mr. Forsati belonged to, became more open, and also came into more open conflict with the members of the more conservative Muslim Students' Association. Once the classes resumed, I began to see Mr. Forsati more often. Films were his passion, and he wanted to start a company related to videos and films. It was with his help that I managed to organize a series of cultural programs for the university at large. He was not very creative himself; his creativity went into a benign form of self-promotion and self-improvement.

At first it seemed to me as if gradually, like an old film's fade-out,

Mr. Ghomi disappeared from my life. He had not disappeared: he continued to come to class, and was no less virulent in his assaults against James and other novelists I taught. If anything, his resentment and anger grew, degenerating into almost childish outbursts. The difference was in the rest of us. Somehow we did not pay much attention to him anymore; when he talked, others answered back. He and his friends had to remind us daily that although Saddam was gone, the threat of the West, of imperialism, of the Zionists and their internal agents, had not vanished. Most of us were too tired even to respond.

In the next-to-last row on the window side, where Mr. Ghomi and Mr. Nahvi would sit, I find a quiet young man, an elementary school teacher. Let us call him Mr. Dori and move on. My glance hovers over Mr. Forsati, and Hamid, and then moves to the other side of the room, the girls' side, past Mahshid, Nassrin and Sanaz. In the middle row, the seat on the aisle is occupied by Manna. I pause for a moment on Manna's laughing face and then glance sideways towards the aisle—it is Nima that I seek.

As I shift from Manna to Nima and back, I remember the first time I saw them in my class. Their eyes were shining in unison, reminding me of my two children whenever they entered a conspiracy to make me happy. By now, more than a few interested outsiders audited my classes. They were former students who continued to come to classes long after they had graduated, students from other universities, young writers and strangers who simply drifted in. They had little access to discussions about English literature and were prepared to spend extra time for no academic credit to attend these classes. My only condition was that they should respect the rights of the regular students and refrain from discussion during class hours. When one morning I found Manna and Nima standing by my office door, both smiling and eager to audit my seminar on the novel, I agreed without much hesitation.

Gradually, the real protagonists in class came to be not my regular students, although I had no serious complaints against them, but these others, the outsiders, who came because of their commitment to the books we read.

Nima wanted me to be his dissertation adviser, because no one in the faculty at the University of Tehran knew Henry James. I had promised myself never to set foot again at the University of Tehran, a place filled with bitter and painful memories. Nima coaxed me in many different ways, and in the end he convinced me. After class, the three of us usually walked out together. Manna was the quiet one and Nima would weave me stories about the absurdities of our everyday life in the Islamic Republic.

Usually, he would walk beside me, and Manna would trail at a slightly slower pace by his side. He was tall and boyishly good-looking; not overweight but bulky, as if he had not yet lost his baby fat. His eyes were both kind and naughty. He had a surprisingly soft voice; not feminine, but soft and low, as if he could not raise it above a certain level.

It had become a habit with us, a permanent aspect of our relationship, to exchange stories. I told them that listening to their stories, and through living some of my own, I had a feeling that we were living a series of fairy tales in which all the good fairies had gone on strike, leaving us stranded in the middle of a forest not far from the wicked witch's candy house. Sometimes we told these stories to one another to convince ourselves that they had really happened. Because only then did they become true.

In his lecture on *Madame Bovary* Nabokov claimed that all great novels were great fairy tales. So, Nima asked, do you mean to say that both our lives and our imaginative lives are fairy tales? I smiled. Indeed, it seemed to me that at times our lives were more fictional than fiction itself.

33

Less than a year after the peace agreement, on Saturday, June 3, 1989, Ayatollah Ruhollah Khomeini died. His death was not officially announced until the next morning at seven A.M., although many Iranians, in fact the majority, already knew or suspected it by then, and thousands had gathered outside his house on the outskirts of Tehran waiting to hear the news. Before the announcement, the government had taken the precaution of shutting down the airports, the borders and the international telephone lines.

I remember the morning we heard the news of Khomeini's death.

Our whole family had gathered in the living room, lingering in that state of dull shock and bewilderment that death always brings with it. And this was no ordinary death. The radio announcer had broken down and sobbed. This would be the way with every public figure from then on, whether they appeared in mourning ceremonies or were interviewed individually; weeping seemed to be a requirement, as if there was no other way of expressing the magnitude of our grief.

It gave us all a feeling of unity and closeness to be sitting in the living room, with the inevitable smell of coffee and tea, speculating about that death: desired by many, feared by many, expected by many and, now that it had occurred, oddly anticlimactic to both friends and foes. Ever since Khomeini's first heart attack and hospitalization in the early eighties, rumors of his impending death would crop up like persistent weeds, only to be rooted out again. Now the event itself was less stupendous than the anxious expectations its possibility had created. The overwhelming mourning ceremonies that swept the country could not make up for this sense of disappointment.

The event had brought together a strange mix of people in our living room. My father, who had been separated from my mother for a few years but was living temporarily, after an accident, in my brother's vacant apartment, was present and so was my brother's ex-mother-in-law, who had also taken up temporary lodging in his apartment. She and my mother did not get along and had not been on speaking terms for several days now. But on this day a provisional truce was called due to the extraordinary nature of the occasion.

My son was in my lap, sprawled in a posture that is peculiar to very young children. His utter comfort in my lap transferred his sense of ease to me as I unconsciously stroked his fine, still-curly hair and every once in a while touched his soft skin. As we grown-ups talked and speculated, my five-year-old daughter looked intently out of the window. Suddenly, she turned around and shouted, "Mommy, Mommy, he is not dead! Women are still wearing their scarves." I always associate Khomeini's death with Negar's simple pronouncement—for she was right: the day women did not wear the scarf in public would be the real day of his death and the end of his revolution. Until then, we would continue to live with him.

The government announced five days of national mourning and forty days of official mourning. Classes were canceled and universities shut. But I felt restless sitting in the living room and ruminating, so I decided to go to the university anyway. Everything felt blurry, like a mirage in the intense heat. The blur remained with me throughout that day and all those days of mourning, when we spent most of our time by the television watching the funeral and the endless ceremonies.

When I arrived on campus, only a few people were inside the building. The silence was so deep that it drowned the mourning chants and marches from the loudspeakers. I climbed up to my office and picked up some books, and as I was coming down the hallway, I met Mr. Forsati and a friend of his from the Persian Department. They both looked solemn; their eyes were moist. I looked at them with an awkward sympathy, at a loss for the appropriate words. They had some leaflets with Khomeini's picture that they were about to post on the walls. I took two and left.

Later, Khomeini's book of Sufi poems, which he had dedicated to his daughter-in-law, would be published. In death there was a need to humanize him, an act he had opposed during his life. And there was, in fact, a human side to him, one that we seldom saw, in his regard for his beautiful young daughter-in-law, in whose notebooks he had written his last poems. In an introduction to this book of poems, she described how he had devoted time to talking to her and teaching her philosophy and mysticism and how she had given him the notebook in which he had composed the poems. It was reported that she had long blond hair and I imagined her walking with the old man in the garden, making circles around the flowers and bushes, and talking philosophy. Did she wear a scarf in his presence? Did he perhaps lean on her as they walked around and around those flower beds? I bought a copy of the slim volume and carried it with me to America, along with the leaflets, relics from a time whose reality seems so fragile at times that I need such hard evidence to prove its fugitive existence.

I am not good with dates and figures—I had to double-check the date of Khomeini's death—but I remember feelings and images. Like bothersome dreams, images from those days mix with sounds in my memory as they did in reality: the announcer's shrill and exaggerated voice, always on the verge of breaking, the mourning marches, the prayers, the messages from high-ranking officials and the chanting mourners, drowning all other sounds: "Today is the day of mourning! Khomeini, the breaker of idols, is with God."

At dawn on Monday, Ayatollah Khomeini's body was transferred from his residence in Jamaran, in Tehran, to a vast wasteland in the hills to the north, an area known as Mosalla, designated as a place of prayer. The body was set up on a temporary podium made of containers. Khomeini lay in an air-conditioned glass case covered in a white shroud, his feet pointing towards Mecca. His black turban, indicating his religious status as a direct descendant of the Prophet Muhammad, rested on his chest.

The events of that frenetic day come to me in fragments. The glass coffin I remember well, and the flowers arranged around the container were gaudy gladiolas. I also remember the swarms of mourners—it was reported that hundreds of thousands had started to pour into Tehran, a black-clad army waving black flags, the men tearing their shirts, beating their chests, the women in their black chadors wailing and moaning, their bodies writhing in ecstatic grief.

Now I remember the hoses: because of the heat and the size of the crowd, the fire department had brought out hoses, which they aimed at people, spraying them at intervals with water to cool them off, but the effect made the scene oddly sexual. As I re-enact it in my mind, I can hear the swish of water, each spray silhouetted against the sky. Every once in a while someone would faint and in the midst of that frenzy, with a shocking sense of order, as if it were all rehearsed, the mourners would lift the person over their heads and pass him along until he reached a point of safety.

When I heard that many had died that day and that tens of thousands were injured, I asked myself stupidly what sort of status these dead would be given. We gave people more rank and space in death than in life. Opponents of the regime and the Baha'is had no status; they were denied headstones and were thrown into common graves. Then there were the martyrs of war and revolution, each of whom had his own special space at the graveyard, with artificial flowers and photographs to mark the grave. Could these people be ranked as martyrs? Would they be granted a place in heaven?

The government had set aside huge supplies of food and drink for the mourners. Alongside the frenzy of beating chests and fainting and chanting, rows upon rows of mourners were to be seen on the roadside, eating their sandwiches and drinking their soft drinks as if they were out on a holiday picnic. Many who actively disliked Khomeini in his lifetime attended the funeral. Dissatisfaction at the time of Khomeini's death was so high that at first, the officials had thought of burying him in the night so as to cover the sparse attendance. But millions had come from all around the country. I remember talking to a middle-aged man on the staff at the university, who lived in the poorer, more traditional part of town. He described the busloads of neighbors, disenchanted with Khomeini and his revolution, who had gone nonetheless, like him, to the funeral. I asked him why he went. Was he forced to go? No, but it seemed the thing to do. Everyone was going—how would it look if he didn't? He paused and then added, After all, an event like this happens only once in a lifetime, doesn't it?

As the procession began to take Khomeini's body through the streets to the cemetery on the outskirts of Tehran, the pressure of the crowd was so enormous that the officials changed their minds and decided to transport the body by helicopter. The crowd surged towards the helicopter, and as it took off, a golden dust rose up from the ground, like a flying skirt, and gradually all that remained were particles of dancing dust, whirling like minuscule dervishes in a bizarre dream.

In the Behesht-e Zahra cemetery, as an attempt was being made to carry the body out of the helicopter, the crowd rushed forward once more and this time actually got hold of its prize, tearing pieces of the white shroud from the dead man's body, revealing a leg dangling from the white cloth. The body was finally retrieved, and rushed back to Tehran to be shrouded again. And when it was returned a few hours later, inside a metal case, the Revolutionary Guards and some members of the inner circle forced the people back. A friend remembered seeing Hojatol-Islam Nategh Nouri—who would later lose the election to President Khatami—standing near the container with a whip and lashing those who tried to approach the dead body. And thus they finally buried Ruhollah Khomeini, whose given name meant "the soul of God."

The government, in a move to turn Khomeini into a sacred figure, tried to create a shrine for him close to the Behesht-e Zahra cemetery. It was hastily built, without taste or beauty: a country famous for some of the most beautiful mosques in the world now created the gaudiest shrine to this last imam. The monument was built close to the burial place of the martyrs of the revolution: a small fountain gushed sprays of red water, symbolizing the everlasting blood of the martyrs.

Khomeini's death carried its own illuminations. Some, like me, felt like aliens in their homeland. Others, like the taxi driver I came across a few weeks after the funeral, were disillusioned with the whole religious fraud, as he put it. Now I know how fourteen hundred years back they created the imams and prophets, he said—just like this guy. So none of it was true.

At the start of the revolution, a rumor had taken root that Khomeini's image could be seen in the moon. Many people, even perfectly modern and educated individuals, came to believe this. They had seen him in the moon. He had been a conscious mythmaker, and he had turned himself into a myth. What they mourned after a well-timed death—for after the defeat in the war and the disenchantment, all he could do was die—was the death of a dream. Like all great mythmakers, he had tried to fashion reality out of his dream, and in the end, like Humbert, he had managed to destroy both reality and his dream. Added to the crimes, to the murders and tortures, we would now face this last indignity—the murder of our dreams. Yet he had done this with our full compliance, our complete assent and complicity.

34

I stray for no good reason to a dark and musty antique shop in downtown Tehran. I had gone to a street lined with secondhand stores in search of an old book to give Nima, who had recently brought me rare videos of an old television series popular before the revolution. When I entered the shop, the owner, sitting behind the counter, was too busy reading the morning paper to bother to glance at me.

As I browsed around the semi-lit room, lost in the objects scattered haphazardly on old wooden tables and shelves, my eyes fell on an odd-looking pair of scissors. They were beautifully handcrafted; one of the handles was much bigger than the other, and they were shaped like a rooster. The blades were blunter than those of ordinary scissors. I asked the shopkeeper what it was. He shrugged. I'm not sure—maybe for trimming the mustache or beard. It probably came from somewhere in Europe, maybe Russia.

I don't know why I was so fascinated by this object, but I found it quite extraordinary that perhaps a hundred years ago this pair of scissors—or mustache trimmer, or whatever it was—had been brought over all the way from Europe to finally end up on an old table in the farthest reaches of this dusty shop. Yet so much work had gone into this quite dispensable object. I decided to buy it for my magician. I had a theory that some gifts should be bought for their own sake, exactly because they were useless. I was sure he would appreciate it, that he would be pleased to receive something he did not need, a luxury item that was not luxurious. Instead of buying something for Nima, I left with my rooster-headed scissors.

When I gave them to my magician with my explanation, he was making coffee and was seemingly so involved in his task that he did not respond. He carried the tray with two mugs and his box of chocolates to the table, and went into the library. A few moments later he returned with a leather-bound book, in solemn green with gold lettering. It was *The Ambassadors*. Since you bought me the gift you should have gotten Nima, I have a gift for him: tell him to reread the scene in Gloriani's garden. Your Nima sounds like a chap who needs to be reminded of things by someone such as myself. So why don't you ask him to reread that scene?

In the book, my magician had marked two passages. One was in the preface, where James mentions a famous and oft repeated scene as the "essence" of his novel; the other was the scene itself. It occurs at a party given by the famous sculptor Gloriani. Lambert Strether, the hero of the novel, tells a young painter, little Bilham, whom he has unofficially appointed as his spiritual heir: "Live all you can; it's a mistake not to. It doesn't so much matter what you do in particular so long as you have your life. If you haven't had that what *have* you had? I'm too old—too old at any rate for what I see. What one loses one loses; make no mistake about that. Still, we have the illusion of freedom; therefore don't, like me to-day, be without the memory of that illusion. I was either, at the right time, too stupid or too intelligent to have it, and now I'm a case of reaction against the mistake. For it *was* a mistake. Live, live!"

35

We work in the dark—we do what we can—we give what we have.
Our doubt is our passion, and our passion is our task. The rest is the
madness of art.—Henry James

It was early in the morning, the first class of the day; the classroom was filled with light. I was summing up James. Last time we talked about certain traits in James, how they appear in different characters and within different contexts, and today I want to talk about the word *courage,* one that we bandy about a great deal these days in our own culture.

There are different kinds of courage in James. Can you think of an example? Yes, Nassrin? The most obvious example is Daisy, Nassrin said. She pushed herself forward with an effort, tried to brush an imaginary strand of hair from her forehead and continued. Daisy tells Winterbourne at the very start not to be afraid. She means not to be afraid of conventions and traditions—that is one kind of courage.

Yes, I said encouragingly. Daisy is a good example, and then there are other characters, others whom we never credit with courage, because we never think of their kind as courageous; we think of them as meek. Mahshid's face lit up, and before she had bolstered the courage to raise her hand, I turned to her and said, Yes? The light withdrew from her face and she hesitated. Tell us, Mahshid, I insisted. Well, when you said "meek," I suddenly thought of Catherine. She is shy and retreating, not like Daisy, yet she stands up to all these characters, who are much more outgoing than her, and she faces up to them at a great cost. She has a different kind of courage from Daisy, but it is still courage. I . . .

It was at this point that we heard a commotion in the hall. I paid no attention to it. Over the years I had come to see such interference from outside the class as part of the class itself. One day, two janitors had walked in with two chairs and placed them in one corner. They left without a word and a few minutes later came back with two more chairs. Another time, a janitor with a crooked neck came in with a broom and started sweeping the floor while I continued to talk about *Tom Jones* and pretended not to notice him.

And then there is *The Ambassadors,* I continued, where we find several different kinds of courage, but the most courageous characters here are those with imagination, those who, through their imaginative faculty, can empathize with others. When you lack this kind of courage, you remain ignorant of others' feelings and needs.

Maria, the soul mate Strether finds in Paris, has "courage," while Mrs. Newsome has only "exultation." Madame de Vionnet, the beautiful Parisian whom Mrs. Newsome is determined to expel from her son's life, demonstrates courage when she risks all the known quantities of her life for the unknown quantity of her love for Chad. But Mrs. Newsome chooses to play it safe. Having imagined what everyone is like, having imagined their function and role, she refuses to change her formulations. She is a tyrant much in the way of a bad novelist, who shapes his characters according to his own ideology or desires and never allows them the space to become themselves. It takes courage to die for a cause, but also to live for one.

I could tell by the restless movements of my students and their glances towards the door that they could not wholly concentrate on this most intriguing point, but I was determined to be undisturbed for as long as possible, so I continued. The most dictatorial character in the novel is the invisible Mrs. Newsome. If we want to learn about the essence of a dictatorial mind, we would do well to study her. Nima, could you please read the passage where Strether describes her—" 'That is just her difficulty—' "

" 'That is just her difficulty—, that she doesn't admit surprises. It's a fact that, I think, describes and represents her . . . she's all, as I've called it, fine cold thought. She had, to her own mind, worked the whole thing out in advance, and worked it out for me as well as for herself. Wherever she has done that, you see, there's no room left; no margin, as it were, for any alteration. She's filled as full, packed as tight, as she'll hold. . . . I haven't touched her. She won't *be* touched. I see it now as I've never done; and she hangs together with a perfection of her own . . . that does suggest a kind of wrong in *any* change of her composition.' "

By this time the disturbance outside had grown louder. There were sounds of feet running and people shouting. Miss Ruhi and

Miss Hatef were now visibly agitated and whispered loudly, casting significant glances at the door. I sent them outside to find out what was happening, and tried to go on.

"Let us return to the quotation . . ." I was instantly interrupted by Miss Ruhi and her breathless mate, who stood on the threshold as if they did not intend to stay. They reported that a student had set fire to himself in an empty classroom and had then started to run down the hall, shouting revolutionary slogans.

We all rushed out. From both sides of the long hall, students were running in the direction of the staircase. I found a place near the stairs, close to one of my colleagues. Three people were carrying a stretcher, trying to make their way through the crowd towards the stairs. From the way they were carrying the stretcher, their burden seemed light. On the stretcher, under a white sheet, I could make out a remarkably pink face, marked by patches of dark gray. A pair of black minstrel hands extended out motionless above the white sheet, creating the impression that they were trying to avoid contact with the sheet at all costs. Two huge black eyes seemed to be attached to the face by invisible wires. They appeared completely motionless, as if fixed on a scene of unbelievable horror, and yet, paradoxically, they also seemed to be roving, but from side to side. Of all the wild images of that morning, those roaming eyes have continued to haunt me.

The loudspeakers urged everyone to return to their classes. No one moved. We were watching the pink face, the minstrel hands and the sooty eyes as they were carried down the staircase in what seemed like a spiral motion. The murmurs died down and rose again with the stretcher's approach and descent. It was one of those scenes which, while happening in front of one's eyes, have already acquired the quality not just of a dream, but of a memory of a dream.

As the stretcher moved down the stairs and out of sight, the murmurs became more articulate and clear. The almost magical creature on the stretcher became more tangible, acquired a background, a name, an identity. This identity was mainly impersonal. He had been one of the most active students in the Muslim Students' Association. To say that he was "active" meant that he was one of the more fanatical. He belonged to the group responsible for the posters and slogans on the walls, the group that had authorized the notices at the entrances to the university listing the names of those who had transgressed the dress code.

I thought of him on that stretcher, going down the staircase, passing the now irrelevant photographs of the war, passing by Ayatollah Khomeini, who even after death was glaring down on the procession with his usual stern and impenetrable gaze and passing his precious slogans about the war: WHETHER WE KILL OR ARE KLLED WE ARE VICTORIOUS! WE WILL FIGHT! WE WILL DIE! BUT WE WON'T ACCEPT COMPROMISE!

There were so many young men like him on all our campuses, those who had been very young at the beginning of the revolution, many from the provinces or from traditional families. Every year, more students were admitted to the universities based on their loyalty to the revolution. They belonged to the families of the Revolutionary Guards or the martyrs of the revolution and were called the "government's share." These were the children of the revolution, those who were to carry its legacy and eventually replace the Westernized workforce. The revolution must have meant many things to them—mainly power, and access. But they were also the usurpers, who had been admitted to the university and given power not because of their own merit or hard work but because of their ideological affiliations. This, neither they nor we could forget.

I went down the stairs, slowly this time, surrounded by a group of students who were talking excitedly among themselves. Who he was had already become an excuse for our remembrances, and our stories. My students spoke heatedly about the humiliations they had suffered at the hands of members of his organization. They repeated the story of another leader of the Muslim Students' Association, one who had died during the war, who claimed to have been sexually aroused by the sight of a white patch of skin peeking out from under a head scarf. Not even death could erase the memory of that white patch and the penalty the young girl had been made to pay for it.

There were no public articulations of these humiliations, so we took refuge in accidental occasions to weave our resentments and hatreds into little stories that lost their impact as soon as they were told. Of the injured student's background very little was known, and no one seemed to care. It dawned on me only much later that despite the precision with which I remembered all the stories related to him and his comrades, I could not remember his name. He had turned himself into a revolutionary, a martyr and a war veteran, but not an individual. Did he ever fall in love? Did he ever desire to hold one of those girls whose throats, under their black scarves, blazed so white?

Like many others at that university, I had climbed the stairs and walked the halls with resentment. Resentment had erased all ambiguity in our encounters with people like him; we had been polarized into "us" and "them." It did not occur to me or to my students and colleagues as we shared stories and anecdotes that day, like conspirators delighting in the setback of a far more powerful adversary, that he who seemingly wielded so much power was in fact the one with the strongest urge to self-destruction. Had he, by burning himself, usurped our right to revenge?

He who in life had been nothing to me in death had become an obsession. All we ever found out about his personal life was that he came from a poor family and that his only close relative was a very old mother, whom he supported. He had gone to the war as a volunteer. He had been shell-shocked and sent home early. Apparently, he never fully recovered. After "peace" with Iraq, he returned to the university. But the peace had created a sense of disillusionment. The excitement of the war was gone, and with that, many young revolutionaries had lost their power.

THIS WAR HAS BEEN A BLESSING FOR US! For us, it was a war that we never felt quite a part of. Yet for people like him, in a strange way the war must have been a blessing. It gave them a sense of community and purpose and power. He lost all that as soon as he returned from the front. His privilege and power meant nothing to him now, and his fellow Islamic students had already moved on. What must have gone through his mind when he saw that his old comrades were more eager to watch the Oscar celebrations, via forbidden satellite dishes, than clips from the war? He could deal with us, but what could he do with a Mr. Forsati, who had become as unfamiliar and as baffling to him as characters in a novel by Henry James?

I kept thinking of him coming early to the university with two full cans of gasoline—probably not searched, because he was a privileged war veteran. I see him going into an empty classroom and pouring gasoline over his head. Next, he would have struck a match and slowly set fire to himself—did he light himself just once, or in several places? Then he ran down the hall and burst into his classroom, shouting, "They betrayed us! They lied to us! Look at what they did to us!" And that was the last of his rhetoric.

One did not have to agree with him or approve of him to understand his position. He had returned from a war where he belonged to a university he had never been a part of. No one wanted to hear his stories. Only his moment of death could spark interest. It was ironic that this man, whose life had been so determined by doctrinal certainty, would now gain so much complexity in death.

He died that night. Did his comrades mourn him in private? Nothing was said about him—no commemoration, no flowers or speeches, in a country where funerals and mourning were more magnificently produced than any other national art form. I, who prided myself on speaking out against the veil or other forms of harassment, also kept quiet. Apart from the murmurs, the only thing out of the ordinary about that day was that the loudspeakers for some reason kept announcing in the halls that classes would be held as usual that afternoon. We did have a class that afternoon. It did not go on as usual.

PART IV

Austen

I

"It is a truth universally acknowledged that a Muslim man, regardless of his fortune, must be in want of a nine-year-old virgin wife." So declared Yassi in that special tone of hers, deadpan and mildly ironic, which on rare occasions, and this was one of them, bordered on the burlesque.

"Or is it a truth universally acknowledged," Manna shot back, "that a Muslim man must be in want not just of one but of many wives?" She glanced at me conspiratorially, her black eyes brimming with humor, knowing she would draw a reaction. Unlike Mahshid, Manna had a way of secretly communicating with the few people she liked. Her chief means of contact were her eyes, which she focused or withdrew from you. We had developed a hidden code between us and only when she felt offended—and she could easily be offended—would she lower and divert her gaze to one side, the playful inflections wiped from her words.

It was one of those cold, gray early-December mornings when the overcast sky and the chill in the air seem to promise snow. I had asked Bijan to light a fire before leaving for work, and it sparkled now with a soothing warmth. *Cozy*—a word too common for Yassi's usage—would be the right term for how we felt. All the necessary components were there: misty windows, steaming mugs of coffee, a crackling fire, languorous cream puffs, thick wool sweaters and the mingling smells of smoke, coffee and oranges. Yassi was sprawled on the couch, in her usual place between Manna and Azin, making me wonder again how such a tiny body could take up so much space. Azin's flirtatious laughter rang in the air, and even Mahshid bestowed upon us a hint of a smile. Nassrin had moved her chair near the fireplace, her restless hands tossing orange peels into the fire.

It was a tribute to the degree of intimacy that had developed among us that we could easily shift from light banter to serious discussions of the novels. What we had with all the writers, but especially with Austen, was fun. Sometimes we even went wild—we became childish and teasing and just plain enjoyed ourselves. How could one read the opening sentence of *Pride and Prejudice* and not grasp that this was what Austen demanded of her readers?

That morning, we were waiting for Sanaz. Mitra, her dimples making a temporary appearance, had informed the class that Sanaz wanted us to wait for her—she had a surprise. All our wild speculations were met with a reticent smile.

"Only two things could have happened," Azin speculated. "Another row with her brother and she's finally decided to leave home and move in with her wonderful aunt." She raised her hand with a tinkling of gold and silver bangles. "Or she's marrying her sweetheart."

"The sweetheart seems the more likely of the two," said Yassi, straightening herself up a little, "judging by Mitra's expression."

Mitra's dimples widened, but she refused to respond to our provocation. Looking at her, I thought of her own recent marriage to Hamid; their furtive courtship must have taken place right under my unsuspecting nose. They had invited me to their wedding, but Mitra had never mentioned her relations with Hamid before then.

"Did you fall in love?" I had asked Mitra anxiously, causing Manna to say, "That boring question again." It was a joke among my friends and colleagues that I could never resist posing my obsessive question to married couples. "Did you fall in love?" I'd ask urgently and eagerly, provoking almost invariably an indulgent smile. Mitra blushed and said, "Well, yes, of course."

"But who is thinking about love these days?" said Azin with mock chastity. Her hair was pulled back in a ponytail and clusters of tiny turquoise beads trembled slightly on her ears as she turned her head. "The Islamic Republic has taken us back to Jane Austen's times. God bless the arranged marriage! Nowadays, girls marry either because their families force them, or to get green cards, or to secure financial stability, or for sex—they marry for all kinds of reasons, but rarely for love."

I looked at Mahshid, who, although quiet, seemed to be saying, "Here we go again."

"And," Azin continued, reaching for her mug, "we're talking about educated girls—girls like *us,* who've gone to college, who one might think would have higher ambitions."

"Not *all* of them," Mahshid said quietly, without looking at Azin. "Many women are independent. Look at how many businesswomen we have, and there are women who have chosen to live alone." Yes, and you are one of them, I thought, a studious working girl still living with her parents at thirty-two.

"But most don't have a choice," said Manna. "And I think we're *way* behind Jane Austen's times." This was one of the few instances I can remember when Manna implicitly sided with Azin against Mahshid. "My mother could choose whom she wanted to marry. I had less choice, and my younger sister has even less," she concluded gloomily.

"How about a temporary marriage?" said Nassrin, rearranging the orange peels on her plate like pieces of a puzzle. "You seem to have forgotten our president's enlightened alternative." She was referring to an Islamic rule peculiar to Iran, according to which men could have four official wives and as many temporary wives as they wished. The logic behind this was that they had to satisfy their own needs when their wives were unavailable, or unable, to satisfy them. A man could enter into such a contract for as short a period as ten minutes or as long as ninety-nine years. President Rafsanjani, then honored with the title of reformist, had proposed that young people should enter into temporary marriages. This angered both the reactionaries, who felt it was a shrewd move on the president's part to curry favor with the young, and the progressives, who were equally skeptical of the president's motives and, in addition, found it insulting, especially to women. Some went so far as to call the temporary marriage a sanctified form of prostitution.

"I'm not in favor of the temporary marriage," said Mahshid. "But men *are* weaker and *do* have more sexual needs. Besides," she added cautiously, "it's the girl's choice. She isn't forced into it."

"The girl's choice?" said Nassrin with evident disgust. "You *do* have funny notions of choice."

Mahshid, lowering her eyes, did not respond.

"Some men, even the most educated," Nassrin continued fiercely, "think of this as progressive. I had to argue with a friend—a *male* friend—that the only way he could convince me this was progressive was if the law gave women the same rights as men. You want to know how open-minded these men are? I'm not talking about the religious guys—no, the secular ones," she said, tossing another orange peel into the fire. "Just ask them about marriage. Talk about hypocrisy!"

"It's true that neither my mom nor my aunts married for love," Yassi said, furrowing her brow, "but *all* my uncles married for love. It's strange when you think about it. Where does that leave us—what sort of legacy, I mean?

"I suppose," she added, brightening up after a moment's reflection, "that if Austen were in our shoes, she'd say it's a truth universally acknowledged that a Muslim man, regardless of his fortune, must be in want of a nine-year-old virgin wife." And this was how we started our play on Austen's famous opening sentence—a temptation that almost every Austen reader must have felt at least once.

Our merrymaking was interrupted by the sound of the bell. Mahshid, who was closest to the door, said, I'll get it. We heard the street door close, steps on the stairs, a pause. Mahshid opened the front door to sounds of greetings and laughter. Sanaz came in, smiling radiantly. She was holding a big box of pastries. Why the pastries? I asked. It isn't your turn.

"Yes, but I have good news," she said mysteriously.

"Are you getting married?" Yassi asked lazily from the depths of the couch.

"Let me sit down first," said Sanaz, taking off her long overcoat and woolen scarf. She tossed her head to one side, with the proud ease of women with beautiful hair, and pronounced: "It's going to snow."

Would she apologize for being late, I wondered, even on this occasion, when she has such a good excuse and no one would blame her?

"I'm so sorry I'm late again," she said with a disarming smile that showed no sign of repentance.

"You usurped my rights," said Azin. "Being late is my specialty."

Sanaz wanted to defer her news until the break. Our rule was that the personal narratives that were increasingly creeping into our Thursday session should not interfere with class. But in this case, even I was too excited to wait.

"It was all done very quickly," Sanaz explained, caving in to our demands. Suddenly, out of the blue, he had called and asked her to marry him—said something about running out of time. He told her he had already talked to his parents, who had talked to her parents (without asking her first, I noted in passing). They were delighted, and since he couldn't come to Iran because of the draft, perhaps she and her family could come to Turkey? Iranians didn't need a visa for Turkey, and the trip could be arranged quickly. She was dumbfounded. It was something she'd always expected, but somehow she couldn't believe it was actually happening. "Your fire is almost out," she said, interrupting herself. "I'm really good with fires. Let me fix it." She added some logs to the languishing fire and poked at it with energy. A long flame leapt out and died just as quickly.

At the start of the twentieth century, the age of marriage in Iran—nine, according to sharia laws—was changed to thirteen and then later to eighteen. My mother had chosen whom she wanted to marry and she had been one of the first six women elected to Parliament in 1963. When I was growing up, in the 1960s, there was little difference between my rights and the rights of women in Western democracies. But it was not the fashion then to think that our culture was not compatible with modern democracy, that there were Western and Islamic versions of democracy and human rights. We all wanted opportunities and freedom. That is why we supported revolutionary change—we were demanding *more* rights, not fewer.

I married, on the eve of the revolution, a man I loved. At that time, Mahshid, Nassrin, Manna and Azin were in their teens, Sanaz and Mitra were a few years younger and Yassi was two years old. By the time my daughter was born five years later, the laws had regressed to what they had been before my grandmother's time: the first law to be repealed, months before the ratification of a new constitution, was the family-protection law, which guaranteed women's rights at home and at work. The age of marriage was lowered to nine—eight and a half lunar years, we were told; adultery and prostitution were to be punished by stoning to death; and women, under law, were considered to have half the worth of men. Sharia law replaced the existing system of jurisprudence and became the norm. My youthful years had witnessed the rise of two women to the rank of cabinet minister. After the revolution, these same two women were sentenced to death for the sins of warring with God and spreading prostitution. One of them, the minister for women's affairs, had been abroad at the time of revolution and remained in exile, where she became a leading spokesperson for women's rights and human rights. The other, the minister of education and my former high school principal, was put in a sack and stoned or shot to death. These girls, my girls, would in time come to think of these women with reverence and hope: if we'd had women like this in the past, there was no reason why we couldn't have them in the future.

Our society was far more advanced than its new rulers, and women, regardless of their religious and ideological beliefs, had come out onto the streets to protest the new laws. They had tasted power and were not about to give it up without a fight. It was then that the myth of Islamic feminism—a contradictory notion, attempting to reconcile the concept of women's rights with the tenets of Islam—took root. It enabled the rulers to have their cake and eat it too: they could claim to be progressive and Islamic, while modern women were denounced as Westernized, decadent and disloyal. They needed us modern men and women to show them the way, but they also had to keep us in our place.

What differentiated this revolution from the other totalitarian revolutions of the twentieth century was that it came in the name of the past: this was both its strength and its weakness. We, four generations of women—my grandmother, my mother, myself and my daughter—lived in the present but also in the past; we were experiencing two different time zones simultaneously. Interesting, I thought, how war and revolution have made us even more aware of our own personal ordeals—especially marriage, at the heart of which was the question of individual freedom, as Jane Austen had discovered two centuries before. *She* had discovered it, I reflected, but what about us, sitting in this room, in another country at the end of another century?

Sanaz's nervous laughter brought me out of my reverie. "I'm so scared," she said, her right hand going to her brow to push back an absent strand of hair. "Up till now, marrying him has been sort of a dream, something to think about when I was fighting with my brother. I never knew—I still don't know—how it would all work out in real life."

Sanaz was worried about the trip to Turkey and what it would be like to see him again. "What if he doesn't like me?" she said. She did not ask, What if *I* don't like him? or, What if *we* don't get along? Would her brother become more vicious and her mother more depressed? Would her mother, with her martyr's look, make Sanaz feel guilty, as if she had failed her on purpose? These were serious questions for Sanaz. It was hard to tell if she was going to Turkey to please the others or because she was in love. This was my problem with Sanaz—one never knew what she really wanted.

"After six years, God knows what he'll be like," said Nassrin, absentmindedly rotating the coffee mug in her hands. I looked at her with some concern, as I almost always did when our talks turned to marriage and men. I couldn't help but wonder how she dealt with her buried memories. Did she compare herself with her friends who were free of such experiences? And *were* they free of such experiences?

Sanaz glanced at Nassrin reproachfully. Did she really need to hear this now? At any rate, going to Turkey would be good for her, even if it didn't work out. At least she'd get him out of her system.

"Do you love him?" I asked her, trying to ignore the girls' sardonic smiles. "You'll always be taking a risk when you decide to marry, but the question is, Do you love him *now*?"

"I loved him when I was very young," Sanaz said slowly, too excited to participate in their joke. "I don't know anymore. I've always loved the idea of him, but he's been away for so long. He's had so many chances to meet other women. . . . What chance have I had of meeting other men? My aunt says I don't have to say yes or no. She says if we want to find out how we really feel about each other, we should meet in Turkey *alone*. We should spend some time together without our families' interfering presence."

"What an unusually wise aunt," I said, unable to stop myself from breaking in like a referee. "She's right, you know."

Mahshid raised her eyes in my direction for a fraction of a second before lowering them again. Azin, quickly catching Mahshid's look, said, "I agree with Dr. Nafisi. You'd be wise to try to live together for a while before making any decisions."

Mahshid decided not to take the bait, and remained demurely silent. Was it my imagination or did she cast a reproachful glance in my direction as she lowered her eyes, fixing them once more on an imperceptible spot in the carpet?

"The first thing you should do to test your compatibility," said Nassrin, "is dance with him."

At first we were puzzled by her statement, which seemed far-fetched even for Nassrin. It took me a second before I grasped her meaning. But of course! She was referring to the Dear Jane Society we'd invented in my last year at Allameh! The idea for that society— defunct even before it started—had begun with a memorable dance.

2

I see it now as if through the large window of a house in the middle of an empty garden. I've pressed my face to the window, and here they come: five women, all in black robes and head scarves. As each passes by the window, I can begin to differentiate their faces; one is standing and watching the other four. They are not graceful; they bump into one another and into the chairs. They are boisterous in a peculiarly subdued manner.

In my graduate seminar that spring, I had compared the structure of *Pride and Prejudice* to an eighteenth-century dance. After class, some of the girls had stayed behind to talk this over—they were confused by what I'd meant. I thought it best to explain myself by going over the motions of the dance with them. Close your eyes and imagine the dance, I suggested. Imagine you are moving back and forth; it would help if you could imagine that the man standing opposite you was the incomparable Mr. Darcy, or maybe not—whoever is on your mind, imagine him. I heard a giggle from one of the girls. Suddenly hit by inspiration, I took Nassrin's reluctant hands and started to dance with her, one-two and one-two. Then I asked the others to form a line, and pretty soon we were all dancing, our long black robes twirling as we bumped into one another and into the chairs.

They stand opposite their partners, give a slight bow, step forward, touch hands and twirl. I say, Now, as you touch hands, look into each other's eyes; okay, let's see how much of a conversation you can hold. Say something to each other. They can barely keep their faces straight. Mojgan says, The trouble is we all want to be Elizabeth and Darcy. I don't mind being Jane, says Nassrin—I always wanted to be the most beautiful. We need a Mr. Collins. Come on, Mahshid, won't you enjoy stepping on my toes? Mahshid demurs. I've never danced in my life, she says awkwardly. This is one dance you needn't worry about, I said. In fact as your professor, I command you to do it. As part of your homework, I added, and it was one of the rare times I actually enjoyed my authority. Forward, backwards, pause, turn, turn, you have to harmonize your steps with the rest in the set, that's the whole point; you are mainly concerned with yourself and your partner but also with all the others—you can't be out of step with them. Well, yes, that is the difficult part, but for Miss Eliza Bennet it comes naturally.

All dance is performance and presentation, I tell them, but do you see how different dances invite different interpretations? Oh yes, says Nassrin. Compare this to the Persian dance. If those British could quiver their bodies the way we do . . . next to us, they are so chaste!

I ask, Who can dance Persian-style? Everyone looks at Sanaz. She is shy and refuses to dance. We start to tease her and goad her on, and form a circle around her. As she begins to move, self-consciously at first, we start to clap and murmur a song. Nassrin cautions us to be quieter. Sanaz begins shyly, taking graceful little steps, moving her waist with a lusty grace. As we laugh and joke more, she becomes bolder; she starts to move her head from side to side, and every part of her body asserts itself, vying for attention with the other parts. Her body quivers as she takes her small steps and dances with her fingers and her hands. A special look has appeared on her face. It is daring and beckoning, designed to attract, to pull in, but at the same time it re-tracts and refracts with a power she loses as soon as she stops dancing.

There are different forms of seduction, and the kind I have wit-nessed in Persian dancers is so unique, such a mixture of subtlety and brazenness, I cannot find a Western equivalent to compare it to. I have seen women of vastly different backgrounds take on that same ex-pression: a hazy, lazy, flirtatious look in their eyes. I found Sanaz's look, years later, in the face of my sophisticated French-educated friend Leyly as she suddenly began to dance to music that was filled with stretches of *naz* and *eshveh* and *kereshmeh,* all words whose sub-stitutes in English—*coquettishness, teasing, flirtatiousness*—seem not just poor but irrelevant.

This sort of seduction is elusive; it is sinewy and tactile. It twists, twirls, winds and unwinds. Hands curl and uncurl while the waist seems to coil and recoil. It is calculated. It predicts its effect before another little step is taken, and then another little step. It is flirtatious in a way Miss Daisy Miller and her likes could never dream of being. It is openly seductive but not surrendering. All this is there in Sanaz's dance. Her large black robe and black head scarf—framing her bony face, her large eyes and very slim and fragile body—oddly enough add to the allure of the movements. With each move she seems to free herself from her layers of black cloth. The robe becomes diaphanous; its texture adds to the mystery of her dance.

We were surprised by a startled student who opened the door. The lunch hour was over; we had not noticed the time. Looking at the student standing on the threshold, with one foot in the classroom, we started to laugh.

That meeting created a secret pact among us. We talked about creating a clandestine group and calling it the Dear Jane Society. We would meet and dance and eat cream puffs, and we would share the news. Although we never formed any such secret society, the girls referred to themselves from then on as Dear Janes, and it planted the seed for our present complicity. I would have forgotten all about it had I not recently started to think about Nassrin.

I now remember that it was that day as Mahshid, Nassrin and I walked to my office that quite suddenly, without thinking of it, I asked them to participate in my secret class. Looking at their astonished faces, I quickly sketched out the concept, improvising perhaps on what I had dreamed of and planned for so many years in my mind. What will be required of us? Mahshid asked. *Absolute* commitment to the works, to the class, I said with an impetuous air of finality. More than committing them, I had now committed myself.

3

I am too much of an academic: I have written too many papers and articles to be able to turn my experiences and ideas into narratives without pontificating. Although that is in fact my urge—to narrate, to reinvent myself along with all those others. As I write the road is clear, the tin man recovers his heart and the lion his courage, but this is not my story. I walk down a different road, whose end I cannot foresee. I know as little about where this road leads as Alice knew when she first ran after the White Rabbit, the one who was wearing a waistcoat and a watch and muttering, "I'm late, I'm late."

I could not find a better way of explaining the overall structure of *Pride and Prejudice* to my classes than to compare it to the eighteenth-century dance, the kind one imagines Darcy and Elizabeth performed in one of the numerous balls they attended. Although balls and dances are instruments of plot in some of Austen's other novels—in *Mansfield Park,* for example, and *Emma*—in no other novel does dance play such a focal role. It is not the specific number of dances that I am concerned with here. As I said, the whole structure of the novel is like a dance, which is both a public and a private act. The atmosphere in *Pride and Prejudice* does carry the festive air of a ball.

So the structure is that of dance and digression. It moves in parallels, contrapuntally, in terms not only of events and characters but also settings. First we see Elizabeth in her setting, then we see her out of her setting and in Darcy's, then we see Darcy in his true setting—each of these shifts in perspective brings them closer. Darcy's proposal to Elizabeth runs parallel to Collins's proposal. There are also parallels between the characters of Darcy and Wickham. Like a camera, Darcy's view of Elizabeth pans in to a close-up; in the second part of the novel, the reverse happens as Elizabeth moves closer to Darcy.

All the main actors are introduced at the first dance, and the conflict sparked there is the tension that will carry us through the novel. Elizabeth becomes Darcy's enemy at that first dance, when she overhears him telling Bingley she is not handsome enough to dance with. Later, when he meets her at the next ball, he has begun to change his mind, but she refuses his offer to dance. At Netherfield they meet again, and this time they dance, a dance that, despite its civilized appearance, is charged with tension; his attraction to her increases in direct ratio to her repulsion. The discordant notes in their dialogue contradict the smooth movements of their bodies on the dance floor.

Austen's protagonists are private individuals set in public places. Their desire for privacy and reflection is continually being adjusted to their situation within a very small community, which keeps them under its constant scrutiny. The balance between the public and the private is essential to this world.

The backwards-and-forward rhythm of the dance is repeated in the actions and movements of the two protagonists, around whom the plot is shaped. Parallel events bring them closer together and then thrust them apart. Throughout the novel, Elizabeth and Darcy constantly move towards and away from each other. Each time they move forward, the ground is prepared for the next move. Moving backwards is accompanied by a re-appraisal of the former forward move. There is a give-and-take in the dance, a constant adapting to the partner's needs and steps. Note for example how terrible Mr. Collins is on the dance floor, as is the uncouth Thorpe in *Northanger Abbey*. Their inability to dance well is a sign of their inability to adapt themselves to the needs of their partners.

The centrality of dialogue in *Pride and Prejudice* fits well into the dancelike structure of the novel. It seems that in almost every scene there is an ongoing dialogue between Elizabeth and Darcy. This dialogue is either real or imagined, but it is a constant preoccupation, leading from exchanges with the other to exchanges with the self. This central dialogue, between Elizabeth and Darcy and Elizabeth and herself, is accompanied by a multiplicity of other conversations.

One of the most wonderful things about *Pride and Prejudice* is the variety of voices it embodies. There are so many different forms of dialogue: between several people, between two people, internal dialogue and dialogue through letters. All tensions are created and resolved through dialogue. Austen's ability to create such multivocality, such diverse voices and intonations in relation and in confrontation within the cohesive structure of the novel, is one of the best examples of the democratic aspect of the novel. In Austen's novels, there are spaces for oppositions that do not need to eliminate each other in order to exist. There is also space—not just space but a necessity—for self-reflection and self-criticism. Such reflection is the cause of change. We needed no message, no outright call for plurality, to prove our point. All we needed was to read and appreciate the cacophony of voices to understand its democratic imperative. This was where Austen's danger lay.

It is not accidental that the most unsympathetic characters in Austen's novels are those who are incapable of genuine dialogue with others. They rant. They lecture. They scold. This incapacity for true dialogue implies an incapacity for tolerance, self-reflection and empathy. Later, in Nabokov, this incapacity takes on monstrous forms in characters such as Humbert Humbert in *Lolita* and Kinbote in *Pale Fire.*

Pride and Prejudice is not poetic, but it has its own cacophonies and harmonies; voices approach and depart and take a turn around the room. Right now, as I flip through the pages, I can hear them leaping out. I catch Mary's pathetic, dry voice and Kitty's cough and Miss Bingley's chaste insinuations, and here I catch a word by the courtly Sir Lucas. I can't quite hear Miss Darcy, shy and reserved as she is, but I hear steps going up and down the stairs, and Elizabeth's light mockery and Darcy's reserved, tender tone, and as I close the book, I hear the ironic tone of the narrator. And even with the book closed, the voices do not stop—there are echoes and reverberations that seem to leap off the pages and mischievously leave the novel tingling in our ears.

4

"Our Sanaz has so many qualifications," Azin was saying as she meticulously inspected her fingernails. "She doesn't need a two-bit boy whose greatest accomplishment has been to dodge the draft and move to England." Her tone was needlessly ferocious, and at the moment, she was targeting no one in particular. This was when I began to pay serious attention to Azin's nails. She had taken to polishing them a bright tomato red and appeared totally preoccupied by their shape and color. Throughout class, whenever she found the opportunity, she would scrutinize her nails as if the red varnish connected her to a different dimension, a place known only to Azin. When she stretched her hand to take a pastry or an orange, her eyes attentively followed the movement of her red-tipped fingers.

We were discussing Sanaz during the break. She was due back from Turkey the following week. Mitra, the only one who was in touch with her, updated us: he was very sweet, she loved him, they were engaged. They had gone together to the seaside; there will be pictures, lots of pictures. The aunt doesn't think he's such a catch.

She thinks he's a nice boy, better as a boyfriend, needs someone to help him hold up his pants (dimples widen). That didn't seem to bother our Sanaz.

"Nothing wrong with being young," Yassi chirped in. "That's how my uncle and his wife started—and on top of that, they had no money. Actually, come to think of it, three of my uncles married that way. All but the youngest, who never married—he joined a political organization," she added, as if that explained why he had never married.

We were hearing about the uncles more often now, because the eldest was in Iran for a three-week vacation. He was Yassi's favorite. He listened to her poetry, looked over her sister Mina's paintings, commented on their shy mother's stories. He was patient, attentive, encouraging and at the same time a bit critical, pointing out this little flaw, that weakness. Yassi was elated whenever he came for visits, or on the rare occasions he wrote home or called from the States and asked specifically to talk to her. He was the only one who was allowed to put ideas into Yassi's head without any reproach. And he did put ideas into her head. First, he had encouraged her to continue her musical practices; then he had said, Why not go to the university in Tehran? Now he advised her to continue her studies in America. Everything he told Yassi about life in America—events that seemed normal and routine to him—gained a magical glow in her greedy eyes. She regularly checked these stories with me, and I always had something of my own to add. I felt as if her uncle and I were co-conspirators, leading young Yassi astray. And I worried: what if we were encouraging her into a life that was essentially not good for her? I could see how our encouragements also made Yassi, an affectionate and loyal girl, very much attached to her affectionate family, feel conflicted and depressed for days on end. She'd make fun of herself and say that she constantly feels . . . Indecisive? I'd ask. Nooo, what's the word? Suddenly her face would light up. Cantankerous! No, Yassi, that's not it. Definitely not cantankerous. Yes, well, indecisive as well as inadequate—that I do feel; maybe I also feel cantankerous.

Nowadays all my girls seemed to want to leave Iran—all except Mahshid, who was more than ever preoccupied by her job. She wanted a promotion and permanence, which she was denied on the basis of her past political affiliation with a religious opposition group. Mitra had already applied for a visa to Canada, although she and

Hamid had their doubts. His mother was against it, and then there was the prospect of an unknown future in Canada, while this life, despite its flaws, was a known quantity. Hamid had a good job; they were secure. "Over here, as his mother keeps reminding us, we are somebody, but over there . . ."

"I'm thinking of going," Azin said suddenly. "If Sanaz had an inkling of sense, she'd just go, or marry the guy, go there and then divorce him. What?" she asked defensively, confronted by the others' startled look, nervously fishing a cigarette out of her bag. "What did I say now?"

She did not light the cigarette—she never did during class sessions—but she held it between her long white fingers, with their tomato-red nails. Suddenly she noticed our silence and, like a child caught stealing a chocolate, she looked at her unlit cigarette and crushed it in the ashtray with a disarming smile.

How do you get away with those nails? I asked her, to change the subject. I wear gloves, she said. Even in summer I wear dark gloves. Polished nails, like makeup, were a punishable offense, resulting in flogging, monetary fines and up to one year imprisonment. Of course they know the trick, she said, and if they really want to bug you, they'll tell you to take off the gloves. She babbled on, talking about gloves and fingernails, and then she came to a sudden halt. It makes me happy, she said in a thin voice that did not suggest any trace of happiness. It's so red it takes my mind off things.

"Off what things?" Nassrin asked, gently for once.

"Oh, things. You know." And then she burst into tears. We were startled into silence. Manna grudgingly, with an obvious attempt to resist Azin's tears, passed her the box of tissues. Mahshid recoiled into her shell, and Nassrin leaned forward, her hands locked together in a ferocious grip. Yassi, who sat closest to Azin, leaned towards her, gently pressing her right shoulder.

5

I will never now discover the real wounds Azin hid, and the unreal ones she revealed. I look for some answer in the photograph we took on my last night in Tehran, my eyes diverted by a glint in Azin's round, gold earrings. Photographs can be deceptive, unless, like my magician, one has the gift of discovering something from the curve of a person's nose. I do not possess such gifts.

As I look at that photograph, none of Azin's troubles can be imagined. She looks carefree; her blond hair suits her pale skin and dark-honey eyes. She loved to seem outrageous, and the fact that she had been married three times supported her claims to this title. She had married her first husband before she'd turned eighteen and had divorced him within a year. She never explained what had happened with her second husband. Perhaps she married so often because marriage was easier in Iran than having a boyfriend.

Her husband, she told us, seemed to be frustrated by all that interested her. He was jealous of her books, her computer and her Thursday mornings. With a fixed smile, she related how he felt humiliated by what she called her "independent spirit"; he beat her up and then tried to placate her by swearing his undying love. I was almost physically hurt by her account. More than the beatings, it was his taunts that disturbed me—how he shouted that no one would marry her, that she was "used," like a secondhand car, that no man would want to have a secondhand wife. He would tell her that he could marry an eighteen-year-old girl; he could marry a fresh, first-hand eighteen-year-old any old time. He would tell her all this and yet he could not leave her. I remember not so much her words but how, as she continued her terrible story, her smile was belied by the shine of tears. After she told us her story, she said, And now you know why I am so often late for class. Later, Manna would say, without much sympathy, Trust Azin to try to get something cheap even out of her own troubles.

Soon we were all involved in Azin's marital problems. First I recounted them to Bijan after dinner, and then I talked to my best friend, a great lawyer with a weakness for lost causes, and convinced her to accept her case. From then on Azin—her vacillations, her husband, her complaints, her sincerity or lack of it—became a constant topic of our discussions.

These forays into the personal were not supposed to be part of the class, but they infiltrated our discussions, bringing with them further incursions. Starting with abstractions, we wandered into the realm of our own experiences. We talked about different instances in which the physical and mental abuse of women had been considered insufficient grounds for divorce by the ruling judge. We discussed cases in which the judge not only refused the wife's request for divorce but tried to blame her for her husband's beatings, ordering her to reflect on the wrongs she had committed to bring on his displeasure. We joked about the judge who used to regularly beat his own wife. In our case, the law really was blind; in its mistreatment of women, it knew no religion, race or creed.

6

It is said that the personal is political. That is not true, of course. At the core of the fight for political rights is the desire to protect ourselves, to prevent the political from intruding on our individual lives. Personal and political are interdependent but not one and the same thing. The realm of imagination is a bridge between them, constantly refashioning one in terms of the other. Plato's philosopher-king knew this and so did the blind censor, so it was perhaps not surprising that the Islamic Republic's first task had been to blur the lines and boundaries between the personal and the political, thereby destroying both.

When I am asked about life in the Islamic Republic of Iran, I cannot separate the most personal and private aspects of our existence from the gaze of the blind censor. I think of my girls, who came from very different backgrounds. Their dilemmas, regardless of their backgrounds and beliefs, were shared, and stemmed from the confiscation of their most intimate moments and private aspirations by the regime. This conflict lay at the heart of the paradox created by Islamic rule. Now that the mullahs ruled the land, religion was used as an instrument of power, an ideology. It was this ideological approach to faith that differentiated those in power from millions of ordinary citizens, believers like Mahshid, Manna and Yassi, who found the Islamic Republic their worst enemy. People like me hated the oppression, but these others had to deal with the betrayal. Yet even for them, the contradictions and inhibitions in their personal lives involved them more directly than the great matters of war and revolution. I lived in the Islamic Republic for eighteen years, yet I did not fully grasp this truth during the first years of upheaval, in the midst of the public executions and bloody demonstrations or over the eight years of war, when the red and white sirens mixed with the sounds of rockets and bombs. It became clear to me only after the war and after Khomeini's death, the two factors that had kept the country forcibly united, preventing the discordant voices and contradictions from surfacing.

Wait, you will say—discord, contradictions? Was this not the time of *hope,* of *reform* and *peace*? Were we not told how Mr. Ghomi's star was descending and that of Mr. Forsati was in ascension? You will remind me of the end of the previous section, where the choices for the radical revolutionaries appeared to be either to set fire to themselves or to change with the times. As for Mahshid, Nassrin and Manna, you will say, They *survived—they were given a second chance.* Are you not overdramatizing a bit, you will inquire, for the narrative effect of your story?

No, I am not overdramatizing. Life in the Islamic Republic was always too explosive, too dramatic and chaotic, to shape into the desired order required for a narrative effect. Times of peace often bring to the surface the extent of the damage, placing in the foreground the gaping craters where houses used to be. It is then that the muted voices, the evil spirits that had been trapped in the bottle, fly out in different directions.

Manna used to say that there are two Islamic Republics: the one of words and the one of reality. In the Islamic Republic of words, the decade of the nineties began with promises of peace and reform. One morning we had woken up to hear that the Council of Guardians, after deliberations, had chosen former president Hojatol-Islam Ali Khamenei as the successor to Ayatollah Khomeini. Before his election, Khamenei's political position was dubious; he was linked to some of the most conservative and reactionary groups within the ruling elite, but he was also known to be a patron of the arts. He had consorted with poets and had earned a severe rebuke from Khomeini for softening the tone of the fatwa against Salman Rushdie.

But this same person, the new Supreme Leader—who now held the highest religious and political title in the country, demanding the greatest respect—was a fake. He knew it, we knew it and, what was worse, his own colleagues and fellow clerics, who had chosen him, knew it. The media and government propaganda had omitted the fact that this man had been raised overnight to the rank of ayatollah; such a position had to be earned before it could be bestowed, and his elevation was a clear violation of the clerical rules and regulations. Khamenei chose to join the side of the most reactionary. It was not just his religious beliefs that guided his decision; he did it out of necessity, for political support and protection, to compensate for the lack of respect from his own peers. From a tepid liberal he turned overnight into an irredeemable hard-liner. In a moment of rare candor Mrs. Rezvan had said, I know these people better than you; they change their words more often than their clothes. Islam has become a business, she went on, like oil for Texaco. These people who deal in Islam—each one tries to package it better than the next. And we are stuck with them. You don't think they'd ever admit that we could live better without oil, do you? Can they say Islam is not needed for good government? No, but the reformers are shrewder; they will give you the oil a little cheaper, and promise to make it cleaner.

Our president, the powerful former speaker of the house, Hojatol-Islam Rafsanjani, the first to earn the title of reformist, was the new hope, but he who called himself the general of reconstruction and was nicknamed Ayatollah Gorbachev was notorious for financial and political corruption and for his involvement in terrorizing dissidents both at home and abroad. He did talk about some liberalization of the laws—again, as Manna reminded us, these reforms meant that you could be a little Islamic, you could cheat around the edges, show a bit of hair from under your scarf. It was like saying you could be a little fascist, a moderate fascist or communist, I added. Or a little pregnant, Nima laughingly concluded.

The result of such moderation was that Sanaz and Mitra were not afraid to wear their scarves more daringly, show a bit of hair, but the morality police also had the right to arrest them. When they reminded the police of the president's words, the Revolutionary Guards would immediately arrest and jail them, hurling insults against the president, his mother and any other son of a . . . who issued such orders in the land of Islam. But the president's liberalism, as would later be the case with his successor, President Khatami, stopped there. Those who took his reforms seriously paid a heavy price, sometimes with their lives, while their captors went free and unpunished. When the dissident writer Saidi Sirjani, who had the illusion of presidential support, was jailed, tortured and finally murdered, no one came to his assistance—another example of the constant struggle between the Islamic Republic of words and deeds, one that continues to this day. Their own interests precede everything, Mrs. Rezvan was fond of reminding me. No matter how liberal they claim to be, they never give up the Islamic façade: that's their trademark. Who would need Mr. Rafsanjani in a democratic Iran?

This was a period of hope, true, but we harbor the illusion that times of hope are devoid of tensions and conflicts when, in my experience, they are the most dangerous. Hope for some means its loss for others; when the hopeless regain some hope, those in power—the ones who had taken it away—become afraid, more protective of their endangered interests, more repressive. In many ways these times of hope, of greater leniency, were as disquieting as before. Life had acquired the texture of fiction written by a bad writer who cannot impose order and logic on his characters as they run amok. It was a time of peace, a time for reconstruction, for the ordinary rhyme and rhythm of life to take over again, and instead a cacophony of voices overwhelmed us and came to supersede the somber sounds of war.

The war with Iraq had ended, but the government continued its war against internal enemies, against those it considered to be representatives of cultural decadence and Western influence. Rather than weakening these enemies and eliminating them, this campaign of oppression had in some ways strengthened them. Political parties and political enemies were in jail and banned, but in the field of culture—literature, music, art and philosophy—the dominant trend was with the secular forces; the Islamic elite had failed to gain ascendancy in any of these areas. The battle over culture became more central as more radical Muslim youths, intellectuals, journalists and academics defected to the other side. Disillusioned with the Islamic Revolution and confronted by the ideological void that followed the collapse of the Soviet Union, they had nowhere to turn but to the Western democracies they had once so vehemently opposed. Those whom the regime had tried to destroy or silence by accusing them of being Westernized could not be silenced or eliminated; they were as much a part of Iranian culture as these others, its self-appointed guardians. But what most frightened the Islamic elite was that these very elements had now become models for the increasingly disenchanted former revolutionaries, as well as for the youth—the so-called children of the revolution.

Many in the Ministry of Islamic Culture and Guidance started taking sides with the writers and artists, allowing books that previously would have been deemed un-Islamic to be published. My book on Nabokov was published in 1994 with the support of some of the enlightened elements in that ministry. Experienced directors whose films had been banned after the revolution were allowed to show their work thanks to the progressive head of the Farabi Film Foundation, who would later be opposed and impeached by the reactionaries within the regime. The ministry itself became a battleground between different factions, what we would now call the hard-liners and the reformists. Many former revolutionaries were reading and interpreting works of Western thinkers and philosophers and questioning their own orthodox approaches. It was a sign of hope, if an ironic one, that they were being transformed by the very ideas and systems they had once set out to destroy.

Unable to decipher or understand complications or irregularities, angered by what they considered betrayals in their own ranks, the officials were forced to impose their simple formulas on fiction as they did on life. Just as they censored the colors and tones of reality to suit their black-and-white world, they censored any form of interiority in fiction; ironically, for them as for their ideological opponents, works of imagination that did not carry a political message were deemed dangerous. Thus, in a writer such as Austen, for example, whether they knew it or not, they found a natural adversary.

7

"You should stop blaming the Islamic Republic for all our problems," said my magician. I frowned, digging into the snow with the tip of my boots. We had woken up to a snowy, sunny morning, the best part of a Tehran winter. The smooth blanket covering the trees and piling up high on the sidewalks appeared to shine with millions of tiny suns.

It was the kind of day that made you feel exhilarated and childlike despite your protests against the pollution and the less tangible but more important complaints you carried in your heart and mind. Even as I tried to air my grievances, the pale memory of my mother's homemade cherry syrup, which she used to mix with fresh snow, rebelled against my expressions of gloom. But I was not one to give way easily; I was overburdened with thoughts of Azin's husband and Sanaz's young man. For the past fifteen minutes, I had been trying to convey my girls' trials and tribulations to my magician, peppering my account with justified and unjustified accusations against the root cause of all our woes: the Islamic Republic of Iran.

Her first week back after her trip, Sanaz had returned to class in a mood of becomingly restrained elation. Photographs were spread out on the glass-topped table: the family in the hotel lobby; Sanaz and a young man with dark brown hair and gentle brown eyes, in jeans and a blue shirt, leaning against a balustrade; the engagement party; Sanaz, in a red dress, her magnificent hair caressing her bare shoulders, looking up at this personable young man in his dark suit and pale blue shirt, and he gazing into her eyes with tender affection—or there he was, slipping an engagement ring on her finger, she looking at it wistfully (it's a shame his parents had bought the ring without consulting us, she said later). And here is the renegade aunt, and the depressed mother, and the obnoxious brother. Before she knew it, he had to return to London and she to Tehran. (There was so little Ali and I said to each other, Sanaz would tell us with some frustration—we were always surrounded by family.)

Two weeks later, she was subdued throughout the class discussion. During the break, a woeful Sanaz, apologizing for taking up class time with her personal stories, her eyes brimming with tears and her right hand pushing an absent strand of hair from her forehead, announced that everything was off, the marriage was off. She had been jilted. A phone call again: he just couldn't see how he could make her happy. He was still a student; how could he support her? How long would it take before they could actually live together? It wasn't fair, he kept saying, not fair to her; he was making up all sorts of excuses. I can see his point, she said, I'd shared the same worries, but still, I wish he didn't feel he had to be so goddamn fair! He would always love her, he pleaded. What else could he say? Sanaz had asked us. Bloody coward, I thought.

Everyone as a result was being was extra nice to Sanaz. His family was very angry with him. He had been corrupted by the years he'd spent among the cold and unfeeling English, his mother said. They—Westerners—don't have personal feelings like we do. He'll change his mind, his father said with conviction; just give him time. None of them had seen that perhaps their own meddling and pressure had forced him into taking a step he was not sure of.

It was all so intolerable to Sanaz, all this commiseration. Even her brother had been sympathetic. There were rumors of another woman—there *always* are, Azin chimed in; that's men for you. No, Sanaz said in response to Mahshid's questions, she wasn't Persian, not that it mattered. Some said Swedish, others English. *Of course!* A foreign girl: always a catch—who had said that? Sanaz was made even more desperate by the silent, funereal way her family and friends walked around her. If only her brother would throw a tantrum, she said, forcing a smile through her tears—confiscate her car or something. Today was the first time she'd had a chance to get away from them, and already she felt better.

Men are always more likable, more desirable, when they're unavailable, Manna said in a surprisingly bitter tone. After a pause, she added enigmatically, And I'm not saying this to be nice to Sanaz.

Men! Nassrin said angrily. Men! echoed Azin. Yassi, who seemed to have suddenly shrunk to her normal size, sat up straight with her hands locked in her lap. Only the aunt was happy, Sanaz informed us. "Thank God, he saved you from your own folly" had been her first words. What do you expect? Only a fool would think it normal that a boy his age, or any age, could live alone for five years without having affairs. I did, Sanaz told her. Well, you were a fool.

Sanaz's reaction on the whole had been calm and collected. She was almost relieved. In the back of her mind, she had always thought it couldn't work, not in this way. But the hurt remained: why had he rejected her? Had she become too provincial for him in comparison with other girls, say, a fine English girl, not coy, not afraid of staying the night? Heartbreak is heartbreak, I reasoned. Even English or American girls are jilted by their lovers. We had read some fine stories—"The Jilting of Granny Weatherall," remember? And then of course there was "A Rose for Miss Emily." Sanaz later joked that she was thinking of making herself more memorable by imitating

Miss Havisham, her heroine of the moment. Only she had not even bought a wedding dress, she added wistfully.

How had we digressed from Sanaz's predicaments to life in the Islamic Republic? We had somehow managed to end our discussions with anecdotes about the regime: the number of clerics and high-ranking officials with green cards, the ruling elite's inferiority complex, burning the American flag on the one hand and being obsequious to Westerners, especially American journalists, on the other. And then there was Faezeh Rafsanjani, the president's daughter, with her blue jeans and Reeboks and her bleached hair peeking out from under her chador.

I had explained all this in detail to my magician, drawing for him vivid and heartrending pictures of Sanaz's heartbreak and Azin's grief. I had concluded, dramatically, that this regime had so penetrated our hearts and minds, insinuating itself into our homes, spying on us in our bedrooms, that it had come to shape us against our own will. How could we, under such scrutiny, separate our personal woes from the political ones? It felt good to know where to put the blame, one of the few compensations of victimhood—"and suffering is another bad habit," as Bellow had said in *Herzog*.

There was a raising of the right eyebrow, followed by a quizzical ironic look. "Tell me," he said sardonically. "How exactly does the jilting of a beautiful girl relate to the Islamic Republic? Do you mean to say that in other parts of the world women are not abused by their husbands, that they are not jilted?" I felt too petulant and perhaps too helpless to react reasonably, although I could see the logic of his argument; so I kept my silence.

"Because the regime won't leave you alone, do you intend to conspire with it and give it complete control over your life?" he continued, never one not to drive his point home. "Of course you *are* right," he said a little later. "This regime has managed to such an extent to colonize our every moment that we can no longer think of our lives as separate from its existence. It's become so omnipotent that perhaps it isn't so far-fetched to hold it responsible for the success or failure of our love affairs. Let me remind you of Mr. Bellow, your latest beau." He paused on the word *beau* for a few seconds. "Remember that sentence you were quoting from him—one of the many we have been regaled with in the past two weeks—'first these people murdered you, then they forced you to brood over their crimes.'

"Are you listening?" he said, bringing his quizzical eyes closer to my face. "Where have you wandered off to?"

"Oh, I'm here all right," I said. "I was just thinking."

"Right," he said, remembering his British training.

"Really, I was listening," I said. "You've just clarified something for me, something I'd been thinking of a lot lately." He waited for me to continue. "I was thinking about life, liberty and the pursuit of happiness, about the fact that my girls are not happy. What I mean is that they feel doomed to be unhappy."

"And how do you propose to go about making them understand that it *is* their right?" he asked. "Surely not by encouraging them to act like victims. They have to learn to fight for their happiness."

I continued to dig my boots deeper into the snow, struggling to keep pace with him at the same time. "But so long as we fail to grasp this, and keep fighting for political freedom without understanding its dependence on individual freedoms, on the fact that your Sanaz shouldn't have to go all the way to Turkey to be courted, we don't deserve those rights."

Having listened to his lecture and not finding anything in it to contradict, I allowed myself my own train of thought. We walked for some time in silence. "But don't you see that in trying to make them understand this, I might be doing these girls more harm than good?" I said, perhaps rather dramatically. "You know, being with me, hearing about my past experiences, they keep creating this uncritical, glowing picture of that other world, of the West. . . . I've, I don't know, I think I've . . ."

"You mean you've been helping them create a parallel fantasy," he said, "one that runs against the fantasy that the Islamic Republic has made of their lives."

"Yes, yes!" I said excitedly.

"Well, first of all, it's not all your fault. None of us can live in and survive *this* fantasy world—we all need to create a paradise to escape into. Besides," he said, "there *is* something you can do about it."

"There is?" I said eagerly, still dejected and dying for once to be told what to do. "Yes, there is, and you are in fact doing it in this class, if you don't spoil it. Do what all poets do with their philosopher-kings. You don't need to create a parallel fantasy of the West. Give them the best of what that other world can offer: give them pure fiction—give them back their imagination!" he ended triumphantly, and looked at me as if he expected hurrahs and the clapping of hands for his wise advice. "You know it might do you some good if you practiced what you preached for a change. Take the example of one Jane Austen," he said with what appeared to me a patronizing munificence.

"You used to preach to us all that she ignored politics, not because she didn't know any better but because she didn't allow her work, her imagination, to be swallowed up by the society around her. At a time when the world was engulfed in the Napoleonic Wars, she created her own independent world, a world that you, two centuries later, in the Islamic Republic of Iran, teach as the fictional ideal of democracy. Remember all that talk of yours about how the first lesson in fighting tyranny is to do your own thing and satisfy your own conscience?" he continued patiently. "You keep talking about democratic spaces, about the need for personal and creative spaces. Well, go and create them, woman! Stop nagging and focusing your energy on what the Islamic Republic does or says and start focusing on your Austen."

I knew he was right, although I was too frustrated and too angry with myself to admit it. Fiction was not a panacea, but it did offer us a critical way of appraising and grasping the world—not just our world but that other world that had become the object of our desires. He was right. I was not listening, otherwise I would have had to admit that my girls, like millions of other citizens, by refusing to give up their right to pursue happiness, had created a dent in the Islamic Republic's stern fantasy world.

When he resumed, his voice seemed to come from afar and to reach me through a fog. "When you were talking of creating this secret class of yours, I thought it might be a good idea," he was saying, "partly because it would divert your attention from politics. But I see it's done the opposite—it has involved you even more."

When I first told him about my decision to resign from the university and to create this secret class he had said, How are you going to survive? You have severed your public contacts, your teaching is your last refuge. I said I wanted to teach a class, a literature workshop at home, with only a few select students who really love literature.

Will you help me? I will help you, he said, of course, but do you know what this means? What? You will be leaving us soon. You are withdrawing more and more into yourself. You have gradually resigned from all activities. Yes, but what if I have my class? Your class will be at home. You used to talk about writing your next book in Persian. Now all we talk about is what you will be saying at your next conference in the U.S. or in Europe. You are writing for other readers. I said, I have you. He said, I am not a good example. You use me as part of your dreamworld.

When we parted and I headed back home, my mood had already changed. I was thinking of the new novel I had lately been planning to add to our list—Saul Bellow's *The Dean's December*—one that dealt with the ordeals of the East and those of the West. I felt guilty about my complaints to my magician. I had so much wanted him to change everything right there and then, to rub the magic lamp and make the Revolutionary Guards vanish, along with Azin's husband and Mahshid's boss. I wanted him to put a stop to all this, and he was telling me not to get so involved. I felt ashamed of myself for refusing to understand him, for acting like a petulant child carelessly punching a beloved parent.

The sun had already started to set as I returned home; it seemed to withdraw one by one the brilliant specks it had scattered over the snow. When I got home I felt grateful to see a fire blazing in the fireplace. Bijan looked serene in a chair drawn closer to the fire, a small glass of bootleg vodka near him on the table, reading *The Long Goodbye*. From the window I could see the snow-covered branches and the faded outlines of the mountains, barely discernible behind the haze.

8

"They tried to be very modern about it," Yassi said with a hint of sarcasm, sprawled in her usual place on the couch. Yassi was narrating her latest adventure with a "gentleman caller"—her term. There was a great pressure on her to get married: her best friends and closest cousins were either married or spoken for. "Both his family and mine agreed that we had to get to know each other before coming to any decisions. So we go to this park, and we're supposed to become intimately acquainted by walking and talking for the next hour," she said in the same sarcastic tone but with an expression that suggested she was enjoying herself.

"He and I walk in front, followed by my parents, my older sister and two of his sisters. I can almost hear them as they pretend to talk casually about all kinds of things while the two of us pretend to ignore their presence. I ask him about his field: mechanical engineering. Reading anything interesting? Doesn't have time to read. I have a feeling he wants to look at me, but he can't. When he came to my uncle's house to officially ask for my hand, he had to keep his head down the whole time, and here again it's impossible to get a good look. So we walk side by side, our eyes glued to the ground. All the time I'm thinking crazy thoughts, like, How would a man know that the woman he was intending to marry was not bald?"

"That's easy," said Nassrin. "In the old days, women from the man's family used to scrutinize the would-be bride. Even her teeth."

"Thank God I have all my teeth! Anyway, we were passing our time in this fashion, until suddenly I got a brilliant idea: I started to walk faster, catching them all by surprise. As they tried to adjust to my pace, I came to a sudden halt, forcing them to almost collide into us. He was genuinely startled but tried to hide it by adjusting to my pace. I made some futile attempts to catch his eyes. Here's what I was thinking: if he gets it and laughs, I'll give it a chance. If he doesn't, that's it—I won't waste my time. I knew *every* one of my uncles would have immediately joined me in the game." After this, she fell silent.

Well, what happened? "Oh," she said as if she'd woken from a trance, "nothing." Nothing? "No, the idiot didn't even ask me why I was suddenly walking faster. Out of politeness, he just tried to fall into step with me. After a while I got tired of it and then we said good-bye and I didn't respond to their inquiries until they stopped asking. I'm sure he's by now happily married to a girl with less flesh on her," she said, looking at us merrily. She always loved telling a good story, even when she herself was the butt of the joke.

It had been an exhausting week for Yassi, what with this new suitor and her uncle's departure for the States. Every time her uncle visited Iran—and it was not often—he provoked doubts and questions in Yassi, who would be plagued for weeks with vague and uneasy longings that made her yearn, without exactly knowing what for. She knew now that she must go to America, as she had known when she was twelve that she must play the forbidden musical instrument. Her playing of the instrument, her insistence on going to university in Tehran, her choosing to come to this class—all were preparations that led her towards her final goal: to be physically where her uncles were and to get a taste of the tantalizing fruit that had always dangled over the lives of her mother and aunts, beckoning and just out of reach. They, the women, had lacked nothing in intelligence and intellect, but they had lacked freedom. Yassi had no choice but to want to be like her uncles—not necessarily like them, but to be possessed of what seemed to her their inalienable rights.

I didn't want her to be married. I wanted her to go through the whole ordeal and conquer the obstacles. The odds were overwhelmingly against her, from family opposition—it was unprecedented for a girl to go abroad to study—to enormous financial difficulties. Then there was the problem of getting accepted to an American college and obtaining a visa. I wanted her to succeed not only for herself but also for the rest of us. I always had a hankering for the security of impossible dreams.

This was a day for gentleman callers; Sanaz, too, was full of stories. After the failure of her engagement, Sanaz went on a spree, going on dates with different suitors and giving us meticulous accounts of the American-educated engineer with a green card—a status symbol—who had picked her out in a family photograph and, on arrival in Tehran, had sought her out and invited her to a Swiss restaurant; the rich merchant who loved the thought of an educated, attractive wife and wanted to buy a whole library for her so that she wouldn't leave home, and so on. These outings were a matter of binge and purge for Sanaz.

"Learn from us," said Azin. "Why do you need to be married?" The flirtatious note had briefly returned to her voice. "Don't take these people seriously—just go out with them to have fun."

My lawyer friend was having a great deal of difficulty in trying to help Azin. At first Azin had been adamant about wanting a divorce. Ten days later she had come to the lawyer's office with her husband, mother-in-law and sisters-in-law. She thought reconciliation was possible. Soon after that, she barged in without an appointment; she was all bruised, claimed that he had beaten her again and taken their little girl to his mother's house. Then at night he had knelt by her bedside, weeping and pleading with her not to leave him. When I mentioned this to Azin, she broke into tears again, saying that he would take the child away from her if she went through with the divorce. That girl was her whole life, and you know the courts, child custody always went to the father. She knew the only reason he wanted the child was to hurt her. He would never care for her; most probably he'd send her to his mother's. Azin had applied for a visa to Canada, but even if her application was accepted, she couldn't leave the country without her husband's permission. Only if I take my own life can I act without my husband's permission, she said, desperately and dramatically.

Manna agreed with Azin, but it was difficult for her to admit it. "If I were you, I'd get out of this country while I can" had been her advice to Sanaz. "Don't stay here and don't marry anyone who'll have to stay here. You'll only rot."

Mahshid looked at her reproachfully. "This is your country," she said, pursing her lips. "There's a lot you can do."

"There's nothing you can do—*nothing*," said Manna with a firm finality.

"You can write and you can teach," said Mahshid, throwing a passing glance at me. "We need good critics. We need good teachers."

"Yes," said Manna, "like Professor Nafisi. Work your head off for so many years, and then what? The other day Nima was saying he would be making more money if he'd become a street vendor instead of spending all those years getting an M.A. in English lit."

"If everybody leaves," said Mahshid, her eyes glued to the floor, "who will help make something of this country? How can we be so irresponsible?"

This was a question I asked myself day and night. We can't all leave this country, Bijan had told me—*this* is our home. The world is a large place, my magician had said when I went to him with my woes. You can write and teach wherever you are. You will be read more and heard better, in fact, once you are over there. To go or not to go? In the long run, it's all very personal, my magician reasoned. I always admired your former colleague's honesty, he said. Which former col-

league? Dr. A, the one who said his only reason for leaving was because he liked to drink beer freely. I am getting sick of people who
cloak their personal flaws and desires in the guise of patriotic fervor.
They stay because they have no means of living anywhere else, because if they leave, they won't be the big shots they are over here; but
they talk about sacrifice for the homeland. And then those who do
leave claim they've gone in order to criticize and expose the regime.
Why all these justifications?

He had a point, but things were not that simple: I knew Bijan
wanted to stay not because he couldn't find a job or a place in the
States—most of his immediate family was there, and he himself had
lived there more years than in Iran. I want to stay because I love this
country, he told me. We should stay as a form of resistance, to show
that we are not out-maneuvered. Our very presence is a thorn in their
side. Where else in the world, he asked me, would a talk on *Madame
Bovary* draw such crowds and nearly lead to a riot? We can't give up
and leave; we are needed here. I love this country, he repeated. Did I
not love this country? I asked myself.

Bijan agrees with you, I told Mahshid. He is more rooted to the
idea of home. He created this home, literally building our apartment
and our place in the mountains, and established routines like watching the BBC and cooking barbecues for friends. It's much harder to
dismantle that world and to rebuild it somewhere else. I guess the
point is we all have to make our own choices according to our potentials and limitations, I said, and as I was saying it, I knew how superficial my words must have sounded to them.

"I have the best excuse for going to America," said a cheeky Yassi.
"It's because I am so plump. Fat girls, I'm told, have a much better
time over there. They say Americans like them with a little meat on
their bones."

"It depends on the girl," Mitra offered with a slight jab at Yassi.
Mitra, of course, would have no problem anywhere on earth, with her
dimples and large brown eyes. She and Hamid had decided to head to
Syria for a week to interview for Canadian residency—Canada did
not accept immigrant visa applications in Iran. Although she still vacillated between leaving and staying.

"Over here we have an identity," she said doubtfully. "We can
make something of our lives. Over there, life is unknown."

"The ordeal of freedom," Nassrin said elliptically, echoing my favorite line from Bellow.

Only Mahshid was silent. She, I knew, was more confident than the rest about what she wanted. She didn't want to marry. Despite all her traditional beliefs and moral imperatives, Mahshid was less of a marrying type than Sanaz. She disapproved of the regime, but her problems were more practical than existential. Long disappointed about the prospects of marrying her ideal man, and utterly without illusions about her ability to survive abroad, she had set her whole heart and mind on her work. At the moment, her problem was how to surmount the stupidity and ignorance of her bosses, who rewarded her exceptional work with something akin to envy and held her political past over her head like a sword.

I worried about Mahshid and the solitary path she had chosen for herself. And about Yassi and her irrepressible fantasies about that never-never land where her uncles lived. I worried about Sanaz and her broken heart and about Nassrin and her memories and about Azin. I worried about them all, but I worried most about Manna. She had one of these honest, demanding intelligences that is hardest on itself. Everything in her present situation offended her, from the fact that she and her husband were still financially dependent on her family to the mediocre state of intellectuals and the everyday cruelties of the Islamic regime. Nima, sharing the same feelings and desires, reinforced her imposed isolation. Yet unlike Yassi, Manna obstinately refused to do anything about her situation. She seemed to take an almost gleeful satisfaction from the knowledge that her powers were going to waste. She, like my magician, was determined to be harder on herself than on the world around her. They both blamed themselves for the fact that such inferior people had control of their lives.

"How is it that we keep coming back to marriage," Mitra said, "when we're supposed to be here to talk about books?"

"What we need," I said with a laugh, "is for Mr. Nahvi to remind us how trivial we are to read Austen and talk about marriage." Mr. Nahvi, with his dusty suit, buttoned-up shirt, layered hair and squishy eyes was every once in a while resurrected as an easy target of our jokes. He earned my eternal contempt the day he announced that the protagonist in Gorky's *Mother* was a far finer specimen of womanhood than all the flighty young ladies in Jane Austen's novels.

9

Olga was silent.

"Ah," cried Vladimir, "Why can't you love me as I love you."

"I love my country," she said.

"So do I," he exclaimed.

"And there is something I love even more strongly," Olga continued, disengaging herself from the young man's embrace.

"And that is?" he queried.

Olga let her limpid blue eyes rest on him, and answered quickly: "It is the Party."

Every great book we read became a challenge to the ruling ideology. It became a potential threat and menace not so much because of what it said but how it said it, the attitude it took towards life and fiction. Nowhere was this challenge more apparent than in the case of Jane Austen.

I had spent a great deal of time in my classes at Allameh contrasting Flaubert, Austen and James to the ideological works like Gorky's *Mother*, Sholokhov's *And Quiet Flows the Don* and some of the so-called realistic fiction coming out of Iran. The above passage, quoted by Nabokov in his *Lectures on Russian Literature*, caused a great deal of mirth in one of my classes at Allameh. What happens, I asked my students, when we deny our characters the smallest speck of individuality? Who is more realized in her humanity, Emma Bovary or Olga of the limpid blue eyes?

One day after class, Mr. Nahvi followed me to my office. He tried to tell me that Austen was not only anti-Islamic but that she was guilty of another sin: she was a colonial writer. I was surprised to hear this from the mouth of someone who until then had mainly quoted and misquoted the Koran. He told me that *Mansfield Park* was a book that condoned slavery, that even in the West they had now seen the error of their ways. What confounded me was that I was almost certain Mr. Nahvi had not read *Mansfield Park*.

It was only later, on a trip to the States, that I found out where Mr. Nahvi was getting his ideas from when I bought a copy of Edward Said's *Culture and Imperialism*. It was ironic that a Muslim fundamentalist should quote Said against Austen. It was just as ironic that the most reactionary elements in Iran had come to identify with and co-opt the work and theories of those considered revolutionary in the West.

Mr. Nahvi kept following me to my office and spouting these pearls of wisdom. He seldom brought them up in class; there, he usually kept silent, preserving a placid and detached expression, as if he had agreed to remain in class as a favor to us. Mr. Nahvi was one of the few students in whom I was unable to find a single redeeming quality. I could say, like Eliza Bennet, that he was not a sensible man. One day, after a really exhausting argument, I told him, Mr. Nahvi, I want to remind you of something: I am not comparing you to Elizabeth Bennet. There is nothing of her in you, to be sure—you are as different as man and mouse. But remember how she is obsessed with Darcy, constantly trying to find fault with him, almost cross-examining every new acquaintance to confirm that he is as bad as she thinks? Remember her relations with Wickham? How the basis for her sympathy is not so much her feelings for him as his antipathy for Darcy? Look at how you speak about what you call the West. You can never talk about it without giving it an adjective or an attribute—*decadent, vile, corrupt, imperial.* Beware of what happened to Elizabeth!

I still remember the look on his face as I said this and, for once, used my privilege as his teacher to have the last word.

Mr. Nahvi exercised a great deal of influence in our university, and he once reported Nassrin to the disciplinary committee. His eagle eyes had detected her running up the stairs one day when she was late for a class. Nassrin at first refused to sign a retraction stating that she would promise never again to run on the university premises, even when she was late for class. She had finally conceded, persuaded by Mrs. Rezvan, who had reasoned with her that her obstinate resistance was not worth expulsion from the university.

During our reminiscences about Mr. Nahvi, I noticed Mitra and Sanaz whispering and giggling. When I asked them to share with us the source of their mirth, Sanaz encouraged a blushing Mitra to tell her story. She confessed that among their friends, they called Mr.

Nahvi the Mr. Collins of Tabatabai University, after Jane Austen's pompous clergyman.

One evening after class, Mr. Nahvi had suddenly appeared in front of Mitra. He had not seemed his usual . . . "Redoubtable self?" the incorrigible Yassi suggested. No, not exactly. "Pontificating? Pompous? Ponderous?" Yassi continued, unabashed. No. Anyway, Mr. Nahvi did not seem himself. His arrogance had given way to extreme nervousness as he handed Mitra an envelope. Sanaz nudged Mitra to describe the envelope. It was a hideous blue, she said. And it reeked. It reeked? Yes, it smelled of cheap perfume, of rosewater.

Inside the envelope, Mitra had found a one-page letter, with the same dreadful color and smell, written in immaculate handwriting, in black ink. "Tell 'em how he started the letter," Sanaz encouraged Mitra.

"Well, he, he actually began by writing . . ." Mitra trailed off, as if lost for words.

"*My golden daffodil!*" shouted Sanaz, bursting into laughter.

Really? Golden daffodil? Yes, and he had gone on to express his undying love for Mitra, whose every move and every word were ingrained in his heart and mind. Nothing—no power—had ever done to him what her smile, which he hoped was for him and him alone, could do. And so on and so forth.

What had Mitra done? we all wanted to know. All this had taken place in the middle of Mitra and Hamid's highly secretive courtship, Sanaz reminded us. The next day, when Mr. Nahvi happened to jump out of nowhere and waylay her in the street, she tried to explain to him how impossible it was for her to return his affections. He nodded philosophically and went away, only to reappear two days later. She had parked her car in an alley near the university and was in the process of opening the door to her small car when she became aware of a presence right behind her. "Like the shadow of Death," Nassrin ominously interjected. Well, she had turned to find Mr. Nahvi, wavy hair, squished eyes, ears jutting out—he had a book in his hands, a book of poems by e. e. cummings. And the blue of another envelope could be detected from between its pages. Before Mitra had time to protest, he thrust the book into her hands and disappeared.

"Tell Dr. Nafisi what he wrote," prompted Sanaz. "She'd love to know that her classes were of some use to Mr. Nahvi." Inside he had

written, *To my bashful rose.* And what else? And, well, he reproduced a
poem that you used to teach in your introduction to literature class:

> somewhere i have never travelled,gladly beyond
> any experience,your eyes have their silence:
> in your most frail gesture are things which enclose me,
> or which i cannot touch because they are too near
>
> your slightest look easily will unclose me
> though i have closed myself as fingers,
> you open always petal by petal myself as Spring opens
> (touching skilfully,mysteriously) her first rose
>
> or if your wish be to close me,i and
> my life will shut very beautifully,suddenly,
> as when the heart of this flower imagines
> the snow carefully everywhere descending;
>
> nothing which we are to perceive in this world equals
> the power of your intense fragility:whose texture
> compels me with the colour of its countries,
> rendering death and forever with each breathing
>
> (i do not know what it is about you that closes
> and opens;only something in me understands
> the voice of your eyes is deeper than all roses)
> nobody,not even the rain,has such small hands

It's enough to put you off teaching poetry, I said, infected by their
girlish mood.

"From now on, you should only teach morbid poems like *Childe
Harold* or 'The Rime of the Ancient Mariner,' " suggested Mahshid.

This time, Mitra felt she had to resort to more drastic measures
before things got out of hand. After several consultations with her
friends, she reached the conclusion that a plain outright *no* would be
dangerous to deliver to someone as influential as Mr. Nahvi. Best to
tell him a convincing lie that would put him in an impossible position.

By the time they next crossed paths, Mitra had plucked up the courage to stop Mr. Nahvi. Blushing and stammering, she told him that she had been too bashful to reveal the real reason for her rejection: she was engaged to be married to a distant relative. His family was influential and very traditional, and she was scared of what they would resort to if they found out about Mr. Nahvi's outpourings. The young man paused for a fraction of a second, as if rooted to the ground, and then turned away without a word, leaving Mitra, still slightly trembling, in the middle of the wide street.

10

The last New Year Mrs. Rezvan was in Tehran, she bought me three small clips. They were hair clips that many women used to keep their head scarves in place. I never learned to wear my scarf properly, and it had become a ritual between us that before talks or lectures she would check and make sure that it was more or less in place. She said, My dear Mrs. Nafisi, I'm sorry that this is what you will remember me by, but I do worry about you. Will you promise me you will wear these when I am gone? I want to see you here when I return.

Mrs. Rezvan was preparing to go to Canada. She had finally, after years of toil, managed to get her coveted scholarship to pursue her Ph.D. For years she had dreamed of this, but now she was too anxious to enjoy the moment. She constantly fretted about whether she would succeed, whether she was up to the task. I was happy that she was leaving, both for her sake and for my own. It came almost as a relief.

I felt at the time that she was overly ambitious, and that she used me and people like me to get where she wanted to go. Later I discovered there was more to the story. Hers was not a mere ambition to go places, to become president of the faculty, although she had that in mind too. She yearned to become a literary personage: her love of literature was real, yet her talents were limited and her ambition for power and control sometimes surpassed and even came to clash with that love. She managed to evoke such contradictory feelings in me. I felt she was always on the verge of telling me something important about herself, something that would reveal her to me. Perhaps I should have been more curious. Perhaps if I had been less wrapped up in her intrusions and demands, I would have noticed more.

In the late summer of 1990, for the first time in eleven years, my family and I left for Cyprus for a vacation and to meet up with my sisters-in-law, who had never seen our children. For years I was not allowed to leave the country, and when they finally did give me permission to leave, I felt paralyzed and could not make myself apply for a passport. If it were not for Bijan's patience and persistence, I never would have followed through. But I got my passport in the end, and we did really leave, without any misadventures. We stayed with a friend, one of Mrs. Rezvan's former students. She said Mrs. Rezvan used to ask her about me, my work and my family.

Later, after we had returned home, my friend informed me that the day we left, probably on the same plane aboard which we had flown to Tehran, Mrs. Rezvan had come to Cyprus on vacation. She was alone. She called my friend inquiring after me and was told that I was gone. My friend told me Mrs. Rezvan wanted her to take her to the same places we had visited together during my stay. She asked what I had done there, where I had gone. One day, they went to the beach where we had gone swimming.

Mrs. Rezvan was shy. She hesitated about putting on a swimsuit, and when she did, she wanted to go to a deserted part of the beach, where no one could see her. She ran into the water but came out after a short while, telling my friend that no matter how hard she tried, she could not get used to parading around in a swimsuit.

When she left Iran, Mrs. Rezvan disappeared from my life. Her absence was as complete as her presence had been pervasive. She did not write or call when she came back for her occasional visits; I heard about her from the secretary at the English Department. Twice she had asked for an extension in order to finish her dissertation. At times, walking down the halls or passing by her office, I was reminded of Mrs. Rezvan, whose absence was both a relief and a sorrow.

A few months after I came to America, I heard she was ill with cancer. I called her; she was not home. She called me back. Her voice was filled with the intimate formality of Tehran. She wanted to know about some of our common students and my work. And then for the first time she opened up and started talking about herself. She could not write—it involved so much pain—and she was always weak and fatigued. Her eldest daughter helped her. She had so many dreams, and she was hopeful. The openness was not so much in what she said as in her tone of voice, which conferred a certain air of confidence to her simple report of her weakness, her inability to write, her dependence on her daughter. She was optimistic about the latest treatment, although her cancer had spread far. She asked me about my work. I did not tell her that I was healthy and writing a book and, on the whole, enjoying myself.

That was the last time I talked to her; she was soon too sick to speak on the telephone. I thought of her almost obsessively. It seemed so unfair that she should have cancer when she was so near to reaching her goal. I did not want to talk to her to remind her that once again I had been the lucky one—I was granted a little more time on earth, the time she was so unfairly cheated of.

She died soon after our last conversation. Her intrusions now have taken a different form. In my mind from time to time, I resurrect and re-create her. I try to penetrate the unsaid feelings and emotions that hung between us. She keeps coming towards me through the flickering light, as in our first meeting, with that ironic sideways glance, and passes through me, leaving me with my doubts and regrets.

II

It was around the spring of 1996, early March in fact, that I first noticed Nassrin's metamorphosis. One day she came to class without her usual robe and scarf. Mahshid and Yassi wore different-colored scarves, and they took these off once they came into my apartment. But Nassrin was always dressed identically; the one variety she allowed herself was the color of her robe, which was interchangeably navy, black or dark brown.

That day, she had come to class later than usual and had casually taken off her coat, revealing a light blue shirt, a navy jacket and jeans. Her hair was long and soft and black, woven into a single plait that moved from side to side with the movement of her head. Manna and Yassi exchanged looks, and Azin told her she was looking good, as if she had changed her hairstyle. Yassi said in her mocking tone, You look . . . you look absolutely intrepid! I mean, divine. By the end of the class, Nassrin seemed so natural in her new attire that I already had a hard time envisioning the other Nassrin.

When Nassrin walked around in her chador or veil, her gait was defiant; she walked as she did everything else—restlessly, but with a sort of bravado. Now, without the veil, she slumped, as if she were trying to cover something. It was in the middle of our discussion of Austen's women that I noticed what it was she was trying to hide. Under the chador, one could not see how curvy and sexy her figure really was. I had to control myself and not command her to drop her hands, to stop covering her breasts. Now that she was unrobed, I noticed how the chador was an excuse to cover what she had tried to disown—mainly because she really and genuinely did not know what to do with it. She had an awkward way of walking, like a toddler taking its first steps, as if at any moment she would fall down.

A few weeks later, she stayed after class and asked if she could make an appointment to see me. I told her to come to our house, but she had become very formal and asked if we could meet at a coffee shop that my students and I were in the habit of frequenting. Now that I look at those times, I see how many of their most private stories, their confidences, were told in public places: in my office, in coffee shops, in taxis and walking through the winding streets near my home.

Nassrin was sitting at a small wooden table with a vase of blood-red wax carnations when I entered the coffee shop. We gave our orders: vanilla and chocolate ice cream for Nassrin and *café glacé* for me. Nassrin had called this meeting to officially register the existence of a boyfriend. Do I know him? I asked her as she ferociously dipped her spoon into the ice cream. No. I mean—she fumbled with her words—you may have seen him. He obviously knows you. I've known him for a long time, she continued, as if finally admitting to a shameful act. For over two years now, she sighed, but we have been sort of going together for the past few months.

I was startled by her news. I tried to hide my surprise, searching for something appropriate to say, but her expression did not allow such evasion. I've wanted to introduce him to you for a long time, she said, but I just didn't know how to go about it. And then I was afraid. Afraid of what? Is he a frightening person? I said, my feeble attempt at a joke. No, I was afraid you might not like him, she said, making swirls with her melting ice cream. Nassrin, I said. I'm not the one who should like him.

I felt sorry for her. She was in love—this should have been the best time of her life—but she was worried and anxious about so many things. Of course, she had to lie to her father—more time on translating texts. She lived in so many parallel worlds: the so-called real world of her family, work and society; the secret world of our class and her young man; and the world she had created out of her lies. I wasn't sure what she expected of me. Should I take on the role of a mother and tell her about the facts of life? Should I show more curiosity, ask for more details about him and their relationship? I waited, trying with some effort to pull my eyes off the hypnotic red carnation and to focus on Nassrin.

"I wouldn't blame you if you made fun of me," she said with great misery, twirling her spoon in the puddle of ice cream.

"Nassrin, I would never do such a thing," I protested. "And why should I? I am very happy for you."

"It is pathetic," she said, without paying attention to my words, following her own thoughts. "My mother had a grown-up kid when she was my age. You were already teaching, and here I am acting like a ten-year-old kid. This is what we should be talking about in class."

"About your being ten years old?" I asked, in an awkward attempt to lighten her mood.

"No, no, about"—she put her spoon down—"about how all of us—girls like me, who have read their Austen and Nabokov and all that, who talk about Derrida and Barthes and the world situation—how we know nothing, *nothing* about the relation between a man and a woman, about what it means to go out with a man. My twelve-year-old niece probably knows all about this, has probably gone out with more boys than I have." She spoke furiously, locking and unlocking her fingers.

In a sense she was right, and the fact that she was prepared to talk about it made me feel tender and protective towards her. Nassrin, I told her, none of us are as sophisticated in these matters as you think. You know I always feel, with every new person, as if I am starting anew. These things are instinctive. What you need to learn is to lay aside your inhibitions, to go back to your childhood when you played marbles or whatever with boys and never thought anything of it.

Nassrin did not respond. She was playing with the petals of the wax flowers, caressing their slippery surface.

"You know," I said, "with my first husband . . . Yes, I was married before Bijan, when I was barely eighteen. You know why he married me? He told me he liked my innocence—I didn't know what a French kiss was. I was born and bred in liberal times, I grew up in a liberal family—my parents sent me abroad when I was barely thirteen—and yet there you are: I chose to marry a man I despised deep down, someone who wanted a chaste and virginal wife and, I am sorry to say, chose me. He had been out with many girls, and when I went to Oklahoma with him, where he went to college, his friends were surprised, because right up to the day he returned to Iran for the summer, he had been living with an American girl he had introduced to everyone as his wife. So don't feel too bad. These things are complicated.

"Are you happy?" I asked her anxiously. There was a long pause during which I picked up the vase and pushed it to the side, next to the wall.

"I don't know," she said. "No one ever taught me how to be happy. We've been taught that pleasure is the great sin, that sex is for procreation and so on and on and forth. I feel guilty, but I shouldn't—not because I am interested in a man. *In a man,*" she repeated. "At *my age*! The fact is I don't know what I want, and I don't know if I am doing the right thing. I've always been told what is right—and suddenly I don't know anymore. I know what I don't want, but I don't know what I want," she said, looking down at the ice cream she had hardly touched.

"Well, you're not going to get an answer from me," I said. I leaned over, wanting to touch her hand, to provide her with some consolation. Only I didn't touch her. I didn't dare; she seemed so distant and withdrawn. "I'll be here for you when you need me, but if you're asking for my advice, I can't give it—you'll have to find out for yourself." Enjoy yourself, I pleaded lamely. How could one be in love and deny oneself a little joy?

Nassrin's young man was called Ramin. I had seen him on several occasions, the first time at a gathering for my book on Nabokov. He had a master's degree in philosophy and taught part-time. Nassrin had met him at a conference where he was presenting a paper and they had started talking afterward. Was it love at first sight? I wanted to ask her. How long had it taken them to confess their feelings? Did they ever kiss? These were some of the details I badly wanted to know, but of course I did not ask.

As we were leaving the coffee shop, Nassrin said hesitantly, Would you go to a concert with us? A concert? Some of Ramin's students are playing. We could get you and your family some tickets . . .

12

I should put the word *concert* in quotation marks, because such cultural affairs were parodies of the real thing, performed either in private homes or, more recently, at a cultural center built by the municipality in the south of Tehran. They were the focus of considerable controversy, because despite the many limitations set upon them, many in government considered them disreputable. The performances were closely monitored and mostly featured amateur players like the ones we went to see that night. But the house was always packed, the tickets were always sold out and the programs always started a little late.

Bijan was reluctant to go. He preferred listening to good music in the comfort and privacy of our home to subjecting himself to these mediocre live performances with their long lines and the inevitable harassment that ensued. But in the end, he gave in to the children's enthusiasm, and to me. After the revolution, almost all the activities one associated with being out in public—seeing movies, listening to music, sharing drinks or a meal with friends—shifted to private homes. It was refreshing to go out once in a while, even to such a desultory event.

We met them at the entrance. Nassrin looked nervous and Ramin was shy. He was tall and lanky, in his early thirties but with an air about him of an eternal graduate student, attractive in a bookish way. I had remembered him as confident and talkative, but now that he was introduced to us in his new role, he seemed to have lost his usual articulateness and his desire to talk. I thanked Ramin for the invitation and we all proceeded towards a long line filled with mainly young men and women. Nassrin busied herself with the children and I, who had suddenly become tongue-tied, tried to ask Ramin about his classes. Only Bijan seemed unconcerned by the awkwardness of the moment. He had made a sacrifice by leaving his comfortable home on a weeknight and felt no obligation to socialize as well.

When we finally entered the auditorium, we found people stuffed into the concert hall, sitting in the aisles, on the floor and standing clustered against the wall. We were among the guests of honor, so our place was in the second row, and we actually got seats. The program began late. We were greeted by a gentleman who insulted the audience for a good fifteen or twenty minutes, telling us that the management did not wish to entertain audiences of "rich imperialists" contaminated by decadent Western culture. This brought smiles to many of those who had come that evening to hear the music of the Gipsy Kings. The gentleman also admonished that if anyone acted in an un-Islamic manner, he or she would be kicked out. He went on to instruct women to observe the proper rules and regulations regarding the use of the veil.

It is hard to conjure an accurate image of what went on that night. The group consisted of four young Iranian men, all amateurs, who entertained us with their rendition of the Gipsy Kings. Only they weren't allowed to sing; they could only play their instruments. Nor could they demonstrate any enthusiasm for what they were doing: to show emotion would be un-Islamic. As I sat there in that packed house, I decided that the only way the night could possibly be turned into an entertainment was if I pretended to be an outside observer who had come not to have fun but to report on a night out in the Islamic Republic of Iran.

Yet despite these restrictions and the quality of the performance, our young musicians could not have found anywhere in the world an audience so receptive, so forgiving of their flaws, so grateful to hear their music. Every time the audience, mostly young and not necessarily rich, started to move or clap, two men in suits appeared from either side of the stage and gesticulated for them to stop clapping or humming or moving to the music. Even when we tried to listen, to forget these acrobats, they managed to impose themselves on our field of vision, always present, always ready to jump out and intervene. Always, we were guilty.

The players were solemn. Since it was almost impossible to play with no expression at all, their expressions had become morose. The lead guitarist seemed to be angry with the audience; he frowned, trying to prevent his body from moving—a difficult task, since he was playing the Gipsy Kings.

At Bijan's suggestion, we tried to get out early—before, as he said, we were trampled by the mob, which, not being able to emote during the show, might choose to exercise its vengeance by trampling fellow concertgoers. Outside, we stood for some minutes by the entrance. Bijan, who seldom talked, was moved by the occasion.

"I feel sorry for these kids," he said. "They're not entirely without talent, but they'll never be judged by the quality of their music. The regime criticizes them for being Western and decadent, and the audience gives them uncritical praise—not because they're first-rate but because they play forbidden music. So," he added, addressing us in general, "how will they ever learn to play?"

"It's true," I said, feeling an obligation to fill the silence that followed. "No one is judged on the merit of their work. People without the least knowledge of music are running around calling themselves musicians." Nassrin was sullen, and Ramin quiet and mortified. I was astounded by his metamorphosis and decided not to add to his discomfort by forcing him to talk.

Suddenly Nassrin became animated. "Nabokov would've had nothing to do with this," she said excitedly. "Look at us—it's pathetic, running to *this* for entertainment." She moved her arms and spoke breathlessly, eager to hide her embarrassment behind a volley of nervous talk. "He would have had a field day if he'd been here—talk about poshlust!"

"What?" said Negar, who'd enjoyed not so much the music as the excitement of a night out.

"*Poshlust,*" Nassrin repeated and, uncharacteristically, left it at that.

13

I was grumbling to myself as I put the plates on the table absent-mindedly for dinner. Bijan turned to me and said, What are you mumbling about? You wouldn't be interested, I said unnecessarily sharply. Try me, he said. Okay, I was thinking about menopause. He turned back to the BBC. You're right—I'm not interested, he said. Why shouldn't he be interested? Shouldn't he want to know about something that has happened to his mother, that will happen to his wife, his sisters, his daughter and, I went on morosely, if ever he has an affair, even to his mistress? I knew I was being unfair to him. He was not insensitive to the hardships of life in the Islamic Republic, but he was on the defensive these days whenever I complained. I protested as if he were responsible for all the woes brought upon us by the regime, and this in turn made him withdraw into himself and act as if he were indifferent about things he actually felt very strongly about.

Our last class meeting had ended on a strange note: we were discussing my girls' mothers—their trials and tribulations and the fact that they really knew nothing about menopause. The discussion had begun with Manna. The night before, she and Nima had seen for the third time Vincente Minnelli's *Designing Woman,* which they'd picked up on their satellite dish. Watching the film had made Manna very sad. It occurred to her that she had never imaginatively experienced love in a Persian context. Love is love, but there are so many ways of articulating it. When she read *Madame Bovary,* or saw *Casablanca,* she could feel and experience the sensual texture of the work; she could hear, touch, smell, see. She had never heard a love song, read a novel or seen a film that made her think that this could be her experience. Even in Persian films, when two people are supposed to be in love, you didn't really feel it in their looks and gestures. Love was forbidden, banished from the public sphere. How could it be experienced if its expression was illegal?

That discussion had been an eye-opener. I had discovered that almost all of my girls separated what they described as intellectual or spiritual love (good) from sex (not good). What mattered, apparently, was the more exalted realm of spiritual affinity. Even Mitra had dimpled her way through the argument that sex was not important in a relationship, that sexual satisfaction had never mattered to her. The worst blow, I felt, came from Azin. With a flirtatious tone that implied she was back to normal—this was a period of semi-truce with her husband—Azin had said that the most important thing in life was the mystical union one felt with the universe. She added, philosophically, that men were just vessels for that higher spiritual love. Vessels? There went all her claims to sexual pleasure and physical compatibility. Even Mahshid, who exchanged a quick glance with Manna, was surprised.

"So," said Nassrin, who had been quiet until then, "when your husband beats you, you can pretend it's all in your mind, since he's just an empty vessel to fill up your fantasies. And it's not just Azin," she said. "The rest of you are basically saying the same thing."

"What about you and Nima?" Mitra asked Manna. "You seem to have a balanced relationship."

"I like him because there is no one in the world I can talk to like Nima," Manna said with a shrug.

"Poor Nima," said Yassi.

"He's not so poor." Manna was feeling savage that day. "He too has no one else to talk to. Misery loves company—and can be as strong a force as love."

"You all disappoint me," Yassi said. "I was hoping you'd tell me how physical attraction does matter, how love isn't just spiritual and intellectual. I was hoping you'd tell me that I'd learn to love physically and see that I was wrong. I'm utterly flabbergasted," she said, sinking deeper into the couch. "In fact, I'm discombobulated," she concluded with a triumphant smile.

Ouch! I shouted. Bijan glanced up from the TV and said, "Nothing wrong, is there?" No, I just cut myself. I was slicing cucumbers to go with Bijan's famous chicken kebab. He went to the bathroom and returned with a Band-Aid, which he carefully put on my finger. Without saying a word, smiling indulgently, he then went to the cabinet, poured a measure of homemade vodka into the small glass, put it on the side table beside a dish of pistachio nuts and settled back in front of the BBC. I went in and out of the kitchen, grumbling to myself. No wonder he enjoys life; this is what he'd do if we lived in the States. It's hard on me, I grumbled, pleading with some unknown interlocutor, who always questioned and mocked my every complaint. It's really hard on me, I repeated one more time, ignoring the guilty knowledge that Bijan bore his hardships without much complaint and should not be begrudged his vodka and his BBC.

By the time I had chopped the cucumbers and the herbs, adding them to the yogurt, I had come to a conclusion: our culture shunned sex because it was too involved with it. It had to suppress sex violently, for the same reason that an impotent man will put his beautiful wife under lock and key. We had always segregated sex from feeling and from intellectual love, so you were either pure and virtuous, as Nassrin's uncle had said, or dirty and fun. What was alien to us was eros, true sensuality. These girls, my girls, knew a great deal about Jane Austen, they could discuss Joyce and Woolf intelligently, but they knew next to nothing about their own bodies, about what they should expect of these bodies which, they had been told, were the source of all temptation.

How do you tell someone she has to learn to love herself and her own body before she can be loved or love? By the time I added the salt and pepper to my dish, I had come up with an answer to this question. I went to the next session armed with a copy of *Pride and Prejudice* in one hand and *Our Bodies, Ourselves*—the only book I had available on sexuality—in the other.

14

Charlotte Brontë did not like Jane Austen. "The Passions are perfectly unknown to her," she complained to a friend, " . . . even to the Feelings she vouchsafes no more than an occasional graceful but distant recognition; too frequent converse with them would but ruffle the elegance of her progress." Knowing Charlotte Brontë and her proclivities, one can understand how one perfectly good novelist could dislike another as much as Brontë disliked Austen. She was fierce and insistent in her dismissal, and had written to G. H. Lewes in 1848: "Why do you like Miss Austen so very much? I am puzzled on that point. . . . I had not seen *Pride and Prejudice* till I read that sentence of yours, and then I got the book. And what did I find? An accurate, daguerreotyped portrait of a commonplace face; a carefully-fenced, highly-cultivated garden, with neat borders and delicate flowers; but no glance of a bright, vivid physiognomy, no open country, no fresh air, no blue hill, no bonny beck. I should hardly like to live with her ladies and gentlemen, in their elegant but confined houses."

There is something to this perhaps, yet Brontë's indictment is not entirely fair. One cannot say that Austen's novels lack passion. They lack a certain kind of overripe sensuousness, an appetite for the more unfiltered romantic abandon of Jane Eyre and Rochester. Theirs is a more muted sensuality, desire by indirection.

Please turn to page 148, and try to visualize the scene as you read the passage. Darcy and Elizabeth are alone in Mr. Collins's house. Darcy is gradually coming to the realization that he cannot live without Elizabeth. They are talking about the significance of the distance between a woman's married home and her parents' home.

> Mr. Darcy drew his chair a little towards her, and said, "*You* cannot have a right to such very strong local attachment. *You* cannot have been always at Longbourn."
>
> Elizabeth looked surprised. The gentleman experienced some change of feeling; he drew back his chair, took a newspaper from the table, and, glancing over it, said, in a colder voice,—
>
> "Are you pleased with Kent?"

Let us return to the aforementioned scene. The insistence in Darcy's voice is a symptom of his passion for Elizabeth; it emerges even in their most mundane interactions. We can trace the development of Darcy's feelings for Elizabeth in the tone of his voice. This reaches its climax in the scene in which he proposes to her. His negative persistence, beginning his speech with "In vain have I struggled. It will not do," becomes almost violent, in part because the novel itself is so restrained and Darcy is the most restrained of all the characters.

Now, please listen carefully to that "you." Darcy seldom if ever addresses Elizabeth by her name, but he has a special way of saying "you" when he addresses her a few times that makes the impersonal pronoun a term of ultimate intimacy. One should appreciate such nuances in a culture such as ours, where everyone is encouraged to demonstrate in the most exaggerated manner his love for the Imam and yet forbidden from any public articulation of private feelings, especially love.

There is seldom a physical description of a character or scene in *Pride and Prejudice* and yet we feel that we have seen each of these characters and their intimate worlds; we feel we know them, and sense their surroundings. We can see Elizabeth's reaction to Darcy's denunciation of her beauty, Mrs. Bennet chattering at the dinner table or Elizabeth and Darcy walking in and out of the shadows of the Pemberley estate. The amazing thing is that all of this is created mainly through tone—different tones of voice, words that become haughty and naughty, soft, harsh, coaxing, insinuating, insensible, vain.

The sense of touch that is missing from Austen's novels is replaced by a tension, an erotic texture of sounds and silences. She manages to create a feeling of longing by setting characters who want each other at odds. Elizabeth and Darcy are placed near each other in several scenes, but in public places where they cannot communicate privately. Austen creates a great deal of frustrated tension by putting them in the same room yet out of reach. The tension is deepened by the fact that while everyone expects Jane and Bingley to be in love, the exact reverse is expected of Elizabeth and Darcy.

Take, for instance, the party scene at Elizabeth's house towards the end of the novel, when she is desperate to find private time to talk with him. The whole event is spent in a state of anxiety. She stands by her sister, helping her pour the tea and coffee, and she tells herself, "If he does not come to me, *then,* I shall give him up for ever." He does approach her, but one of the girls attaches herself to Elizabeth and says in a whisper, "The men shan't come and part us, I am determined. We want none of them; do we?" Darcy moves away, forcing her to follow him with her eyes. She "envied every one to whom he spoke, had scarcely patience enough to help anybody to coffee, and then was enraged against herself for being so silly!" This game continues all night. Darcy approaches her table again, bringing back his cup, lingers for a while, they exchange a few pleasantries and again he has to leave.

Austen manages to make us aware of the most intriguing aspect of a relationship: the urge, the longing for the object of desire that is so near and so far. It is a longing that will be gratified, a suspense that will end in unity and happiness. The scenes of actual lovemaking are almost nonexistent in Austen's novels, but her tales are all one long and complicated process of courtship. It is obvious that she is more interested in happiness than in the institution of marriage, in love and understanding than matrimony. This is apparent from all of the mismatched marriages in her novels—Sir Thomas and Lady

Bertram, Mr. and Mrs. Bennet, Mary and Charles Musgrove. Like Scheherazade in her tales, one finds an infinite variety of good and bad marriages, good and bad men and women.

Nor is Brontë's claim about boundaries completely true. Boundaries are constantly threatened by the women in Austen's novels, who feel more at home in the private than the public domain, the domain of heart and of intricate individual relations. The nineteenth-century novel placed the individual, her happiness, her ordeals and her rights at the center of the story. Thus, marriage was its most important theme. From Richardson's hapless Clarissa to Fielding's shy and obedient Sophia to Elizabeth Bennet, women created the complications and tensions that moved the plots forward. They put at the center of our attention what Austen's novels formulate: not the importance of marriage but the importance of heart and understanding in marriage; not the primacy of conventions but the breaking of conventions. These women, genteel and beautiful, are the rebels who say no to the choices made by silly mothers, incompetent fathers (there are seldom any wise fathers in Austen's novels) and the rigidly orthodox society. They risk ostracism and poverty to gain love and companionship, and to embrace that elusive goal at the heart of democracy: the right to choose.

15

Imagine a summer night. We are at a party, sitting outdoors in a fragrant garden. On a large terrace overlooking the swimming pool, our tasteful host has set up small tables with fragile candles. In one corner, against the wall, colorful cushions have been spread out over a Persian carpet. Some of us are sitting propped up against the cushions. The wine and vodka are homemade, but you can't tell by the color. The sound of laughter and small talk wafts among the tables. The company is as good as any you might find anywhere in the world—cultured, witty, sophisticated, full of stories.

What are we all listening to, those of us sitting on the carpet, playing with our wineglasses, leaning back against the cushions? Our host is recounting the bus story. It is fresh from the oven. Many of us have heard bits and pieces of it in the past two days, but the story is too in-credible even for us, with our seasoned knowledge of so many stories unbelievable to believe. Our host is a reliable source, and what is more, he has heard it from the horse's mouth, or at least from the mouth of one of the horses involved in the incident.

About two months earlier, the board of the writers' association re-ceived an invitation to participate in a conference in Armenia. The in-vitation was extended to all the members. At first, many received phone calls from the intelligence service threatening them and in-structing them not to go, but later on, the regime seemed to relent, and even to encourage the trip. In the end, twenty-odd members ac-cepted the invitation. They decided to hire a bus for their journey. Ac-counts differ here as to the details—some claim to have suspected something fishy was going on from the start; others accuse one an-other of being complicit in the plot. But what all agree is that on the morning of the trip, twenty-one writers made their way to the bus sta-tion. Some found it a little odd that the bus was not on time and that the driver had been changed. Others noticed that certain colleagues had reneged and decided not to go, on the very morning of the trip.

Finally, they were on their way. The journey went smoothly until after midnight, or some say until around two in the morning, when all of the passengers were asleep—all but one single insomniac, who noticed that the bus had stopped and the driver had disappeared. He glanced out the window and saw that the bus had stopped at the tip of a very high precipice. At this point, he ran—all the time shouting to wake up the others—to the front of the bus, got behind the wheel and turned the bus around. The other passengers, waking startled from their sleep, filed off the bus in a certain commotion, only to be met by members of security, who were there with their Mercedes-Benzes and helicopters. The passengers were taken to different interrogation outposts, and after being detained and expressly advised not to say a word, they were released. The next day, the whole of Tehran had heard the news. Apparently there had been a plot to push the bus over the cliff and claim it was an accident.

There were many jokes about this incident, as there were about similar events. Later that night, on our way home, Bijan and I dis-cussed the writers' terrible ordeal. It's so strange, he said. Usually when you talk about most of these writers, it's because of your frustrations with their ideological stance towards literature, but something like this makes all that irrelevant. No matter how much you might disagree with some of these people or think of them as bad writers, pity will ultimately overtake all other considerations.

Not long after that, we were awoken early one morning by a friend who was married to one of the founders of the writers' association. Her voice was frightened. She wanted to know if we could call the BBC and let them know what was going on. She and her husband had been forced to leave Tehran for a while until things cooled down, and she wanted to know if their son could stay with us for a few days.

This incident was preceded by many others: the attack on a small party given by a German consul at his house for intellectuals and writers, and their arrest; the disappearance of a well-known leftist journalist, the editor of a popular magazine who had been arrested with others and kept after they were released. Later it was said that he had left for Germany, where his wife and family lived, but he never arrived there. The Iranian government claimed he had left Iran and that the Germans were keeping him. The German government denied the allegations. The international hue and cry surrounding his disappearance helped keep the matter in the public eye. Then one day he appeared in the Tehran airport with a strange story about having gone to Germany and from there to a third country. A few days later, he wrote an open letter in which he described his tortures at the hands of the regime and he was promptly rearrested. Finally, he was released after much international pressure. Shortly afterward, an Iranian publisher who had helped him and other dissident writers left his home and never returned. His body was dumped in a deserted place on the outskirts of Tehran, like those of so many other dissidents.

In the mid-nineties, in an effort to reach out to Europe, a number of Western intellectuals were invited to Iran. Paul Ricoeur came for a series of lectures. He gave three talks; for every one of them, audiences spilled out into the hall and stairs. Some time afterward, V. S. Naipaul came to Iran. In Isfahan, he was taken around by a well-known translator and publisher, Ahmad Mir Alai. I can still see Mir Alai in his bookshop in Isfahan, which had become a place for intellectuals and writers to gather and talk. He was a pale man; his skin seemed oddly faded. He was pudgy and wore round-rimmed brown glasses. Somehow, the combination of paleness and pudginess made you trust him and want to share your stories with him. He had a sharp wit and was the kind of man who seemed to listen and empathize with you. This came partly from the fact that, unlike his more militant friends, he was not a confrontational person. I could call him a victim because he was not political—he was caught in the cross fire and at times had to take radical political stances despite his nature. He had excellent taste in his translations, choosing Naipaul and Kundera and a host of other writers.

A few months after Naipaul left Iran, Mir Alai's body was found in a street, near a stream. He had left the house in the morning and had not returned. Late that night, his family was informed of his death. A small bottle of vodka was found in his pocket. Vodka had been spilled all over his shirtfront in an attempt to make it look as if Mir Alai, in the middle of the day, had gone off on a drunken binge and had a heart attack in the middle of the street. No one believed the story. A big bruise had been found on his chest and the mark of an injection on his arm. He had been interrogated and either accidentally or deliberately killed by his interrogators.

Shortly afterward, Jahangir Tafazoli, the best-known expert on ancient Iran, was found murdered. I knew him well. He was very shy and slight and had a shock of black hair and large eyes that looked huge under his glasses. Tafazoli was not politically involved, although he had written for the Encyclopedia Iranica, a project that was overseen by a prominent Iranian scholar at Columbia who was greatly denounced by the Iranian government. His subject of expertise—pre-Islamic Iran—was hated by the Islamic regime. He had left the University of Tehran to go home and had made a suspicious phone call en route from a car to his daughter at home. His body was found alongside a road far from his home and from the university. It was claimed that he had been trying to change a tire and was hit by a car.

Time and again in memorial services, in parties and gatherings, I went over these deaths with friends and colleagues. We obsessively resurrected and evoked the manner of death as reported by the officials and then we remurdered them, trying to envision the way they had really died. I still imagine Tafazoli sitting in a car between two thugs, forced to make a call home to his daughter, and then I draw a blank and ask myself, When and where did they kill him? Was it with a blow inside the car? Or did they take him to one of their safe houses, kill him there and then throw him on the deserted road?

16

If you promise you'll behave, my magician said on the phone, I have a nice surprise for you. We arranged to meet at a popular coffee shop that opened into a restaurant and had its own pastry shop in the front. The name eludes me, although I am sure, like so many other places, it must have been changed after the revolution.

When I arrived with my bag of books, I found my magician sitting at a corner table, surveying a stack of his own. You were looking for an English edition of *A Thousand and One Nights,* he said. I've found you an Oxford edition. We ordered a cappuccino for me, an espresso for him and two napoleons, the pastry for which the café was famous. I also brought you that Auden poem you were looking for, though I'm not sure why you want it, he said, handing me a typed sheet of paper with Auden's "Letter to Lord Byron."

We had a really interesting discussion in class the other day, I said. We were talking about *The Dean's December* and *Lolita* and other books we'd covered in class. One of my girls, Manna—you remember my Manna? Yes, I remember Manna, he said, your poet. Yes, well, Manna asked how we could relate these other authors to Jane Austen, who is so much more optimistic about the world and its people.

Most people make that mistake about Austen, he said. They should read her more carefully.

Yes, that's what I told her—Austen's theme is cruelty not under extraordinary circumstances but ordinary ones, committed by people like us. Surely that's more frightening? And that's why I like Bellow, I said with a flourish, thinking of my new flame.

How fickle you are, he said. What happened to Nabokov? One book and he's old news! No, but really, I said, trying to ignore his mocking tone. Bellow's novels are about private cruelties, about the ordeal of freedom, the burden of choice—so are James's, for that matter. It's frightening to be free, to have to take responsibility for your decisions. Yes, he said, to have no Islamic Republic to blame. And I'm not saying they're blameless, he added after a brief pause—far from it.

Look here, I said, rummaging through *More Die of Heartbreak,* which I had brought along for the sole purpose of quoting my favorite passages to him: "The meaning of the Revolution was that Russia had attempted to isolate itself from the ordeal of modern consciousness. It was a sealing off. Inside the sealed country, Stalin poured on the *old* death. In the West, the ordeal is of a *new* death. There aren't any words for what happens to the soul in the free world. Never mind 'rising entitlements,' never mind the luxury 'life-style.' Our buried judgment knows better. All this is seen by remote centers of consciousness, which struggle against full wakefulness. Full wakefulness would make us face up to the *new* death, the peculiar ordeal of *our* side of the world. The opening of a true consciousness to what is *actually* occurring would be a purgatory."

I love this "poured on the *old* death," I told him. He talks somewhere about the "atrophy of feeling"—the West is gripped by an "atrophy of feeling . . ."

Yes, he said. Mr. Bellow, Saul as your students call him, is highly quotable. I don't know if that's a virtue or a fault.

Who started me on this? Who gave me *The Bellarosa Connection*? I asked him accusingly. I think this is important for my class. They tend to look at the West too uncritically; they have a rosy picture of the West, thanks to the Islamic Republic. All that is good in their eyes comes from America or Europe, from chocolates and chewing gum to Austen and the Declaration of Independence. Bellow gives them a truer experience of this other place. He allows them to see its problems and its fears.

Look here, I said. This is the whole point. This is what we're going through. . . . He was not looking at me. You're not listening, I said impatiently. He was looking behind me and making motions to the waiter, who was soon at our table. What's going on? he asked. What's all the commotion about? For there was a commotion behind us, which I had missed in my eagerness to propound the virtues of Mr. Bellow.

The waiter explained that this was a raid. Guards were standing at the entrance door, monitoring those who had started to leave. He delicately suggested that if we were not related, my magician should move to another table and I could explain, were I asked what I was doing there, that I was waiting for my order from the pastry shop.

I said, We are not doing anything wrong—I am not going to move—and, turning to my magician, added, Nor are you. Don't be stupid, he said. You don't want to create a scandal. I'll call Bijan right now, I said. What good will that do? he shot back. Do you really think they will listen to him, since he has no control over his wife? He rose with his coffee cup in his hands. You forgot something, I said, handing him the copy of *A Thousand and One Nights*. He said, in English, Now you're being childish. I think you need something to keep you busy, I said, and besides, I already photocopied the other one you gave me. He walked to a distant table with his coffee and the books, and I sat alone, trying to eat my napoleon, ferociously leafing through *More Die of Heartbreak,* as if cramming for the next day's exams.

When the Revolutionary Guards entered the coffee shop, they started going from table to table. A few young people had slipped away in time; others were not so lucky. A family of four, my magician, two middle-aged women and three young men were left behind. When my order was ready, I rose, tipped the waiter extravagantly, dropped my parcel of books, which broke open and spread all over the floor, waited for the waiter to fetch me a bag and left without looking at my magician.

In the taxi, I felt confused and angry and a little repentant. I am going to leave, I told myself. I can't live like this anymore. Every time something like this happened, I, like many others, would think of leaving, of going to a place where everyday life was not such a battleground. Recently, the thought of leaving Iran had become more than a defense mechanism and incidents like this were slowly tipping the scales. Among friends and colleagues some had tried to adjust to the situation. We are not with the regime in our hearts and minds, one had said, but what can we do but comply? Should I go to jail and lose my job for the sake of two loose strands of hair? Once Mrs. Rezvan had said, By now we should be used to all of this; these young girls are a little spoiled—they expect too much. Look at Somalia or Afghanistan. Compared to them, we live like queens.

"I can't get used to it," Manna had said one day in class. And I couldn't blame her. We were unhappy. We compared our situation to our own potentials, to what we could have had, and somehow there was little consolation in the fact that millions of people were unhappier than we were. Why should other people's misery make us happier or more content?

When I arrived home, Bijan and the children were downstairs in my mother's apartment. I put the napoleons I had brought for them in the refrigerator and left the carrot cake out to take to my mother. Then I went straight to the freezer, made myself a big bowl of ice cream, poured coffee and walnuts over it, and by the time the kids and Bijan had come upstairs, I was already in the bathroom throwing up. All evening and all night, I threw up. My magician called at some point. I am very sorry, he said. One feels so tainted. I'm sorry, too, I said back. We're all sorry—don't forget to date and autograph my book.

I could not keep anything in my stomach that night, not even water, and in the morning when I opened my eyes, the room started to rotate; tiny specks of light formed brightly spiked coronets, dancing in the dizzying air. I closed my eyes, opened them again and the deadly coronets reappeared. I held on to my stomach, went to the bathroom and vomited nothing but bile. All day I stayed in the luxury of my bed, my skin sensitive to the touch of the sheets.

17

You could not shock her more than she shocks me;
    Beside her Joyce seems innocent as grass.
It makes me most uncomfortable to see
    An English spinster of the middle class
    Describe the amorous effect of "brass",
Reveal so frankly and with such sobriety
The economic basis of society.

A girl is raped, carried in the trunk of a car and murdered. A young student is killed and has his ears cut off. There are discussions of prison camps, of death and destruction in Bellow, in Nabokov we have monsters like Humbert, who rape twelve-year-old girls, even in Flaubert there is so much hurt and betrayal—What about Austen? Manna had asked one day.

Indeed, what about Austen? Austen's comedies and her generosity of spirit sometimes led my students to share the common belief that she was a prim spinster, at peace with the world and unaware of its brutality. I had to remind them of Auden's "Letter to Lord Byron," in which he asks Byron to tell Jane Austen "How much her novels are beloved down here."

Austen's heroines are unforgiving, after their own fashion. There is much betrayal in her novels, much greed and falsehood, so many disloyal friends, selfish mothers, tyrannical fathers, so much vanity, cruelty and hurt. Austen is generous towards her villains, but this does not mean that she lets anyone, even her heroines, off easy. Her favorite and least likable heroine, Fanny Price, is in fact the one who also suffers the most.

Modern fiction brings out the evil in domestic lives, ordinary relations, people like you and me—Reader! *Bruder!* as Humbert said. Evil in Austen, as in most great fiction, lies in the inability to "see" others, hence to empathize with them. What is frightening is that this blindness can exist in the best of us (Eliza Bennet) as well as the worst (Humbert). We are all capable of becoming the blind censor, of imposing our visions and desires on others.

Once evil is individualized, becoming part of everyday life, the way of resisting it also becomes individual. How does the soul survive? is the essential question. And the response is: through love and imagination. Stalin emptied Russia of its soul by pouring on the old death. Mandelstam and Sinyavsky restored that soul by reciting poetry to fellow convicts and by writing about it in their journals. "Perhaps to remain a poet in such circumstances," Bellow wrote, "is also to reach the heart of politics. The human feelings, human experiences, the human form and face, recover their proper place—the foreground."

18

Our decision to leave Iran came about casually—at least that is how it appeared. Such decisions, no matter how momentous, are seldom well planned. Like bad marriages, they are the result of years of resentment and anger suddenly exploding into suicidal resolutions. The idea of departure, like the possibility of divorce, lurked somewhere in our minds, shadowy and sinister, ready to surface at the slightest provocation. If anyone asked, I would recount the usual reasons for our departure: my job and my feelings as a woman, our children's future and my trips to the U.S., which had once more made us aware of our choices and possibilities.

For the first time, Bijan and I had serious fights, and for a while we talked about nothing but leaving or staying. When Bijan discovered that this time I was determined to leave, he went into a period of mortified silence; then a phase began when we had long, torturous arguments, in which family and friends participated as well. Bijan said it wasn't a good idea, we should at least wait until the children were older, ready for college; my magician said it was the only thing to do; my friends were divided. My girls didn't want me to leave, but then so many of them had themselves decided to go. My parents wanted us to leave, despite the fact that our departure would mean their loneliness. The offer of a better life for their children—even if it is an illusion—is so attractive to most parents.

In the end, Bijan, always judicious and far too reasonable, had agreed that we should leave—for a few years at least. His acceptance of our new fate had set him in motion. His way of dealing with our impeding departure was practical; he kept himself busy with dismantling eighteen years of life and work and fitting them into the eight suitcases we were allowed to take with us. Mine had been to evade the situation to the point of denial. The fact that he was taking it so graciously made me feel guilty and hesitant. I deferred packing, and refused to talk about it seriously. In class, the light and flippant attitude I espoused made it difficult for my girls to know how to react.

We had never properly discussed in class my decision to leave. It was understood that the class could not continue indefinitely, and I had voiced the hope that my girls would form their own classes, to bring more friends into the fold. I had felt the tension in Manna's silences and Mahshid's oblique allusions to duty towards home and country. The others showed a certain anxiety and sadness at the thought of the class coming to an end. Your place will be so empty, Yassi had said, using a Persian expression—but they too began to nurture their own plans to leave.

As soon as our decision was final, everyone stopped talking about it. My father's eyes became more withdrawn, as if he were looking at a point beyond which we had already vanished into the horizon. My mother was suddenly angry and resentful, implying that my decision had once more proven her worst suspicions about my loyalty. My best friend energetically took me shopping for presents and talked about everything but my journey, and my girls barely registered the change; only my children mentioned our impending departure with a mixture of excitement and sadness.

19

There is a term in Persian, "the patient stone," which is often used in times of anxiety and turbulence. Supposedly, a person pours out all his troubles and woes into the stone. It will listen and absorb his pains and secrets, and this way he will be cured. Sometimes the stone can no longer endure its burden and then it bursts. My magician was not my "patient stone," although he never told his own story—he claimed people were not interested in that. Yet he spent sleepless nights listening to and absorbing others' troubles and woes, and to me his advice was that I should leave: leave and write my own story and teach my own class.

Perhaps he saw what was happening to me more clearly than I did. What I now realize is that, ironically, the more attached I became to my class and to my students, the more detached I became from Iran. The more I discovered the lyrical quality of our lives, the more my own life became a web of fiction. All of this I can now formulate and talk about with some degree of clarity, but it was not at all clear then. It was much more complicated.

As I trace the route to his apartment, the twists and turns, and pass once more the old tree opposite his house, I am struck by a sudden thought: memories have ways of becoming independent of the reality they evoke. They can soften us against those we were deeply hurt by or they can make us resent those we once accepted and loved unconditionally.

We sit again with Reza around the same round dining table, under the painting of green trees, talking and eating lunch, the forbidden ham-and-cheese sandwiches. Our magician does not drink. He refuses to compromise with the counterfeits: the bootleg videos and wine, censored novels and films. He does not watch television, nor does he go to the movies. To watch a beloved film on video is anathema to him, although he obtains tapes of his favorite movies for us. Today he has brought us homemade wine, its color a sinful pale pink, poured into five vinegar bottles. Later, I take the wine home and drink it. Something has gone wrong and the wine tastes like vinegar, though I do not tell him.

The hot subject of the day was Mohammad Khatami and his recent candidacy. Khatami, mainly known to intellectuals for his brief stint as minister of Islamic Culture and Guidance, had within a few weeks become a household name. In buses and taxis, at parties and at work, everyone talked about Khatami, whom it was our moral duty to vote for. It was not enough that for over seventeen years the clerics had announced that voting was not just a duty but a religious duty; we ourselves had now adopted the same stance. There were fights and ruptures in friendships over this matter.

That day as I was walking to my magician's house, struggling with my scarf and trying to keep it around my neck, I noticed a campaign poster for Khatami on the opposite wall. There was a big picture of the candidate ornamented in huge letters: IRAN HAS FALLEN IN LOVE AGAIN. Oh no, I said to myself despondently—not again.

As we sat around my magician's table, the site of so many stories we told or created, I was telling them about the posters. We love our family, our lovers, our friends, but do we have to fall in love with our politicians? Even in my class we're fighting over him. Manna can't see how anyone could vote for him; she says it doesn't make much difference to her if she can wear a lighter-color scarf or let a bit more hair show. Sanaz says that given a choice between bad and worse, you choose the bad, and Manna shoots back that she doesn't want a nicer jail warden—she wants to be out of jail. Azin says, This guy wants the rule of law? Isn't this the same law that allows my husband to beat me and take my daughter away? Yassi is confused, and Mitra says, Even in these elections there are rumors that they'll check your passports and won't let you leave if you don't vote. Another rumor, Mahshid says tartly, that you don't need to listen to.

"People usually deserve what they get," said Reza, biting into his ham and cheese. I gave him a reproachful look. "I mean it," he said. "If we are prepared to be duped by every so-called election—we all know they aren't real elections when only Muslims with impeccable revolutionary credentials, chosen by the Council of Guardians and approved by the Supreme Leader, can become candidates. Anyway, the point is that as long as we accept this charade called elections and hope that some Rafsanjani or Khatami can save us, we deserve our later disenchantments."

"But this frustration is not one-sided," my magician added. "How do you think Mr. Khamenei feels"—he turned a quizzical eye to me and raised an eyebrow—"to see your Mitra and Sanaz going on their merry way and corrupting good Muslim girls like Yassi and Mahshid in the bargain? Or hearing their former radical revolutionaries quoting Kant and Spinoza instead of Islamic sources? And then we have our president's daughter, peddling votes by promising to give women the right to ride bicycles in public parks."

"But all of this is so ridiculous," I said.

"It might be ridiculous to you," he said, "but it is not very funny to this president and his followers, who have to win the hearts and minds of the children of the revolution by promising them—at least implicitly—access to all things Western. And still," he added with relish, "these young people listen more to Michael Jackson and read your Nabokov with more enjoyment and enthusiasm than you and I ever did in our decadent youth.

"Besides, what are you worrying about anyway?" he said. "You'll be leaving us and our problems very soon."

"I won't be leaving either you or your problems," I said. "I'm counting on you to keep me posted."

"No, I won't," he said. "We won't communicate once you go."

In response to my startled look, he said, "Call it self-defense or cowardice; I don't want to be in touch with those of my friends who are lucky enough to leave."

"But you encouraged me," I said, bewildered by what I was hearing.

"Well, yes, that's another matter. But anyway, these are my rules. Seldom seen, soon forgotten; out of sight, out of mind and all that. A chap needs to protect himself."

He did everything in his power to help me leave, and yet when he saw that I was finally leaving, when it all came out well in the end, he was not happy with me. Was he disenchanted? Did he think my departure was a comment of sorts on those I was leaving behind?

20

I was on the phone when Nassrin arrived. Negar, who had opened the door, kept shouting, quite unnecessarily, Mom, Mom, Nassrin is here! A few minutes later a shy Nassrin entered, standing by the door as if already regretting her visit. I gestured for her to wait for me in the living room. I'll have to call you later, I told my friend. One of my girls is here to see me. Girls? she said—she knew very well what I meant. Students, I said. Students! Get a life, woman. Why don't you return to teaching? But I am teaching. You know what I mean. By the way, talking of your students, your Azin is going to drive me crazy. That girl doesn't know her own mind—either that or she's playing a game I don't understand. She's worried about her daughter, I said hurriedly. But listen, I really have to go. I'll call you later.

When I entered the living room, Nassrin was staring at the birds-of-paradise and chewing her nails with the distracted focus of a professional nail chewer. I should have guessed before that she belonged to the category of people who bite their nails, I remember thinking—she must have exercised a great deal of restraint in class.

At the sound of my voice, she turned around abruptly and impulsively hid her hands behind her back. To cover the awkwardness she had brought into the room, I asked her what she wanted to drink. Nothing, thank you. She had not taken her robe off, only unbuttoned it, revealing the outlines of a white shirt tucked into a pair of black corduroys. She was wearing Reeboks and her hair was pulled back into a ponytail. She looked like a pretty girl, young and fragile, like any other girl from any other part of the world. She shifted restlessly from one leg to another, reminding me of the first time I had seen her, almost sixteen years earlier. Nassrin, stand still for a moment, I said quietly. Better yet, sit. Sit down, please—no, let's go downstairs to my office; it's more private.

I was trying to delay what she had come to tell me. We made a stop in the kitchen. I handed her the fruit bowl and put a jug of water, two glasses and some plates on a tray. On our way down the stairs, she caught me: I'm going away, she said. I knew from experience that I should not throw her any further off balance by showing too much surprise. Where are you going? To London, to live with my sister for a while. And what about Ramin? We had reached my office. She waited for me to open the door, shifting her weight from one leg to another, as if neither leg would take responsibility for its burden. I could tell by her pale color and the stunned expression on her face that I had asked the wrong question. I'm done with him, she muttered as we entered the room.

How are you leaving? I asked her once we had sat down, she with her back to the window and I slumped on the couch against the wall with its large painting—much too large for the small room—of the Tehran mountains. Smugglers, she said. They still won't issue me a passport. I'll have to make my way to Turkey by land and wait for my brother-in-law to pick me up.

When? In about a week or so, she said. I'm not sure of the exact date; they will let me know. You will know through Mahshid, she added after a pause. She's the only one in our class who knows.

Is anyone going with you? No. My father's against it. The only thing he finally agreed to do was help pay for part of the trip. My sister is taking care of the rest—she calls it my rescue operation. My father says if I insist on going ahead with this crazy plan, I'm on my own. To him these people, no matter what we think of them, they're our people. He lost one daughter, now this other one. He says first it was the class, and now this. I thought he didn't know about the class, I said. Apparently, he did; he too was keeping up appearances.

She rubbed her hands obsessively and refrained from looking at me directly. This was Nassrin, or to be honest, this was the two of us together: sharing the most intimate moments with a shrug, pretending they were not intimate. It wasn't courage that motivated this casual, impersonal manner of treating so much pain; it was a special brand of cowardice, a destructive defense mechanism, forcing others to listen to the most horrendous experiences and yet denying them the moment of empathy: don't feel sorry for me; nothing is too big for me to handle. This is nothing, nothing really.

She told me that of all the years she had spent in jail, all the years of the war, this period of adjustment had been the hardest for her. At first she had thought she needed to leave only for a while. But gradually she had realized that she just wanted to leave. They would not issue her a passport, so she would have to go illegally, and that suited her fine.

I acted as if we were talking about a normal trip, a routine visit to her older sister in London—it's far too wet at this time of year; do ask them to take you to the Globe. . . . And why did you end it with Ramin? I could not stop myself from asking her. Was he opposed to your move, or did he inspire it? No, he, he—well, he knew how much I wanted to leave, because of this illness I have, you know, from my jail time. We, my sister, my mother and I, have been thinking for a long time that there might be a better way of handling it over there. I never asked her what exactly the illness was.

At first Ramin, he's an honorable man—a genuine grin brought back for a brief glimpse her girlishness—agreed that I should go, but he thought we should at least be engaged. I waited for her to continue. But then, well, then I broke it up. Nassrin? She paused and lowered her head, concentrating on her hands. She said, very fast: He was . . . he is no better than the others. Do you remember that line you read from Bellow about people emptying their garbage of thought all over you? Again she smiled. Well, that's Ramin and his intellectual friends for you.

This was too much, even for an experienced evader like myself. Taking a sip of water, as we know from novels, is a good way of gaining time. What do you mean no better than the others? Which others?

My uncle was cruder, she said slowly. You know, more like Mr. Nahvi. Ramin was different. He had read Derrida; he had watched Bergman and Kiarostami. No, he didn't touch me; in fact he was very careful not to touch me. It was worse. I can't explain, it was his eyes. His eyes? The way he looked at people, at other women. You could always tell, she said. She lowered her head miserably, her fingers touching one another. Ramin thought there was a difference between the girls that you were sexually attracted to and the girls you married— a girl who'd share your intellectual life with you, a girl you'd respect. *Respect,* she said again, with a great deal of anger. *Respect* was the word he used. He respected me. I was his Simone de Beauvoir, minus the sex part. And he was too much of a coward to just go and have sex with others. So he looked at them. It got to the point where he'd look at my older sister while he was talking to me. He just looked. He stared at women in the way . . . in the way my uncle touched me.

I felt sorry for Nassrin and, oddly, for Ramin too. I felt that he too needed help—he too needed to know more about himself, his needs and desires. Couldn't she see that he was not like her uncle? Perhaps it was too much to ask of her to sympathize with Ramin. She was quite ruthless to him; she had convinced herself she couldn't afford any feelings there. She had told him they were through, had made it clear that in her eyes, he was no better than the men he criticized and despised. At least you know where you stand with Ayatollah Khamenei, but these others, the ones with all sorts of claims and politically correct ideas—they were the worst. You want to save mankind, she had told him, you and your bloody Arendt. Why don't you start by saving yourself from your sexual problems? Find a prostitute. Stop looking at my sister.

Whenever I think of Nassrin, I always begin and end with that day in my room when she told me she was leaving. It was evening. Outside, the sky was the color of dusk—not dark, not light, not even gray. Rain was coming down in heavy sheets, the drops hanging from the bare brown leaves of the pear tree.

She said, "I am going away." She said she was twenty-seven now and didn't know what it meant to live. She had always thought that life in jail would be the hardest, but it hadn't been. She brushed a few strands of hair from her face. She said, There, in jail, I like the rest of them thought we would be killed and that would be the end, or we would live, we would live and get out, and begin all over. She said, There, in jail, we dreamed of just being outside, free, but when I came out, I discovered that I missed the sense of solidarity we had in jail, the sense of purpose, the way we tried to share memories and food. She said, More than anything else, I miss the hope. In jail, we had the hope that we might get out, go to college, have fun, go to movies. I am twenty-seven. I don't know what it means to love. I don't want to be secret and hidden forever. I want to know, to know who this Nassrin is. You'd call it the ordeal of freedom, I guess, she said, smiling.

21

Nassrin had asked me to tell the class about her departure. She couldn't face them—it was too intolerable. Better just to leave without good-byes. How should I break the news to them? "Nassrin won't be coming to class anymore." The statement was simple enough; it was how you said it, where you put the emphasis, that counted. I said it abruptly and rather crudely, forcing everyone into a stunned silence. I registered Yassi's nervous titter, Azin's startled glance and the quick exchange of looks between Sanaz and Mitra.

"Where is she now?" asked Mitra after a long pause.

"I don't know," I said. "We have to ask Mahshid."

"Nassrin left for the border two days ago," Mahshid quietly informed us. "She's waiting for the smugglers to get in touch with her, so by next week she should be riding a camel or a donkey or a jeep across the desert."

"*Not Without My Daughter,*" said Yassi with an uneasy giggle. "I'm so sorry," she said, putting her hand to her mouth. "I feel so terrible."

For a while everyone speculated about Nassrin's journey: the perils of traveling from the Turkish border, her loneliness, her future options. "Let's not talk about her as if she's dead," said Azin. "She's much better off where she's going, and we should be happy for her." Mahshid threw her a sharp glance. But Azin was right. What else could we have wished for her?

The person who reacted most strongly, not to Nassrin's departure but to my own now that Nassrin's sudden vanishing act had made concrete the threat of separation, was the one who identified with me most—Manna.

"This class will be over very soon anyway," she said without looking at anyone. "Nassrin has gotten the message from Dr. Nafisi." What message? "That we should all leave."

I was rather startled by the bitterness of her accusation. I felt guilty enough on my own, as if my decision to leave was a betrayal of some promise I had made to them. (Guilt has become part of your makeup. You felt guilty even while you had no notion of leaving, my magician said later, when I complained to him.)

"Don't be silly," Azin said, turning to Manna, her voice full of reproach. "It isn't her fault if you feel trapped living here."

"I am not being silly," said Manna savagely, "and, yes, I do feel trapped. Why shouldn't I?"

Azin's hand went to her bag, perhaps to fish out a cigarette, and came out empty. "How could you? You talk as if it's all Mrs. Nafisi's fault," she said to Manna, her hand shaking.

"No, let Manna explain what she means," I said.

"Perhaps she means . . ." Sanaz started lamely.

"I can explain myself, thank you," said Manna crossly. "I mean, you set up a model for us"—she turned to me—"that staying here is useless, that we should all leave if we want to make something of ourselves."

"That's not true," I told her with some irritation. "I never suggested that my experience should be yours. You can't follow me in everything, Manna. I mean each one of us has to do what's best for her. That's all the advice I can give you."

"The only way I can convince myself that it's okay for you to leave us here," said Manna (I remember she said to *leave us here*), "is that I know if I had half a chance, I would too. I would leave everything," she said as an afterthought. Even Nima? "Especially Nima," she shot back with a wicked little smile. "I am not like Mahshid. I don't think any of us has a duty to stay. We have only one life to live."

For so many years now I had acted as their confessor. They'd poured out their heartaches, their troubles, as if I never had any troubles of my own to cope with, as if I lived under a magical spell that allowed me to avoid all the pitfalls and hardships not just of life in the Islamic Republic but of life in general. And now they wanted me to carry the burden of their choices as well. People's choices were their own. The only way you could help them was if you knew what they wanted. How could you tell someone what she should want? (Nima would call later that night. "Manna is afraid you don't like her anymore," he said half jokingly. "She asked me to call.")

Other people's sorrows and joys have a way of reminding us of our own; we partly empathize with them because we ask ourselves: What about me? What does that say about my life, my pains, my anguish? For us, Nassrin's departure entailed a genuine concern for her, and anxieties and hopes for her new life. We also, for the moment at least, were shocked by the pain of missing her, of envisioning the class without her. But in the end we finally turned back towards ourselves, remembering our own hopes and anxieties in light of her decision to leave.

Mitra was the first to express her own anxieties. Lately, I had observed an anger and bitterness in her that was all the more alarming because it was so unprecedented. She had started to raise her voice in her diaries and notes, beginning with her account of her visit with her husband to Syria. The first thing that struck her was the humiliations Iranians suffered, quite meekly, at the Damascus airport, where they were segregated into a separate line and searched like criminals. Yet what had shocked her most were her sensations in the streets of Damascus, where she had walked freely, hand in hand with Hamid, wearing a T-shirt and jeans. She described the feel of the wind and the sun on her hair and her skin—it was always the same sensation that was so startling. It had been the same with me and would be so later with Yassi and Manna.

In the Damascus airport she had been humiliated by what she was assumed to be, and when she returned home, she felt angry because of what she could have been. She was angry for the years she had missed, for her lost portion of the sun and wind, for the walks she had not taken with Hamid. The thing about it, she had said with wonder, was that walking with him like that had suddenly transformed him into a stranger. This was a new context for their relationship; she had become a stranger even to herself. Was this the same Mitra, she asked herself, this woman in jeans and a tangerine T-shirt walking in the sun with a good-looking young man by her side? Who was this woman, and could she learn to incorporate her into her life if she were to live in Canada?

"You mean you don't have any sense of belonging here?" Mahshid asked, looking defiantly at Mitra. "I seem to be the only one who feels she owes something to this place."

"I can't live with this constant fear," said Mitra, "with having to worry all the time about the way I dress or walk. Things that come naturally to me are considered sinful, so how am I supposed to act?"

"But you know what is expected of you, you know the laws," said Mahshid. "This is nothing new. What has changed? Why is it bothering you so much more now?"

"Maybe for you, it is easier," said Sanaz, but Mahshid did not let her continue.

"You think I have it easy?" she said, turning a sharp eye towards Sanaz. "Do you think only people like you suffer in this country? You don't even know what fear is. Just because of my faith and the fact that I wear the veil, you think that I don't feel threatened? You think I don't feel fear? It's rather superficial, isn't it, to think that the only kind of fear is *your kind,*" she said with a rare show of bitterness.

"I didn't mean that," said Sanaz more gently. "The fact that we know about these laws, the fact that they are familiar, doesn't make them any better. It doesn't mean that we don't feel the pressure and the fear. But for you, at least, wearing the veil is natural; it's your religion, your choice."

"My choice," said Mahshid with a laugh. "What else do I have but my religion, and if I lose that . . ." She left her sentence unfinished, and turned her gaze once more to the ground, murmuring, "I'm sorry. I got too emotional."

"I know what Mahshid's talking about," Yassi broke in. "The worst fear you can have is losing your faith. Because then you're not accepted by anyone—not by those who consider themselves secular or by people of your own faith. It's terrible. Mahshid and I have been talking about that, about how ever since we could remember, our religion has defined every single action we've taken. If one day I lose my faith, it will be like dying and having to start new again in a world without guarantees."

My heart went out to Mahshid, sitting there trying to look composed, her face flushed, strong emotions like thin veins moving under her pale skin. Mahshid, I thought, more than my more secular students, has the most troubling questions about religion. In her class diary and papers, with a rage as restrained as her smile, she reviewed and questioned minute details of life under Islamic law. Mahshid later wrote in her class diary: "Both Yassi and I know that we have been losing our faith. We have been questioning it with every move. During the Shah's time, it was different. I felt I was in the minority and I had to guard my faith against all odds. Now that my religion is in power, I feel more helpless than ever before, and more alienated." She wrote about how ever since she could remember, she had been told that life in the land of infidels was pure hell. She had been promised that all would be different under a just Islamic rule. Islamic rule! It was a pageant of hypocrisy and shame. She wrote about how at work her male superiors never look her in the eye, about how in movies even a six-year-old girl must wear a scarf and cannot play with boys. Although she wore the veil, she described the pain of being required to wear it, calling it a mask behind which women were forced to hide. She talked about all of this coldly, furiously, always with a question mark after each point.

"This decision to leave was a difficult one," I said, feeling for the first time that I was ready to speak to them honestly about what I was doing and what it meant. "I had to go through many torturous deliberations. I even contemplated leaving Bijan." (You did? Bijan asked me later, when I recounted our conversation to him. You never told me.) This had the effect of diverting them momentarily from their anger and frustrations. I told them about my own fears, about waking up at night feeling as if I were choking, as if I would never be able to get out, about the dizzy spells and nausea and pacing around the apartment at all hours of the night. For the first time I opened up to them, talking about my own feelings and emotions, and it seemed to have an oddly soothing effect on them. By the time Azin suddenly jumped up, remembering that today was her turn to visit her daughter—named after my own Negar—who now lived temporarily with her husband's family, we felt lighter. We joked about Sanaz's various gentleman callers and Yassi's attempts to lose some weight.

Before they left, Mahshid picked up a little parcel she had brought with her. She said, "I have something for you. Nassrin sends her regards. She asked me to give this to you." She handed me a thick folder and a bundle of notes. I have the folder here on this other desk, in this other office, right now. It is brilliantly colored: white with bright bubble-gum-orange stripes and three cartoon characters. In vivid green and purple characters it says: *Be Seeing You in Fabulous Florida. Things Go Better with Sunshine!* Inside the folder, Nassrin had transcribed every word of my classes during my last three terms at Allameh, neatly written in her handwriting, with headings and subheadings. All the sentences and anecdotes were recorded. James, Austen, Fielding, Brontë, Poe, Twain—all of them were there. She left behind nothing else—no photograph, and no personal note—except for one line on the last page of the folder: *I still owe you a paper on Gatsby.*

22

Living in the Islamic Republic is like having sex with a man you loathe, I said to Bijan that evening after the Thursday class. He had come home to find me sitting in my customary chair in the living room, Nassrin's folder on my lap, my students' notes scattered on the table and beside them a dish of melting coffee ice cream. Boy, you must be feeling rotten, he said after a glance at the ice cream. He took a seat opposite me and said, Don't just let that sentence hang in the air. Explain a little.

Well, it's like this: if you're forced into having sex with someone you dislike, you make your mind blank—you pretend to be somewhere else, you tend to forget your body, you hate your body. That's what we do over here. We are constantly pretending to be somewhere else—we either plan it or dream it. Ever since my girls left this afternoon, I have been thinking of this issue.

Bijan and I had become surprisingly closer after our period of arguments, which had been heated and painful. Bijan was most articulate in his silences. Through him I had learned the many moods and nuances of silence: the angry silence and the disapproving one; the appreciative silence and the loving one. Sometimes his silences accumulated and overflowed into torrents of words, but recently we had found ourselves talking for long stretches. It all started when we both decided to describe to each other how we felt about Iran. For the first time, we began seeing the matter through each other's eyes. Now that he had begun to dismantle his life in Iran, he needed to articulate and share his thoughts and emotions. We spent long hours talking about our feelings, our ideas of home—for me portable, for him more traditional and rooted.

I told him in detail about the arguments we had had in class that day. After they left, I couldn't get rid of this idea of sexual molestation. I said, I keep tormenting myself with the thought that that's how Manna must feel.

Bijan didn't respond—he seemed to be waiting for me to elaborate—but suddenly I had nothing more to say. Feeling a little lighter, I stretched and picked at a few pistachio nuts. Have you ever noticed, I said, cracking a nut, how strange it is when you look in that mirror on the opposite wall that instead of seeing yourself, you see the trees and the mountains, as if you have magically willed yourself away?

Yes, as a matter of fact I have, he said, going into the kitchen for his usual vodka, but I haven't lost sleep over it. You, however, must have been thinking about it day and night, he added, placing his glass and a new dish of pistachio nuts on the table. As for your most eloquent analogy, your girls must resent the fact that while you're leaving this guy behind, they have to keep sleeping with him—some of them, at least, he said, taking a sip of his drink. He looked at his glass speculatively. I'm going to miss this, you know. You have to admit, we've got the best bootleg vodka in the world.

Cutting through his speculations on the merits of our vodka, I said, Going away isn't going to help as much as you think. The memory stays with you, and the stain. It's not something you slough off once you leave.

I have two things to say to that, he said. First, none of us can avoid being contaminated by the world's evils; it's all a matter of what attitude you take towards them. And second, you always talk about the effect of "these people" on you. Have you ever thought about your effect on them? I looked at him with some skepticism. This relationship is not equal in both good and bad ways, he continued. They have the power to kill us or flog us, but all of this only reminds them of their weakness. They must be scared out of their wits to see what's happening to their own former comrades, and to their children.

23

It was a warm summer day, about a fortnight after my conversation with Bijan. I had taken refuge in a coffee shop. It was really a pastry shop, one of the very few that still remained from my childhood. It had great piroshki for which people stood in long lines, and near the entrance, next to the large French windows, two or three small tables. I was sitting at one of these with a *café glacé* in front of me. I took out my pen and paper and, staring into the air, started to write. This staring into the air and writing had become my forte, especially in those last few months in Tehran.

Suddenly I noticed in the long line of people waiting for piroshki a face that seemed familiar, but not so familiar that I could place it. A woman was looking at me, more like staring. She smiled and, giving up her precious place in line, came towards me. Dr. Nafisi, she said. Don't you remember me? Clearly, she was a former student. Her voice was familiar, but I could not place her. She reminded me of my classes on James and Austen, and gradually her ghost took shape in my memory and hovered into focus alongside her present self and I recognized Miss Ruhi, whom I had not seen for some years. I would have recognized her more quickly if she had been dressed in a chador that emphasized her small upturned nose and defensive smile.

She was dressed in black, but not in a chador, and had curled a long black scarf around her neck, fastened with a silvery pin that seemed to quiver like a spider's web against the black cloth. Her makeup was pale, and a few strands of dark brown hair showed from under the scarf. I kept remembering her other face, the austere one, so withdrawn that her lips seemed constantly pursed. I noticed now that she was not plain, as I had believed her to be.

She lingered by my table. I asked her, since she had lost her coveted place in the line, to sit down and have a coffee with me. She hesitated and then perched herself precariously on the edge of the chair. After college, she had become active in one of the militia organizations, but she'd left it after a short while. They didn't care much for English literature, you know, she said with a smile. . . . And then she had been married for two years. She said she missed her college years. At the time, she had often wondered why she continued with English literature, why she didn't find something useful—here she smiled— and now she was glad she had continued. She felt she had something others did not. Do you remember our discussions of *Wuthering Heights*?

Yes, I remembered them, and as we talked I remembered her more clearly too; images chased away her present unfamiliar face and replaced it with another, now also unfamiliar. I returned in my mind to that classroom, on the fourth floor, to the third—or was it the fourth?—row near the aisle. I can just about pick out two faces, almost identical in their bland disapproval, taking notes. They were there when I entered the class and would linger after I left. Most of the others looked on them with suspicion. They were quite active in the Muslim Students' Association and did not mix well even with the more liberal elements in the Islamic Jihad, like Mr. Forsati.

I remember her. I remember that particular discussion of *Wuthering Heights,* because I remember how Miss Ruhi had unglued herself from her friend and followed me out of the classroom, pushing me almost into a corner of the hall. She leapt at me and spluttered out her indignation over the immorality of Catherine and Heathcliff. There was so much passion in her words—I had been taken aback. What was she talking about?

I was not about to put another novel on trial. I told her it was immoral to talk about a great novel in this manner, that characters were not vehicles for pedantic moral imperatives, that reading a novel was not an exercise in censure. She said something about other professors, their delicacy in censoring even the word *wine* out of the stories they taught, lest it offend the Islamic sensibilities of their students. Yes, I thought, and they have been stuck teaching *The Pearl.* I told her she could drop the class or take the matter to higher authorities, that this was the way it would be in my class and that I would continue to teach what I taught. I left her there in the darkened corner of that very long hallway. Though I saw her afterward, in my mind I left her there forever. And now she had excavated herself and polished up her image.

She had also objected to *Daisy Miller:* she found Daisy not only immoral but foolish and "unreasonable." But then, despite our differences and her obvious disapproval of the novels I taught, she had enrolled in my class again the following year. There were rumors that she was having an affair with one of the big shots in the Muslim Students' Association. Nassrin was always bringing these rumors to my attention, trying to prove how hypocritical "these people" were.

She said now that she missed college. It didn't seem like much at the time, but later she noticed how much she missed it. She missed the films we watched together and the class discussions. Do you remember your Dear Jane Society? I was puzzled—how did she know about that? It was a joke shared by me and a handful of my students. She said, I always wanted to be in on it. I always thought it would be a great deal of fun. I really liked Jane Austen—if you only knew how many girls swooned over Darcy! I said, I didn't know you were allowed to have a heart in your group. She said, Believe it or not, we fell in and out of love all the time.

She had tried to study Arabic and had translated some short stories and poems from English into Persian—for herself, she added as an afterthought. She used the Persian expression "for my own heart." After a pause she added, And then I got married and now have a daughter. I wondered if she had married the man of our rumors; he was a man I had no fond memories of.

I asked her how old her daughter was. She said, Eleven months, and, after a pause, with a playful shadow of a smile: I named her after you. After me? I mean, she has a different name on her birth certificate—she is called Fahimeh, after a favorite aunt who died young—but I have a secret name for her. I call her Daisy. She said she had hesitated between Daisy and Lizzy. She had finally settled on Daisy. Lizzy was the one she had dreamed of, but marrying Mr. Darcy was too much wishful thinking. Why Daisy? Don't you remember Daisy Miller? Haven't you heard that if you give your child a name with a meaning she will become like her namesake? I want my daughter to be what I never was—like Daisy. You know, courageous.

Daisy was the character my female students most identified with. Some of them became obsessed. Later, in my workshop, they would go back to her time and again, speaking of her courage, something they felt they had lacked. Mahshid and Mitra spoke of her with regret in their writings; like Winterbourne, they felt they were bound to make a mistake about her. When she rose to say good-bye, I looked at her with some hesitation and said, May I ask you a rather personal question? You said you were married. And your husband? I married someone outside the university, she said. He is in computers. And open-minded, she added with a smile.

She had to go, she had an eleven-month-old daughter with a secret name waiting for her at home. You know, I didn't think about it then, but we did have fun, she said. All the fuss we made over these writers, as if what they said was a matter of life and death to us—James and Brontë and Nabokov and Jane Austen.

24

Certain memories, like the imaginary balloons Yassi made with her delicate hands when she was happy, rise from somewhere in the depths of what we call memory. Like balloons, these memories are light and bright and irretrievable, despite the "air sadness" (Bellow's term) surrounding them. During my last weeks in Iran, my girls and I met, in addition to Thursdays, on other days in different parts of town. We even went shopping together, as I had decided I had to buy presents for friends and family in America.

I went into my favorite café one afternoon, looking for my girls, but could not find them. I waylaid a waiter, an ancient one, his black trousers a little too short, carrying a tray of pastries and two steaming cups of coffee, and asked him if he had seen a handful of young girls come through. Are they unaccompanied? he asked. I looked at him in surprise. Why, yes. I suppose they are unaccompanied. Well then, they must be in the back room. He nodded to my left, where the main restaurant was. You know the rules, he said. Unaccompanied women cannot sit in this section.

My girls were sitting near the window. The only other table in this vast space that was occupied was a small one near the wall, where two women were drinking coffee. "No men, no privileges," Manna exclaimed merrily. "This is one time when Nima might have been of some use." Nassrin's absence was more obvious in those last weeks when we were all together. I asked Mahshid for news of her. She had no news. And, she added with some bitterness, no news is good news, anyway.

Both Manna and Azin had brought their cameras—café memories, said Manna. As my departure drew closer, I became obsessed with taking pictures of all the details of our life. When I did not have an actual camera with me, I became a camera myself, writing feverishly about the flight of birds in Polur, our mountain resort near Tehran, the quality of air that was so tactile, especially early mornings around sunrise and all the beloved faces that surrounded us during those last weeks.

Mitra was subdued. Before I arrived, she had been telling the others about her problems at home and now she continued. Hamid's mother was strongly opposed to their going to Canada, and her disapproval was causing Hamid to vacillate constantly in his decision. What makes me resent this, Mitra said, is not just that she doesn't want us to leave but that she always meddles in our affairs. Before, it was her wanting us to have children—she wanted a grandson before she was too old to enjoy him—and now this. Both Mitra and Hamid were also wavering. He had a good job and financial security and in Canada they would have to start from scratch. She said she felt she was changing—she had become more anxious, more sensitive; she had started having nightmares. One night she woke up feeling that the whole house was shaking, but it was only her shaking the bedside table. Sometimes I think men just can't relate to how difficult it is to be a woman in this country, she said with frustration. For them it's easier, said Yassi. In a way, this place can be a man's paradise. Hamid tells me, said Mitra, that if we make a good living, we can always take our vacations abroad.

Things are definitely better for men, said Azin. Look at the marriage and divorce laws; look at how many so-called secular men have taken second wives. Especially some of the intellectuals, said Manna, those who make the headlines with their claims about freedom and all that.

Not all men are like that, Sanaz objected.

Azin, suddenly brightening up, turned to Sanaz. Well, yes. Some men, like your new beau . . .

He's not a beau, Sanaz objected, giggling now, clearly enjoying herself after a long period of depression. He's a friend of Ali's. He's here on a visit from England, she informed me, feeling that an explanation was in order. We knew each other before—we were sort of friends, she said, through Ali. He was supposed to be our best man, you see. So he came to pay me a visit, just to be nice.

Mitra's dimples and Azin's knowing smile suggested that there was more to "nice" than met the eye. What? said Sanaz. He's not good-looking. Actually, she said, narrowing her eyes, he's sort of ugly. Perhaps more like rugged? suggested Yassi hopefully. No, no, more like, well, more like ugly, but a very nice man, considerate and kind. My brother keeps making fun of him, she said, and you know sometimes I feel like going with him or something. The other day, he was saying how he can't wear short sleeves or go swimming over here. After he left, my brother kept mimicking him and saying, Very clever new method of seduction and my silly sister is just the kind of girl to fall for it.

The waiter came in to take my order. I ordered a *café glacé,* and then, looking at Manna, said also, Could you bring all of us some Turkish coffee a little later? Ever since my mother had established the ritual of serving our class Turkish coffee, we had gotten into the habit of telling our fortunes from the dregs. Manna and Azin always vied for the privilege of fortune-telling. The last time Azin had told mine, and I had promised Manna that she would get her turn soon.

After the waiter left, Azin said, Boy I'd love to take a picture of him. Why don't you guys divert his attention and I'll take the picture. How can we divert his attention? said Manna. You don't want us to go to jail for flirting with this decrepit creature!

When the waiter returned with my order, I saw Azin bring up her camera, making signs to Yassi, who was sitting beside me, and idly move the camera in my general direction, as if focusing on the wall. Could I have my coffee without sugar? Yassi asked the waiter. I don't know; it's usually already mixed in, said the waiter peevishly. He turned around sharply at the sound of a click, glanced suspiciously at our innocent expressions and left. I don't know how it will come out, said Azin. We'll see. In the photograph he's standing over me, but his face is turned towards Yassi; only we can't see his face from the chin up. His headless torso is slightly bent and he has an empty tray in one hand; both Yassi and I are looking in his direction and I am holding on to my frosted glass protectively, as if it might be snatched from me at any moment.

Later, I showed the pictures we'd taken in those last few weeks to my magician. You get a strange feeling when you're about to leave a place, I told him, like you'll not only miss the people you love but you'll miss the person you are now at this time and this place, because you'll never be this way ever again.

The waiter brought us our coffee in small different-colored cups, and while drinking, we pondered the trials and tribulations of being a writer in Iran, having so much to say but not being allowed to say it. I looked at my watch; I was already behind schedule. Let's hear Manna's reading of my fortune and then I'll have to go, I said. I told Manna as I took up my pencil and diary, ready to write, that I would record every word and that she would be beholden for what she was telling me. Remember what Cary Grant said in that fabulous film: a word, like a lost opportunity, cannot be taken back once it has been uttered.

Manna took up my coffee cup and starting telling my fortune: "I see a bird like a cock, which means good news, but you yourself are very agitated. A road that looks bright. And you are on the first step. You are thinking of a hundred things at the same time. One road is closed and dark, and the other is open and full of light. Both could happen; it is your choice. There is a key; a problem will be solved. No money. A small ship that is still in the harbor and has not yet started to set sail."

25

Does every magician, every genuine one, like my own, evoke the hidden conjurer in us all, bringing out the magical possibilities and potentials we did not know existed? Here he is on this chair, the chair I am in the process of inventing. As I write, the chair is created: walnut, a brown cushion, a little uncomfortable, it keeps you alert. This is the chair, but he is not sitting on that chair; I am. He sits on the couch, the same brown cushions, softer perhaps, looking more at home than I do; it is his couch. He sits as he always does, right in the middle, leaving a vast empty space on either side. He does not lean back but sits up straight, his hands on his lap, his face lean and sharp.

Before he talks, let me have him go to the kitchen, because he is a very hospitable person and would definitely not leave me talking for so long without some offer of tea or coffee, or perchance some ice cream? Today, let it be tea, in two mismatched mugs, his brown, mine green. His graceful, aristocratic poverty, his mugs, his faded jeans, his T-shirts, his chocolates. While he is in the kitchen, let me be silent and consider how meticulously he has created his rituals—reading the paper at a certain hour after breakfast, the morning and evening walks, the answering of the phone after two rings. I am overtaken by a sudden tenderness: how tough he seems to us, yet how fragile is his life.

As he carries in the two mugs of tea, I tell him, You know, I feel all my life has been a series of departures. He raises his eyebrows, placing the mugs on the table, and looks at me as if he had expected a prince and all he could see was a frog. Then we both laugh. He says, still standing, You can say this sort of crap in the privacy of these four walls—I am your friend; I shall forgive you—but don't ever write this in your book. I say, But it is the truth. Lady, he says, we do not need your truths but your fiction—if you're any good, perhaps you can trickle in some sort of truth, but spare us your real feelings.

He's back in the kitchen, rummaging through the refrigerator. He comes back with five pieces of chocolate on a small plate. He sits opposite me, almost on the edge of the couch. We are out of everything, I'm afraid. Just a few chocolates is all I have in the fridge.

I said to him that I wanted to write a book in which I would thank the Islamic Republic for all the things it had taught me—to love Austen and James and ice cream and freedom. I said, Right now it is not enough to appreciate all this; I want to write about it. He said, You will not be able to write about Austen without writing about us, about this place where you rediscovered Austen. You will not be able to put us out of your head. Try, you'll see. The Austen you know is so irretrievably linked to this place, this land and these trees. You don't think this is the same Austen you read with Dr. French—it was Dr. French, wasn't it? Do you? This is the Austen you read here, in a place where the film censor is nearly blind and where they hang people in the streets and put a curtain across the sea to segregate men and women. I said, When I write all that, perhaps I will become more generous, less angry.

So we sit, eternally weaving stories, he on his couch, I in my chair; behind us, the oblong circle of light in front of the rocking chair becomes narrower and smaller, and now it disappears. He turns on the lamp and we continue our talk.

26

"I have a recurring fantasy that one more article has been added to the Bill of Rights: the right to free access to imagination. I have come to believe that genuine democracy cannot exist without the freedom to imagine and the right to use imaginative works without any restrictions. To have a whole life, one must have the possibility of publicly shaping and expressing private worlds, dreams, thoughts and desires, of constantly having access to a dialogue between the public and private worlds. How else do we know that we have existed, felt, desired, hated, feared?

"We speak of facts, yet facts exist only partially to us if they are not repeated and re-created through emotions, thoughts and feelings. To me it seemed as if we had not really existed, or only half existed, because we could not imaginatively realize ourselves and communicate to the world, because we had used works of imagination to serve as handmaidens to some political ploy."

That day when I left my magician's house, I sat on the top steps of the apartment house and wrote those words in my notebook. I dated the entry June 23, 1997, and wrote beside the date: "For my new book." It took me another year after that day to think again about writing this book, and another before I could bring myself to take up my pen, as the saying goes, and write about Austen and Nabokov and those who read and lived them with me.

That day, when I left my magician's house, the sun was fading and the air was mild, the trees a verdant green, and I had many reasons to feel sad. Every object and every face had lost its tangibleness and appeared like a cherished memory: my parents, friends, students, this street, those trees, the withdrawing light from the mountains in the mirror. But I was also vaguely elated and, to paraphrase Muriel Spark's heroine in her wonderful novel *Loitering with Intent,* I went about my way rejoicing, thinking how wonderful it is to be a woman and a writer at the end of the twentieth century.

Epilogue

I left Tehran on June 24, 1997, for the green light that Gatsby once believed in. I write and teach once again, on the seventh floor of a building in a town without mountains but with amazing falls and springs. I still teach Nabokov, James, Fitzgerald, Conrad as well as Iraj Pezeshkzad, who is responsible for one of my favorite Iranian novels, *My Uncle Napoleon,* and those others whom I have discovered since I arrived in the United States, like Zora Neale Hurston and Orhan Pamuk. And I know now that my world, like Pnin's, will be forever a "portable world."

I left Iran, but Iran did not leave me. Much has changed in appearance since Bijan and I left. There is more defiance in Manna's gait and those of other women; their scarves are more colorful and their robes much shorter; they wear makeup now and walk freely with men who are not their brothers, fathers or husbands. Parallel to this, the raids and arrests and public executions also persist. But there is a stronger demand for freedom; as I write, I open the paper to read about the recent student demonstrations in support of a dissident who was sentenced to death for suggesting that the clergy should not be blindly followed like monkeys and calling for a revision of the constitution. I read the writings of young students and former revolutionaries, the slogans and demands for democracy, and I know now as much as I will ever know anything that it is this dogged desire for life, liberty and the pursuit of happiness by young Iranians today, the children of the revolution, and the anguished self-criticism of former revolutionaries that will determine the shape of our future.

Since I left Iran, respecting his wishes, I have not talked or written to my magician, but his magic has been so much a part of my life that sometimes I ask myself, Was he ever real? Did I invent him? Did he invent me?

Sometimes I get e-mail messages on my computer, like fireflies, or letters postmarked from Tehran or Sydney, and they are from my former students, telling me about their lives and memories.

Nassrin, I know, arrived safely in England. I do not know what happened to her after that.

Mitra left for Canada a few months after we moved to the U.S. She used to write me e-mails or call me regularly, but I have not heard from her for a long time. Yassi tells me that she enrolled in college and now has a son.

I heard from Sanaz, too, when I first came to the States. She called me from Europe to inform me that she was now married and intended to enroll at the university. But Azin tells me she dropped that plan and is keeping house, as the saying goes.

When I first came to America, I did not hear from Azin often; she usually called me on my birthday. A former student had told me that Azin was teaching at Allameh, the same courses and books that I once taught. The last she had heard of Azin, she added mischievously, she was moving into the room next to my old office on the fifth floor. I often thought of her and her beautiful little Negar. A few months ago, she called out of the blue, from California. Her voice was filled with that buoyant and flirtatious tone whose notes I seem to have memorized. She has remarried; her new husband lives in California. Her former husband had taken Negar from her and there was not much else to stay in Tehran for. She was full of ideas about enrolling in classes and starting a new life.

Mahshid, Manna and Yassi continued to meet after I left. They read Virginia Woolf and Kundera and others, and wrote about films, poetry and their own lives as women. Mahshid got her much deserved tenure and is now a senior editor, publishing books of her own.

During her last year in Iran, Yassi held her own private class, with students who loved her and with whom she went mountain climbing, about which she wrote me e-mails delirious with this newfound capability. She also worked hard to come to America for her graduate studies. She was finally accepted at Rice University, in Texas, in 2000 and is currently working on her Ph.D.

Nima teaches. He, I always thought, is what we call a born teacher. He also writes brilliant and unfinished essays on James,

Nabokov and his favorite Persian writers. He still regales me with his stories and anecdotes. Manna writes her poetry, and when I recently told her I wanted to write an epilogue for my book and was wondering what to say about her, she sent me this:

> Five years have passed since the time when the story began in a cloud-lit room where we read *Madame Bovary* and had chocolate from a wine-red dish on Thursday mornings. Hardly anything has changed in the nonstop sameness of our everyday life. But somewhere else I have changed. Each morning with the rising of the routine sun as I wake up and put on my veil before the mirror to go out and become a part of what is called reality, I also know of another "I" that has become naked on the pages of a book: in a fictional world, I have become fixed like a Rodin statue. And so I will remain as long as you keep me in your eyes, dear readers.

ACKNOWLEDGMENTS

There are numerous individuals whose real selves, ghosts or shadows make cameo appearances in the pages of this book. Some I have known for a long time, sharing with them many of the experiences narrated in the preceding chapters; others I feel as if I have known all my life, even if they were not there then. There is no way that I can acknowledge their contributions in these few words. Like the good fairies and genies protecting Nabokov's Pnin, they have been the guardian angels of my book. To them I owe more than I can ever articulate.

My mother, Nezhat Nafisi, died on January 2, 2003. I could not be with her through her last months of illness and her death. That grief will always be accompanied by a hatred I shared with her of evil totalitarian systems which Nabokov denounced for holding their citizens hostage by their heartstrings. For her, the fight against tyranny was not a political but an existential struggle. As a daughter and an individual I could never reach the standards of perfection she expected of me, but she did take genuine pleasure in my work and we believed in the same ideals and values. She had looked forward to reading this book, and I dedicate it to her in memory of her courage and sense of integrity, which were the main causes of her passionate failings. She and my father were the first, most enthusiastic and selfless supporters of my work.

My father was the first storyteller in my life, creating stories for me and with me. He taught me many things, among them how to believe in ideals and how to confront the real world with the possibilities created by fictional ones. With my brother, Mohammad, I shared my earliest dreams and stories (an experience I continue to share with my beloved niece, Sanam Banoo Nafisi); although we lived apart during the writing of this book, his critical and compassionate eye has been my constant companion. My husband, Bijan, with whom I shared so many of the experiences in this book, has been literally my better half throughout this ordeal as all others. He was the only one apart from my editor who read the finished manuscript of my book, helping me much through his impartial judgment, moral integrity and love. My children, Dara and Negar, provided me with the kind of love and support that at times reversed our roles.

Other family members and friends made the writing of this book easier with their support and encouragement: Manijeh and Q Aghazadeh; Taraneh and Mo Shamszad; Parvin, whose invaluable friendship and constant support cannot be acknowledged in words, and also Khosrow, Tahmineh joon, Goli, Karim, Nahid and Zari; my good friend Mahnaz Afkhami, who offered friendship and wise counsel during a difficult and lonely time and to whom I am especially grateful for her invaluable support and suggestions and ideas for my private class; Paul (thank you for introducing me to *Persecution and the Art of Writing,* among many other things), Carl Gershman, Hillel Fradkin and the wonderful colleagues and staff at the University of Freedonia; Bernard Lewis (who opened the door); Hayedeh Daragahi, Freshteh Shahpar, Farivar Farzan, Shahran Tabari and Ziama (for teaching me about the relation between Beethoven and freedom); Lea Kenig for her friendship, support and love of books, which she generously shared with me; my retrieved childhood friends Farah Ebrahimi and Issa H. Rhode; and my voices of conscience and bosom friends Ladan Boroumand, Roya Boroumand and Abdi Nafisi.

I will always remain indebted to my students, who provided me with a new outlook on life and literature, but especially to Azin, Yassi, Sanaz, Mitra, Mahshid, Manna, Ava, Mozhgan, Nassrin and Nima. Almost every page of this book resonates with memories of my teaching experiences and in a sense every page is dedicated to them.

Since I left Iran in 1997, the Paul H. Nitze School for Advanced International Studies (SAIS) at Johns Hopkins University has been my academic and intellectual home. I have benefited from the openness, curiosity and intellectual freedom shown by past and present colleagues and staff. I would like to thank them for providing an atmosphere that is academically exciting and adventurous but never intellectually stilted or confining. My thanks especially to Fouad Ajami and the Middle East department and to the staff and my colleagues at the Foreign Policy Institute and to its director, Dr. Tom Keaney.

A generous grant from the Smith Richardson Foundation provided me with the opportunity to work on this book as well as pursue my projects at SAIS. My thanks especially to Marin Strmecki and Samantha Ravich for their belief in the rights of all individuals, no matter what part of the world they live in, to life, liberty and the pursuit of happiness. For quotations from Ayatollah Khomeini and facts about his life, I am grateful to Baqer Moin's *Khomeini: Life of the Ayatollah* (I.B. Tauris, 1999).

I would like to thank the staff at Random House for their support, enthusiasm and professionalism. I am grateful to Veronica Windholz for her scrupulous copyediting as well as her compassionate hatred of tyrannies, and to Robin Rolewicz, on whose smiles and generous and timely support, which went far beyond the call of duty, I came so much to rely. I had often wondered why some writers waxed lyrical over their editors until I started to work with Joy de Menil. Although very young, Joy decided to become this book's fairy godmother. I appreciate her friendship, developed over the course of writing this book, her imaginative insights and suggestions, her meticulous editing and not least her own passion for and appreciation of great works of fiction.

And then there is always the inimitable, incorrigible Mr. R, wherever he may be at this moment and whatever story he may be inventing or participating in.

AZAR NAFISI is a professor and director of the SAIS Dialogue Project at Johns Hopkins University–SAIS. She taught English literature at the University of Tehran from 1979 to 1981, when she was expelled for refusing to wear the veil, and later at the Free Islamic University and the University of Allameh Tabatabai in Iran. In 1997, she left Iran for the United States with her family. She has written for *The New York Times, The Washington Post, The Wall Street Journal* and *The New Republic,* among other publications, and is the author of *Anti-Terra: A Critical Study of Vladimir Nabokov's Novels,* published in Iran. She lives in Washington, D.C., with her husband and two children.

ABOUT THE TYPE

This book was set in Bembo, a typeface based on an old-style Roman face that was used for Cardinal Bembo's tract *De Aetna* in 1495. Bembo was cut by Francisco Griffo in the early sixteenth century. The Lanston Monotype Company of Philadelphia brought the well-proportioned letterforms of Bembo to the United States in the 1930s.